Tell Me What Happened

Questioning Children About Abuse

Second Edition

Michael E. Lamb, Deirdre A. Brown,
Irit Hershkowitz, Yael Orbach,
and Phillip W. Esplin

WILEY Blackwell

This edition first published 2018
© 2018 John Wiley & Sons Ltd

Edition History
John Wiley & Sons Ltd (1e, 2008).

All rights reserved. No part of this publication may be reproduced, stored in a retrieval system, or transmitted, in any form or by any means, electronic, mechanical, photocopying, recording or otherwise, except as permitted by law. Advice on how to obtain permission to reuse material from this title is available at http://www.wiley.com/go/permissions.

The right of Michael E. Lamb, Deirdre A. Brown, Irit Hershkowitz, Yael Orbach, and Phillip W. Esplin to be identified as the authors of this work has been asserted in accordance with law.

Registered Offices
John Wiley & Sons, Inc., 111 River Street, Hoboken, NJ 07030, USA
John Wiley & Sons Ltd, The Atrium, Southern Gate, Chichester, West Sussex, PO19 8SQ, UK

Editorial Office
111 River Street, Hoboken, NJ 07030, USA

For details of our global editorial offices, customer services, and more information about Wiley products visit us at www.wiley.com.

Wiley also publishes its books in a variety of electronic formats and by print-on-demand. Some content that appears in standard print versions of this book may not be available in other formats.

Limit of Liability / Disclaimer of Warranty
While the publisher and authors have used their best efforts in preparing this work, they make no representations or warranties with respect to the accuracy or completeness of the contents of this work and specifically disclaim all warranties, including without limitation any implied warranties of merchantability or fitness for a particular purpose. No warranty may be created or extended by sales representatives, written sales materials or promotional statements for this work. The fact that an organization, website, or product is referred to in this work as a citation and/or potential source of further information does not mean that the publisher and authors endorse the information or services the organization, website, or product may provide or recommendations it may make. This work is sold with the understanding that the publisher is not engaged in rendering professional services. The advice and strategies contained herein may not be suitable for your situation. You should consult with a specialist where appropriate. Further, readers should be aware that websites listed in this work may have changed or disappeared between when this work was written and when it is read. Neither the publisher nor authors shall be liable for any loss of profit or any other commercial damages, including but not limited to special, incidental, consequential, or other damages.

Library of Congress Cataloging-in-Publication Data

Names: Lamb, Michael E., 1953– author. | Brown, Deirdre Ann, 1973– author. | Hershkowitz, Irit, author.
Title: Tell me what happened : questioning children about abuse / Michael E. Lamb, Deirdre A. Brown, Irit Hershkowitz, Yael Orbach, Phillip W. Esplin.
Description: Second Edition. | Hoboken : Wiley, [2018] | Series: The psychology of crime, policing and law | Revised edition of Tell me what happened, 2008. | Includes bibliographical references and index. |
Identifiers: LCCN 2018008932 (print) | LCCN 2018025471 (ebook) | ISBN 9781118881637 (pdf) | ISBN 9781118881651 (epub) | ISBN 9781118881675 (pbk.) | ISBN 9781118881637 (ePDF)
Subjects: LCSH: Child abuse–Investigation. | Interviewing in child abuse. | Abused children. | Child witnesses.
Classification: LCC HV8079.C46 (ebook) | LCC HV8079.C46 L36 2018 (print) | DDC 363.25/95554–dc23
LC record available at https://lccn.loc.gov/2018008932

Cover image: © ClarkandCompany/iStockphoto
Cover design by Wiley

Set in 10/12pt NewCenturySchlbk by SPi Global, Pondicherry, India
Printed in Singapore by C.O.S. Printers Pte Ltd

10 9 8 7 6 5 4 3 2 1

This newly-revised volume on interviewing children is up-to-date, comprehensive, and accessibly written, including recent scientific evidence as well as actual case studies. The authors are outstanding contributors to this field, both as scientists and practitioners. This new edition goes beyond considering children's memory in isolation and embeds it within what is known of their social and emotional functioning. It will be a major resource for both child protection professionals and researchers.

— **Stephen J. Ceci, Ph.D.,
The H. L. Carr Chaired Professor
of Developmental Psychology,
Cornell University**

Such a joy to read the new edition of "Tell Me What Happened". For two decades Lamb and colleagues have profoundly shaped the field and practice of forensically interviewing children and adolescents through meticulous research, exceptional and sensitive presentation of information, clear guidance, and practical suggestions. Building on the early work introducing us to a structured protocol and promoting the use of retrieval prompts and strategies for mining children's recall memory for personal experiences, the revised protocol tackles the barriers encountered by interviewers questioning reluctant children. The authors invite us to appreciate the great hurdles faced by children during the investigative process and interview, observe closely children's active and passive forms of resistance, and provide non-suggestive support through statements and behaviors. We are encouraged once again to move into more sensitive and skillful practice.

— **Linda Cordisco Steele, M.Ed., LPC,
National Children's Advocacy Center**

Wiley Series in
the Psychology of Crime, Policing and Law

Series Editors
Graham M. Davies[1] and Ray Bull[2]
[1]*University of Leicester, UK*
[2]*University of Derby, UK*

The Wiley Series in the Psychology of Crime, Policing and Law publishes concise and integrative reviews on important emerging areas of contemporary research. The purpose of the series is not merely to present research findings in a clear and readable form but also to bring out their implications for both practice and policy. Books in this series are useful not only to psychologists, but also to all those involved in crime detection and prevention, child protection, policing and judicial processes.

For other titles in this series please see www.wiley.com/go/pcpl

We dedicate this book to the memory of Kathleen Sternberg, a passionate advocate for evidence-based practice who died tragically young. She was integrally involved in the research leading to development of and initial evaluation of the NICHD Protocol.

Contents

About the Authors		ix
Series Preface		xi
Preface		xv
1	Interviewing Children About Abuse: An Overview and Introduction	1
2	Contributions to Children's Testimony: The Child and the Event	11
3	Contributions to Testimony: Preparation for the Interview and Questioning Strategies	47
4	How do Investigators Typically Interview Alleged Victims?	67
5	The NICHD Investigative Interview Protocols for Young Victims and Witnesses	87
6	When Interviewers Follow the Protocol, What Impact Does it Have on Their Interviewing and on Children's Responding?	101
7	Interviewing Suspected Victims under Six Years of Age	119
8	Interviewing Children with Developmental Disabilities	137
9	The Revised Protocol: Effectively Supporting Reluctant Witnesses	161
10	Using Tools and Props to Complement the Protocol	189
11	Training and Maintaining Good Interviewing Practice	201
12	Case-related Outcomes When the Protocol is Used	213
13	Progress to Date and the Challenges Ahead	225

Revised Investigative Interview Protocol: Version 2018	239
References	251
Index	315

About the Authors

Michael E. Lamb is Professor of Psychology at the University of Cambridge, where he moved in 2004 after serving 17 years as Head of the Section on Social and Emotional Development at the National Institute of Child Health and Human Development (NICHD) in Bethesda, MD. It was here that he and his colleagues launched the program of research and developed some of the interview procedures outlined in this book.

Deirdre A. Brown is Senior Lecturer in Psychology at the Victoria University of Wellington. After completing her PhD and training in clinical psychology at the University of Otago, she began a postdoctoral fellowship at NICHD and the University of Lancaster, where she led the research on children with intellectual disabilities described in this book. She was appointed to her current position in 2007.

Irit Hershkowitz is Professor of Social Work at the University of Haifa. After completing her PhD at the University of Haifa, she completed a postdoctoral fellowship at NICHD, where she played a crucial role in the development of the Investigative Interview Protocol described in this book. She returned to the University of Haifa in 1994 and has since spearheaded efforts to evaluate and improve the training of investigative interviewers.

Yael Orbach worked as a Senior Researcher in the Section on Social and Emotional Development of the National Institute of Child Health and Human Development for nearly 15 years. After retiring from her position as Staff Scientist in 2006, Dr. Orbach continued to conduct collaborative research with the other co-authors, focusing on the application of cognitive and developmental research to criminal investigation of children until 2015. She was integrally involved in the development of the NICHD Investigative Interview Protocol and participated in much of the research on forensic interviewing described in this book.

Phillip W. Esplin has worked as a forensic psychologist based in Phoenix, AZ for more than 40 years. After interviewing alleged victims and evaluating interviews by other professionals, he began conducting field research designed to enhance the quality of practice and became a senior consultant to the NICHD Protocol research team in 1989. In that role, he was integrally involved in the development and evaluation of the Investigative Interview Protocol described in this book.

Series Preface

The Wiley Series in the Psychology of Crime, Policing, and the Law publishes both single and multi-authored monographs and edited reviews of important and emerging areas of contemporary research. The purpose of this series is not merely to present research findings in a clear and readable form, but also to bring out their implications for both practice and policy. Books in this series are useful not only to psychologists, but also to all those involved in crime detection and prevention, child protection, policing, and judicial processes.

Recent years have seen a welcome increase in the number of successful prosecutions for child sexual or physical abuse in countries which employ the adversarial principles of English common law. This increase has been facilitated by the advent of video- and later, digital-recording of investigative interviews of alleged victims conducted by trained police officers or social workers. In the United Kingdom and other common-law countries, such interviews may be played to the jury at trial as the sole or principal element of the prosecution case. A properly conducted interview, where the child describes in a consistent and detailed manner the circumstances and nature of the offence allegedly committed by the defendant, can provide powerful evidence against an adult who might otherwise escape justice. However, as with all witness statements, children can misunderstand or be misled in their evidence, risking miscarriages of justice (Ceci & Bruck, 1995).

In the first edition of *Tell Me What Happened* (2008), Lamb, Hershkovitz, Orbach, and Esplin argued that such injustices arose primarily from poor investigative practice: In particular, research showed that interviewers used few open-ended questions, relying instead on closed or specific questions. They argued that open-ended questions (e.g., "And then what happened?") encourage children to actively shape and detail their own account of events, while specific ("What color was the bedspread?") or closed ("Were you on your back or on your front?") questions induced a passivity and a greater readiness to agree with the interviewer's preconceptions. To address this concern, Michael Lamb, the late Kathy Sternberg, and others at the National Institute for Child Health and Human Development (NICHD) in the United States fashioned a new interviewing procedure: the NICHD Protocol. The Protocol drew upon the principal authors' extensive knowledge of children's cognitive and social development and placed the need for children to give their own account as the central requirement. This was best fostered by the use of open-ended questions by interviewers. This style of discourse ran counter to everyday carer-child interactions and needed to be laboriously learned and practiced if it was to be maintained consistently in the interview room. The book summarizes the evidence for the effectiveness of the Protocol, drawing upon both experimental and field studies conducted in different countries and its superiority to other current interviewing techniques in eliciting detailed and forensically useful content from child complainants.

The first edition of *Tell Me What Happened* proved to be a popular and influential guide for practitioners and researchers alike and has generated a good deal of research and comment, not merely from the original research team, but from others who have been stimulated by the issues it raised. It has remained the primary source of guidance outside government publications for practitioners and professionals involved in child protection. The new edition which features the same writing team, with the addition of Deirdre A. Brown, summarizes much of this new information and features a major revision to the original Protocol: the additional consideration of emotional and motivational factors, which experience has shown can influence whether an abused child will fully disclose the nature of any abuse and the identity of the abuser. In making these additions, the Revised Protocol mirrors a wider movement within memory research to complement purely cognitive influences with consideration of social and affective factors as determinants of recall (e.g. Eysenck, Derakshan, Santos, & Calvo, 2007; Harris, Rasmussen, & Berntsen, 2014).

This new emphasis has emerged from recent research on interviewing reluctant witnesses and also provides a more comprehensive understanding of the issues faced by professionals when interviewing very young children, and those with developmental issues, including autistic spectrum disorders, which, as the authors note, are all disproportionately represented among victims of abuse. As with the original, this new book is written with child protection professionals as well as scholars in mind and offers advice and opinions drawn from actual investigative interviews as well as academic research. Like the original, the Revised Protocol requires interviewers to maintain a rigorous program of refresher training, monitoring, and feedback in order to ensure their continuing adherence to protocol requirements (Lamb, 2016). Police Child Protection Units in England and Wales who wish to adopt this new tool must fight for adequate funding to support its use against the demands of other policing priorities in a climate of ever-shrinking budgets.

Professor Lamb's continuing contribution to psychology and society in general and the field of investigative interviewing in particular has been internationally recognized: In 2015 he achieved a rare double when the American Psychological Society honored him with both their "Distinguished contribution to psychology in the public interest" award and the "Distinguished award for the application of psychology." Along with his co-authors, this new book represents a scholarly and ambitious attempt to make a difference to the general quality of interviews received by the courts and minimize the risks of miscarriages of justice, for victim or defendant. It deserves to be read by all practitioners involved in child protection, whether as investigators, judges, or lawyers.

Graham M. Davies
University of Leicester

REFERENCES

Ceci, S. J., & Bruck, M. (1995). *Jeopardy in the courtroom: A scientific analysis of children's testimony.* Washington, DC: American Psychological Association.

Eysenck, M. W., Derakshan, N., Santos, R., & Calvo, M. G. (2007). Anxiety and cognitive performance: Attentional control theory. *Emotion, 7,* 336–353.

Harris, C. B., Rasmussen, A. S., & Berntsen, D. (2014). The functions of autobiographical memory: An integrative approach. *Memory, 22,* 559–581.

Lamb, M. E. (2016). Difficulties translating research on forensic interview practices to practitioners: Finding water, leading horses, but can we get them to drink? *American Psychologist, 71,* 710–718.

Preface

When *Tell Me What Happened* first appeared in 2008, it provided a comprehensive overview of the literature on the frailties and strengths of young victim witnesses. After summarizing the results of numerous experimental and field studies, we described how a careful examination of those findings could inform practice and introduced a structured interviewing guide, the NICHD Investigative Interview Protocol, which had been successfully employed in several jurisdictions.

A decade later, our collective understanding of these issues had grown so dramatically that a revision of the book seemed necessary. Indeed, this revision is a completely new book, written with the involvement of a new author. It not only reviews the topics covered in the first edition but also incorporates a myriad of relevant findings published since the first edition went to press. This means that the book provides a comprehensive survey of both classic and new research informing best practice interviewing and reviews more recent studies exploring the utility and effectiveness of the Protocol.

Whereas the Protocol initially emphasized cognitive factors affecting the retrieval and reporting of experienced events, recent research has focused on the emotional and motivational factors that affect the willingness to disclose abuse and describe it in detail. Accordingly, this book introduces and explains the Revised Protocol, which has been developed, tested, validated, and implemented by the authors and their colleagues since publication of the first edition.

The Revised Protocol is designed to help interviewers establish the cognitive and emotional conditions that together maximize the likelihood that abused children will disclose and describe their experiences of maltreatment when formally interviewed. The revised version of *Tell Me What Happened* describes the Revised Protocol, as well as the research on which it is based, and shows how its use affects the behavior of interviewers and suspected victims.

Tell Me What Happened also includes a summary of recent research on the eyewitness capacities of children with intellectual and learning difficulties, Autism Spectrum Disorder, and other vulnerabilities. As we show, there is growing evidence that the Protocol and Revised Protocol are well-suited to guide investigative interviews of such individuals, who are disproportionately likely to be victimized.

We also review research on the utility and risks associated with the widespread use of the various props and tools that are being used very frequently in the absence of a thorough understanding of what effects they might have. In general, as we show, there is little evidence that these tools help interviewers obtain evidence that could not be obtained in the course of well-structured verbal interviews, conducted in accordance with the guidelines summarized earlier in the book.

Tell Me What Happened, like the first edition, has been written with practitioners in mind. We have made considerable efforts to ensure that our discussion is readily accessible to practitioners in the field—particularly social workers, agency staff, and police officers—as well as to academics and researchers. Although we pay close attention to the scholarly research literature, we do so in order to ensure that the advice and guidance we provide for interviewers is grounded in a thorough understanding of what we know about investigators' characteristics and needs as well as children's tendencies, strengths, and limitations. Our goal in writing this book is to foster improved practice, thereby ensuring that young and vulnerable victims of abuse can be protected from further harm while just outcomes are pursued for those who have maltreated them.

In writing this book, we have benefited from insights and observations made by countless professionals and researchers, as well as from feedback from the many practitioners whose own interview experiences have informed both our research and the continued development and optimization of the Investigative Interview Protocol we describe in the book. Researchers' contributions are recognized in citations throughout the text; here we acknowledge and thank the many unsung practitioners without whose tireless efforts this book would not have been possible.

We are proud of this book, and hope that readers will find it as useful as colleagues found the first edition.

Michael E. Lamb, Deirdre A. Brown, Irit Hershkowitz, Yael Orbach, and Phillip W. Esplin
December 2017

Tell Me What Happened

1

Interviewing Children About Abuse: An Overview and Introduction

A mother contacts Child Protective Services, concerned about a comment her daughter, Sarah (3 years old), made during bath time. Sarah pointed to her vagina and said "Daddy does that to me".. Sarah's parents recently separated, and her father lives out of town, only seeing her one weekend a month. Sarah's class has recently been working through a trial of an educational model about "good touch, bad touch." When Sarah was asked during an investigative interview what she was there to talk about she replied, "Mummy is mad because Daddy rubbed me there and that's bad touch."

Ben (4 years) recently developed an infection around his bottom. During examination his doctor noted that Ben appeared to have some partially healed abrasions that might be consistent with abuse. During the rapport building stage of an investigative interview Ben talked about his interest in pirates. During the substantive phase Ben told the interviewer that his friend Joey (8 years) "stabbed him in the butt with his sword and then I punched him in the face and he died."

Theresa (6 years) lives with her mother and stepfather (Shane). She often stays up late with them and falls asleep on the couch while they watch television. Two weekends a month Theresa stays with her father (Steve), stepmother (Melissa), and stepsister (Molly—4 years). Melissa became concerned when she observed Theresa playing with two dolls, one on top of the other, saying "see Molly, this is how you show someone you love them, this is how you are a real special girl." Melissa asked Theresa how she knew that, and Theresa replied "I'm Shane's special girl." Melissa told Theresa that grownups should not love children like that and she needed to tell her father that Shane was playing with her the wrong way. An investigation was initiated.

Imagine you were to interview Sarah, Ben, or Theresa to investigate the concerns raised. What might you be wondering about? Perhaps how well children can describe their experiences for child welfare officials or legal investigators? Or perhaps, how others' concerns might affect how children behave in an interview? Or even whether the inclusion of highly improbable details (e.g., a claim about punching someone in the face and killing them, in the absence of a dead body) renders the entire account unreliable. These vignettes highlight just a few of the many challenges that practitioners and researchers working in the area of child maltreatment investigation must grapple with. Children's ability to provide detailed, coherent and reliable accounts of their experiences may also be evaluated by lawyers (e.g., considering what aspects of a case might be subject to challenge), judges, and jury members, all of whom may also be wondering about children's ability to provide reliable eyewitness testimony.

In this book, we update our previous review of research examining children's testimony and of how the way children are questioned affects the quality of information they provide. We integrate the substantial body of research published in the ten years since the first edition was prepared and reflect upon questions that the field should continue to address. Although much has been learned about children's competencies and shortcomings, the lessons remain difficult to translate effectively into practice. Amidst many international studies demonstrating the persistence of interviewing techniques that do not help children provide detailed and accurate accounts, studies continue to show that use of the evidence-based NICHD Investigative Protocol is effective in that regard. In the following chapters, we review what research has demonstrated about young witnesses' strengths and difficulties, the challenges that interviewers face when eliciting testimony from children, how to effectively prepare children to be interviewed, and the evidence showing how the NICHD Protocol can help interviewers conduct high quality, developmentally sensitive interviews with witnesses, especially those who are young or have additional vulnerabilities. As we explain in some detail, forensic interviews with children can be invaluable sources of information, but they should always be recognized as parts of the forensic investigation, not seen as synonymous with the investigation as a whole.

THE BACKGROUND: INTERVIEWING AND CHILD DEVELOPMENT

Our understanding of children's capacities to recount their experiences has emerged from two distinct but complementary approaches to the study of eyewitness testimony. Many researchers have studied what children can tell us when interviewed in developmentally sensitive and supportive ways, whilst others have focused on how children's accounts can be compromised by various influences, such as suggestive questioning and exposure to misinformation. Together, the resultant knowledge about the conditions which foster *accurate responding*, and conversely, those that promote *false responding* has shown us how to establish optimal conditions so that children can describe their experiences in a complete, organized, and accurate manner.

Just as there have been two broad approaches to developing key research questions about children's testimonial ability, there have also been disparate and yet complementary methodologies employed to examine the issues. Most research examining children's eyewitness testimony has been conducted using laboratory-based analogue experiments. In a typical laboratory study, for example, children experience staged events, or watch short video clips, before their recall is tested using scripted questions that vary depending on the focus of the study (e.g., children's recall vs. suggestibility). The advantages of such approaches are that researchers can systematically examine variables thought to influence recall (or suggestibility), whilst limiting the impact of confounding factors. Importantly, the accuracy or reliability of children's statements can be evaluated against an objective record of what actually occurred. Invariably, however, such approaches are limited in the extent to which they mimic many of the features that may characterize investigations of possible maltreatment, thus their ecological validity is often questioned.

In attempts to bridge the gap between tightly controlled laboratory-based research and actual forensic interviews, researchers have also studied children's recall of naturally occurring events that more closely parallel aspects of maltreatment (e.g., medical procedures, traumatic events), and their recount of self-nominated events that were emotionally salient (e.g., happy, sad, or scary events). Although the events described are presumed to have been more salient and thus memorable than staged events, there may be no objective record of them, meaning accuracy cannot be ascertained.

Researchers have also conducted field studies, examining forensic interviews of children believed to have been victims of maltreatment. Such work has illuminated interviewing practice in the absence of strict experimental control and identified areas in need of further research. Whilst field studies uniquely provide the opportunity to study the impact of interviewing techniques on children's recall in real world settings, they are typically limited by the absence of objective records or incontrovertible corroborating evidence from which to assess the accuracy of children's statements. The field has benefited from the combined outputs of both approaches in constructing evidence-based practice recommendations (Lamb & Thierry, 2005). Despite very different approaches to examining the impact of interviewing strategies on children's responses, the conclusions reached regarding children's limitations *and* competencies have been remarkably consistent.

We have no litmus test to assess the accuracy of children's accounts. What we do have is a convergent body of findings showing the range of influences that interact to shape children's testimony. Broadly speaking, these can be grouped into factors that relate to 1) the kind of experience children are being asked to describe, 2) characteristics of the child, and 3) the way in which children are interviewed. Given the limited (if any) opportunity to intervene to mitigate the influence of factors relating to the experience itself, much attention has been focused on what the child brings to the interview context, what the interviewer brings, and how their mutual interactions shape the nature of the testimony elicited. In brief, the research reviewed at greater length later in this book has shown that, although children clearly *can* remember incidents they have experienced, the relationship between age and memory is complex, with a variety of factors influencing the quality of information provided. For our present purposes, perhaps the most important of these factors pertain to the interviewer's ability to *elicit* information and the child's willingness and ability to *express* it, rather than the child's ability to *remember* it. Recognizing that, like adults, children *can be* informative witnesses, a variety of professional groups and experts have offered recommendations regarding the most effective ways of conducting forensic or investigative interviews with children (e.g., American Professional Society on the Abuse of Children (APSAC), 2012; Home Office, 2011; Lamb, La Rooy, Malloy, & Katz, 2011; Lyon, 2014; Saywitz & Camparo, 2013). Clearly, it *is* often possible to obtain valuable information from children, but doing so requires careful investigative procedures as well as a realistic awareness of their capacities and tendencies. Specifically, accounts elicited using open-ended questions ("Tell me what happened") that tap recall rather than recognition memory are typically more accurate, regardless of the children's ages. The completeness of these initially brief accounts can be increased when interviewers use the information provided by children in their first spontaneous utterance as prompts for further elaboration (e.g., "You said the man touched you, tell me more about that touching") (Lamb et al., 2003). Unfortunately, however, forensic interviewers frequently ask very specific questions ("Did he touch you?") that draw upon recognition rather than recall memory. Such questions typically elicit less accurate responses than open-ended prompts and may even cause erroneous information to be incorporated into children's testimony. What we have learned about children's memories and reporting capacities, as well as the implications for forensic interviewers, are the focus of **Chapter 2**.

In **Chapter 3** we outline how children's contributions and informativeness can be enhanced significantly by preparing them for their task as informants. Research has demonstrated the positive impact of establishing "ground rules" and conducting a brief practice interview with children before introducing the focus of enquiry. We outline some relevant caveats—for example, that children need to have the opportunity to practice ground rules for maximum effect and that practice interviews need to follow the same principles that apply to the substantive interview (namely, they should emphasize the use of open questions). We discuss research evaluating responsive interviewing and exploring the impact of interviewers' responses to requests for clarification and "I don't know" statements on children's subsequent reporting. We also review evidence regarding the effectiveness of different kinds of questioning strategies.

Just as the research examining children's capacities in forensic interviews shows remarkable consensus, so too does research evaluating the conduct of those interviews, regardless of country and training method. Unfortunately, the research-based and expert-endorsed recommendations are widely proclaimed but seldom followed. As discussed more fully in **Chapter 4**, descriptive studies of forensic interviews in various parts of the United States, United Kingdom, Canada, Sweden, Finland, Norway, New Zealand, and Israel, amongst other countries, consistently highlight common and continuing challenges for forensic interviewers. Such studies show that forensic interviewers use open-ended prompts quite rarely, even though such prompts reliably elicit more information than more focused prompts do and are universally recommended as the preferred means of eliciting information from young children (and, indeed, adults too). Interviewers often use untested or unsupported techniques in their interviews, and in doing so may exacerbate the tendency to ask more focused prompts. As well as the addition of undesirable practices, interviewers often omit recommended practices (e.g., ground rules, pre-substantive practice narratives), known to promote children's engagement with and contribution to interviews. To the distress of trainers, interviewers, and administrators, furthermore, deviations from "best practice" are commonly evident even when the interviewers have been trained extensively, are well aware of the recommended practices, and often believe that they were adhering to those recommendations! Both intensive and brief training programs for investigative interviewers appear to impart knowledge about desirable practices but have little if any lasting effect on the actual behavior of forensic investigators (Lamb, 2016).

Because forensic interviewers often have difficulty adhering to recommended interview practices in the field, the authors and their colleagues developed a structured interview Protocol designed to translate professional recommendations into operational guidelines that were first published as an appendix to a report by Orbach and her colleagues (2000). The structured Protocol featured in this book guides interviewers by illustrating techniques designed to maximize the amount and quality of information elicited from alleged victims. As detailed in **Chapter 5**, the NICHD Protocol (named after the research institute where most of the developers worked and from which they received financial support for their work) covers all phases of the investigative interview. The most recent version of the interview protocol includes guidance about how to enhance a child-centered approach to interviewing, by improving rapport and support offered to the child throughout (this version is included at the end of the book as the **Appendix**). In this chapter we describe the structure and progression of interviews following the Protocol, and provide a review of the evidence-base that has supported the Protocol's development and implementation with children of different ages.

We then turn to field studies designed to determine whether interviewers using the Protocol indeed conduct interviews that conform better to the universally recognized "good practices" described earlier in the book, and how such practices affect children's reporting (**Chapter 6**). Independent field studies in several different countries (Canada, Israel, Japan, Korea, the United Kingdom, and the United States) demonstrated convincingly that interviewers using the Protocol used at least three times more open-ended and many fewer risky and suggestive prompts than when exploring comparable incidents, involving children of the same ages, without the Protocol, and that the children, in turn, provided much more forensically relevant information (including disclosures) that was more likely to be accurate because of the ways in which it was elicited. Recent laboratory-based studies examining children's responses when interviewed about a known event using the Protocol have provided additional evidence of its effectiveness in eliciting *accurate* as well as detailed accounts with minimal interviewer input or contamination. Contrary to widespread concerns that younger children could not be helped by use of the structured Protocol, furthermore, research discussed in this chapter shows that children as young as 4 years of age benefit and are more informative when interviewed in this way. Younger and older children are different, of course, and we will explain strategies especially designed to capitalize on the capacities and tendencies of younger (3- to 5-year-old) children (**Chapter 7**).

Children with developmental disorders are particularly vulnerable to maltreatment. Despite this, relatively little attention has been focused on understanding the capacities of such children to provide meaningful information when forensically interviewed. In a series of studies using the Protocol we examined various aspects of testimonial capacity in children with intellectual disabilities of varying severity as well as those with autism spectrum disorders (ASD) and present the findings and recommendations for practice in **Chapter 8**.

Most of the published research on forensic interviewing has focused on interviews with cooperative suspected victims who were ready to disclose, had often made specific allegations of abuse prior to the formal investigation, and were especially responsive to open-ended prompts. However, there is ample evidence that many victims of abuse report the abuse belatedly, if at all, with many denying or failing to report the abuse even when they are directly asked or formally interviewed. In **Chapter 9**, we describe work examining interviews with reluctant victims, as well as witnesses who are not also victims (Lamb, Sternberg, Orbach, Hershkowitz, & Horowitz, 2003), and with youthful suspects (Hershkowitz, Horowitz, Lamb, Orbach, & Sternberg, 2004).

In **Chapter 10** we discuss the findings of studies that have examined the effectiveness of alternative or complementary ways of eliciting information from suspected victims. The use of visual aids (e.g., dolls, diagrams, and drawing) is common in forensic interviewing, despite a relatively limited or non-existent evidence-base. We present research examining additional approaches interviewers might use to support children's recall and reporting, such as mental context reinstatement, a component of the Cognitive Interview, drawing, body diagrams, and dolls, concluding that some of these techniques are unnecessarily risky.

Chapter 11 discusses how ongoing supervision and the review of interviewing practice with interviewers serves to maintain and enhance the quality of their forensic interviews. In this chapter, we reflect upon training approaches and post-training practices that contribute to good interviewing. We also consider possible difficulties accessing supervision and consider recent innovations designed to overcome them.

Because use of the Protocol enhances the quality and informativeness of forensic interviews with suspected victims, it should enhance the value and conclusiveness of investigations into suspected incidents of sexual abuse by making it easier for investigators to judge whether victims are telling the truth (because the children provide more information in a narrative form which is more amenable to credibility assessment) and to extract more clues that may guide their search for corroborative evidence. More child-centered interviews with multiple opportunities for children to provide their own accounts of their experiences may also influence the likelihood that clear allegations will emerge during the interviews, and the quality of the children's testimony (and indeed, of the interviews themselves) has an impact on how cases proceed through the criminal justice system. These issues are explored more fully in **Chapter 12**.

The final chapter (**Chapter 13**) summarizes the information provided in the preceding chapters and briefly describes what we do not yet know. We believe that development of the Protocol has permitted considerable progress in the way in which children are interviewed forensically, although we hope that future research may shed further light on effective interviewing strategies and continue to inform forensic practices.

CONCLUSION

The research reviewed in this book demonstrates both 1) how much we have collectively learned about children's communicative and memory retrieval capacities and 2) that this information can be used by interviewers to maximize the value of their investigative interviews with alleged or suspected victims of abuse. The Protocol operationalizes the principles about which there has been clear expert professional consensus and has been shown to actually improve the behavior of investigative interviewers by helping them to elicit information that is more likely to be accurate because it is recalled by the child freely rather than in response to information and probes provided by the interviewer.

Of course, the Protocol does not address all the problems facing those investigating the possible abuse of young children. Efforts are still being made to refine safe ways of providing emotional support and addressing motivational factors that make many children—more than a third of suspected victims and unknown numbers of children about whom no suspicions have been raised—reluctant to disclose abuse. Likewise we have shown that some children with developmental, intellectual, and communicative difficulties, are able to participate effectively in Protocol interviews, provided they are evaluated from a developmentally sensitive perspective. Whether children with particular types of developmental disorders (e.g., language impairments) require particular modifications to the interviewing context and strategies used remains unknown. Likewise we have not examined how well the Protocol works when used to interview adults—typically developing adults as well as those with particular mental, intellectual, or communicative challenges. There is considerable scope for further work with young suspects, and especially those who have language and/or intellectual disabilities as well.

So to return to the cases outlined at the beginning of the chapter, what does the sum of our research tell us? Let's for a brief moment consider Ben, Sarah and Theresa, and some of the issues that their cases raise. Can very young children describe their experiences sufficiently well to inform those who must ensure their welfare or investigate possible crimes? Does the inclusion of highly improbable or fantastic details in a report irrevocably undermine the child's reliability or credibility? What are the effects of others' agendas on how children behave when interviewed? Our research would suggest that, with appropriate preparation and use of a child-centered interviewing approach, even very young children can provide investigatively useful information, and that disclosures of improbable events can be clarified by follow-up questioning using open-ended prompts. The preparation phase of an interview can also act as a protective strategy by clearly communicating to children the interviewers' expectations about how they should behave during the interview. The third issue is not so clear—a good interview may assist by highlighting inconsistencies or script-like language that could indicate pre-interview coaching or the negative influences of informal (suggestive) interviewing (e.g., from concerned parents, or doctors, teachers, and so forth) but that certainly cannot be assumed. The potentially long-lasting effects of pre-interview suggestions have been demonstrated in many studies, highlighting the need to conduct forensic interviews as soon as possible, to both facilitate recall and to minimize opportunities for the contamination of children's memories.

In all, although development of the Protocol has improved the way in which some children are interviewed forensically, considerably more work is needed before we can feel confident that we are collectively doing all we can both to protect vulnerable children from further abuse and to ensure that innocent adults are not accused of crimes they did not commit because forensic interviewers failed to elicit accurate information from young informants. The Protocol remains a "work-in-progress" and must continue developing to accommodate the results of new research. We present here an update of this work-in-progress and the implications for interviewing, and children's role in investigations, and highlight future directions for research.

2

Contributions to Children's Testimony: The Child and the Event

If we were to try to predict how well Sarah, Ben, or Theresa (Chapter 1) could contribute to the investigations that followed their comments, we would most likely focus our assessment on three broad categories of factors shown to influence children's recall and reporting, i.e., child-related, event-related, and interview-related. Examples of the kinds of factors that we would group in each category are shown in the text boxes below.

In the three cases we introduced, the children were the only available sources of information about what had happened to them; no one could provide additional or corroborative eyewitness testimony, which is a common challenge for investigations of maltreatment. As a result, the outcome of an investigation will often rest on the quality of what the child can recount in an investigative interview, with other kinds of corroborative evidence seldom available. In this chapter, we review important aspects of children's development that affect their ability to provide useful information when interviewed about events they have experienced, and consider how characteristics of the event in question may influence what children remember and report.

Tell Me What Happened: Questioning Children About Abuse, Second Edition.
Michael E. Lamb, Deirdre A. Brown, Irit Hershkowitz, Yael Orbach, and Phillip W. Esplin.
© 2018 John Wiley & Sons Ltd. Published 2018 by John Wiley & Sons Ltd.

Event

How many times did it happen?
How long ago did it happen?
How involved was the child?
What kind of event was it?

Child

How old?
Language skills?
Intellectual ability?
Developmental disorder?
Responsiveness to questions?
Information-processing skills?
   Theory of Mind
   Source monitoring
   Encoding
   Processing speed
   Attention
   Knowledge
   Strategy use
Motivation?

Interview

How long since the disclosure?
How many interviews?
Any pre-interview assessment?
Who has talked to the child about this event already?
How was the interview explained to the child?
How was the child "prepared" for the interview?
What rapport was established?
What types of questions were asked?
How were the questions distributed throughout the interview?
Was the interview child-led or interviewer-led?
Were other aids or techniques used?

WHAT THE CHILD BRINGS TO AN INTERVIEW

When we think of child development, we tend to think of a range of skills and attributes that increase and become more sophisticated as children develop.

Researchers have identified typical age ranges or stages in which children first demonstrate skills or achieve mastery of them. While such estimates are helpful in understanding what we might expect from children, it is important to recognize that, in practice, the "average child" may never face an interviewer. Within any group of children, there is immense variation in the age of attainment of most skills, and it is therefore problematic to apply to any individual child group-based age estimates of when children attain skills. For example, it is difficult to translate our knowledge of how children's memory abilities develop into predictions of how a specific child may describe an event because multiple factors are at play. Generally speaking, there is no easy answer to the question "At what age can children …?" because, typically, the answer starts with "It depends on …." That is, children's performance reflects a complex interaction among a number of factors, rather than any single ability in isolation. Moreover, a single child may show various levels of different skills such as attentional or linguistic skills. That said, it is well accepted that one of the most robust predictors of children's memory performance is age, and we provide a brief discussion of the development of memory below.

The Emergence of Long-Term Memory in Children

There is robust scientific evidence that our earliest experiences are not available to us as adults, with very few adolescents or adults able to recall life events from before about 3 years of age This phenomenon is referred to as *"infantile amnesia"* and has posed a puzzle to developmental scientists, especially given substantial evidence that very young children are capable of forming autobiographical memories that they retain over days, months, or even longer, from a much younger age than 3 (Jack, MacDonald, Reese, & Hayne, 2009; Peterson, Wang, & Hou, 2009; Peterson, Warren, & Short, 2011; Tustin & Hayne, 2010). Indeed, even before the acquisition of language, very young infants clearly remember experiences, sometimes over long time periods, if appropriate nonverbal measures of memory are used (see Rovee-Collier & Hayne, 2000, for review). Recent research has shown that the age of our earliest memories is influenced by how old we are when asked to recall them—children and adolescents may recall events from earlier ages than adults, well below the typical cut-off of 3 years (Jack et al.,

2009; Peterson et al., 2009, 2011; Tustin & Hayne, 2010). Children's earliest memories start to become less accessible around 7 years of age; thereafter, children's recall of early experiences begins to fall away or become less detailed, much like adults' recall of events from this period (Bauer, 2015; Bauer & Larkina, 2014a).

Infantile amnesia occurs for memories of all kinds of early experiences—even highly distinctive events are not protected from forgetting. Although some events are more likely than others to be recalled from early ages (Fivush, Sales, Goldberg, Bahrick, & Parker, 2004; Neisser, 2004; Peterson, 2015), traumatic events are also forgotten when the events occurred very early in life.

There are several theories seeking to explain why we may have difficulty as adults retrieving early memories about our childhood. **Neurobiological** accounts emphasize the role of physical maturation of brain regions and neurotransmitter systems that are implicated in learning and memory (Madsen & Kim, 2016). Some researchers have suggested that infantile amnesia ends as **language development** begins—implying that language is an essential component for us to be able to retain and communicate our experiences. Language clearly plays a role: Memories acquired during infancy are very fragile, in part because these memories are only encoded in nonverbal modalities, involving perceptually-based attributes (Hayne & Rovee-Collier, 1995). In order to recall and describe nonverbal representations of events verbally, these memories must be recoded into language. The ability to translate early nonverbal experiences into a language-based format when children have acquired the necessary vocabulary seems fragile, and dependent on contextual support—for example, the presence of objects that were part of the experience and can thus serve as cues or reminders (Bauer et al., 2004; Dahl, Kingo, & Krøjgaard, 2015). When such cues are not available, children are unable to verbally describe experiences they had prior to developing language, although they can sometimes do so through behavioral re-enactment (Simcock & Hayne, 2002). Social-interactionist perspectives on the emergence of autobiographical memory (Fivush, 2011) also highlight the importance of language development. For instance, Nelson and her colleagues argued that children start to form long-term memories only when they begin talking about their experiences with others, thereby creating meaningful and enduring autobiographical records of their experiences. This social construction of personal narratives influences the quantity and quality of children's narratives (Nelson, 2013). The emergence of memory as part of a dynamic exchange where an individual is shaped by many levels of a system (family, culture, context) is recognized in socio-cultural perspectives on autobiographical memory development (Wang, 2016).

Other scholars have suggested that infantile amnesia dissipates with the **emergence of a sense of self** and an understanding that other people are separate entities from ourselves, with different thoughts, experiences, beliefs, and knowledge (Prebble, Addis, & Tippett, 2013). It is only when we understand that there is an "I" or self that is separate (Howe, 2014) that we need to process and recall information from our own experiences because we understand that others may not share them (see Howe, Courage, & Edison, 2003; Nelson & Fivush, 2004; Perner, 2000).

Still other researchers have suggested that infantile amnesia reflects **basic memory processes** that continue to occur throughout the lifespan (Bauer & Larkina, 2014a, 2014b). As very young infants, we encode our memories in a very primitive way that is dependent on the exact context of the experience and this is stored in a nonverbal way (because we have not yet developed language). We have limited capacity for storage and retention of these experiences, and as they become less relevant, or more automatic (less novel and informative), they are displaced by subsequent experiences. As a result, they are no longer available to us as adults. Memories encoded as we age are likely to be richer in detail and therefore likely to contain more cues that we can use to later trigger recall of them (Hayne, 2004).

How Old is the Child? Age Differences in Eyewitness Testimony

Numerous studies have shown a developmental progression in the amount of information that children report, with younger children typically reporting less than older children and adolescents (e.g., Brown, Lewis, & Lamb, 2015; Brown, Lewis, Lamb, & Stephens, 2012; Jack, Leov, & Zajac, 2014; Jack, Martyn, & Zajac, 2015). Age in itself is not sufficient to account for these differences, however, because within groups there are often younger children who do better than older children. Specifically, although measures of the average performance may show older children to be more competent, there is often overlap between adjacent age groups, such that there are high performing younger children who are better than the poorer performing older children (Geddie, Fradin, & Beer, 2000; Leichtman, Ceci, & Morse, 1997; Pipe & Salmon, 2002; Quas, Goodman, Ghetti, & Redlich, 2000; Quas, Qin, Schaaf, & Goodman, 1997). Furthermore, when the demands of the task are changed (e.g., to allow children to demonstrate knowledge in different ways) age group differences may be minimized or even eliminated (Ceci, Ross, & Toglia, 1987b; Cole & Loftus, 1987; Jones, Swift, & Johnston, 1988; Saywitz, 1987), indicating that age-related differences in performance reflect factors other than memory ability (e.g., the way in which knowledge was assessed). In some respects, younger children may actually outperform older children—for example, younger children are *less* likely than older children and adults to falsely include non-presented information that is strongly related to the theme of the to-be-remembered material (Brainerd & Reyna, 2012). Age, it seems, does not determine children's ability to recount personal experiences but rather serves to encapsulate the influence of a number of variables relating to children's abilities, the effects of which may differ across interview/recall contexts.

Responsiveness to Questions: Developmental Changes in Children's Verbal Accounts

Once children are able to talk about their experiences, their abilities to recall events are often impressive, although significant developmental changes continue through early childhood. Young children typically recall significantly less information than older children, particularly in response to very general prompts such as "Tell me what happened," and may not include the kinds of details that adults might mention (Strange & Hayne, 2013). What they spontaneously include in their reports, however, is as likely to be accurate as information provided by older children. Four- and 5-year-olds thus typically require more specific prompts from interviewers (Hamond & Fivush, 1991; Hershkowitz, Lamb, Orbach, Katz, & Horowitz, 2012), but in responding to such prompts their accounts may be more inaccurate than older children's (Bjorklund, Bjorklund, Brown, & Cassel, 1998; Goodman, Quas, Batterman-Faunce, Riddlesberger, & Kuhn, 1994). Nevertheless, recent field research shows that children as young as 4 years of age provide proportionally as much information in response to open-ended questions as older children, although the brevity of their responses makes it necessary for interviewers to prompt for additional information, using the children's prior responses as cues to trigger further recall (Lamb et al., 2003; Hershkowitz et al., 2012 and Chapter 7).

Developmental differences in the quality and extent of children's recall are not restricted to mundane experiences or those with a positive emotional valence, but are also evident when children are interviewed about painful, distressing, and traumatic experiences, such as accidental injuries, intrusive medical procedures (e.g., Peterson, 2012), and abusive experiences (Lamb, Sternberg, & Esplin, 2000; Sternberg, Lamb, Orbach et al., 2001). Although most studies do not report developmental changes in the *accuracy* of open-ended free narrative reports, the accuracy of responses to prompts and questions is likely to decrease markedly for the younger children, particularly when they must disagree with the interviewer to answer correctly (Myers et al., 2003).

In sum, even though young children can accurately describe previous experiences, developmental changes in remembering nonetheless take place. Age emerges as an important determinant of event memory in part because it is correlated with other variables that influence memory, including children's prior knowledge and understanding of events, and the effectiveness of the retrieval strategies used. As we shall see, it is sometimes possible to eliminate or reduce developmental differences in memory when the confounding effects of variables usually associated with age, such as knowledge, are controlled.

Individual Differences

There are often marked individual differences in the amount and/or accuracy of information children recall. Individual differences may be forensically relevant to the extent that they predict, for example, whether or not a child is likely to be suggestible or easily misled, to lie, or to benefit from a particular interview strategy (Gordon et al., 1993; Pipe & Salmon, 2002). Although we have learned much from studies examining the contribution of various aspects of children's development and functioning to their memory ability, the associations reported have not been strong enough for us to safely predict the testimonial ability of any particular child. More generally, however, understanding sources of variation in children's recall may help place their testimony in context, and help interviewers understand why some children may say less about their experiences than others do. Most studies examining the role of individual differences in memory have focused on identifying those children likely to be vulnerable to suggestive questioning (see Quas et al., 1997). A small but growing number of studies have also been concerned with both cognitive and personality variables that moderate the accuracy of children's recall.

Intelligence

There is some evidence that, within the typical range of intelligence, higher scores are positively correlated with children's event recall (Elischberger & Roebers, 2001; Geddie, Fradin, & Beer, 2000; Melinder et al., 2010) although the relation may be stronger for older (e.g., 8- to 10-year-old) children (Roebers & Schneider, 2001) and may also depend on how interviews are conducted (Brown & Pipe, 2003a; Melinder et al., 2010). As we discuss in Chapter 8, when comparisons are made between children with significantly impaired cognitive function and those whose intellectual ability falls in the normal range, the impact of low intellectual ability is more evident.

Attachment and Temperament

Attachment and temperament may affect the quality of children's event reports by affecting the way in which children attend to various aspects of their experiences, and the meaning they attribute to events, which, in turn, can affect the ways in which events are recalled (Chae, Goodman, & Edelstein, 2010; Chae, Ogle, & Goodman, 2009; Melinder et al., 2010). For example, children who do not have secure attachments to significant adults may be more focused on seeking sources of security during stressful experiences and so not process the same amount of information about them as children who have more secure attachments (Goodman, Quas, Batterman-Faunce, Riddlesberger, & Kuhn, 1997). In turn, securely attached children should be better able to regulate their emotions, aiding both encoding and subsequent recall. There is some evidence to support these predictions: Goodman and colleagues found children whose parents reported insecure attachments were both more stressed during painful and distressing medical procedures and subsequently made more errors when recounting them than children whose parents reported secure attachment styles (Goodman et al., 1994, 1997). Further, a laboratory-based study with young (3-year-old) children indicated that children with secure attachments may do better recalling positive events whereas children with insecure attachments focus more on negative events (Belsky, Spritz, & Crnic, 1996). Melinder et al. (2010) showed that young (4-year-old) children were more accurate recalling a medical examination and were more able to resist suggestion when lower levels of parental attachment anxiety were evident.

Research has not established a clear link between different types of temperament and event memory. Gordon et al. (1993) found that three dimensions of temperament (approach-withdrawal, emotionality, and adaptability) were related to recall of a medical examination by both 3- and 5-year-old children. Merritt, Ornstein, and Spicker (1994) likewise found that adaptability and approach-withdrawal were related to children's recall of the procedure. However, Baker-Ward, Burgwyn, Ornstein, and Gordon (1995) did not find any association between temperament and recall of minor surgery for facial lacerations, although coping style during the surgery was related to recall (see Pipe & Salmon, 2002; Quas, 1998; Quas et al., 1997, for review). Zajac, Jury, and O'Neill (2009) showed that children with lower levels of self-confidence, self-esteem, and assertiveness (as rated by their teachers) performed more poorly than children rated more highly on these dimensions during cross-examination-style questioning. Other researchers have found that shy children answered specific questions less accurately than did children who were less shy and that manageability was positively related to the number of intrusions reported by 3-year-olds when re-enacting an event using dolls and props (Greenhoot, Ornstein, Gordon, & Baker-Ward, 1999; Roebers & Schneider, 2001)). Greenhoot et al. (1999) suggested that more manageable or "easy" children may be more compliant and eager to please, which, in turn, may have led them to produce more intrusion errors. Additionally, Greenhoot et al. found that less persistent 3-year-olds were more likely to produce errors than children who were more persistent and thus better able to attend to the tasks. Salmon, Roncolato, and Gleitzman (2003) found that children with higher levels of "effortful control" (i.e., the ability to shift and refocus attention in order to regulate behaviors and emotions) produced more details than children with lower levels of effortful control when behaviorally re-enacting events. Children who are more prone to anxiety, and those who are anxious during recall are more likely to be suggestible than children with lower levels of general and in-context anxiety (Almerigogna, Ost, Bull, & Akehurst, 2007), and levels of anxiety may also predict children's responses to challenging questions such as those encountered during cross-examination (Bettenay, Ridley, Henry, & Crane, 2015).

Fantasy
Fantasy and pretend play are normative and developmentally appropriate behaviors for children. However, children's beliefs in fantastical characters or their judgments about fantasy versus reality may be used to discredit their testimony as victims/witnesses. Children are often portrayed as confused about and unable to distinguish between fantasy and reality, and their belief in fantastical characters is often seen to exemplify their difficulties in this area (see Woolley & Ghossainy, 2013, for a review), with "a disproportionate amount of attention" paid to children's tendency to believe in fantastical beings. Three and 4-year-olds are also prone to erroneously label real events or entities as "pretend," presumably because they are relying on their limited knowledge and experience when making such judgments. Like adults, children over 6 years of age can discriminate easily between imagined and experienced events (Carrick, Rush, & Quas, 2013; Lindsay & Johnson, 1987; Roberts, 2000). Studies show that even 3-year-olds can make some "fantasy versus reality" judgments accurately (e.g., they are aware that imaginary objects cannot simply appear in real life and that pretend actions are not real actions; Estes, Wellman, & Woolley, 1989; Flavell, Flavell, & Green, 1987; Woolley & Wellman, 1993). For example, Carrick and Quas (2006) presented preschoolers (3- to 5-year-olds) with real versus fantastical emotional images from children's storybooks (e.g., a mother yelling at a child versus a cat yelling at kittens;

mice dancing in clothes versus people celebrating) and then asked children to indicate whether the scenes depicted "could happen in real life." Regardless of how realistic the images were, children were more likely to say that the positive images "could happen in real life."

The presence of fantastic elements in children's accounts of abuse is affected by the presence of props (such as toys or dolls) usually associated with fantasy (Thierry, Lamb, Orbach, & Pipe, 2004), or by interviewers prompting children to "imagine" or "pretend," and may also be influenced by the instructions that interviewers give alongside interview techniques (e.g., drawing: MacLeod, Gross, & Hayne, 2016). As a result, forensic investigators have been urged to avoid having props present during investigative interviews and to avoid making reference to play or imagination-based processes (Lamb, Sternberg, & Esplin, 1995; Lamb, Sternberg, & Esplin, 1998; Poole & Lamb, 1998).

Information-processing Skills

A broad range of information-processing skills must be applied to the task of remembering experiences. Beginning with what is perceived during the experience, and therefore encoded, these skills can enhance or detract from children's ability to provide detailed and accurate testimony.

Knowledge

Children's understanding or knowledge of what is happening around them influences what they encode about it (Haden, 2013). Knowledge can be more important than age in explaining how well a person might recall information. For example, children who are experts about a topic (e.g., dinosaurs, cartoons) may be able to recount more information relating to these topics than novice adults (e.g., Bjorklund, 1987; Bjorklund & Thompson, 1983; Bjorklund & Zeman, 1982; Chi, 1978; Chi & Ceci, 1987; Chi & Koeske, 1983; Landis, 1982). Researchers have shown that both adults and children can encode (and therefore remember) information better if it makes sense to them. It is much easier to remember information that is presented in a story with all of the elements relating to each other than to remember a list of isolated words or concepts, especially if those words are unfamiliar to us. Similarly, children who can make some sense of an event can encode more about what is happening while children who have more knowledge about certain types of events later recall more details about those events than children with less knowledge (Greenhoot, 2000; McGuigan & Salmon, 2004; Sutherland, Pipe, Schick, Murray, & Gobbo, 2003). Conversely, if the events that children experience or witness fall outside their knowledge base, they may have difficulty making sense of them and encoding information that can later be retrieved and communicated.

However, children may also attempt to use existing knowledge and concepts and apply them to their experiences incorrectly, leading to confusion about what has actually occurred. Think about Ben, for example, and his assertion that he was stabbed by his friend. It is possible that Ben may have been using his knowledge base or frame of reference to explain something unfamiliar, interpreting the pain of penetration in a place he could not see by reference to a sword that might be wielded by a pirate. Increasing knowledge about an event may also increase the likelihood of false memories developing, if children embed additional knowledge or information into their recollection, draw upon script knowledge, or use knowledge as a cue to report related information (Brainerd & Reyna, 2012; Otgaar, Candel, Scoboria, & Merckelbach, 2010; Otgaar, Smeets, & Peters, 2012).

Source Monitoring
The credibility and reliability of children's testimony may be influenced by how well they can identify how they learned about the things they are recounting, and how well they can distinguish between different versions of similar events. Identifying where one's knowledge came from involves source monitoring (Johnson, Hashtroudi, & Lindsay, 1993). Source monitoring may be particularly challenging for very young children in part because they are still learning how to keep distinct two representations for their experiences—a general framework (or script) that describes what the core components of such experiences are, and the memory of particular instances of the class of experiences. In order to recall details about specific incidents from among many similar instances, children must discriminate the source of the detail, including which occasion it was associated with, which location it happened in, when it occurred, and so forth. When describing their experiences, children must also be able to differentiate between knowledge they possess from direct experience as distinct from knowledge gained from other sources, such as the media, conversations with others, or even their own imagination (see Principe & Schindewolf, 2012). Think about Theresa for a moment—she may have been repeating dialogue and demonstrating actions with the doll that she saw on television programs when she stayed up with her mother and stepfather. Field work examining the associations between children's source awareness and their recall of multiple experiences of alleged abuse underline the importance of source monitoring for episodic recall. For example, Thierry, Lamb, and Orbach (2003) found that 3- to 11-year-old alleged sexual abuse victims who were more aware of the source of their knowledge recalled more episodic details (but not more generic details) about multiple experiences of abuse than children who were less aware of source.

Attempts to improve children's source monitoring performance and ability to recall specific events without intrusion of information about other similar experiences have met with mixed success. In general, children are less likely to make source errors when asked for open-ended, free-recall accounts than when asked specific questions (Roberts & Powell, 2001). Older children are better able than younger ones to distinguish between components of events that have similar general structure but differing content (Brubacher, Glisic, Roberts, & Powell, 2011), as inferred from their higher likelihood to generate event-specific labels for repeated incidents of abuse (Brubacher, Malloy, Lamb, & Roberts, 2013). Explicitly asking children about the source of information they have reported –for example, whether it was something that they saw or something that someone told them about –can be useful with older children (Lindsay & Johnson, 1989; Zaragoza & Lane, 1994), but not with very young (3- or 4-year-old) children (Leichtman, Morse, Dixon, & Spiegel, 2000; Quas, Schaaf, Alexander, & Goodman, 2000; see Roberts & Powell, 2001; Roberts, 2002 for reviews). Using children's disclosed labels for different incidents when requesting additional event-specific episodic information may help children of all ages to provide event-specific details, often necessary for ensuring successful prosecution (Brubacher et al., 2013). A study of misinformation also demonstrated that instructions to ignore information from another source may as well improve children's accuracy (Schaaf, Bederian-Gardner, & Goodman, 2015).

Strategy use
Strategy use (employing a conscious approach to enhancing memory during encoding or retrieval) develops with age (Schwenck, Bjorklund, & Schneider, 2009), and usually improves recall (Flavell, 1970; Ornstein, Haden, & Hendrick, 2004). Compared with younger children, older children are more proficient at using strategies to help them pay attention to information, and to retrieve it from memory, and are more likely to do so spontaneously (Schneider & Bjorklund, 1998). As children become older, they also become better at generating their own retrieval cues, which makes them less reliant on support provided by the interviewer (Quas et al., 2000). Younger children may be able to benefit from strategies when explicitly instructed to use them, although whether they benefit may reflect how difficult the strategy is for them to use, and they may fail to transfer their strategy learning to a new task (Clerc, Miller, & Cosnefroy, 2014). Demanding strategies may over-tax children's cognitive processing (e.g., working memory) resources meaning they have less available for memorizing (Flavell, Miller, & Miller, 1993; Miller, 1990). Alternatively, children may be able

to implement strategies, but not efficiently (Clerc et al., 2014). In real-life situations, children may be unlikely to recognize that they might employ strategies to strengthen their encoding of their experiences because this would require them to recognize that they may be required to access this information in the future. Rehearsal (repeated remembering) is one strategy that may occur naturally—through conversations with friends and family, or re-exposure or re-experiencing of the event—although such conversations increase the chance that false details may be incorporated (e.g., suggestions from others, Principe & Schindewolf, 2012), or that unrehearsed information becomes inaccessible in later interviews (Aslan & Bäuml, 2010).

LANGUAGE SKILLS

The clarity and completeness of children's testimony is clearly affected by their developing communicative abilities (Poole, 2016; Walker, Kenniston, & Inada, 2013). Young children often do not articulate individual sounds consistently even after they seem to have mastered them (Reich, 1986), so it is quite common for interviewers to misunderstand children, especially preschoolers. In addition, the vocabularies of young children are much more limited and less descriptive than those of adults (Brown, 1973; Dale, 1976; De Villiers & De Villiers, 1999), and their statements are likely to lack adjectival and adverbial modifiers. Misunderstandings between children and interviewers may also occur because children's rapid vocabulary growth often leads adults to overestimate their linguistic capacities and thus use words, sentence structures, or concepts that are age-inappropriate and exceed the children's competencies (Orbach & Lamb, 2007; Saywitz & Camparo, 1998; Saywitz, Nathanson, & Snyder, 1993; Walker, 1994; Walker et al., 2013). Despite their apparent maturity, young children—especially preschoolers—frequently use words before they know their conventional adult meaning, may use words that they do not understand at all, and may understand poorly some apparently simple concepts, such as "any," "some," "touch," "yesterday," and "before" (Harner, 1975; Walker et al., 2013). Moreover, children who have been maltreated are more likely to show generalized language delays than non-maltreated children (Eigsti & Cicchetti, 2004), which may further exacerbate developmental limitations in language proficiency. Positive associations between different aspects of children's language competency and their memory performance have been demonstrated (Kulkofsy, 2010), with the particular contribution of language varying according to which aspect of language and what kind of memory task is assessed. For example, Klemfuss (2015) showed that children's productive language skills were associated with the accuracy of their spontaneous accounts, whereas receptive language skills were associated with resistance to suggestive questions.

The accuracy of children's accounts is greatly influenced by the linguistic style and the complexity of the language addressed to them by questioners, especially in legal contexts (Carter, Bottoms, & Levine, 1996; Imhoff & Baker-Ward, 1999; Perry et al., 1995). For example, children are often asked to negate adult statements or to confirm multifaceted "summaries" of their accounts (e.g., "Is it not true that…?"), and are expected to understand unfamiliar words and syntactically complex or ambiguous compound sentences (Brennan & Brennan, 1988; Dent, 1982; Pea, 1980; Perry & Wrightsman, 1991; Saywitz, 1988; Walker, 1993; Walker & Hunt, 1998; Walker et al., 2013; Warren, Woodall, Hunt, & Perry, 1996). Such questions are particularly prevalent in the courtroom, and during cross-examination (Andrews & Lamb, 2017; Klemfuss, Quas, & Lyon, 2014; Stolzenberg & Lyon, 2014; Zajac, Gross, & Hayne, 2003; see Zajac, O'Neill, & Hayne, 2012 for a review). The style of questioning that children experience in court is particularly worrisome in light of evidence that young children may not recognize that they do not understand such questions and should thus seek clarification (Malloy, Katz, Lamb, & Mugno, 2015; Perry et al., 1995), and that children frequently attempt to answer unanswerable or nonsensical questions, especially if the questions are phrased in a closed manner, even when they are able to identify that the questions do not make sense (Waterman, Blades, & Spencer, 2000, 2001, 2004). Even when interviewers and lawyers attempt to ask more open-ended questions, they commonly preface these with phrases that turn the question into a yes/no format. For example, young children often respond in a very literal manner to questions such as "Do you remember where it was?," answering "yes" without elaboration, rather than to the intent of the question ("Where was it?") (Evans, Stolzenberg, Lee, & Lyon, 2014). Lawyers, particularly for the defense, typically pose suggestive questions, often repeatedly (Andrews & Lamb, 2016; Andrews, Lamb, & Lyon, 2015a; Klemfuss et al., 2014; Stolzenberg & Lyon, 2014), which are especially likely to elicit self-contradictions, and even prosecutors are unlikely to use optimal questioning techniques with young witnesses (Andrews & Lamb, 2016; Andrews, Lamb, & Lyon, 2015b; Klemfuss et al., 2014).

Unfortunately, forensic interviewers also frequently ask very specific questions (such as "Did he touch you?"). Young children (those under 6) have special difficulty answering specific questions, and may exhibit a response bias (e.g., Fivush, Peterson, & Schwarzmueller, 2002; Peterson,

Dowden, & Tobin, 1999), or a reluctance to give "don't know" responses in the absence of knowledge (Davies, Tarrant, & Flin, 1989; Saywitz & Snyder, 1993). Children often choose a response from the set of options presented in an option-posing question, even when the response options do not include the correct answer (Rocha, Marche, & Briere, 2013). Interviewers are often advised to minimize the likelihood that children will choose from the options presented by also offering "or something else" as a response. London, Hall, and Lytle (2017) showed, however, that, at least with very young children (3–5 years), this strategy does not overcome the problem of children's tendency to simply select one of the response options. Including a "something else" alternative improved accuracy when there was no correct answer included in the response set (but not when the options included a correct answer, or the question was unanswerable). Despite the improvement, furthermore, children's response accuracy was still unacceptably low (31% compared to 15% without this option).

Even when children *do* respond "I don't know," interviewers frequently ignore such responses and continue to probe the topics, often using increasingly closed questions (Earhart, La Rooy, Brubacher, & Lamb, 2014). Stolzenberg and Pezdek (2013) showed how detrimental it can be to force children to respond. In their study, children (6- and 9-year-olds) were asked answerable and unanswerable questions about a brief video clip, with some of the children being encouraged to use "I don't know" as a response, and others asked to respond even if they were uncertain (i.e., take a guess). Children were re-interviewed one week later. The researchers found that, regardless of age, children encouraged to answer unanswerable questions did so in the initial interview (more so than children who were encouraged to say "I don't know" when appropriate). Further, in the later interview, the older children were more likely to repeat the incorrect answers they had been encouraged to give in the earlier interviews (i.e., they carried the earlier errors over into the later interviews). The type of questions asked and the context in which they are introduced thus determine whether they enhance or degrade the reliability of children's reports (Brown & Lamb, 2017).

The more impoverished the children's language, the greater the likelihood that their statements will be misinterpreted or that the children will misinterpret the interviewers' questions and purposes (King & Yuille, 1987; Perry & Wrightsman, 1991; Walker et al., 2013). When interviewers misrepresent what children say, furthermore, children tend not to correct them, and thus the mistakes, rather than the correct information, may be reported by the children later in the interview (Hunt & Borgida, 2001; Roberts & Lamb, 1999). Indeed, researchers have shown that children rarely challenge or correct interviewers when the interviewers have inaccurately paraphrased their statements (Evans, Roberts, Price, & Stefek, 2010; Hunt & Borgida, 2001). This further underscores the extent to which the interviewers' behavior—particularly their vocabularies, the complexity of their utterances, their suggestiveness, and their success in motivating children to be informative and forthcoming—profoundly influences the course and outcome of their interviews.

In addition, children frequently interpret words very concretely and restrictedly (e.g., a child may not respond to a question about something that happened at "home" if the child lives in an "apartment"), or make references that fall outside of the listener's knowledge base (e.g., "he looked like my English teacher"), thus making their accounts ambiguous. Emerging understanding of prepositions (e.g., "on," "under," "down") and concrete interpretation and use or under-extensions of such linguistic tools may lead children to describe important aspects of their experiences differently from adults. For example, when describing the placement of their (or the alleged perpetrator's) clothing, children may deny that clothing was pulled "down" unless they were standing, because they associate "down" (and "up") with verticality (Stolzenberg & Lyon, 2016). Children's vocabularies, of course, may also be very idiosyncratic. Limitations in theory of mind development (the ability to understand that other people have different perspectives, beliefs, and knowledge) may also lead children to communicate in this way.

Conversational Ability and Experience

Children also *learn* how to participate in conversations (Poole, 2016). They must learn how to stay on topic, how to adapt their speech appropriately to different audiences (e.g., "strange" interviewers who do not know their family members and were not present during the events in question), and how to structure coherent narratives about past events (Warren & McCloskey, 1997). The challenge confronting investigators is to obtain organized accounts that are sufficiently rich in descriptive detail to permit an understanding of the children's testimony. Unlike adults and older children, furthermore, young children cannot draw upon an array of past experiences to enrich and clarify their descriptive accounts (Johnson & Foley, 1984).

The richness and usefulness of children's accounts of abusive experiences are also influenced by social or pragmatic aspects of communication. For example, when asked questions such as "Do you remember his name?" "Do you know why you are here today?" or "Can you show me where he touched you?," older children usually read between the lines and provide the desired information, whereas younger children may simply answer literally, "Yes" or "No" (Evans, Stolzenberg, & Lyon, 2015; Evans, Stolzenberg, Lee, & Lyon, 2014; Klemfuss et al., 2014; Walker & Warren, 1995; Warren et al., 1996).

Children are significantly influenced by early exposure to conversations by the adults around them. The way in which adults talk to young children at home and in other settings (e.g., daycare) models to children how to talk about the past (e.g., what kinds of details to include or omit, and how to structure their accounts, Salmon & Reese, 2015, 2016). The socio-cultural theory of autobiographical memory (Nelson, 2013), for example, explains how early conversational exchanges between parents and their children help to shape children's subsequent memory development and their abilities to recount experiences. The level of detail sought in forensic interviews stands in stark contrast to the typical conversational descriptions of experienced events (Lamb & Brown, 2006). In addition, young witnesses are typically accustomed to being the junior partners in exchanges with adults, and the goal of their conversations is often for them to learn, be tested, or get feedback, rather than to serve as the expert informants. If children fail to appreciate that interviewers have little, if any, knowledge of the alleged events, or attribute superior knowledge to the adult interviewers, they may refrain from reporting all they know. As a result, interviewers need to communicate their needs and expectations clearly, motivating children to provide as much information as they can.

Increases in the amounts of information reported by children as they grow older may also reflect their increasingly sophisticated skills as narrators. Young children are still developing their meta-linguistic abilities—coming to know what listeners want to know, and how to report information coherently, monitor the success of their communication, and modify strategies as necessary to ensure that listeners have understood (Lamb & Brown, 2006; Saywitz & Camparo, 2013). The ability to organize the remembered details into a coherent form is important for both communication (e.g., how well a listener will understand the experience being recounted) and for long-term memory; research has shown that the thematic coherence of an account is a stronger predictor of how long a memory is retained than the level of detail contained (Bauer & Larkina, 2015; Morris, Baker-Ward, & Bauer, 2010; Peterson, Morris, Baker-Ward, & Flynn, 2014; Wang, Bui, & Song, 2015). Long-term retention of accounts is important because children often experience substantial delays between their initial disclosures, subsequent investigative interviews, and testifying in court. It is thus important for interviewing strategies to promote coherent, as well as detailed, narratives. The NICHD Protocol, by relying heavily on an approach to encouraging children to elaborate upon their initial statements by using the children's own words to form cues and asking broad open questions which are known to increase coherence (Feltis, Powell, Snow, & Hughes-Scholes, 2010; Snow, Powell, & Murfett, 2008), is likely to enhance this important aspect of testimony.

Young children are also still developing their theory of mind—their ability to recognize that others' mental states, knowledge, beliefs, experiences, and emotions may be different from their own. They are also developing their skill in monitoring their own and others' comprehension of the content and exchanges in a conversation. For this reason, young children may not be able to flexibly describe their experiences, provide additional elaboration to clarify statements, or tell things in different ways when interviewers require more information. In addition, if children infer that interviewers would prefer particular responses, they may compromise their accounts rather than communicate their actual experiences in order to appear cooperative (Ceci & Bruck, 1993, 1995). In the forensic context, therefore, interviewers must be sensitive to children's perceptions of their knowledge and status. To facilitate comprehensive and accurate reporting by children, for example, interviewers should emphasize that they do not know what the children experienced, and that it is thus important for the children to tell as much as they know (e.g., Sternberg, Lamb, Esplin, Orbach, & Hershkowitz, 2002).

SUGGESTIBILITY OF CHILD WITNESSES

The enormous publicity accorded to allegations of multi-victim sexual abuse in daycare centers in the 1980s and early 1990s spurred many researchers to study the accuracy of children's recollections and the unreliability of their responses when questioned suggestively (see Lamb, Malloy, Hershkowitz, & La Rooy, 2015, and Poole, 2016, for reviews). Suggestive interviewing is defined by the use of statements or questions that introduce or assume undisclosed allegation-related input and are formulated so as to strongly communicate the expected responses (e.g., "He forced you to do that, didn't he?"; or "He lay on you or you lay on him"? when the child said: "We lay on the sofa"; e.g., Lamb et al., 2009; Lamb, Orbach, Hershkowitz, Esplin et al., 2007; Orbach, Lamb, Abbott, Hershkowitz, & Pipe, unpublished research, 2016).

Children's suggestibility is mediated by several distinct cognitive and social processes. For example, children may be exposed to pre-event misinformation or stereotypes that might influence how subsequent events are interpreted and encoded. Children may also be exposed to post-event misinformation, prior to or during the forensic interview (e.g., when asked to imagine or speculate about what might have occurred or describe aspects of the allegation that the interviewer introduces before a child has raised them), which may become integrated into their recollection. Children may also be reinforced (positively or negatively) during an interview for giving particular types of responses or influenced by other kinds of social pressures (e.g., incentives to tell, or references to other children telling). The extent to which such influences compromise children's accounts increases when repeated, or when more than one kind of suggestive technique is employed (e.g., Garven, Wood, Malpass, & Shaw, 1998; Garven, Wood, & Malpass, 2000). Laboratory-based research has demonstrated that suggestibility declines with age (Paz-Alonso & Goodman, 2016), but even adults are not immune to the impact of suggestive interviewing and exposure to misinformation (Sharman & Powell, 2012).

Analyses of the notorious daycare cases helped draw attention to a number of potentially problematic suggestive investigative techniques (see text box). Such practices alarmed developmentalists and helped stimulate a number of studies that clarified our understanding of suggestibility (Kuehnle & Connell, 2008; Lamb, Sternberg, Orbach, Hershkowitz, & Esplin, 1999; Poole, 2016), while fueling an intense controversy about the value of laboratory analogue studies (e.g., Ceci & Bruck, 1995; Ceci & Friedman, 2000; Lyon, 1999, 2002a). Several decades of studies followed; they demonstrated how each of the influences identified in the daycare cases resulted in substantial numbers of children making erroneous reports (e.g., Cleveland, Quas, & Lyon, 2016; Garven

---

Suggestive techniques identified in the daycare cases

- Attributing negative stereotypes to the suspected perpetrators
- Casting doubt on the truthfulness of the witness' testimony
- Embedding assumptions in prompts
- Introducing unreported information
- Implying the expected responses (tag questions)
- Referencing interviewers' high status
- Exerting peer pressure (reference to what other witnesses said)
- Reinforcing desired responses, using rewards or threats
- Requesting that children pretend, imagine or speculate about what occurred
- Using anatomical dolls as interview aids
- Repeating any of the above
- Employing multiple suggestive techniques

et al., 1998, 2000; Gilstrap, 2004; Howie, Nash, Kurukulasuriya, & Bowman, 2012; Leichtman & Ceci 1995; Poole & White, 1991; Schreiber, Wentura, & Bilskey, 2001; Uhl, Camilletti, Scullin, & Wood, 2016; Zajac, Gross, & Hayne, 2003). In conjunction with studies examining children's recall when they were interviewed under optimal conditions, this research has helped to identify the characteristics of both effective and risky techniques, and shown how some children can be induced to acquiesce to interviewer suggestions, to integrate inaccurate suggested details into their (otherwise accurate) accounts, and even to provide elaborate and convincing accounts of entirely false experiences (for a discussion see Ceci, Kulkofsky, Klemfuss, Sweeney, & Bruck, 2007).

We do not provide a detailed or exhaustive review here of the various factors that can lead children to produce inaccurate reports (see Ceci, Hritz, & Royer, 2015 for an overview). In general, research has demonstrated that, while adults are certainly susceptible to the above influences and can be suggestible, children are more so. Importantly, in many of the studies, even when multiple suggestive techniques were employed in several interviews, some children remained resistant to suggestion. Conversely, other studies showed that very mildly suggestive questions enticed many (but again, not all) children to acquiesce and subsequently report the suggested information (see Ceci et al., 2007 for a discussion). Clearly, suggestibility, like accurate reporting, reflects an interaction between child and interview factors, including factors that children are exposed to *before* their first interview.

Elements of the NICHD Protocol described in subsequent chapters offer ways in which interviewers might minimize the likelihood that the kinds of factors or processes listed in the text box might occur in their interviews, and thus elicit more reliable testimony from child witnesses. Orbach et al. (2016) showed that even when following the Protocol, however, interviewers sometimes used suggestive prompts (albeit at a lower rate than when they were not using the Protocol; e.g., Lamb et al., 2009). Interviewers suggestively introduced undisclosed information or made allegation-related assumptions in their prompts, and even confronted child witnesses regarding their testimony. Consistent with earlier findings from both laboratory (e.g., Hunt & Borgida, 2001) and field (e.g., Evans et al., 2010; Roberts & Lamb, 1999; Walker & Hunt, 1998) studies, Orbach and colleagues (2016) demonstrated that, when responding to suggestion, children were more inclined to acquiesce (in 52% of 2,642 responses) than to resist interviewers' suggestions. Furthermore, they demonstrated that children's responses to interviewers' suggestions were differentially associated with acquiescing and resisting, depending on the type of suggestion and children's ages. Resisting interviewers' suggestions was significantly more likely in responses to "confrontational" (casting doubt on the truthfulness of the child by questioning the plausibility of her/his statements) than to "suppositional" (implicitly or explicitly assuming that an allegation-related action happened during the investigated incident) or "introductory" (non-confrontationally introducing undisclosed allegation-related contents) suggestive prompts (41.0%, 27.1%, and 23.1%, respectively). The overall likelihood of resisting interviewers' suggestions increased 5% for each one-year increase in child age. Observed percentages of acquiescing were 36.7%, 53.4%, and 53.9% for confrontational, suppositional, and introductory suggestive prompts, respectively. However, contradictions of earlier assertions were significantly more likely to occur (96%) when children acquiesced to rather than resisted interviewers' suggestions. Indeed, some acquiescing responses may actually confirm accurate incident-related information introduced by interviewers, perhaps because the information had been independently verified by them prior to the interview (using case files, police reports, etc.). However, the inability to assess the accuracy of most contents introduced during forensic interviews makes it impossible to differentiate between "accurate" and "inaccurate" information or "leading" and "misleading" questions. Importantly, the legal system requires that all testimonial evidence would be provided by witnesses, based on their own memory of allegedly experienced incidents, thus forensic interviewers are typically encouraged to "introduce as little information as possible while encouraging children to provide as much information as possible in the form of narratives elicited using open-ended prompts" (Lamb, Orbach, Hershkowitz, Esplin et al., 2007, p. 1203; Orbach & Lamb, 2000).

THE EVENT

Encoding Personal Experiences—How Involved was the Child?

For very young children, especially, direct experience is an important source of event knowledge (e.g., Nelson, 1986, 1996b). In general, directly participating in an event is likely to result in stronger and/or more accessible memory traces, for both adults and children, than being a bystander, observer, or audience for a story about the same event (Murachver, Pipe, Gordon, Fivush, & Owens, 1996; Pathman, Samson, Dugas, Cabeza, & Bauer, 2011). Tobey and Goodman (1992), for example, found that 4-year-old children who participated in a real-life event (a Simon Says game) freely recalled central actions more accurately than children who merely observed the same event on video, and Rudy and Goodman (1991) found that 4-year-olds who were direct participants in a real-life event were less susceptible to misleading questions than children who observed the real-life event. Similarly, Murachver et al. (1996) found that children who participated in a contrived interaction with an adult "pirate" recalled more information than those who read a story about "visiting the pirate." Their free recall was also more accurate than that of children who only watched the event or heard about the event. Even when recall was supported by behavioral re-enactment, children who were read the story were significantly less accurate than those who had participated or observed. Whether direct participation leads to stronger memories than other sources for younger children has not been examined directly, however.

A common explanation for the enhanced recall of direct experiences is that participation strengthens the resulting memory trace. Theorists agree that memory trace strength can vary (Brainerd & Reyna, 1990, 2012; Ceci, Toglia, & Ross, 1988), such that stronger or weaker memory traces can be created. Comparing 3- and 5-year-old children's memories of events about which they heard a story (narrative condition) or in which they directly participated, Gobbo, Mega, and Pipe (2002) found that children who participated recalled more details accurately than children in the narrative condition. To determine whether this difference in recall was due to differences in the strength of the memory traces created by participating rather than only hearing a story about the event, Gobbo et al. (2002) equated children's level of learning (or encoding) by having children in each condition reach a criterion level of learning. This criterion was achieved by exposing children to the event repeatedly. Children who heard about the event to a criterion level of learning recalled as many details as children who participated in the event (see Murachver et al., 1996, for compatible findings). Thus, although participating in an event creates a stronger memory trace than merely being told about it, repeated exposure to the information can reduce or eliminate these differences.

Adults often talk to children about anticipated as well as past events, and discuss the activities in which they are taking part (Fivush, 1998b; Fivush, Haden, & Adam, 1995; Haden & Fivush, 1996). Talking about events while (Ornstein, Principe, Hudson, Gordon, & Merritt, 1997; Tessler & Nelson, 1994) or after (Goodman et al., 1994; Hudson, 1990b) they are taking place may enhance children's event recall. In Tessler and Nelson's (1994) study, children's recall of an event in which they had participated reflected those aspects of the event talked about by the parent and/or the child during the event. Ornstein, Principe et al. (1997) reported compatible findings in a study of children's memory of a painful medical procedure (see also Haden, Ornstein, Eckerman, &

Didow, 2001). Goodman et al. (1994) similarly found that parents' retrospective reports of their post-event discussions with their children about a painful medical procedure that the children had experienced were correlated with the children's subsequent ability to resist misleading questions about the procedure. In other words, although parental discussion was not related to correct recall, it was negatively correlated with errors in response to misleading questions.

Parent-child discussion about events *before they* occur can also influence children's subsequent recall (Salmon, Champion, Pipe, Mewton, & McDonald, 2008; Salmon, Mewton, Pipe, & McDonald, 2011; Sutherland et al., 2003), although talk during and after an event is more effective than talk before (McGuigan & Salmon, 2004). Of course, parental (or other) conversations can also *compromise* children's reports if those conversations include misinformation. Such conversations may occur because the parents are concerned about what the children may have experienced and are thus trying to establish what happened (e.g., Teresa and Molly in our case examples, or the parents in the daycare cases described earlier), or because parents are deliberately coaching their children to influence what they say to investigators. Lyon, Malloy, Quas, and Talwar (2008) showed how young (4- to 7-year-old) children can be encouraged to lie about experiences (either that something that did happen did not happen—a false denial, or that something that did not happen did, in fact, happen—a false allegation) following extensive coaching.

Event-related discussion may strengthen memories for several reasons. Discussing events in advance, for example, increases knowledge about the event, thereby rendering it more memorable, whereas post-event discussion may ensure rehearsal, which consolidates the memory or, following long delays, fosters retrieval and reactivation of the memory. Moreover, prior, contemporaneous, or retrospective discussions may all highlight important factors on which children should focus, and provide appropriate verbal labels for actions and objects, thereby facilitating memory.

Many of the experiences explored in forensic investigations may have been poorly understood by alleged victims, especially when the alleged victims were young children. In addition, disclosures of sexual abuse are often made months or even years after the abusive incident(s) (see Hershkowitz, Horowitz, & Lamb, 2005, 2007; Hershkowitz et al., 2006; Hershkowitz, Orbach et al., 2007; London, Bruck, Ceci, & Shuman, 2005, 2007 and Chapter 9) with little or no discussion with others in the intervening period. Victims of childhood sexual abuse are frequently embarrassed, afraid, or have been threatened not to tell (Cederborg, Lamb, & Laurell, 2007). In the absence of discussion and opportunities for verbal recall, such experiences may not be remembered in detailed or coherent narrative form.

In all, research on the development of autobiographical memory shows that younger children's impoverished reports, relative to those of older children and adults, may be due, in part, to limited retrieval skills, meta-linguistic deficits, and immature narrative skills. Encoding and retrieval strategies develop with age and experience, and the use of effective retrieval strategies is usually associated with improved recall and reporting of information. Developmental differences in the selection and use of cognitive strategies affect children's ability to talk about past events, and therefore the amount of support they may need to help them describe events completely. As they grow older, children learn to use strategies automatically, allowing them to allocate more attention and effort to retrieval, whereas younger children may need explicit instruction in the use of specific strategies, although they still do not benefit from such instructions as much as older children do (Flavell et al., 1993). As children become older, they also become better at generating internal retrieval cues, which makes them less reliant on external support provided during the interview (Quas et al., 2000).

Repeated Experiences—How Many Times Did it Happen?

Children's knowledge and the resulting memory representations can also be affected by the number of times they have experienced an event. Victims of sexual abuse are frequently abused repeatedly, sometimes over long periods of time. When this happens, children may be asked (in investigative interviews or in the courtroom) to provide chronologically organized information about the various events. Children's ability to accurately order multiple events, to sequence their components, and to identify the number of events they have experienced has been mostly examined in laboratory studies, where accuracy could be assessed, using objectively recorded contrived or naturally occurring events. The most influential recent research on the development and understanding of temporal concepts (e.g., dating, sequencing, frequency) and their related linguistic markers (e.g., after, before, during) by children has been conducted by Friedman, who systematically examined the temporal processes involved in reconstructing the time of past events and how these processes are affected by the specific temporal category, task characteristics, context familiarity, and children's age in determining the accuracy of children's temporal judgments (e.g., Friedman, 1990, 1991, 1992, 1993, 2000; Friedman & Lyon, 2005). Friedman and Lyon (2005) reported that, when 4- to 13-year-olds were prompted to recount their memories of two recent contrived school events, experienced within 2 days of one another, children from first grade onward recalled the order of the two events accurately following a 3-month delay. However, they almost never produced information about contiguity and order of events in response to open-ended questions. In a study of 4- to 8-year-olds' memories of repeated events after a short delay (1 week) Roberts and colleagues (2015) showed that, whereas children were highly accurate in identifying whether they had experienced one or multiple events, all children, especially the youngest, struggled to order components of repeated events across the four experiences and to correctly describe the order of each occurrence. Similarly, Sharman, Powell, and Roberts (2011) showed that young children who experienced either one event or multiple events were accurate at responding to a general question about the number of occurrences ("did that happen one time or more than one time?"), but the children who experienced multiple events had difficulty accurately specifying the number of occurrences they had experienced.

Orbach and Lamb (2007) examined the kinds of temporal references (i.e., sequencing, dating, number of occurrences, duration, and frequency) made by children when describing allegedly experienced incidents of abuse during forensic interviews. The findings highlighted significant shifts around the age of 10 years in the ability to report temporal information. Number of occurrences was mostly referenced by children globally, using a nonspecific response (e.g., "more than one time") in response to the recognition prompt scripted in the NICHD Protocol (i.e., "Did it happen one time or more than one time?"), and spontaneous references to discrete number of occurrences were rare. The dominant temporal attribute used in children's retrospective accounts for structuring event components was forward-sequencing ("he did x and then he did y"; nearly 72% of the children used this spontaneously). Seventy four percent of the total number of temporal references provided by children in that study was elicited using free-recall and cued-recall prompts.

When children experience similar events, they tend to form general event representations (or scripts) of "typical" events rather than representations of particular incidents (Hudson & Mayhew, 2009). As such, they may be able to recount the overall "gist" of recurring events but struggle with specific details of any one occurrence (Odegard, Cooper, Lampinen, Reyna, & Brainerd, 2009; Connolly, Gordon, Woiwod, & Price, 2016). Nelson (1986) argued that memories serve to facilitate predictions about the future, and that, as a rule, repeated experiences permit better predictions than experiences that happened only once. As a result, children should be particularly attuned from an early age to "what usually happens." These general event representations can help children to predict what is going to occur, understand what is happening during an event, and guide the recall of familiar events (Brainerd & Ornstein, 1991; Brewer & Nakamura, 1984; Hudson, 1986; Nelson, 1986, 1993a, 1993b; Nelson & Gruendel, 1981). Repeated experience may strengthen event memories, with children recalling more details than if they experienced the event only a single time (Bauer & Fivush, 1992; Connolly et al., 2016; Fivush, Kuebli, & Clubb, 1992; Hudson & Nelson, 1986; see Powell & Thomson, 2003 for review). Memories of repeatedly experienced events may also differ from memories of events occurring a single time because there are repeated opportunities to reactivate the memories by rehearsal. Further, children's memories of details that recur across experiences are also more accurate and more resistant to suggestion and misinformation effects (Connolly & Lindsay, 2001; Gobbo et al., 2002; McNichol, Shute, & Tucker, 1999; Powell, Roberts, Ceci, & Hembrooke, 1999).

Prior experiences can also have adverse effects on children's event recall, particularly if there are variations across the different instances of the event. When events recur with any regularity, children's accounts are likely to be skeletal, reflecting common components and the basic structure without the details that may vary from one occasion to another (Brubacher et al., 2011; Brubacher, Malloy, Lamb, & Roberts, 2013; Powell, Roberts, & Guadagno, 2007). The changing components may also be more vulnerable to suggestion, at least under some conditions (Connolly & Lindsay, 2001; Fasig, 1999; McNichol et al., 1999; by contrast, see Powell et al., 1999; Powell, Roberts, & Thomson, 2000).

The effects of knowledge and repeated experience on memory are quite significant from a practical perspective. In forensic contexts, especially when child sexual abuse is alleged, it is not uncommon for children to be asked about incidents that have occurred repeatedly, sometimes over long periods of time. In the courtroom, what happened on one specific occasion is often critically important. Yet the requirement that children recall a single episode distinct from other similar experiences may be very challenging for young children. Despite remarkable memory for details of what happened (Fivush & Hamond, 1990; Powell et al., 1999), young children are generally not as accurate when identifying details associated with *one particular incident* of a repeated experience (Farrar & Goodman, 1990; Roberts & Powell, 2001). Although children may be able to include the details that varied across occurrences they may struggle to link the details to a particular occurrence (Brubacher, Roberts, & Powell, 2012; Connolly & Gordon, 2014). Researchers have examined whether prompting for particular instances of events that may hold some distinctiveness (e.g., the first or last time, or a time that was different) assists in overall recall and in eliciting episode-specific information. Several studies have demonstrated superior recall for the first instance of a series of recurring events (primacy effect: Hudson, 1990a, 1990b; Powell, Thomson, & Ceci, 2003; Connolly et al., 2016), with somewhat weaker evidence for improved recall of the last instance (recency effect: Powell et al., 2003 (short delay only); Powell & Thomson, 1997 (older children only), Connolly et al., 2016). Focusing children on a time that was different (in an unexpected way) may help children to recall details about a particular experience (Connolly et al., 2016), however more research is needed to identify when and with whom such an instruction is most likely to be effective. The way in which children are prepared for talking about repeated experiences also appears to be important: Brubacher, Roberts, and Powell (2011) showed that young (5- to 6-year-old) children who practiced narrating a repeated event included more distinctive details about a series of repeated events than children who practiced narrating a single event first. Older children (7- to 8-year-olds) benefited from either type of practice, relative to children who had no practice at all. Brubacher et al (2012) highlighted the importance of *how* children's accounts of repeated experiences are elicited: 4- to 8-year-old children were asked to provide either an account of what usually happened during a series of repeated events and then asked to describe a specific occurrence or were prompted about a specific occurrence first and then asked to describe what usually happened. Prompting for a generic account resulted in children reporting more details overall and more distinctive features from the various episodes.

The fact that children may have difficulty recalling specific incidents of multiply-experienced events has led many court systems in the United States to relax the requirement that child witnesses identify the time of the individual incidents of multiply-experienced events (Roberts, 2002) because confusions between episodes do not necessarily cast doubt on the accuracy or credibility of young witnesses (see also Roberts, 2002).

Despite these issues, children are often asked to describe the number of times they experienced an event, which may prove challenging. Malloy, Brubacher, Lamb, and Benton (2013) examined transcripts of investigative interviews with 4- to 8-year-old suspected victims of child sexual abuse to see how they responded to the question, "Did that happen one time or more than one time?" The majority of children responded appropriately, with just 12% (all of whom were 4- to 6-year-olds) responding with providing an inappropriate response (e.g., responses that used incorrect terminology or involved implausible numbers). Roberts et al. (2015) showed that older children (6 to 8 years) are more likely to be able to put repeated events into chronological order than younger children (4 to 5 years)—in their study of children's recall of a series of repeated staged events all children were likely to recall the first instance of a recurring event better than one that occurred subsequently, and older children showed enhanced recall of the latest incident relative to those occurring in the middle of the series.

Wandrey, Lyon, Quas, and Friedman (2012) also explored children's abilities to make legally relevant judgments about how often an event had occurred, and had access to data that made it possible to objectively verify children's responses, and therefore measure accuracy. Specifically, 6- to 10-year-old maltreated children judged how many times they had attended court hearings and the number of placements that they had experienced after being removed from home. The children often gave surprisingly inaccurate answers, although they were better at reasoning about more extreme values (e.g., when the number of actual experiences differed substantially from the number of experiences that they were asked about; "Did you come to the court building more than 10 times?" versus "Did you come to the court building more than five times?" when they had visited twice). One-third (35%) of the children provided inaccurate responses to the basic event question often recommended, "Did that happen one time or more than one time?" It is thus crucial for interviewers and legal professionals to recognize both that children may fail to answer, or give implausible or inappropriate responses to, questions concerning event temporal location or numerosity even when they are able to use numbers and quantifiers correctly in some contexts and that "inaccurate responses to time and number questions may say little about whether the event actually occurred" (Wandrey, Lyon, Quas, & Friedman, 2012, p. 100). Unfortunately, children rarely mention how often an event occurred spontaneously, meaning that interviewers may need to prompt children for this information.

Traumatic, Distressing, and Other Unpleasant Experiences—What Kind of Event Was It?

In the past, forensic professionals often dismissed the relevance of experimental research on children's memory by arguing that the stressful nature of sexual abuse makes memories thereof distinctly different. In fact, considerable controversy persists in the experimental literature concerning the effects of increased arousal or stress on the accuracy of children's memories. The entire range of possible associations between stress and memory have been reported in research studies—enhanced memory for stressful events, degraded memory, and no impact at all of stress. For example, Howe, Courage, and Peterson (1994) found no relationship between the amount of stress (reported by the parents) and the amount of information recalled by their children either 3–5 days or 6 months after an emergency room procedure. By contrast, Goodman, Hirschman, Hepps, and Rudy (1991b) found that children who showed higher levels of arousal during a medical procedure reported the incident more accurately than children who simply had a washable tattoo applied. When Bahrick, Parker, Fivush, and Levitt (1998) classified 3- and 4-year-old children into high, medium, and low-stress groups based on the extent of their exposure to Hurricane Andrew, however, they found that children in the high- and low-stress groups recalled the least information about the hurricane whereas children in the medium-stress group recalled the most information, suggesting that some stress improves recall while too much stress impedes it.

At least some of the variation in study outcomes can be explained by methodological differences across studies, including how stress was defined and measured and the kind of event that was examined. Clearly, however, the relationship between stress and recall is complex and likely reflects (as with eyewitness testimony) interaction between characteristics of the child (e.g., how distressed they were; Peterson & Noel, 2012), the event (e.g., how long ago the event occurred; Peterson, 2015), and how they are interviewed (e.g., Quas & Lench, 2007; Quas, Rush, Yim, & Nikolayev, 2014; Rush et al., 2014; Sales, Goldberg, & Parker, 2001). Importantly, it appears that, even when stress enhances recall, memories are still susceptible to the same deleterious effects of suggestion and delay as more mundane memories (Cordón, Pipe, Sayfan, Melinder, & Goodman, 2004; Fivush, 1998a; Howe, 1997; Sales et al., 2001).

Many factors can make some events more memorable than others. Few researchers have studied the association between the severity of abuse (presumably a correlate of stressfulness) and children's recall, probably because there is no consensus regarding the ways in which the severity of abuse should be measured, and a variety of events (ranging from exposure by a "flasher" to rape at gunpoint) are defined as sexual abuse. Children may also experience varying degrees of distress in response to the same category of event, meaning that using externally- (rather than internally-) generated definitions may not capture the influence of stress. In addition, whether or not the abuse is even stressful to children may vary depending on such factors as the age of the child, the identity of the perpetrator, and the coping mechanisms, discussion, and support later available. With better definitions of child abuse and access to accounts of a larger number of cases, researchers may be able in the future to determine whether different types of abuse are recalled differently as a function of the many interrelated factors that characterize real-world experiences of abuse.

Given concerns about whether findings from studies examining the impact of lower levels of stress than might be associated with maltreatment, researchers have examined children's memories of naturally occurring experiences that were more similar, with respect to the intensity and duration of distress, to the experiences children might be asked to recount during a forensic interview. Some of the studies examined children's recall of a medical procedure—a voiding cystourethrogram (VCUG)—a painful diagnostic procedure involving genital contact, meaning the to-be-remembered experience is also likely to have involved pain, embarrassment, or shame.

In general, children's accounts of painful and/or distressing medical procedures (Brown et al., 1999; Goodman et al., 1994, 1997; Ornstein, 1995; Quas et al., 1999; Steward, 1993; Steward, O'Conner, Acredolo, & Steward, 1996), accidental injuries and their treatment (e.g., Howe et al., 1994; Peterson, 1999, 2015; Peterson & Bell, 1996; Peterson & Whalen, 2001; see Peterson, 2012 for a review), natural disasters (Fivush et al, 2004; Parker, Bahrick, Lundy, Fivush, & Levitt, 1998), and forensic accounts of suspected or alleged sexual abuse (Lamb et al, 2000; Lamb et al., 2003; Sternberg, Lamb, Orbach et al., 2001) appear to be influenced by many of the same variables, including age, that affect memory for neutral or mundane experiences (see Cordón et al., 2004, Peterson, 2012; Peterson & Warren, 2009 for reviews). Moreover, infantile amnesia curtails the ability of children and adults alike to recall their earliest experiences verbally, whether or not they were traumatic (Fivush, 2002; Howe et al., 1994; Nelson & Fivush, 2004; Peterson & Rideout, 1998 Quas et al., 1999). Further, children who have experienced painful inoculations remembered some aspects of it better than those who witnessed another child experiencing the inoculation (Lindberg, Jones, Collard, & Thomas, 2001), thereby reflecting a general tendency for participants to recall events better than observers (Bauer & Larkina, 2015; Murachver et al., 1996; Tobey & Goodman, 1992). Just as understanding and knowledge influence memory of more mundane events (e.g., Greenhoot, 2000; Ornstein, Shapiro, Clubb, Follmer, & Baker-Ward, 1997; Ricci & Beal, 1998; Sutherland et al., 2003), traumatic experiences that are better understood or explained to children are recalled by them more fully and/or more accurately (Goodman et al., 1994).

There is some evidence that memories of negative experiences endure longer than memories of everyday events, however. When children recall neutral or positive events after extended delays, forgetting is often quite marked (e.g., Flin, Boon, Knox & Bull, 1992; Goodman, Batterman-Faunce, Schaaf, & Kenney, 2002; Hudson & Fivush, 1991; Jones & Pipe, 2002; Ornstein et al., 1997; Salmon & Pipe, 2000; but cf.

Fivush & Schwarzmueller, 1998) whereas memories of painful and stressful experiences may change little over periods of several years (e.g., Burgwyn-Bailes, Baker-Ward, Gordon, & Ornstein, 2001; Merritt et al., 1994; Peterson, 1999, 2011; Peterson & Whalen, 2001). In one study, for example, children who were very young (approximately 3 years old) at the time of an experience (a hurricane) reported even more information when interviewed 6 years later than in an initial interview (Fivush et al., 2004), and similar findings were observed by Peterson (2012) when examining children's accounts of an injury and subsequent hospital treatment two years earlier. Of course, these children were probably reminded of their experiences frequently by family members, friends, interviewers, and even by the media. In contrast, retrospective surveys of adults suggest that young victims seldom discussed their abuse with others in childhood (London et al., 2005, 2007) and we know that events not discussed may not be well remembered (Fivush, Pipe, Murachver, & Reese, 1997; Fivush, 2004a, 2004b; Salmon & Reese, 2016). In the only field study examining the effects of delay on children's recall of alleged sexual abuse, Lamb, Sternberg et al. (2000) reported that children interviewed within a month of the alleged abuse were more likely to provide information in response to the interviewers' open-ended prompts and questions than children interviewed following long (5- to 14-month) delays, although, very surprisingly, children interviewed early provided no more details in total than those interviewed following the longest delays. The absence of differences in the total number of details reported may have been attributable to the poor quality of the interviews studied.

In sum, it is unclear whether memories for traumatic experiences involve unique mechanisms or can be accounted for by the same mechanisms that affect memories of other events (Cordón et al., 2004). Traumatic experiences are often distinctive, so memories thereof might be retained over time better than memories of less distinctive or meaningful events (Howe, 1997, 2000; Ornstein, Larus, & Clubb, 1992). Whether or not special mechanisms are involved, however, real-world events such as child abuse may not necessarily be better remembered than memories of events or stimuli studied in the laboratory. First of all, not all incidents of sexual abuse are painful or traumatic, and thus the potentially facilitative effects of arousal and salience cannot be assumed. Relatedly, children's ignorance or misunderstanding of sexual events may make some abusive experiences even less memorable. Second, stress may affect different types of memory encoding and retrieval (e.g., recall, recognition, and reconstructive memory) in different ways. The context in which children are asked to retrieve information about the experienced event—during interviews with child protective service workers, policemen, attorneys, or judges—may be stressful regardless of whether or not the target events were (Goodman et al., 1992). Researchers have not yet studied the effects of stress at the time of recall, although some have studied the effects of social support and of supportive interviewer practices which presumably reduce stress (Almerigogna et al., 2007; Rush et al., 2014; Quas et al., 2014; Quas & Lench, 2007) and it seems reasonable to expect that stress at the time of recall may hinder retrieval (Nathanson & Saywitz, 2003). Third, whether the event involves shame, perceived responsibility, embarrassment, or guilt, and whether it is talked about, reflected on, kept secret, or even negated, may all affect how experiences of abuse or trauma are remembered and recalled over time. Overall, although salience generally affects the memorability of experienced events, we cannot presume that instances of abuse will always be salient and thus easy to remember.

We do not know whether the distinctiveness of traumatic events is retained when multiple instances of abuse are experienced and the stress becomes chronic rather than acute (Peterson & Warren, 2009). Following repeated *traumatic* experiences, over-general memory retrieval may occur, with several episodes summarized by reference to their common characteristics despite requests for specific examples, characterized by distinctive information about particular events, times, locations, people, places, or activities (McNally, 1998; Williams, 1996; Williams & Dritschel, 1992). Williams (1996) hypothesized that stressful childhood experiences lead depressed individuals to adopt generic retrieval strategies, typical of earlier stages of development, in order to minimize the negative affect associated with some specific features of past events. Children who were victims, witnesses, and both victims and witnesses of family violence are significantly more depressed than children who were not victims of physical abuse (Sternberg et al., 1993), and among these children the proportion of generic responses in the children's accounts of earlier family experiences were positively correlated with their depression scores (Orbach, Lamb, Sternberg, Williams, & Dawud-Noursi, 2001).

Effects of Delay—How Long Ago Did it Happen?

Once remembered, how durable are children's memories of their experiences? When children (and adults) recall neutral or positive events over long time periods, forgetting is typically extensive (e.g., Jones & Pipe, 2002; Ornstein, Baker-Ward et al., 1997; Salmon & Pipe, 2000) and children may require many cues and props to facilitate recall (Hudson & Fivush, 1991; but cf. Fivush & Schwarzmueller, 1998) if, indeed, they can do so at all (Goodman et al, 2002; Pillemer, Picariello, & Pruett, 1994). Pillemer and colleagues showed, for example, that although both 3- and 4-year-old children remembered what happened at school when a fire alarm went off and they were interviewed soon after, none of the younger and only some of the older children remembered it when interviewed 7 years later (Pillemer, 1993; Pillemer et al., 1994; see also Drummey & Newcombe, 1995). Jack, Simcock, and Hayne (2012) showed that about 20% of 2- to 4-year-old children who had experienced a single, unique experience were able to describe it in a verbal interview 6 years later, including some who were as young as 2 years old at the time of the event. Bauer and Larkina (2015) compared the *rate* of forgetting by children of different ages (4-, 6-, and 8-years) and adults of parent-recorded (or for adults, self-recorded) events in a series of interviews over 3 years. Children showed faster rates of forgetting than adults, with younger children forgetting at a faster rate than older children.

Children can remember some experiences after very long forensically relevant delays. Ornstein and colleagues showed that even quite young children recalled a pediatric examination extremely well after delays of up to 6 weeks (e.g., Baker-Ward et al., 1993; Ornstein, Larus, & Clubb, 1993; Clubb, Nida, Merritt, & Ornstein, 1993; Merritt et al., 1994; Ornstein, Shapiro et al., 1997). Medical examinations are likely to be familiar events for many young children, and the good recall in this study might reflect children's knowledge about and understanding of the examination. Other studies suggest that some traumatic experiences about which children presumably had little prior knowledge may be remembered better over long delays than more mundane or neutral experiences. In a study of children's recall of the VCUG (the painful diagnostic procedure described earlier), although children did recall somewhat less when interviewed 6 weeks as opposed to shortly after the test, the change was not statistically significant (Merritt et al., 1994). Burgwyn-Bailes et al. (2001) similarly reported good recall of hospital treatment that included suturing of facial lacerations. Children who were between the ages of 3 and 7 years at the time of the injury recalled a similar number of features when interviewed 1 year later as they had both a few days and 6 to 8 weeks after the suturing. However, more false alarms occurred in response to suggestive questions after the long delay, suggesting that the memory representations did change over time.

Children also remembered injuries, and the hospital treatment that resulted, in studies by Peterson and her colleagues (e.g., Peterson, 2011; Peterson & Bell, 1996; Peterson & Whalen, 2001). When children were interviewed 6 months after the injury, they reported significantly less information about both the injury and the hospital events than when they were interviewed soon after the events (Peterson & Bell, 1996), but when re-interviewed 2 years and 5 years after the injury, the children recalled less about the hospital event than they had soon after, but as much as before about the injuries (Peterson, 1999, 2011; Peterson & Whalen, 2001). Nonetheless, the children's accounts of both the injury and hospital events were less accurate after the very long delays than in the initial interview, suggesting changes in the content of the memories, if not in the amount recalled.

Reinterviewing children about Hurricane Andrew, however, Fivush et al. (2004) showed that children's reports can become *more*, rather than less, detailed after long delays. The children, who had been 3 to 4 years old at the time of the hurricane, were re-interviewed 6 years later. The effects were quite dramatic, with the now 9- to 10-year-old children reporting almost twice as much information as when interviewed shortly after the event (Parker et al., 1998). Likewise, in Peterson's (2011) study, whereas the completeness (or structure) of children's accounts of injuries leading to hospital visits remained constant, the degree of elaborative detail reported about the components of the events increased over time, perhaps reflecting the children's greater narrative ability.

Regardless of the research setting, delay between the occurrence of the to-be-remembered event and questioning has adverse effects on the strength of the memory trace. Lamb, Sternberg et al. (2000) have shown that after delays of more than 1 month, children report fewer new details about alleged abuse than do children recalling abuse that allegedly happened more recently. It is thus preferable to question child witnesses as soon as possible after the alleged incident(s). Interviewers should recognize that children interviewed after a substantial delay might require more time to retrieve details from recall memory, and they should also be more cautious when questioning children after long delays because such children are more susceptible to suggestion.

Although children are more likely to be misled about staged events (Ceci, Loftus, Leichtman, & Bruch, 1994; Leichtman & Ceci, 1995) and report fewer event details about them the longer the delay (Baker-Ward et al., 1993; Ornstein et al., 1992), recent research (Roberts & Powell, 2007) shows that the timing of both misinformation and test interviews as well as the type of details mediate children's suggestibility after repeated experiences. Although 5- to 6-year-old children who experienced the to-be-remembered event once were more suggestible when the misleading information was introduced longer after the event than when it was presented shortly after, children who experienced the event repeatedly were more accurate after longer delays between the events and misinformation, but only when questioned about invariant details.

When children are interviewed after a delay, investigators may need to locate the alleged events in time as well as place. As with other aspects of testimony, there is evidence that children can accurately describe some temporal aspects of events, but changes occur through middle childhood and into adolescence (Jack, Friedman, Reese, & Zajac, 2016; Lee, Wendelken, Bunge, & Ghetti, 2016; Orbach & Lamb, 2007; Pathman, Doydum, & Bauer, 2013; Wang, Peterson, & Hou, 2010). The ability to recall different aspects of chronology varies, with recalling the time of day that an event occurred being the most accurate category of response and also the earliest to emerge; Friedman (1991) showed that 4-, 6-, and 8-year-olds were able to identify the relative recency of two events that had previously occurred (1-week and 7-weeks earlier), and the time of the day that the events had occurred, but only the 6-, and 8-year-olds could correctly place the 7-week event with respect to day of the week, month, and season. Wang et al. (2010) showed that 8-, 11-, and 14-year-olds asked to date memories that occurred before they started school (using parental reports as an index of accuracy) overestimated how long in the past events that occurred after they were 4 years of age happened, and underestimated how long in the past events that occurred before they were 4 years of age took place.

The ability to correctly locate past events in time continues to develop across middle childhood and adolescence, with one study showing children (9 to 11 years) being less able than adults to identify the days of the week and the months of the year of experiences that had occurred 8 months earlier, but no differences between children and adolescents (14- to 16-year-olds) or between adolescents and adults (Jack et al., 2016). All three groups were highly accurate and did not differ when describing the time of the day that the events occurred. No differences were observed in children's, adolescents', and adults' abilities to identify the season and the year that the events occurred (Jack et al., 2016). Importantly, the accuracy (or lack thereof) of all groups' time responses was not associated with the accuracy of their reports of the content of the event, and similar findings have been reported by other researchers (e.g., Friedman & Lyon, 2005; Friedman, Reese, & Dai, 2011; Orbach & Lamb, 2007), suggesting that errors or inconsistencies in such information should not be used to discredit the reliability of other information in children's statements.

A common practice to support children in identifying when an event occurred during an interview is to link it to a landmark event (e.g., a season, birthday, or holiday), however recent research suggests that children may not be able to link such events accurately. Children may understand the concepts of events occurring "near" or "before" one another if the landmark event occurred *after* the event of interest. Problems may arise, however if the landmark event occurred *prior* to the event; children appear to take a linear perspective on time and the calendar, rather than appreciating it as cyclic. For example, a child with a birthday in March may not recognize that an injury sustained in April was "near" their birthday, as it is now 11 months until their next birthday (as opposed to just one month since their last birthday). Children's responses about dating events with reference to landmark events may therefore be inaccurate or misinterpreted (McWilliams, Lyon, & Quas, 2016).

CONCLUSION

As shown in this chapter, we can assert with confidence that, although children clearly can remember incidents they have experienced, the relationship between age and memory is complex, with a variety of factors (including the interviewer's skills) influencing the quality of information provided. Clearly, children, like adults, can be informative witnesses. It is often possible to obtain valuable information from children but doing so requires careful investigative procedures as well as a realistic awareness of children's capacities and tendencies. However, we must also recognize that children may need help retrieving, structuring, and reporting their experiences in an elaborative manner and throughout this book we highlight a number of constructive approaches to interviewing that provide appropriate support without degrading the quality of children's accounts. The onus is therefore on interviewers to ensure that they establish the optimal conditions for children to provide accurate and detailed accounts of even very distressing and traumatic experiences. In this way, we can, in turn, maximize the likelihood that children's accounts will be heard and respected in courts of law and can be protected from their abusers, while innocent adults are not falsely accused.

3

Contributions to Testimony: Preparation for the Interview and Questioning Strategies

In Chapter 2, we described how factors relating to the child and to the events under investigation can have a significant influence on how children describe their experiences. In this chapter, we turn to the interview context, summarizing what researchers have learned about how the way in which children are prepared for an interview and how the strategies employed by the interviewer can also have a major impact on what children say. How children's reports are elicited, both during initial disclosures and during investigative interviews, significantly affects the quality of the information provided and children's perceived reliability (Brown & Lamb, 2015; Ceci et al., 2007). As a result, it is widely accepted that forensic interviews with children can be invaluable sources of information, but they should always be recognized as parts of the forensic investigation, not seen as synonymous with the investigation as a whole.

Assuming children have encoded events, stored memories, and are able to retrieve those memories, children still have to report what they remember in order to effectively contribute to the investigation. This (reporting) stage of the process is the one that is most open to intervention

---

Tell Me What Happened: Questioning Children About Abuse, Second Edition.
Michael E. Lamb, Deirdre A. Brown, Irit Hershkowitz, Yael Orbach, and Phillip W. Esplin.
© 2018 John Wiley & Sons Ltd. Published 2018 by John Wiley & Sons Ltd.

or influence by interviewers and provides the best opportunity to ensure good practice. A number of influences can be at play during the reporting stage. Just as children bring their own characteristics and experiences to the interview context, so do the interviewers. To make it even more complex, these contributions interact. The interview situation is a **dynamic** one—with both the interviewer and the child influencing each other, through question and response styles, nonverbal behavior, rapport, engagement, and so forth. How, then, should interviewers prepare to talk with Sarah, Ben, or Theresa about their possible maltreatment? In this chapter we outline some issues relating to the conduct of the interview that interviewers would do well to consider in planning how they can provide the best opportunity for children to provide relevant, accurate, coherent, and complete accounts of their experiences.

Interview

How long since the disclosure?
How many interviews?
Any pre-interview assessment?
Who has talked to the child about this already?
Rapport?
Preparation for the interview?
Types of questions asked?
Distribution of the questions?
Use of other aids or techniques?

HOW LONG SINCE THE DISCLOSURE?

Just as there may be delays between children experiencing maltreatment and telling others about it, so too can delays occur between initial disclosures and the relevant forensic interviews. As outlined in the previous chapter, delay can result in memory decay. Further, as we outline below, conversations that occur in the period between disclosure and the formal interviews may also contaminate children's recall. Recall and rehearsal of some aspects of the event (e.g., the child thinking about the event, or talking about it with someone) can weaken memory traces and later access to the aspects of the event that were not thought/talked about (Murayama, Miyatsu, Buchli, & Storm, 2014). To the extent that children provide a gist-based or generic description of the alleged maltreatment, later access to and recall of specific details of any particular episode may be difficult (Brubacher et al., 2011). It is therefore widely accepted that children should be interviewed as soon as possible after their disclosures.

HOW MANY INTERVIEWS?

The benefits and risks of having more than one interview with a child have been a matter of some contention over the past decades (Bruck & Ceci, 2004; Goodman & Quas, 2008; La Rooy, Lamb, & Pipe, 2009; Malloy & Quas, 2009). To date, research attention has been largely directed towards establishing the extent to which repeated interviewing can increase suggestibility, and this negative effect has been widely debated in both legal and academic circles (see Brainerd & Reyna, 2005, p. 304; Goodman & Quas, 2008; La Rooy, Katz, Malloy, & Lamb, 2010). In particular, a failure to distinguish between the effects of repeated *suggestive* interviewing and the effects of repeated interviewing per se has meant that professional guidance documents, prosecutorial decision making, and judicial fact finding often discourage the practice of repeated interviewing (Criminal Justice System, 2007, sections 2.13, 2.117, 2.188; New Zealand Law Commission, 1997, section 97; Scottish Executive, 2003, section 30; Scottish Executive, 2007, sections 7, 155). However, there are many circumstances in which it is extremely valuable to interview children more than once, so long as the interview context and the types of questions asked conform to those recommended in best-practice interview guidelines (e.g., Orbach, Lamb, La Rooy, & Pipe, 2012). Children may be interviewed on more than one occasion when they appear reluctant to disclose but other investigative leads indicate that maltreatment probably occurred (Cederborg et al., 2007). Additional interviews may also be required when there are multiple events to be recounted, or when children have become fatigued or distressed during the initial interview. Children may be re-interviewed after longer delays when new information comes to light, when cases are re-opened, as a refresher prior to a court appearance, and during the trial process itself (e.g., during direct, cross- and re-examination) (La Rooy et al., 2010).

Repeated interviewing may lead to reminiscence (recollection of new, previously unreported information; e.g., Orbach et al., 2012), or hypermnesia (an increase in the total amount of information reported relative to earlier retrieval attempts) (Brainerd, Reyna, Howe, & Kingma, 1990; Erdelyi, 1996). The act of retrieving and reporting information may also reactivate the original recall, consolidating the strength of memory traces and increasing subsequent access to retrieval cues (Rovee-Collier, Greco-Vigorito, & Hayne, 1993; Howe, Courage, & Bryant-Brown, 1993).

With strengthened memory traces, children may be more likely to generate their own retrieval cues, which, in turn, may prompt additional information (e.g., Orbach et al., 2012).

However, repeated interviewing may also compromise the reliability of children's accounts if errors reported during earlier interviews (either self-generated or in response to suggestive questioning) become incorporated into memory representations (e.g., Ceci, Huffman, Smith, & Loftus, 1994). Additionally, children may be exposed between interviews to information from other sources that is subsequently incorporated into their accounts (via source-monitoring errors or social pressure). Children may also produce inconsistent accounts in successive interviews, reflecting errors of both omission and commission (Peterson, 2011). Such inconsistencies may affect credibility negatively in the eyes of investigators, lawyers, judges, and jurors.

The negative effects of repeated interviewing have typically been demonstrated in the context of suggestive interviews rather than interviews conducted in accordance with recognized evidence-based practice (e.g., Goodman & Quas, 2008; La Rooy et al., 2010; Peterson, 2011). Studies that examine repeated recall using optimal interviewing techniques (i.e., open-ended questioning) show that, as with other dimensions of eyewitness testimony, the length of delay and the questioning strategy employed are both influential (e.g., Goodman & Quas, 2008; La Rooy et al., 2009, 2010). With short delays, reporting of increased amounts of information that is highly accurate is facilitated (i.e., by both reminiscence and hypermnesia: La Rooy, Pipe, & Murray, 2005; Quas et al., 2007). When the delay between interviews is more substantial (6 months or longer), new information reported is often inaccurate, whereas information that is consistently reported tends to be accurate (e.g., La Rooy et al., 2005; Salmon & Pipe, 1997, 2000).

HAS THERE BEEN ANY PRE-INTERVIEW ASSESSMENT?

Planning for the interview helps ensure that relevant and comprehensive information is elicited and that potential challenges can be identified in advance. While it was relatively uncommon in the past for interviewers to have access to good information about children's capacities and limitations, such information can help ensure that they have the best opportunity to communicate what they know. For example, witnesses in the United Kingdom may sometimes be supported by a "registered intermediary" during interviews or court appearances, to mitigate the impact of any developmental or communicative disorders (Lamb, La Rooy, Malloy, & Katz, 2011; Plotnikoff & Woolfson, 2015).

Even when an intermediary is not involved, a good understanding of the child's developmental, communicative, cognitive, and social functioning enhances the interviewer's ability to plan for any necessary modifications to usual procedures (e.g., the nature of questions asked, how many interviews, scheduling of breaks, and so forth: Brown, Lewis, & Lamb, 2015; Brown, Lewis, Stephens, & Lamb, 2017; Henry, Bettaney, & Carney, 2011).

WHO HAS TALKED TO THE CHILD ALREADY?

In forensic interviews, children do not start out as "blank canvasses" and have often been subject to informal interviews by concerned family members or the people to whom they first disclosed (Ceci et al., 2007). Each of these informal interviews, or conversations, some perhaps meant to prepare children for upcoming interviews, are opportunities for the children's recollections of events to become fused with information gleaned from other sources (e.g., their conversational partners; Poole & Lindsay, 1995; Principe & Schindewolf, 2012). As children recall (or rehearse) these new, embellished, versions of the events, the associations between the various aspects strengthen, to the detriment of the original associations, making it more difficult to retrieve and report the undistorted original memories. Thus, in addition to exploring the content of children's disclosures, it is also important to understand how those disclosures came about, the extent to which the events have been talked about prior to an interview, and the way in which those conversations unfolded.

Research suggests that mothers, like interviewers, are good at remembering the general gist of the content of conversations between them and their children, but not who said what, or whether children contributed information spontaneously or in response to questions. Bruck, Ceci, and Francoeur (1999) demonstrated how difficult it is for parents to recall what their children said and how they came to say it. In their study, mothers interviewed their own children (3- to 5-year-olds) about a play activity that had occurred when the mothers were absent. The mothers were told to talk to their children immediately after the play activity to find out what happened. Three days later, the mothers were interviewed to see what they recalled about the conversation. Very little (only 5%) of the conversation was reported (and only 66% of the activities that had been talked about), and mothers attributed over a quarter of the information that was elicited in response to direct questions to spontaneous reporting by their children. As Bruck et al. concluded: "our data indicate that the mother may not be able to accurately recall whether these were the child's own words or if her statement is a reconstruction of a conversation in which the child provided one-word answers to a series of direct and possibly leading questions from the mother. A genuine concern is that a mother might accurately report the gist of a child's disclosure but fail to recognize that this disclosure resulted from a host of repeated leading questions" (p. 105).

Korkman and colleagues obtained similar findings when they evaluated parental reports of disclosures their children had made to them about child sexual abuse (Korkman, Juusola, & Santtila, 2014). Parents who provided the police with self-recorded conversations with their children about the children's disclosures were interviewed about the disclosures. Parents grossly underestimated their own input into the disclosure process and the suggestive nature of the questions they used, and over-reported the children's input and the spontaneous nature of the information the children provided. Similar findings were observed in a subsequent experimental study, in which parents listened to a recording of a mother questioning her child about sexual abuse. Parents incorrectly attributed 51% of the details to the child (when they were provided by the mother), and 12% of details that the parents reported were not in the recording at all (Korkman, Laajasalo, Juusola, Uusivuori, & Santtila, 2015). As the researchers concluded, "it appears, thus, that even under ideal conditions, the human capacity of reporting verbatim questions and answers is weak" (p. 97). Unfortunately, such selective recall is not only characteristic of parents: In an earlier study, Lamb et al. (2000) found that interviewers systematically misattributed elicited information to open-ended rather than more focused prompts, even though they were ostensibly making verbatim contemporaneous transcriptions!

THE IMPORTANCE OF RAPPORT

Children's awareness of the possible consequences of disclosing abuse in forensic interviews may affect their willingness to disclose and discuss their experiences. Children may be reluctant to disclose abuse and/or participate in interviews for a variety of reasons that include close relationships with the perpetrators (Goodman-Brown, Edelstein, Goodman, Jones, & Gordon, 2003; Hershkowitz et al., 2007), a sense of loyalty to perpetrators (Mian, Wehrspann, Kaljiner-Diamond, LeBaron, & Winder, 1986), fear of retribution and abandonment (Burgess & Holmstrom, 1978), feelings of complicity, embarrassment, guilt, and shame (Cederborg et al., 2007; Goodman-Brown et al., 2003; Hershkowitz et al., 2007), fear of consequences for others (Burgess & Holmstrom, 1978; Goodman-Brown et al., 2003), fear of not being believed and therefore punished (Browne & Finkelhor, 1986), and fear of family disruption (Lawson & Chaffin, 1992). Children are often disconcerted by the speed at which investigations are initiated, frequently feel they have little control over the process, and are often uncomfortable with the manner in which they are interviewed (Wade & Westcott, 1997). Forensic interviews require children to talk about subjects that may be embarrassing and/or traumatic, and diverse emotions may adversely affect children's willingness to converse with interviewers. The task of forensic interviewers is thus to create an atmosphere in which children are willing to discuss topics that are not normally sanctioned. When interviewers fail in this task, either by neglecting to establish rapport or by failing to communicate ground rules for the conversations, children are less likely to share their experiences completely and accurately.

Establishing rapport with children before raising the matter under investigation is widely promoted as best practice (see Saywitz, Larsen, Hobbs, & Wells, 2015, for discussion). Although widely promoted, few studies have directly compared different ways of establishing rapport and linked these methods to interview outcomes (Brown et al., 2013; Hardy & van Leeuwen, 2004; Price, Ahern, & Lamb, 2016; Roberts, Lamb, & Sternberg, 2004; Teoh & Lamb, 2010). Similarly, scant research has examined the dynamics of interviewer-child exchanges during the rapport-building stage of an interview, but the evidence emerging from such work is that, just as in the substantive phase, the nature of interviewers' utterances (type and content) influences how productive and responsive children are, even from the very outset of the interview (Ahern, Hershkowitz, Lamb, Blasbalg, & Winstanley, 2014; Price et al., 2016). Collectively, studies of rapport building indicate that (as with a practice narrative, described below) an open-ended style of questioning during this phase successfully encourages children to provide lengthy responses with minimal interviewer input.

Many more studies include some form of simple rapport building at the beginning of their interviewing protocols (e.g., brief introductions and discussions about things the child likes to do), but the effect of including or excluding such interactions has not been tested. A few researchers have examined other ways of establishing a supportive context for the interview (but not examined rapport building directly). These studies typically show that, when interviewers adopt a supportive behavioral style with children (ranging in age from 3 to 11 years), the children are better able to resist suggestive questions, and may also recount target events more accurately (Almerigogna et al., 2007; Carter et al., 1996; Goodman, Bottoms, Schwartz-Kenney, & Rudy, 1991; Rush et al., 2014; Quas & Lench, 2007; Quas et al., 2014). Additionally, in a field study examining children's responsiveness when interviewed about alleged abuse, Lewy, Cyr, and Dion (2015) showed that, when a non-supportive interviewing style was adopted, children reported fewer details during the interview.

Of course, establishing rapport prior to discussion of the events under investigation is no guarantee that rapport will remain intact throughout the interview (Saywitz et al., 2015). Recently, Hershkowitz and colleagues have examined the development and maintenance of rapport and the provision of support throughout the interview, documenting the positive effects on the amount of information children provide (e.g., Ahern, Hershkowitz, Lamb, Blasbalg, & Karni-Visel, 2018; Blasbalg, Hershkowitz, Lamb, & Karni-Visel, 2018; see Chapter 9). In an earlier field study comparing the supportive and standard versions of the NICHD Protocol, Ahern et al. (2014) showed that, when interviewers followed children's statements of reluctance with supportive comments, children were more likely to be responsive rather than reluctant thereafter (a more detailed discussion of the supportive version of the Protocol and associated research is presented in Chapter 9). Thus momentary gains and losses in children's engagement with interviewers can occur as a function of the interviewers' responses to reluctance, and this underscores the importance of monitoring child motivation, state, and rapport throughout the interview.

Much of the research discussed in Chapter 9 explores how best to establish the type of rapport that promotes complete and accurate accounts and to avoid taxing children's limited attentional and cognitive resources (e.g., by making the interview session excessively long). Research using the Revised Protocol described there has also illustrated how to effectively (and safely) establish rapport with more reluctant children, who tend to be less communicative even in the pre-substantive phase of the interview (Orbach, Shiloach, & Lamb, 2007), or those who exhibit particularly high levels of anxiety or distress. Much still remains to be learned about how to establish rapport with children who have varied characteristics, how to monitor the ongoing levels of rapport during the interview, and how best to reinstate rapport should the rapport between the interviewer and child break down.

PREPARING THE CHILD FOR THE INTERVIEW—GROUND RULES

Establishing "ground rules" for the interaction is widely promoted as an important aspect of preparing children to be interviewed. Such ground rules typically include giving any or all of the following instructions to the children to: provide unrestricted accounts of their experiences (e.g., "tell me everything, even the little things"), report only what they are confident about (e.g., "don't guess, just tell me what you really know"), be cognizant of the interviewers' naivety about what occurred (e.g., "I don't know what happened"), tell the truth (e.g., "only tell me what really happened"), signal when they do not know the answer to a question (e.g., "if you don't know the answer to a question, just say "I don't know"), signal when they do not understand a question (e.g. "If I say something that you don't understand, just tell me"), and correct interviewers if they say something wrong (e.g., "If I make a mistake you should correct me") (Brubacher, Poole, & Dickinson, 2015).

Ground rules are thought to mitigate some of the challenges children face during forensic interviews. From an early age, children learn how to construct accounts of their experiences, guided in large part by interactions with their parents (Fivush, 2011; Nelson & Fivush, 2004; Salmon & Reese, 2015), and children may learn that a good story is better than an accurate one. For example, Kulkofsky, Wang, and Ceci (2008) showed that children who told better organized and more detailed narratives about an event were often less accurate about the specific details of the experience than children who provided briefer accounts. Giving priority to telling a good story is, of course, at odds with the goal of a forensic interview. Thus, a ground rule emphasizing the importance of telling the truth may serve to highlight the gravity of the forensic interview and minimize the number of embellishments made in service of creating good stories.

A published evaluation of forensic interviews about alleged abuse showed that children said "I don't know" rarely—they did so in response to fewer than 6% of all prompts (Earhart et al., 2014). Children are unlikely to recognize that "I don't know" is a valued response in this context (Scoboria & Fisico, 2013), given the encouragement (or even pressure) they may receive to answer challenging questions in other settings (e.g., in conversations with parents, or when their knowledge is being tested by teachers). Children may also have difficulty admitting that they do not understand interviewers' requests, and so instructing them that they should indeed do so may be reassuring. Finally, interviewers often make errors when talking to children, perhaps incorrectly paraphrasing a statement (Lamb, Orbach, Sternberg, Hershkowitz, & Horowitz, 2000; Roberts & Lamb, 1999) or introducing misleading or incorrect information. When such errors occur, it is important that children address them directly, because a failure to do so may imply tacit agreement with or confirmation of the incorrect information. Children frequently fail to directly signal such errors, however (Evans, Roberts, Price, & Stefek, 2010; Hunt & Borgida, 2001; Roberts & Lamb, 1999), and they are unlikely to be reinforced for challenging or correcting adults in other settings (Brubacher et al., 2015). An explicit instruction about the importance of correcting the interviewer during an interview may therefore increase the likelihood that children do so.

Ground rules are often referred to collectively, although each particular rule addresses very different aspects of children's behavior in interviews. While some of the rules have been more extensively studied and supported by empirical research (e.g., eliciting a promise to tell the truth; Evans & Lee, 2010; Lyon & Dorado, 2008; Lyon et al., 2008; Talwar, Lee, Bala, & Lindsay, 2002, 2004; encouraging children to say "I don't know" when appropriate but to respond informatively when they do know the answer; Gee, Gregory, & Pipe, 1999; Saywitz & Moan-Hardie, 1994), others have minimal (albeit positive) evidence-based support (e.g., informing the child that the interviewer is ignorant about their experience; Mulder & Vrij, 1996; telling children not to guess; Warren, Hulse-Trotter, & Tubbs, 1991; instructing the child to correct the interviewer if they make a mistake; Warren et al., 1991).

Practice applying or following the ground rules (also known as extended demonstration and teaching, e.g., Danby, Brubacher, Sharman, & Powell, 2015; Krackow & Lynn, 2010) appears to be necessary to ensure that children benefit from the presentation of ground rules (Brubacher et al., 2015) and follow them appropriately. For example, early studies examining the impact of instructing young children to say "I don't know" revealed a tendency for children to *overuse* the term, unless they were also instructed not to do so when they *did* know the answer (Gee et al., 1999; Saywitz & Moan-Hardie, 1994).

There is emerging evidence that children's understanding (Dickinson, Brubacher, & Poole, 2015), use of (Danby et al., 2015), and benefit from (Earhart et al., 2014; Teoh & Lamb, 2013) ground rule instruction varies depending on their age and abilities (Brown et al., 2016). Dickinson et al. (2015) showed that children's comprehension of different ground rules increased with age. Preschoolers (4- to 5-year-olds) had more difficulty when instructed to correct interviewers and to tell interviewers if they said something wrong. By about age 7, most children could demonstrate an accurate understanding of several ground rules in response to practice probes, and when questions were examined individually, children generally did well. Across seven ground rules, however, many (39%) of even the oldest children (8- to 9-year-olds) failed to understand at least one. Danby et al. (2015) extended Dickinson et al.'s research by looking at whether, having demonstrated proficiency during a practice, children then made use of the rules during interviews or in response to some delayed test questions. Danby et al. found that practice with the "don't know" rule increased spontaneous use of it during the interview (relative to children who were just instructed to say "I don't know" but did not practice), but practice did not increase children's accuracy when they recounted their experiences. However, children seldom said "I don't understand" or corrected the interviewer regardless of whether or not they had practiced application.

Although many of the ground rules have not yet been systematically studied in combination with the varied factors known to directly influence the quality of children's testimony, there is little evidence that discussion of the ground rules has detrimental effects on children's reporting. However, we still have much to learn about ground rules and the best ways to present them to children at different developmental levels (Brown et al., 2016; Brubacher et al., 2015), when they should be introduced, the impact of reminding children about the rules at various stages of the interview, and whether children's application of the rules during an interview improves the overall reliability of their accounts.

PREPARING THE CHILD FOR THE INTERVIEW—PRACTICE NARRATIVES

The way in which children are prepared to participate in interviews shapes how they respond to subsequent questioning (see Roberts, Brubacher, Powell, & Price, 2011 for a review) because children are unlikely to recognize on their own that forensic interviews and everyday conversations have very different purposes and needs (see Lamb & Brown, 2006, for discussion). In everyday conversations, children are encouraged to describe events by focusing on key actions and providing a broad summary or overview, rather than including many details, whereas forensic interviews are designed specifically to obtain those rich details (Lamb & Brown, 2006). Additionally, children are still in the process of developing their narrative ability and learning how to construct effective narratives (including details about the context, location, characters and their motivations, consequences, and so forth; Reese et al., 2011). Allowing children to practice narrating recent experiences in the preparation stage of forensic interviews addresses these challenges by 1) orienting children to the types of information interviewers need in order to fully understand their experiences (including level of detail, and descriptions of specific instances rather than generic summaries), 2) providing children with opportunities to respond to the kinds of prompts that will be used to encourage elaboration during the substantive phase of the interview, 3) allowing for extended rapport building, and 4) giving interviewers opportunities to become familiar with the children's communicative styles. Importantly, the way in which practice narratives are conducted affects children's subsequent reporting (e.g., Price, Roberts, & Collins, 2013; Roberts et al., 2004; Sternberg et al., 1997). Encouraging children to describe specific neutral events promotes the use of episodic language when they are recounting target events. Moreover, focusing on specific instances of repeated events helps young children to spontaneously report that there were multiple events and to describe each of them in greater detail (Brubacher et al., 2011). The types of prompts used are also important: The use of broadly open prompts (e.g., "Tell me everything you can remember about that") encourage more detailed reporting (Price et al., 2013; Roberts et al., 2004; Sternberg et al., 1997) than when more narrowly focused questions are used (Brown et al., 2013; Price et al., 2013). Importantly, using an open style during the practice narrative also promotes the continued use of that style by interviewers during the substantive phase (Price et al., 2013), resulting in fewer interviewer prompts overall (Price et al., 2013) and shorter substantive questioning phases (Brown et al., 2013). Other researchers have examined the benefits of explicitly training children to narrate events prior to the substantive interview and have shown that this can improve children's accounts (e.g., Brown & Pipe, 2003a, 2003b; Camparo, Wagner, & Saywitz, 2001; Saywitz & Camparo, 2013; Saywitz & Snyder, 1993, 1996).

Orbach and colleagues (2016) suggested that the pre-substantive phase should include extended opportunities for both children and interviewers to practice retrieval skills (see Lamb, Orbach, Hershkowitz, Esplin et al., 2007; Orbach et al., 2000; Sternberg et al., 1997) while minimizing the use of suggestive prompts. Because interviewers frequently misclassify their own statements/questions (e.g., Cauchi, Powell, & Hughes-Scholes, 2010; Lamb, Orbach, Sternberg, Hershkowitz, & Horowitz, 2000; Yi & Lamb, unpublished data) and because suggestive prompts may take any form (e.g., open-ended invitations, directive questions, or yes/no and forced-choice questions), Orbach and colleagues (2016) focused on enhancing interviewers' awareness of what constitutes "suggestive" input in forensic contexts for increasing their ability to replace suggestive information-requests with non-suggestive alternatives.

Other influences on children's reporting. Interviewers seldom initiate interviews without some knowledge of what has been alleged. Assumptions about likely explanations for the disclosure may shape the kinds of questions interviewers pose and limit the children's opportunities to provide information that would support alternative interpretations. In other words, interviewer bias may result in a line of questioning designed to confirm particular hypotheses or explanations rather than to test a range of possible explanations (Ceci et al., 2007), and thus exert undue influence on what the children report, even if the questions used are open-ended. Children's responding may also be shaped by the nonverbal cues that accompany questions. For example, an interviewer's tone, gestures, and facial expressions may convey information about expected responses or selectively reinforce responding (or non-responding), as might the repetition of questions (Earhart et al., 2014).

Types of Questions Asked

Our understanding of how interviewer questioning strategies influence children's responding has been informed by research using a range of methodological approaches, including tightly controlled laboratory-based experiments manipulating a range of factors thought to influence how and what children recall about events and field-based research examining the conduct of forensic interviews with children to investigate alleged maltreatment. Despite very different approaches to examining the impact of interviewing strategies on children's responses, the research has yielded remarkably consistent conclusions. Although older children typically provide more detailed accounts than younger children, especially during spontaneous or free recall, accuracy remains surprisingly stable with age—at least when children are responding to very open-ended questions (Schneider & Bjorklund, 2003). Question type has a pervasive impact on the amount, accuracy, and organization of children's responses. Broad open-ended prompts (e.g., "tell me everything you remember about that") and those that use disclosed details as cues to encourage children to elaborate upon previously reported information (e.g., "You told me that he did special things. Tell me more about those special things") request "free-recall" responses, which are associated with higher levels of accuracy (Brown et al., 2013), more forensically important information (Phillips, Oxburgh, & Myklebust, 2012), and fewer inconsistencies (Lamb & Fauchier, 2001; Orbach & Lamb, 2001; Orbach et al., 2012) than focused prompts. Children also provide more coherent and organized responses to open as opposed to focused prompts (Feltis et al., 2010).

Focused recall prompts (cued-recall) that refocus on disclosed, allegation-related, information and provide a category for requesting additional specific details, using "Wh-" questions (e.g., "What color was his car?" when "car" was mentioned) understandably tend to elicit fewer details, but also more errors (Brown et al., 2013) and more inconsistencies (Lamb & Fauchier, 2001), than free-recall open-ended prompts. Focused recognition prompts (e.g., Yes/no or multiple choice type questions) introduce interviewer-generated information and tend to elicit fewer details (Cederborg, Orbach, Sternberg, & Lamb, 2000; Korkman, Santtila, & Sandnabba, 2006), as well as more errors and inconsistent statements (Andrews et al., 2015; Friedman & Lyon, 2005; Lamb & Fauchier, 2001; Orbach et al., 2016; Orbach & Lamb, 2001; Waterman et al., 2000) than any of the other types of prompt.

In field contexts, reported details can seldom be verified independently, but researchers have instead used the incidence of internally contradictory information to index inaccuracy. In one such study, Lamb and Fauchier (2001) examined the circumstances in which seven alleged sexual abuse victims repeated or contradicted forensically relevant details. Suggestive questions elicited a disproportionately high number of contradictions in that study, whereas no responses to free recall prompts were ever contradicted.

Like Lamb and Fauchier (2001), Orbach and Lamb (2001) focused on the eliciting conditions associated with the retrieval of contradictory information, but whereas Lamb and Fauchier examined "average" interviews (i.e., interviews similar in structure and quality to the investigative interviews conducted by peer interviewers in investigative agencies around the world at the time), the investigative interview examined by Orbach and Lamb (2001) was selected because it was characterized by excessive reliance on risky practices, and they expected that such an interview would elucidate the extent to which these negative practices fostered internal contradictions. Option-posting and suggestive utterances were posed from the beginning of the interview studied by Orbach and Lamb (2001), with no information provided by the child prior to the investigator's first option-posing or suggestive prompt. Of the 195 substantive utterances in the interview, 143 (73%) were option-posing or suggestive in nature. Fifty-nine (41%) of those option-posing and suggestive utterances were associated with contradictory details, either because they elicited information that was later contradicted (14 utterances, 24%) or because they elicited details that contradicted details reported earlier (45 utterances, 76%). Many (85%) of the utterances eliciting contradictory information in this study were yes/no questions. Moreover, five (25%) of the 20 option-posing utterances and 13 (52%) of the 25 suggestive utterances that elicited contradictory details were repeated.

Likewise, of the 403 details provided by the child during the interview, 138 details (34%) were associated with contradiction, in that 51 details were later contradicted and 87 details contradicted information that had been reported earlier. Moreover, in over 50% of the contradicting utterances, of which 91% were elicited in response to option-posing or suggestive questions, the child provided information contrary to her earlier denials. Eighty-two (94%) of the 87 contradicting details were elicited using option-posing or suggestive utterances. No contradiction occurred in response to an open-ended utterance. Similar findings were obtained in a much larger field study described more fully in Chapter 6 (Lamb, Orbach, Hershkowitz, Horowitz, & Abbott, 2007).

In a recent examination of trial testimonies of 6- to 12-year-old alleged sexual abuse victims, significantly more self-contradictions were elicited in responses to suggestive questions posed by trial attorneys than to any other prompt type (Andrews et al., 2015).

Using within-interview self-contradictions as an index of inaccuracy, Orbach and colleagues (2016) assessed the consistency of 229 children's responses to suggestive prompts, for which their earlier assertions on the same issues (in the same interviews) were available. The 229 pairs of responses were identified in 144 forensic accounts of 4-to 13-year-old alleged victims of sexual abuse. Although overall, children were much more likely to confirm (80.4%) than to contradict (19.7%) their earlier assertions while responding to interviewers' suggestions, the likelihood of self-contradiction and the type of the eliciting suggestive prompt were associated.

Self-contradictions were significantly more likely to occur in response to introductory (introducing an undisclosed allegation-specific content) and confrontational (casting doubt on the truthfulness of a witness' statement) than to suppositional (assuming or implying an undisclosed allegation-specific content) suggestive prompts (the three mutually exclusive and exhaustive categories used by Orbach et al. to differentiate suggestive prompts in relation to the type of suggestive input). Interestingly, although confrontational prompts accounted for only 5% of the total number of suggestive prompts, they elicited 31% of all contradictory responses (Orbach et al., 2016). The riskiness of these confrontational prompts was also evident in Orbach and Lamb's (2001) findings that 40% of the contradictory details elicited during a forensic interview with a 5-year-old child were provided in response to suggestive prompts that questioned the truthfulness of the witness' account.

Unlike confrontational prompts in laboratory studies, which mostly involve game-like or personally insignificant staged events, such prompts in the forensic context involve personally and emotionally meaningful allegedly experienced events (e.g., "You said ... but the police officer told me...."). Thus, interviewers' confrontations in forensic cases may be very challenging, leading children to agree with interviewers' suggestions, even if by doing so they contradict their own earlier assertions (see O'Neill & Zajac, 2013; Zajac et al., 2003). Such inconsistencies may negatively affect children's reliability and perceived credibility in legal contexts, particularly when younger children are involved (e.g., Baugerud, Magnussen, & Melinder, 2014; Ghetti, Goodman, Eisen, Qin, & Davis, 2002; Zajac, O'Neill, & Hayne, 2012).

Recall vs. Recognition Processes

Importantly, the various kinds of prompts that interviewers use invoke different kinds of memory retrieval mechanisms. Invitations and direct questions both rely on *recall*, whereas option-posing and suggestive questions require *recognition* memory processes. When memory is probed using open-ended prompts, children must search their memories and attempt to provide as much relevant information as they "remember." In this way, the information exchange is *child-led,* and allows the child to focus on and report what is best remembered and thus most easily accessible (and perhaps most salient) to them. In contrast, when children have to select, confirm, or reject information provided by interviewers, recognition memory is being used. When such questions are used, the exchange becomes *interviewer-led,* which may interfere with the children's ability to generate and benefit from their own retrieval cues, and result in potentially important information not being included in children's accounts.

Recognition probes refocus children on domains of interest to the investigators and exert greater pressure to respond, whether or not the respondents are sure of their responses. Recognition probes are more likely to elicit erroneous responses in eyewitness contexts because of response biases (i.e., tendencies to say "yes" or "no" without reflection) and false recognition of details that were only mentioned in previous interviews or are inferred from the gist of the experienced events (Brainerd & Reyna, 1996). Effective interviewers should thus maximize the reliance on free recall by offering open-ended prompts so as to minimize the risk of eliciting erroneous information.

Free-recall reports are not always accurate, of course, especially when the events occurred long before the interview or there have been opportunities for either pre- (Leichtman & Ceci, 1995) or post-event contamination (Leichtman & Ceci, 1995; Poole & Lindsay, 1995, 1997; Poole & White, 1993; Warren & Lane, 1995) but they are likely to be much more accurate than reports elicited using recognition cues or prompts. The completeness of brief initial responses can be increased when interviewers use the information provided by children in their early spontaneous utterances as "cues" for further elaboration (i.e., "cued-invitations"; e.g., "You said the man touched you; tell me more about that touching") (Lamb et al., 2003).

Open questions, while the most effective for eliciting detailed and accurate accounts from children, are not, however, silver bullets that guarantee reliable responses. Although they typically elicit more detailed narrative responses from children, open questions are also associated with more frequent non-responding than other types of prompts (e.g., Korkman, Santtila, & Sandnabba, 2006; Korkman, Santtila, Westeråker, & Sandnabba, 2008; Melinder & Gilstrap, 2009; Wolfman, Brown, & Jose, 2016). Additionally, children can provide inaccurate details in response to open questions just as they do when responding to more focused ones, although the accuracy of their responses to open questions is typically higher. The predominant use of open questions during a more formal investigative interview is especially critical because, while such questions may not overcome the effects of any pre-interview suggestion, misinformation, or contamination, they can prevent further suggestive influences on children's recall.

DEVELOPMENTAL DIFFERENCES IN RESPONSES TO INTERVIEWER QUESTIONS

Research examining more subtle differences in children's responsiveness to various question types sheds light on the development of children's ability to answer open-ended questions. While very young children (e.g., 3- to 4-year-olds) are able to report meaningful information in response to open-ended questions (e.g., "tell me everything you can remember about that"), children in this age group appear to be most informative when asked focused recall (i.e., directive) questions (e.g., "What color was his car?'"; when "car" was mentioned by the child). For example, Hershkowitz et al. (2012) showed that 3- and 4-year-old children gave more detailed responses to focused recall ("Wh-") prompts than to open-ended ones, whereas the reverse was true for 5- to 6-year-olds. Other studies have shown that 4- to 6-year-olds and 7- to 8-year-olds provide equivalent numbers of details per prompt in response to open-ended prompts. Thus, from around 4 to 5 years, developmental differences become less apparent than during the preschool years, when children seem to benefit from more structured input from interviewers' narrow specific requests, perhaps because "Wh-" questions provide more concrete retrieval cues for children (e.g., by signaling the category of information to focus on). Indeed, other authors have speculated that open-ended prompts may elicit more non-responding from children because these prompts do not provide enough structure and guidance for them to understand and answer the questions (Korkman et al., 2006, 2008; Melinder & Gilstrap, 2009).

HOW ARE THE QUESTIONS DISTRIBUTED?

The metaphor commonly used for an approach to interviewing is that of a funnel, with very open-ended questions at the beginning followed by progressively narrower or more specific questions as the interview unfolds (Fisher, Ross, & Cahill, 2010). As we describe in the next chapter, such an approach is often mentioned in evaluations of field interviews, with questions appearing in blocks, and open invitations more prevalent in the first compared to the latter half of interviews (Sternberg et al., 2001; Wolfman, Brown, & Jose, 2016a, 2016b). The problem with a funnel approach is that the positive effects of invitations are not then available to children for the entire interview. Further, the negative effects of asking more specific questions are likely to be exacerbated when such questions are introduced later in an interview, by which time the children's recall is likely to have been exhausted. As a result, children may be even more susceptible to the social and cognitive demands such questions place on them. Other commentators have also noted that the presence (and frequency) of suggestive questions do not necessarily make an entire interview problematically suggestive (Ceci et al., 2007). Rather, it is important to consider how such questions are nested within the broader context of the interview. Indeed, in a laboratory-analogue study of the NICHD Protocol, Brown et al. (2013) showed that children's responses to (mildly) leading and misleading questions were impressively accurate. They speculated that this may have reflected 1) the mild levels of suggestion, and 2) the positive impact of the practice of "pairing" promoted by the Protocol. Pairing is the practice of immediately following up any focused (direct, option-posing, or suggestive) question with an invitation (e.g.., "tell me everything you can about [that]"), to encourage child-led elaboration and limit interviewer input. When interviewers follow this principle, they are not only more likely to address children with a greater number of invitations, but also maintain the use of invitations throughout the *entire* interview. This approach may be especially important with younger children, who may benefit from the additional structure and help organizing their responses into a coherent and detailed narrative (Reese et al., 2011).

USE OF VISUAL AIDS OR TECHNIQUES?

Many professional protocols and consultation documents make provision for the use of visual aids (e.g., dolls, body diagrams, drawings) in interviews with children (e.g., APRI, 2003; APSAC, 2002; New Zealand Police/Child, Youth and Family, 2015; Home Office, 2011; Plotnikoff &

Woolfson, 2009). Such provisions suggest that dolls and body diagrams remain a common part of an interviewer's repertoire of techniques. The primary goals of these aids are: 1) to decrease any reluctance that children might have about divulging information about their past experiences; 2) to enhance retrieval from memory of information about the event(s) in question, and 3) to aid in establishing rapport and making children more comfortable during the interview (e.g., Poole & Dickinson, 2014).

We review evidence regarding the effectiveness of visual aids in Chapter 10. To foreshadow the conclusions we reach there, there is little evidence that such aids effectively improve children's recall, at least when they are used alongside an exhaustive, best-practice interview (see Brown, 2011, for discussion). The reliability of children's accounts can be compromised when they are interviewed using such aids, however, due to an increased use of risky questions, which may result in increased numbers of errors in the children's accounts.

There has been very little research on potential contributions of visual aids for purposes other than supporting recall (e.g., establishing a supportive interview context, increasing engagement, and enhancing the quality of the interview experience (e.g., Katz, Barnetz, & Hershkowitz, 2014; Poole & Dickinson, 2014). Although it is possible that using visual aids facilitates recall indirectly, by breaking down some of the social barriers that are likely to arise during face-to-face interviews with strangers, it is also conceivable that such tools might encourage children to lose sight of the focus of the interview and engage in more off-topic verbalization that might develop into false reporting.

CONCLUSION

A forensic interview is likely to be daunting for children for many reasons—the consequences of participating may be disconcerting; they need to interact with unfamiliar adults; the topic may be difficult to talk about (for both emotional and cognitive reasons), and children are unused to taking on the role of experts and to recounting their experiences at length and in minute detail. How children are prepared for such demands, thus, affects how well they are likely to engage and contribute. Such preparation is best done within the interview, however, because pre-interview preparation or coaching (e.g., by parents) could irrevocably change how children come to remember and describe events. Most important are the strategies interviewers use to elicit children's evidence—the kinds of questions asked, how those questions are distributed throughout the interviews, and whether or not other tools (e.g., visual aids) are used. A substantial body of evidence has emerged documenting the benefits and risks associated with different interviewing strategies. This evidence demonstrates that open-ended invitations best support children's recall. As we show in the next chapter, however, interviewers typically do not rely extensively on such prompts in the course of their interviews.

4

How do Investigators Typically Interview Alleged Victims?

The converging outcomes of research examining factors that promote, or detract from, children's ability to provide useful and reliable testimony have informed a series of best-practice guides and protocols. Clearly, how well interviewers understand children's development and the process by which they come to remember and describe their experiences affects how effectively they conduct forensic interviews. In this chapter, we focus on the extent to which interviewers actually adhere to the recommendations that have emerged from the research on children's eyewitness testimony when conducting investigative interviews with alleged victims.

As indicated in Chapters 2 and 3, many researchers have studied children's capacities to provide accurate information about their past experiences, while others have paid special attention to children's limitations and vulnerabilities (e.g., suggestibility). To recap, the research shows that, although children clearly can remember incidents they have experienced, the relationship between age and memory is complex, with a variety of factors influencing the quality of information provided. For our present purposes, perhaps the most important of these factors pertains to the interviewer's ability to *elicit* information

---

Tell Me What Happened: Questioning Children About Abuse, Second Edition.
Michael E. Lamb, Deirdre A. Brown, Irit Hershkowitz, Yael Orbach, and Phillip W. Esplin.
© 2018 John Wiley & Sons Ltd. Published 2018 by John Wiley & Sons Ltd.

and the child's willingness and ability to *express* it, rather than the child's ability to *remember* it. Clearly, it is often possible to obtain valuable information from children, but doing so requires careful investigative procedures, as well as a realistic awareness of children's capacities and tendencies.

RECOMMENDED INTERVIEWING PRACTICE

For many years now, expert professional groups and individuals have published consensus statements or formal guidelines describing evidence-based best-practice for interviewing children (e.g., American Professional Society on the Abuse of Children (APSAC), 2012; Brown & Lamb, 2015; Home Office, 2011; La Rooy et al., 2015; Orbach, Hershkowitz, Lamb, Sternberg, & Esplin et al., 2000; Poole, 2016; Saywitz & Camparo, 2013; Saywitz, Lyon, & Goodman, 2011). Such documents reflect agreement about the following principles:

- Children should be interviewed as soon as possible after the alleged offenses. Interviewers should promote a child-centered interviewing approach by using input-free open-ended prompts ("Tell me what happened") and cues (e.g., "Earlier you mentioned [disclosed content]. Tell me everything about that") to elicit detailed free-recall narratives throughout the entire interview, and avoid introducing any information.
- Interviewers should refrain from introducing focused-recall questions (directive prompts) that request additional information about a specific aspects of an earlier-disclosed issue (e.g., time, appearance; "When did it happen?" or "What color was that car?") until they have exhausted open-ended free-recall prompts.
- The use of recognition prompts ("Did he touch you?") should be delayed until as late in the interview as possible and used only when needed for eliciting undisclosed forensically relevant information.

In addition, most experts agree that children benefit from being prepared for the interview by having their and the interviewer's respective roles, the purpose of the interview, and the "ground rules" (for example, to limit themselves to descriptions of events "that really happened" to them and to correct the interviewer, request explanations or clarification, and acknowledge ignorance, as necessary) explained.

The universal emphasis on the value of free-recall narrative responses, elicited using open-ended prompts, is rooted in the results of many laboratory analogue studies. These studies consistently show that information elicited using free-recall open-ended (invitations) and focused-recall (directive) prompts is much more likely to be accurate than information elicited using focused-recognition (option-posing or suggestive) prompts.

Free-recall invitations and focused-recall directive questions do not involve any interviewer-generated input and demand that the child *recalls* information from memory, whereas focused-recognition prompts ask children to *recognize* one or more options suggested by the interviewer. When it has been possible to assess accuracy in field studies, the same pattern has been observed: Responses to recall prompts posed by forensic interviewers are more likely to be accurate than responses to recognition prompts which are, in turn, more likely to be erroneous. Thus, interviewers are routinely advised to avoid using "yes/no" and "forced-choice" questions, especially when interviewing young children. Such questions may encourage children to acquiesce to interviewer-introduced input and may even mislead them into accepting options describing non-experienced events. Because recognition questions are even riskier when addressed to children aged 6 and under, forensic investigators need to make special efforts to use open-ended prompts when interviewing such young children.

The emphasis on the value of open-ended prompts is also supported by evidence that, in forensic contexts, responses to individual free-recall prompts are three to five times more informative than responses to focused prompts, as we show later in this chapter.

EVALUATIONS OF INTERVIEWING—DIVERGENCE FROM RECOMMENDED PRACTICE

Systematic field studies examining the conduct of investigative interviews with children have only emerged in the last three decades. Lamb and colleagues began to investigate the ways in which interviewers questioned children during formal investigations of maltreatment and how children responded to the questions in a series of studies conducted in Israel, Sweden, the United Kingdom, and the United States. In each study, audio-taped recordings of the interviews were transcribed in full by native speakers of the language used in the interview, and checked carefully to ensure their accuracy and completeness. Coders then focused on the portion of each interview concerned with substantive issues (excluding introductory comments, rapport building, practice narratives, and ground rules in the pre-substantive phase, digressions throughout the substantive phase, and the discussion of neutral topics at the end of the interview). Coders reviewed the transcripts and categorized each interviewer utterance, defined as a "turn" in the discourse or conversation, without distinction between questions and statements. Facilitators such as words of encouragement designed to keep the child talking informatively (e.g., "OK"), were not considered independent utterances (details they elicited were added to those elicited by the utterance type they followed). The primary interviewer utterances examined in the various studies are described in Table 4.1. When two or more interviewers' statements or questions that could be coded differently were included in a single "turn," coders employed a "trumping" system with "mixed" utterances assigned to the category representing the highest degree of interviewer input. Thus, if a statement formulated as an invitation included suggestive input, the utterance was coded as "suggestive." Children's responses to interviewer prompts were categorized as being relevant (on-topic) or not, and the amount of the disclosed information was quantified by counting the first mention of each detail reported about the alleged event(s).

Israel

In the first of these studies Lamb, Hershkowitz, Sternberg, and Esplin et al. (1996b) examined a representative sample of 22 audio-taped interviews drawn from a pool of investigative interviews conducted by Israeli "youth investigators" with young alleged victims (5 to 11 years old). Specially trained youth investigators employed by the Israeli Division of Correctional Services and Services for Youth in Distress (now labeled the "Child Investigation Unit") are the only individuals who are allowed to interview children under the age of 14 in Israel. They are required to begin their investigation within 72 hours of the referral and to record their interviews. Children are routinely interviewed once, with an occasional supplementary interview.

In Lamb et al.'s (1996a, 1996b) study, most of the 3,563 substantive utterances spoken by the interviewers (an average of 162 substantive prompts per interview) were directive utterances, whereas a considerable number were option-posing utterances. Only 77 (2.2%) were invitations. Most (3,214, 87%) of the interviewers' utterances elicited relevant responses from the children (see Table 4.2). The average response was 6 words long and yielded an average of 2 details and there was a high correlation (.83) between the number of details and the length of the children's utterances, with approximately one detail provided for every three words that the children spoke, regardless of the type of interviewer utterance to which they were responding.

Invitations elicited significantly longer and more detailed responses than did directive, option-posing, or suggestive utterances (see Table 4.3).

Table 4.1 Definitions and examples of interviewer prompts used in evaluations of forensic interviewing practice with children

Interviewer utterances	Definitions	Examples
Invitations	Questions or statements that prompt free-recall responses	"Tell me everything you can remember"
Cued-invitations	Questions or statements that utilize details disclosed by the child as cues to prompt free-recall responses	"You told me that you and he did special things. Tell me about those special things"
Directive questions	Recall-based prompts that refocus the child's attention on disclosed allegation-related detail(s) and often use "wh" questions to request information within a particular category (e.g., time, color)	"When did this happen?" "What color was his t-shirt [when the child mentioned "he was wearing a t-shirt"]"
Option-posing	Focused-recognition prompts that introduce undisclosed, interviewer-generated, allegation-related content(s) and request the interviewee to select among given options, using a yes/no or choice questions, but do not imply that a particular response is expected	"Did anyone see what happened?" "Did he touch you under or over your clothes?"
Suggestive	Statements or questions that introduce undisclosed, interviewer-generated, allegation-related content(s) AND imply the expected response	"He touched you, didn't he?" "Did it hurt when he touched you?" [when the child did not mention being touched]
Summaries	Statements that repeat exactly what the child said, without posing any information request. New informative details, if elicited, are attributed to "free-recall" memory	"You said he touched you" [After the child said "He touched me"]

Table 4.2 Relative prominence of the different prompts used by investigators to elicit information from alleged victims

Study	Invitation	Directive	Option-posing	Suggestive
Lamb et al. (1996b); Israel ($n = 22$)	3	57	30	10
Lamb et al. (1996a); U.S. ($n = 24$)	2	39	49	10
Sternberg et al. (1996); U.S. ($n = 45$)	5	33	50	12
Sternberg et al. (2001); U.K. ($n = 119$)	7	54	33	6
Cederborg et al. (2000); Sweden ($n = 72$)	6	41	39	14

Note: Numbers in the table may differ from those in the publications because they have been prorated to include only utterances of the types included in this table; some reports also included other types of prompts, especially facilitators, which comprised 10 to 15 % of the total number of prompts used by the interviewers, but in later studies were not considered independent utterances and their elicited details were added to those elicited by the utterance type they followed. In Lamb et al.'s American "doll study" (1996a), the rates appeared separately for interviews with and without dolls; the combined rates were estimated for the purpose of this table.

Not surprisingly, older children provided significantly longer and more detailed responses than the younger children did, but the different interviewer prompts had similar effects on children's responses, regardless of age. The same results were also obtained when data from the first and second halves of the interviews were analyzed separately, suggesting that invitations did not become progressively less effective as children "ran out" of new details to provide.

These results confirmed expectations, based on the literature reviewed in the previous chapter, that open-ended questions or invitations would yield responses that were longer and more detailed than responses to any of the focused prompts (directive, option-posing, or suggestive), and that younger children would provide fewer details and shorter responses to all types of utterances than older children would. The most striking finding, however, was that the interviewers made very few invitations, even though each yielded much more information than the average focused question. In addition, of course, these results showed that the interviewers were not following expert recommendations to rely as much as possible on open-ended questions, especially invitations, when questioning children about possible abuse.

Because we had ourselves provided training to many of these interviewers in the years before the study, we knew that they were very familiar with these recommendations, but we did not know whether

Table 4.3 Mean numbers of details and length (in words) of children's responses to the different types of prompts

	Invitation		Directive		Option-posing		Suggestive	
	Details	Words	Details	Words	Details	Words	Details	Words
Lamb et al. (1996b) Israel	5.0	15.8	1.7	5.6	2.0	4.9	5.1	2.0
Lamb et al. (1996a) U.S.	9	20	2	5	1.8	3.5	1.5	5
Sternberg et al. (1996) U.S.	8.5	22.1	1.8	6.1	1.9	5.4	1.6	5.1
Sternberg et al. (2001) U.K.	7.8	–	2.7	–	2.8	–	4.7	–
Cederborg et al. (2000) Sweden	3.6	–	1.9	–	2.1	–	3.4	–

Note: In Lamb et al.'s American doll study (1996a), the means appeared separately for interviews with and without dolls; the combined means were calculated for the purpose of this table.

interviewers in other countries might find it easier to follow such guidelines, not least, perhaps, because the Israeli's youth investigators had other professional responsibilities (e.g., probation) that might have distracted them. Since that first study, we have conducted several descriptive studies in the United States, the United Kingdom, Sweden, Canada and Korea, using unselected samples of forensic interviews and the findings are reviewed below, as well as in Tables 4.2 and 4.3.

DESCRIPTIVE STUDIES

United States

Sternberg, Lamb, Hershkowitz, Esplin et al. (1996) studied 45 interviews conducted by six male detectives in a small town in the Southeastern United States. Twenty-three of the interviews involved children who reported being abused on only one occasion; the remainder involved children who reported being abused on three or more different occasions. The sample included all interviews from a 2-year period that involved children (35 girls, 10 boys) ranging in age from 4 to 12 years old (they averaged just over 8 years) who made a clear allegation of sexual abuse by an identified adult and who specifically said that they had been abused only once *or* more than three times.

A total of 4,518 interviewer utterances were identified. Most of these were option-posing (40%) or directive (28%) utterances and only 5% were invitations (see Table 4.2). Most of the interviewers' utterances elicited relevant responses from the children and there were surprisingly few differences between interviews with children who reported one as opposed to three or more incidents of abuse. Interviews of the two types (single vs. multiple) did not differ with respect to the number of interviewer utterances or child responses, the number of words spoken by either the children or the interviewers, or the types of utterances that predominated.

Open-ended invitations yielded responses that were approximately four times longer and up to three times richer in relevant details than responses to directive, option-posing, or suggestive utterances. (The numbers of details and the numbers of words spoken by the children in each response were again very highly correlated.)

As predicted, invitations also yielded more relevant and central details from children who reported multiple incidents of abuse than from children who reported being abused only once. These findings replicated those obtained by Lamb, Hershkowitz, Sternberg, Esplin et al. (1996b) in the Israeli field study and are also consistent with reports of earlier laboratory studies focusing on known or staged events (Dent & Stephenson, 1979; Goodman & Aman, 1990; Goodman, Hirschman, et al., 1991). Interestingly, children who experienced multiple incidents of abuse did not provide more relevant information than children who reported being abused only once, perhaps because open-ended probes were employed so rarely.

This study also examined whether different types of utterances had different effects depending on where in the interview they occurred. In fact, the same results were obtained in analyses of data from the first half and from the second half of the substantive portion of the interview, indicating that invitations did not become less productive as the interview progressed.

Craig, Scheibe, Raskin, Kircher, and Dodd (1999) conducted a similar study involving police interviews with 48 alleged victims who ranged in age from 3 to 16 years (the average age was just under 9 years). Craig and his colleagues were primarily interested in indices of credibility in the children's accounts, and their definitions of interviewer prompts differed from those used in our various studies. More than half of the utterances coded were focused, i.e., either directive or option-posing questions. About 20% were either invitations or facilitators; another 20% were compound questions (i.e., consisting of more than one prompt type), and about 5% were suggestive.

The United States' anatomical doll study

The next field study involved interviews by American forensic social workers who frequently used anatomically detailed dolls in their interviews. Although the American Professional Society on the Abuse of Children (APSAC, 1995) had recommended that anatomical dolls should only be used by knowledgeable and experienced professionals, little was known then (or now) about the actual skill level of the majority of professionals using anatomical dolls. This ignorance is especially alarming in light of the widespread popularity of the dolls, particularly among those conducting protective and investigative interviews that have major implications for decisions about children's custody and supervision (Conte, Sorenson, Fogarty, & Dalla Rosa, 1991; Hlavka, Olinger, & Lashley, 2010).

The videotaped interviews studied by Lamb, Hershkowitz, Sternberg, Boat et al. (1996a) were initially gathered by Boat and Everson (1994, 1996) as part of an effort to describe and understand the utilization of anatomical dolls in protective service investigations. Protective service agencies in a large Southeastern state provided copies of recent videotaped interviews. The agencies were not aware of Boat and Everson's interest in anatomical dolls, because one goal of their study was to see how frequently and typically the dolls were used in the participating counties.

The coding scheme was adapted from that described earlier (see Table 4.1 and Chapter 3), with two additional categories devised to represent nonverbal gestures and enactments:

Technical suggestions. This code was used: (a) when nonverbal actions were not mentioned by the transcriber but were referred to by the interviewer; or (b) when nonverbal actions were not described by the transcriber in as much detail as the interviewer implies. (For example: Interviewer: Where did he touch you? Child: [points to lower part.] Interviewer: On your private.)

Suggestive actions. This code was used when the interviewer demonstrated something with the dolls that the child had not demonstrated or described verbally. This code would be used, for example, if the interviewer removed the doll's clothes before asking (or being told) whether the perpetrator's or child's clothes were on or off at the time of the alleged incident.

As Lamb, Hershkowitz, Sternberg, Boat et al. (1996a) reported, the average number of words spoken or details provided by children in the substantive portions of the interviews did not differ depending on whether (M = 467, 166 details) or not (M = 469 words, 180 details) dolls were used. Whether or not dolls were used, interviewers offered few of the recommended invitations and instead used many focused (directive, option-posing, and suggestive) utterances. The relative prominence of the different interviewer utterances did not change depending on whether or not dolls were used.

As in previous studies, furthermore, the different types of utterances were differentially associated with how long and detailed children's responses were (see Table 4.3), with invitations eliciting longer and more detailed responses than the more focused (directive, leading, and suggestive) utterances. On average, responses were significantly longer and more detailed when dolls were *not* used than when they were employed. In addition, the superiority of invitations over more focused measures was especially marked when dolls were not used. The introduction of anatomical dolls, in other words, reduced the disparity between the length and richness of responses to invitations relative to more focused utterances.

Although children in the two groups were carefully matched, it is still possible that the decisions to use dolls were based on some systematic criteria, such as the child's apparent shyness or reluctance. In order to determine whether investigators chose to use dolls when children seemed less talkative, we tabulated the number of utterances and the number of words spoken by the children in the pre-substantive portions of the interview, but found no significant differences, suggesting that pre-existing differences among children did not explain the adverse "effects" of doll usage.

Independent ratings of these interviews by Boat and Everson (1996) revealed that in all but one of these 16 interviews, the dolls were used as anatomical models for purposes of demonstration—that is, to facilitate the children's description of the alleged abusive events. That being the case, it was somewhat surprising that the average number of relevant details provided by the children was not greater when anatomical dolls were used than when they were not used. Indeed, inspection of the means shows that the children provided more, rather than fewer, details in interviews without dolls, although this difference was not statistically significant. The average responses provided by the children were significantly briefer and less detailed when dolls were employed, furthermore, suggesting that the use of dolls tended to inhibit rather than facilitate informativeness. In part, the difference reflected the continuation of a non-significant tendency for these children to be less talkative than those whose interviews did not include dolls, although this difference appeared to be amplified rather than ameliorated by the introduction of the anatomical dolls.

It may be that these interviewers introduced dolls in an effort to motivate reluctant children to be more informative. Only a random assignment experiment would permit us to determine whether the introduction of dolls was a reaction to uninformativeness or was a cause thereof. On the other hand, the basic interview process was not much different when anatomical dolls were employed: As in earlier field studies, interviewers seldom used the much-recommended open-ended invitations even though invitations yielded longer and richer responses than more focused prompts did.

Sweden

Cederborg, Orbach, Sternberg, and Lamb (2000) studied 72 interviews of 4- to 13-year-old Swedish children (averaging nearly 9 years) by six experienced police officers (two males, four females) from one police district in Sweden to determine whether Swedish forensic interviews were similar to those conducted in the other countries that had been studied. All 110 interviews involving children between the ages of 4 and 13 years that were referred to these police officers for video-recorded interviews between 1986 and 1995 were considered for inclusion in the study. Thirty-eight of the original 110 cases were excluded: 33 because the children made no allegations, one because the child summarized abusive incidents by two different perpetrators, and four because the tape was of poor quality or had been misplaced.

The Swedish Code of Judicial Procedures (SFS, 1942, p. 740) specifies how witnesses should be interviewed for forensic purposes. The Swedish provisions are formulated in a general manner, without specific operational instructions, although they are in agreement with other professional recommendations. They emphasize that witnesses should be allowed to give spontaneous accounts in their own words before any focused questions are posed, and that questions which suggest the expected response should be avoided. The provisions are addressed to court professionals and not to police officers, however, even though police officers are typically the first to interview witnesses. Unfortunately, the Recommendations for Preliminary Investigations (1942, p. 948) compiled for Swedish prosecutors and police officers included very general statements about the administrative and procedural handling of cases but ignored the sections of the Swedish Code of Judicial Procedures that specify desirable and undesirable question types. Except for some modifications in content and language, moreover, no changes regarding investigative techniques had been introduced since 1947. Exactly how Swedish police officers actually conduct their interviews had never been determined before Cederborg et al.'s (2000) study.

The police officers participating in the study received their regular three-year training at the police academy. During this period they attended 4 hours of lectures on the ways in which children should be interviewed, participated in discussions of the Recommendations for Preliminary Investigations, but did not have any supervised experience interviewing children before they started conducting forensic interviews.

The relative prominence of the different utterance types in the Swedish investigative interviews is displayed in Table 4.2. As in previous studies, invitations were quite rare (6%), while more focused prompts were quite common. Together, option-posing and suggestive questions comprised 53% of the investigators' utterances. As in the other studies, invitations on average elicited more ($M = 3.6$) details than directives (1.9 details), option-posing (2.1 details), or suggestive utterances (3.4 details). Because invitations were so rare, only 8% of the total number of details provided by the children were elicited by invitations, 35% were elicited by directive utterances, 41% were elicited by option-posing questions, and 16% were elicited by suggestive utterances.

The mean number of utterances before the interviewer posed the first option-posing or suggestive utterance was 1, or only 2% of the total number of substantive utterances recorded. In 35 of the interviews, in fact, the very first interviewer utterance was suggestive, and in another 11, the first substantive prompt was option-posing. On average, children provided only 4.3 details (4% of the total) before the first option-posing or suggestive utterance, increasing the risk of contaminating information produced later in the interview.

As Table 4.2 makes clear, the Swedish interviews in many ways resembled forensic interviews in Israel, the United Kingdom, and the United States. In all of these countries, interviewers seldom used open-ended invitations to prompt for information and tended to rely heavily on option-posing and suggestive utterances.

The British Study

Sternberg, Lamb, Davies, and Westcott (2001) studied interviews of 119 British children (86 girls, 33 boys) who were interviewed between 1994 and 1997 by police officers ($n = 108$) or social workers ($n = 11$) guided by the Home Office's (1992) Memorandum of Good Practice (MOGP). The children ranged in age from 4 to 13 years (the average was 8¼ years). Consistent with the MOGP, both police officers and social workers were present for many of the investigations but one typically took lead responsibility. In 55 interviews, only one professional was present. Thirteen collaborating police forces provided transcripts for this study, each providing 9 interviews on average (*range* = 2 to 21).

Because the MOGP was so thorough, its recommendations concerning how forensic interviews of alleged child abuse victims should be conducted were adopted throughout England and Wales, and extensive resources had been invested in training, so one might reasonably have expected that interviews conducted in England and Wales would be of higher quality than those conducted in countries where less specific guidance was given to investigative interviewers. Sternberg et al. (2001) predicted that, in contrast with the investigative interviews conducted in Sweden, the United States, and Israel, interviews conducted in England and Wales would be better organized and would include more of the rapport-building techniques recommended in the Memorandum. They also predicted that interviewers in England and Wales would ask a substantial number of open-ended questions and would postpone more focused types of questions, particularly option-posing and suggestive questions, until late in their interviews.

The MOGP recommended that the introductory phase of the interview be used to build rapport with the child, explain the ground rules for the interview, caution the child to tell only the truth, and assess the developmental capacities of the child. In the interviews studied by Sternberg et al. (2001), the importance of truth telling was discussed in almost all the interviews (98%) and nearly half (49%) of the children were encouraged to acknowledge uncertainty if they did not know the answer to a question. Only 8% of the children were told that they had to provide a complete account of their experiences because the interviewers had not been present, however.

Twenty children (17%) disclosed details about the abusive event before the interviewers made any effort to elicit information about the abuse, and in 62 (52%) other cases, the substantive phase began with an invitation, as recommended in the MOGP. In other interviews, the substantive topic was introduced using directive (4; 3%), option-posing (16; 13%), or suggestive (17; 14%) prompts. Substantive sections that began with invitations were more likely than those starting with option-posing or suggestive prompts to continue with other open-ended invitations. The substantive sections of the interviews included an average of nearly 8 invitations (6%), 20 facilitators (13%), 71 directives (47%), 40 option-posing prompts (29%), and nearly 7 suggestive prompts (5%).

In order to avoid contaminating children's responses, the MOGP recommends that open-ended prompts be exhausted before more focused prompts are employed, and it was thus important to determine whether invitations were proportionately more common and focused questions less common earlier as opposed to later in the interviews. Invitations were quite uncommon and option-posing questions were introduced early in the interviews studied, however. On average, interviewers offered only 6 utterances before introducing their first option-posing question. By that time, children had provided only 8% (32 details) of the substantive details they were to provide. On the other hand, proportionally more invitations were asked in the first quartile than in the last three quartiles of the substantive phase. There were no differences between the first and last quartiles in the numbers of suggestive utterances, because these prompts appeared in all quartiles of the interview.

Children provided substantive details in response to 62% of the nearly 15,000 substantive interviewer prompts (excluding facilitators) tabulated. On average, children provided 402 substantive details (the range was from 23 to 1499 details), of which 14% (65 details) were elicited using invitations, 46% (191 details) using directive prompts, 30% (114 details) using option-posing prompts, and 9% (32 details) using suggestive prompts. In other words, nearly 40% of the information obtained was elicited using the option-posing or suggestive prompts, which are known to yield less reliable information than open-ended questions. Sixty percent of the children provided their first substantive details in response to invitations whereas others provided their first substantive details when asked directive (8%), option-posing (17%), or suggestive (15%) prompts. The children's first substantive responses included an average of 11 details (4% of the total number of details provided in the interview). As in our other studies, invitations elicited more details on average (nearly 8 details per prompt) than did responses to the other utterance types (directives, option-posing, and suggestive) combined (just under 3 details per prompt). On average, older children provided more details in response to all types of interviewer prompts than younger children did.

Because the MOGP guidelines were both specific and implemented nationwide, we had correctly expected that MOGP-guided interviews would be superior to those conducted by forensic interviewers in countries lacking similar explicit national guidelines. Unexpectedly, however, these forensic interviewers in Britain relied heavily on option-posing utterances and infrequently on open-ended utterances to elicit information from children. Instead of allowing children to describe their experiences from free-recall memory, option-posing questions were asked early in the interviews. Unlike interviewers in other countries, however, approximately two-thirds of the British interviewers introduced the substantive topic with an open-ended question, and in this regard thus conducted slightly "better" interviews than their peers. In other respects, however, introduction of the MOGP does not appear to have substantially improved the quality of investigative interviews relative to that of investigators in other countries.

Korea

Yi, Lamb, and Jo (2015) surveyed 32 police officers about their interviewing practice with children and examined transcripts from 45 of their interviews with 3- to 13-year-old children. The results indicated a mismatch between officers' self-reports of their practice and an objective analysis of what occurred in practice. For example, officers reported regularly using ground rules and explaining the role of the interviewer, while transcript analysis demonstrated that none included an instruction to provide detailed information, just 18% emphasized the importance of telling the truth, and less than 10% instructed the children about indicating when they did not understand a question, saying "I don't know" when appropriate, and correcting the interviewer when needed. The vast majority (90%) of officers indicated that they included a rapport-building phase in their interviews (estimating an average of 14 minutes spent on such activities), whereas only 31% of the transcripts included rapport building (with an average of 4 questions posed during this part of the interview). Officers reported predominantly using invitations and directive prompts to elicit information, but the transcripts, in fact, included very few (4%) invitations, many directive (37%) and option-posing (39%) prompts, and a substantial number (14%) of suggestive prompts.

Canada

Luther, Snook, Barron, and Lamb (2015) examined 45 interviews conducted by 26 interviewers with 3- to 16-year-old children across a six-year period from 2006. The majority of interviewers omitted at least one of the recommended ground rules: 18% included a discussion about truth and lies, none elicited a promise to tell the truth, 29% encouraged the children to say "I don't know" when needed, 18% gave children permission to indicate when they did not understand something the interviewer said, and 20% encouraged children to correct the interviewers if mistakes were made. Fewer than a third (31%) of the interviews included rapport building and just 11% included narrative practice. The substantive phases of the interviews largely comprised focused (directive: 32%, option-posing: 39%) questions, with very few invitations (7%) used.

RESEARCH BY OTHER INVESTIGATORS

Many similar descriptive analyses of interviews have been conducted in Australia, Finland, New Zealand, Norway, and the United States, each reporting results that were very much in line with our own, despite differences in how various interviewer utterances and child responses were coded. Other researchers have also examined interviewers' reports of their practice, and have shown that interviewers often overestimate the extent to which they adhere to recommended practices.

Australia

Powell and Hughes-Scholes (2009) examined 136 interviews conducted by 95 interviewers in two Australian jurisdictions between 2001 and 2007 with 3- to 15-year-old children. Many recommended ground rules were frequently communicated (e.g., informing the child about the interviewer's naivety, giving permission to say "I don't know" and to ask for a break), but only few interviewers included an instruction to tell everything (27.2%) or not to guess (7.4%) and none instructed children to correct the interviewers if they made a mistake. Invitations comprised 16% of all interviewer utterances, with interviewers predominantly relying on focused directive (45%) and option-posing (37%) questions.

Scotland

Although they did not directly examine forensic interviews, La Rooy, Lamb, and Memon (2011) surveyed 91 police interviewers in Scotland about their adherence to the Scottish Executive Guidelines. The officers were confident that they typically obtained full and complete accounts from children, and attributed any failure to do so to the children (as opposed to, for example, their interviewing approach). Almost all (97%) reported establishing rapport with children and frequently informing them of the ground rules (85%), but few (13%) indicated that they included a practice narrative in their interviews. Many of the officers (20%) reported never or rarely using invitation prompts; the majority (88%) reported always or almost always using directive questions. The extent to which these assessments of practice would be supported by a direct evaluation of transcripts is unknown, however, given the tendency for interviewers to overestimate their use of optimal techniques and underestimate their use of less desirable questioning approaches (e.g., Wright & Powell, 2006; Yi et al., 2015), it is likely that officers adhered to recommended practice even less that these results would suggest.

Finland

Several smaller and less representative samples of forensic interviews in Finland have been studied by Korkman and her colleagues (Korkman, Santtila, & Sandnabba, 2006). One sample involved 27 interviews of 12 3- to 12-year-old children that were chosen for the study because they were considered by professionals to be problematic, and the other sample comprised interviews of 43 3- to 8-year-old children in hospital clinics. It is easy to see why the interviews studied by Korkman et al. (2006) were considered problematic: Only 2% of the interviewer prompts were invitations, 22% were directives, 31% were option-posing, and a remarkable 31% were suggestive. In the second study, Korkman, Santtila, Westeraker, and Sandnabba (2006) used slightly different coding procedures, but the interviews seemed quite problematic as well, although they had not been selected on this basis: Nearly half of the prompts were either suggestive or option-posing, about a third were directives, and only 6% were invitations. In both studies, most of the information was elicited using risky prompts and in both studies, interviewers compounded the problems by using invitations or facilitators following fewer than 20% of the responses in which the children provided forensically relevant details. A subsequent study (Korkman, Santtila, Westeraker, & Sandnabba, 2008) of 43 interviews with 3- to 8-year-old children showed that 48% of all interviewer utterances were option-posing or suggestive and just 6% were invitations. Open-ended (invitations and directives) and facilitative utterances elicited the lengthiest and most descriptive responses from the children. However, interviewers rarely followed up with invitations when children reported important information.

New Zealand

In New Zealand, Wolfman, Brown, and Jose (2016a) evaluated 93 interviews with 6- to 16-year-old children about child sexual abuse, conducted during a 12-month period (2012–2013). Interviews largely included the recommended preparatory components in the pre-substantive phase of the interview, but questioning during the substantive phase deviated from ideal practice both in terms of the proportions of question types used, and the timing of those questions within the interview. Although interviewers predominantly used recall-based questions (79%), just 22% were invitations. Focused (directive) questions (57%) were often introduced within the first 3% of all questions and option-posing (21%) within the first 10% of questions. Invitations were more prominent in the first half of the interview than the latter. Although these statistics suggest that the New Zealand interviewers performed better than their peers in other countries, this was probably because the interviewers volunteered to participate in the study, with many interviewers and entire regions of New Zealand not sampled.

Norway

Thoresen, Lonnnum, Melinder, Stridbeck, and Magnusson (2006) studied 91 interviews conducted between 1985 and 2002, mostly (85) by police officers, although a few were conducted by judges (4) or psychologists (2). The suspected victims ranged in age from just under 4 to just over 14 years, and averaged 8¾ years. Across the time period sampled, open-ended invitations were seldom asked, with the proportions never exceeding 2 to 3%. However, the numbers of prompts equivalent to those we call directives increased to about 14% in 1999–2002, and the numbers of risky prompts declined. Specifically, option-posing prompts declined from a peak of 43% in 1990–1994 to 31% in 1999–2002 while the use of suggestive prompts declined from 20% in 1985–1989 to 8% during both 1995–1998 and 1999–2002. These results indicate that interviewers (perhaps sensitized by the enormous publicity surrounding a large Norwegian multi-victim case in 1992–1994) learned to avoid using the most risky prompts when interviewing alleged victims, but still did not make much use of the most desirable question types. In a follow-up study of 224 interviews conducted with 3- to 16-year-old children during the ten years following 2002, Johnson et al. (2015) found little further change in interviewing practices: Invitations comprised less than 4% of the prompts used in interviews conducted between 2002 and 2005, less than 3% of those used from 2006 to 2009, and less than 2% in interviews conducted between 2010 and 2012. When interviews conducted across the entire 22-year period captured by the two studies were considered, just 2% of all prompts posed were invitations. Fewer option-posing questions and more directive questions were asked in the later interviews than in earlier interviews.

CONCLUSION

The studies described in this chapter paint a remarkably consistent and sobering picture. Many researchers have demonstrated that there are universal challenges that constrain interviewers from conducting high-quality interviews with children. Important components of interviews are frequently omitted (for example, introducing and practicing a range of ground rules, and providing an opportunity for children to practice describing neutral past events before the topic of investigation is introduced). Interviewers also continue to use unsupported or untested techniques (e.g., different visual aids). Across multiple studies in different countries with different systems and protocols, we also see that interviewers typically used very few invitations, even though open-ended questions yield more information than the average focused questions. In fact, focused questions are so much more numerous that the bulk of the forensically relevant information is often obtained in responses to these more specific and risky questions. Such results were evident not only in the initial research evaluating interviewer practice, but also in more recent studies. Thus, despite an increase in knowledge and research evidence about the best ways to elicit rich and accurate information from children, interviewers have difficulty adhering to recommended practices.

This disappointing state of affairs does not reflect a lack of attention to the problem. Considerable resources have been invested in training interviewers, but the yield (as documented above) has been quite disappointing, with rather minor differences between, say, British police officers following the then state-of-the-art Memorandum of Good Practice and their peers in other countries (Sternberg, Lamb, Orbach, Esplin, & Mitchell, 2001), between expert and novice interviewers in

Sweden (Cederborg & Lamb, 2008b), or even between interviews conducted in Norway before and after the notorious case that was the focus of so much attention and anguish in that country (Johnson et al., 2015). Do these findings mean that good interviews must remain the exception rather than the rule?

5

The NICHD Investigative Interview Protocols for Young Victims and Witnesses

As we showed in the previous chapter, forensic interviewers often have extraordinary difficulty adhering to recommended interview practices in the field. To help interviewers adhere to professional recommendations, the authors and their colleagues developed a structured interview procedure that translates research findings into practice. In this chapter, we describe the various phases of the Protocol and the research that informed them. The complete text of the most recent version of the Protocol is provided in the Appendix. In Chapter 6, we describe research evaluating the impact of this Protocol on both interviewer and child behavior.

As we discussed in Chapter 4, there is a substantial degree of consensus among professional and expert groups regarding the ways in which investigative interviews should be conducted and remarkable agreement regarding the results of the relevant experimental and empirical literature. Clearly, it is often possible to obtain valuable information from children but doing so requires a realistic awareness of their capacities and tendencies, as well as careful investigative procedures.

Tell Me What Happened: Questioning Children About Abuse, Second Edition.
Michael E. Lamb, Deirdre A. Brown, Irit Hershkowitz, Yael Orbach, and Phillip W. Esplin.
© 2018 John Wiley & Sons Ltd. Published 2018 by John Wiley & Sons Ltd.

Unfortunately, as shown in the previous chapter, research-based and expert-endorsed recommendations are widely proclaimed but seldom followed, with forensic interviewers typically using open-ended prompts quite rarely, even though such prompts reliably elicit more information than more focused prompts do. To the distress of trainers and administrators, furthermore, such deviations from "best practice" were evident even when the interviewers had been trained extensively, were well-aware of the recommended practices, and often believed that they were adhering to those recommendations.

For this reason, Sternberg and her colleagues (1997) initially developed a partially scripted procedure that provided forensic interviewers and children, respectively, with practice posing and responding to open-ended prompts during the pre-substantive phase of investigative interviews. Following the training, the children's first substantive narratives were significantly longer and more informative than the narratives provided by children "trained" by responding to directive questions. However, the investigators thereafter reverted to focused questioning, using few open-ended questions and prompts during the rest of the interview. Because these findings suggested that interviewers needed guidelines to help them structure the entire interview, we decided to develop a fully structured investigative Protocol (see Appendix). In the subsequent years, much research evaluated the effectiveness of the Protocol in helping interviewers to adopt a child-led and invitational approach to questioning children, and how this, in turn, influenced the quality and quantity of children's reports. Adjustments have been made to the Protocol over the last two decades to reflect feedback from research and practitioners. More recently, we developed and validated a revised version that paid closer attention to interviewer behaviors that support children's emotional and social needs during an interview, while maintaining the focus on cognitive processes. In the sections below, we outline the strategies included in the Revised Protocol, and the evidence demonstrating their effectiveness. In light of the research described in this book, we recommend that interviewers employ the Revised Protocol when conducting investigative interviews with alleged victims of abuse.

PRE-INTERVIEW CONSIDERATIONS

Although the Protocol does not provide prescriptive advice about preparing for an interview, interviewers should consider a number of factors in advance of meeting children. Finding out about a child's usual routines, for example, may assist in determining the best time of day for an interview. Knowing about the child's level of functioning (developmental, communicative, physical, intellectual, social, emotional, behavioral) may assist in determining what, if any, modifications to the interview environment or procedures may be needed, and how many interviews may be required (including any orientation meetings). Learning about a child's culture and how that might affect how s/he interacts with and responds to questions asked by unfamiliar adults is also important. Whether there is need for the use of interpreters, or intermediaries, and what preparation they may need to make, should also be considered. Pre-interview considerations are discussed at greater length at http://www.theadvocatesgateway.org/

The Pre-Substantive Part of the Interview

Supportive Environment
To promote a relaxed and supportive environment, first of all, interviewers are asked to ensure that the room is free of distractions such as other people, noise, toys, and incoming phone calls. A supportive and distraction-free environment is believed to make child-witnesses feel more comfortable and thus more willing to disclose information while also enhancing their retrieval capabilities and accuracy (Cheung, 1997; Geiselman, Saywitz, & Bornstein, 1993; Powell & Thomson, 1994; Sternberg et al., 1997). Likewise, the absence of toys, including dolls, prevents inadvertent suggestions or ambiguous statements relating to pretense or fantasy, rather than to the real experiences of the child.

INTRODUCTORY PHASE: EXPLAINING THE PURPOSE AND GROUND RULES

In the introductory phase, the interviewer introduces him/herself and his/her role, clarifies the child's task (the need to describe events in detail and to tell the truth), and explains the ground rules and expectations. Children are likely to bring to the interview a range of expectations about their role and about how the interaction with the interviewer will unfold (Lamb & Brown, 2006), shaped by socialization processes and previous interactions with adults (Nelson, 2013). Many of these expectations and assumptions can undermine children's responsiveness and reliability if not addressed. From an early age, children learn how to construct stories of their experiences, guided in large part by interactions with their parents (Fivush, 2011; Nelson & Fivush, 2004; Salmon & Reese, 2015) which might lead them to believe that a good story may be more valued than an accurate account. For example,

Kulkofsky, Wang, and Ceci (2008) showed that children who told better stories about an event, from a narrative perspective, were often less accurate about the specific details of the experience than children who provided briefer accounts. Thus, a ground rule emphasizing the importance of telling the truth may serve to highlight the gravity of the forensic interview.

Children are unlikely to recognize that "I don't know" is a valued response in this context (Scoboria & Fisico, 2013), perhaps because they are often encouraged or pressured to answer challenging questions in other settings (e.g., at school). Earhart et al. (2014) also reported that children seldom said "I don't know." Children may also have difficulty admitting that they have not understood interviewers' requests, and so instructing them that this is permissible, and indeed, encouraged, may serve to reassure children. Finally, interviewers may make errors when talking to children, perhaps incorrectly paraphrasing statements (Lamb, Orbach, Sternberg, Hershkowitz, & Horowitz, 2000; Roberts & Lamb, 1999) or introducing misleading prompts. When that happens, it is important that children draw attention to the errors, as a failure to do so may be seen as tacit validation of the interviewers' errors. Children frequently fail to directly signal such errors, however (Hunt & Borgida, 2001; Roberts & Lamb, 1999), and they are unlikely to be reinforced for challenging or correcting adults in other settings (Brubacher et al., 2015). Explicit instructions about the importance of correcting the interviewer during an interview may therefore increase the likelihood that children will apply this rule.

Interviewers therefore attempt to empower children and minimize status differences by explaining that the children are unique sources of information because the interviewers were not present when the alleged events took place and thus do not know what happened. Interviewers also instruct children that they are obliged to tell the truth (Lyon & Saywitz, 1999) and to only report personally experienced events rather than events they heard about or imagined. Eliciting promises to tell the truth increases children's willingness to disclose self-transgressions (Evans & Lee, 2010; Talwar, Lee, Bala, & Lindsay, 2002, 2004) and joint transgressions (Lyon & Dorado, 2008; Lyon et al., 2008) and decreases the likelihood that children will provide coached false reports (Lyon et al., 2008) in laboratory studies. Many cooperating law enforcement agencies also asked us to include questions probing young children's abilities to tell the difference between true and false statements. Children being interviewed using the Protocol can thus be asked whether several simple statements are true or false, for example. Alternately, some jurisdictions simply want children to promise to tell the truth.

Interviewers continue by explaining to children that, in addition to correcting the interviewers when appropriate, they can and should admit lack of knowledge or lack of understanding, by saying "I don't remember," "I don't know," or "I don't understand," instead of guessing.

The inclusion of ground rules in the preparatory phase of the interview rests on the assumption that they promote detailed and accurate responding, and they have become a common feature of international interviewing guidance and practice. As noted earlier (Chapter 3), however, evidence regarding the effectiveness of ground rule presentation is largely wanting.

RAPPORT-BUILDING PHASE

The rapport-building phase that follows the introductory phase comprises two sections. The first is designed to create a relaxed, supportive environment for children and to establish rapport between children and interviewers, primarily by getting to know the children. Children are encouraged to talk openly about both positive and negative issues and are prompted to respond in detail to the gentle questions provided by attentive and manifestly interested adults. Within the Revised Protocol, guidance is provided about how to introduce such topics and respond to them supportively. Research examining the effects of rapport has suggested that higher levels of rapport are associated with heightened responding by children (Davis & Bottoms, 2002a, 2002b; Sternberg et al., 1997) and reduced suggestibility (Wood & Garven 2000, 109–118); Teoh & Lamb, 2010). Surprisingly little research has examined *how* interviewers can best establish rapport with children, however, and no studies have examined how to maintain rapport, or repair it when the interaction between the child and interviewer is compromised (Saywitz, Larson, Hobbs, & Wells, 2015). Although rapport-building is the focus of the interaction early in the pre-substantive interview, interviewers need to ensure that it is maintained throughout the interview so as to avoid children becoming disengaged or uncooperative.

NARRATIVE-TRAINING PHASE

Just as in other contexts where children learn from the adults around them, we see in forensic interviews how children learn from unfamiliar adults even in the course of very brief interactions, with the style of interaction assuming great importance. In both field (Anderson, Anderson, & Gilgun, 2014; Hershkowitz et al., 1998; Price, Roberts, & Collins, 2013;

Sternberg et al., 1997) and laboratory-based (Brown et al., 2013; Brubacher, Roberts, & Powell, 2011; Roberts, Lamb, & Sternberg, 2004) studies, children who practice recalling a past event in response to open-ended prompts are more responsive during the substantive phase of the interview. Providing children with opportunities to talk in detail about recent past events allows practice in retrieving and reporting detailed episodic information, fosters familiarity with the types of prompts used in the substantive interview, and promotes awareness of the level of detail required for interviewers to understand the children's experiences (Brubacher, Roberts, & Powell, 2011; Roberts, Brubacher, Powell, & Price, 2011). In Protocol interviews, children are encouraged to elaborate on issues discussed in the rapport-building phase in this context.

Before the interview, the interviewer is advised to identify a neutral event the child experienced recently (first day of school, birthday party, holiday, celebration, etc.) so that s/he can then ask questions about that event. If possible, interviewers choose events that took place at about the same time as (but not during) the alleged or suspected abuse occurred. If the alleged abuse took place during a specific day or event, interviewers should ask about a different event. Interviewers are advised to monitor the way children describe the event to ensure they are eliciting from the child an *episodic* account of a specific incident or event, to promote and prepare the way for episodic (rather than script) recall during the substantive phase. When children are prompted to provide generic descriptions of repeated experiences, they may maintain this style of remembering and reporting when talking about the alleged events being investigated (Brubacher, Roberts, & Powell, 2011).

THE SUBSTANTIVE PART OF THE INTERVIEW

Following the pre-substantive phase, the interviewer attempts to shift the child's focus to the substantive issues as non-suggestively as possible so that the recollection process can commence.

Although a substantial minority of suspected victims never report abuse when first interviewed (see Chapter 9), the vast majority of those who do disclose (more than 80% in the field studies described by Sternberg, Lamb, & Orbach et al., 2001, and Orbach et al. 2000) did so in response to one of the completely open (i.e., input-free) prompts. Only if the child fails to identify the target event/s in response to either of the input-free prompts does the interviewer employ progressively more focused prompts to identify the suspected abuse when there is good reason to believe that the child was abused and that the risk of damage caused by continued abuse is likely to be greater than the risk of suggesting abuse when none occurred.

At this stage, if the alleged victims have not made an allegation, we recommend that the interviewer pause to consider whether to abort the interview, perhaps proceeding on another occasion. As we reported earlier, few suspected victims disclose abuse in response to these more focused prompts, all of which have attendant risks, although they have been scripted to be as innocuous as possible. In some cases, however, the investigator may have good reason to believe that the child has been abused and may need to explore the possibility further to ensure that the child does not remain in a home or setting where he/she may be abused further. In such circumstances, the investigator may decide to press on, trying a last few frankly though minimally suggestive prompts to see whether the child will disclose.

Investigators are advised, in case they decide to go ahead, that they should have formulated specific versions of these focused questions, using the facts available to them, before they interview. Investigators should ensure that they suggest as few details as possible to the child. If they have not formulated these questions in advance, investigators are urged to take a break to formulate them carefully before proceeding.

If the child confirms or makes an allegation, the interviewer says "Tell me everything about that."

If the child does not confirm or does not make an allegation, the investigator should turn attention to a neutral event (see below) and terminate the interview, leaving open the possibility of another interview at a later date.

THE FREE-RECALL PHASE

When an allegation is made, the free-recall phase begins with the first substantive invitation ("Tell me everything that happened from the beginning to the end as best you can remember"), followed by open-ended prompts ("Then what happened?" "Tell me more about that") aimed at eliciting spontaneous recall accounts of the alleged incident/s.

Younger children (4- to 6-year-olds) typically provide briefer responses than older children, and may therefore require more prompts in order to elicit as full accounts as possible (see Chapter 7). These children often have difficulty responding to the most general open-ended invitational prompts (i.e., utterances requesting that the interviewees report everything they remember about something, e.g., "What happened?").

Unfortunately, many interviewers react by using more focused recognition prompts (i.e., yes/no and multi-choice questions) and even suggestive prompts (e.g., "So he did put his finger in your pee pee?") when questioning young children, even though such prompts are more likely to elicit inaccurate information. Instead of resorting to such risky prompts, the Protocol provides interviewers with alternative open-ended contextual cueing techniques to be used to elicit additional freely recalled information when general open-ended prompts are no longer effective. These cued invitations are invitations that make reference to events, actions, people, places, or objects already mentioned by the children (e.g., "You said that he touched your pee pee. Tell me more about that"). Similarly, time-segmenting invitations make references to a segment of time, demarcated by action/s or event/s that were mentioned by the children (e.g., "You mentioned [an action (or event) mentioned by the child]; Tell me what happened just before/after that," or "Tell me what happened from [an action mentioned by the child] until [another action mentioned by the child]").

As reported more fully in Chapters 6 and 7, 4- to 8- year-old alleged victims provide considerable amounts of forensically relevant information in response to cued invitations, which thus represent productive open-ended alternatives to risky focused questions when general invitations appear to be ineffective. By structuring the recall of experienced events, using details that have been mentioned by the child, contextual cueing techniques enhance the capacity of young children to reconstruct past events and elaborate upon their narrative accounts, avoiding interviewer contamination during the recall. Interestingly, action-based cues (e.g., "Tell me more about the touching") were consistently more effective than all other types of cues, regardless of age, in Lamb, Sternberg, Orbach, Esplin et al.'s (2003) study of 4- to 8-year-olds.

Open-ended questions are thus used exhaustively to elicit free-recall narrative information from children at all ages, with focused questions only used at the end of the questioning phase to elicit essential information that is still missing. The Protocol also recommends returning to open-ended questioning mode following confirmatory responses to focused questions, a practice labeled as "pairing." When interviewers follow this practice, the overall proportion of invitations used in an interview increases, and focused recognition questioning is minimized (Wolfman, Brown, & Jose, 2016b). In addition, the contextual cueing techniques—cued invitations and time segmentation—can be used throughout the interview as open-ended techniques to refocus children on material they have disclosed and request further elaboration.

When There May Have Been Multiple Incidents

Forensic interviewers need to elicit information from event-specific memories of the investigated incident(s), rather than generic or script statements, especially when interviewing children who have experienced multiple incidents of abuse. Like adults, unfortunately, children tend to report features common to multiple incidents on the basis of features shared by all, without describing the distinctive features of each specific event (Bauer & Fivush, 1992; Hudson et al., 1992; Nelson & Gruendel, 1986). Interviewers must thus communicate the need for accounts of specific events and direct children to recount events that are most accessible to memory, such as those that occurred first or last in a series of incidents (Roberts et al., 2015), or, with older children (e.g., 8 years or older), a time they remember best (Danby, Brubacher, Sharman, Powell & Roberts, 2017). The short delay between the last incident and the time of the interview makes it more accessible to memory than earlier incidents (Flin et al., 1992; Poole & White, 1993) and the diminished opportunities for post-event contamination might enhance the accuracy of the memories associated with it. On the other hand, because the first incident was encoded before a general scheme was developed, it might be more accessible to memory than later incidents. Like the first of many incidents, the specific distinctive features of unusual incidents should be better remembered and more easily retrieved than specific features of other incidents that fit a general script (Davidson & Hoe, 1993).

As soon as children complete their initial narratives, therefore, interviewers prompt them to indicate whether the incident occurred "one time or more than one time" and proceed to secure incident-specific information, while communicating the need for accounts of specific incidents and directing children to recount those events that are most accessible to memory.

When children have experienced repeated instances of maltreatment, it can be challenging to elicit episodic details that are linked to a specific instance of maltreatment. Some research suggests that children may give more event-related information overall if they are first asked about "what usually happens" in relation to repeated events, followed by descriptions of specific instances, rather than the reverse (eliciting a specific account first and then gathering a generic account) (Brubacher, Roberts, & Powell, 2012; Hudson & Nelson, 1986). These two studies were conducted using contrived events in experimental studies, however, and so, as yet, it is unclear whether the same benefits would be observed when children are questioned about maltreatment using the Protocol. The current version of the Protocol therefore recommends that interviewers identify particularly unique or memorable instances of the alleged events and elicit episodic detail about those without focusing on a generic, script-based account.

FOLLOW-UP QUESTIONS—THE PAIRING PRINCIPLE

If some central details of the allegation are still missing or unclear after exhausting the open-ended questions, the interviewer may need to ask directive questions. It is important to pair directive questions with open invitations whenever appropriate. In general, interviewers are taught to first focus the child's attention on the detail mentioned, and then ask the directive question (see text box above). When children provide information in response, interviewers encourage elaboration using an invitation prompt (see Figure 5.1).

Interviewers' over-reliance on focused questions may develop, at least in part, from a failure to adhere to the pairing principle. Whereas interview evaluations typically show that open prompts are used at the very beginning of the interview, their use is often limited during the remainder of the substantive phase. Following the pairing principle is likely to assist interviewers in maintaining an open style of prompting throughout the entire interview and prevent the adoption of a progressively narrower style of prompting as the interview progresses (Wolfman et al., 2016b).

Following up on specific details

"You mentioned [person/object/activity], when/what/where [completion of the directive question]?"

For example:

"You mentioned you were at the shop. Where exactly were you? [Pause for a response] *Tell me about that shop.*" [pairing]

"Earlier you mentioned that your mother 'hit you with this long thing.' What is that thing? [Pause for a response] *Tell me everything you can remember about that thing.*" [pairing]

Questions to Avoid

Whereas some factors enhance children's retrieval, others impede children's competency and increase the likelihood of error (Bruck & Ceci, 1995, 1996; Ceci & Bruck, 1995; Ceci & Huffman, 1997; Ceci, Huffman, Smith, & Loftus, 1996; Ceci, Leichtman, & Bruck, 1995). For example,

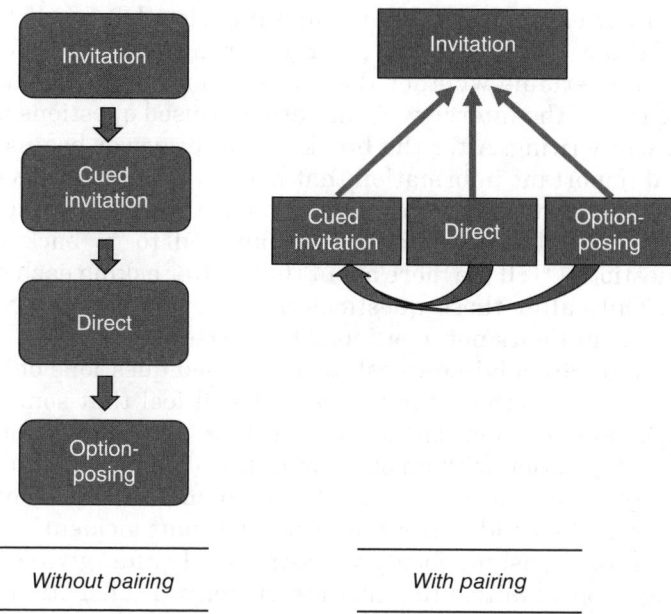

Figure 5.1 Hypothetical progression of an interview without and with pairing.

verbal prompts that encourage children to imagine (Ceci & Bruck, 1995; Lamb et al., 1995; Poole & Lamb, 1998), reliance on option-posing or suggestive prompts (Dale et al., 1978; Leichtman & Ceci, 1995; Orbach et al., 2016; Wood et al., 1998), and the inclusion of "yes/no" questions (Bell, 1984; Goodman & Aman, 1990; O'Callaghan & D'Arcy, 1989; Peterson & Biggs, 1997; Peterson et al., 1999; Price & Goodman, 1990; Saywitz et al., 1991) can all compromise the reliability of children's responses. The use of visual aids (e.g., dolls, drawings, and diagrams) and other props (e.g., toys) may also compromise children's accuracy (Brown, 2011), and are discussed further in Chapter 10. The negative effect of such practices is aggravated when children are very young and when the error-inducing practices occur early in the substantive portion of the interview. In addition to using techniques that facilitate information retrieval, therefore, interviewers should avoid techniques that impede retrieval or induce error.

Break

After the open-ended questioning we have described—ideally before asking any potentially contaminating questions—interviewers are encouraged to give children and themselves a short break to reflect upon the information reported and anything else that needs to be discussed. During the break, the interviewer reviews the information received to determine whether there is any missing information, and plans the rest of the interview, formulating focused questions in detail, preferably in writing. After the break, the interviewer begins to elicit additional important information that has not been mentioned by the child, asking additional open-ended and directive questions, as described above. Interviewers are encouraged to go back to open-ended questions ("Tell me more about that") after asking each directive question. Only after these questions do interviewers proceed to ask questions about topics not mentioned by the child.

Interviewers are advised to ask these focused questions only if they have already tried other approaches and still feel that some forensically important information is missing. It is very important to pair each focused question with an open invitation ("Tell me everything you can about that") whenever possible. In case of multiple incidents, interviewers direct the child's attention to the relevant incidents, using the child's own words, asking focused questions only after giving the child open-ended opportunities to elaborate on central (allegation specific) details. Before shifting attention to the next incident, interviewers make sure that they have obtained all the missing details about each specific incident.

The general format of questions focused on information that has NOT been mentioned by the child is as follows:

"When you told me about [specific incident identified by time, location, or any label used by the child] you mentioned [person/object/activity]. Did/was [focused questions]?"

Whenever appropriate, after the child responds, the interviewer offers an invitation: "Tell me all about that."

Examples include:

"When you told me about the time in the basement, you mentioned that he took off his trousers. Did something happen to your clothes? "[Pause for a response] "Tell me everything you can about that."

"When you told me about the last time, you mentioned that he touched you. Did he touch you over your clothes?" [Pause for a response] "Tell me all about that."

"Did he touch you under your clothes?" [Pause for a response] "Tell me everything you can remember about that."

> "You told me about something that happened on the playground. Did somebody see what happened?" [Pause for a response] "Tell me all about that."
>
> "Do you know whether something like that happened to other children? [Pause for a response]" "Tell me all about that."
>
> "You told me about something that happened in the barn. Do you know when that happened?"

If a child fails to mention information the interviewer expected, it may sometimes be necessary to use other potentially contaminating questions to prompt information. Quite frequently, for example, the child has talked to a friend or a parent, but fails to mention some details when formally interviewed, perhaps because s/he is embarrassed.

Information about the Disclosure

Although it was not initially included in the Protocol, experiences in the field led us to develop a portion of the interview concerned with the disclosure history, in part because asking the child who they spoke to first often provided investigative leads that could be followed in attempts to better understand and document exactly what happened to the child.

Closure

The interviewers complete the questioning phase by asking children whether they have additional information to report before thanking them for their cooperation and shifting the discussion to a neutral topic for closure.

CONCLUSION

The Protocol was developed after it became clear that interviewers had difficulty following the guidelines that had been prepared by various expert groups and individuals. Unlike these rather general guidelines, the Protocol was much more detailed and provided very specific examples of the sorts of questions that interviewers should use at specific stages during the course of the interview. Although many of these examples were scripted, the scripting was generally in the form of a "stem," which the interviewer had to adapt to accommodate the details and circumstances of the specific case and, most importantly, what the child had already said. The Protocol helped interviewers structure their interviews in ways that allowed them to address all important issues in an appropriate sequence—introducing the respective roles of the interviewer and informant, explaining the ground rules, establishing rapport, providing practice opportunities for responding to repeated demands for unusually detailed descriptions of experienced events, providing non-suggestive introduction of the incident under investigation, and examining the disclosure process.

The flexible structure proved comforting to interviewers once they had been trained, and allowed them to improve the quality of their interviews dramatically, as we show in the next chapter. So pleased were they, in fact, that variants of the Protocol were developed for use with witnesses (other than victims) as well. Research documenting the usefulness of the original Protocol, the revised version, and its variants is described in the next chapter.

6

When Interviewers Follow the Protocol, What Impact Does it Have on Their Interviewing and on Children's Responding?

In this chapter, we summarize research examining whether use of the Protocol is associated with improved interviewing practice and enhances the nature of children's responding. We describe the results of seven field studies conducted in Canada, Israel, Japan, Korea, the U.K., and the U.S.; they demonstrate convincingly that interviewers using the Protocol use many more desirable open-ended prompts and substantially fewer risky and suggestive prompts than they do without the Protocol. Importantly, the studies also demonstrate that the children, in turn, provide more forensically relevant information (including disclosures) that is more likely to be accurate because of the ways in which it was elicited. We describe a meta-analysis examining the aggregated data from five of the seven field studies examining the impact of the Protocol on interviewers' questions and children's responses. We also describe some laboratory-based studies that have examined the accuracy of children's responses when they are interviewed about known events; they show high levels of accuracy when children

Tell Me What Happened: Questioning Children About Abuse, Second Edition.
Michael E. Lamb, Deirdre A. Brown, Irit Hershkowitz, Yael Orbach, and Phillip W. Esplin.
© 2018 John Wiley & Sons Ltd. Published 2018 by John Wiley & Sons Ltd.

respond to interviewers' recall prompts, particularly when invitations are employed. In other words, the Protocol demonstrably achieves its objectives: Its use leads interviewers to conduct interviews that conform to recognized good practice *and* encourages young interviewees to provide detailed and accurate information.

Each of the studies described in this chapter was designed to assess the effectiveness of the flexibly structured Protocol. In each study, it was expected that use of the Protocol would affect the behavior of both the interviewers and the children they were interviewing. As far as the interviewers were concerned, it was predicted that the number and proportion of open-ended prompts would be significantly higher in Protocol interviews, especially when interviewers were exploring the allegations. With respect to the children's performance, it was predicted that, in Protocol interviews, the total number of substantive details provided by children would be significantly higher; and that more of the substantive details provided by children would be elicited using open-ended utterances.

CHARACTERISTICS OF PARTICIPANTS IN THE FIELD STUDIES

In each of the field studies, interviews conducted prior to training on use of the Protocol were matched as closely as possible with respect to child and allegation characteristics with those that were conducted after the implementation of the Protocol. In some studies, interviews were conducted by the same interviewer pre- and post-Protocol implementation, whereas in others the interviews were conducted by different interviewers. Interviews explored a range of alleged events of single or multiple occurrences, involving either familiar or unfamiliar perpetrators, and ranging in abuse severity. Children were generally between 3 and 13 years of age with a mean age of 8 to 9 years. The amount of training in use of the Protocol ranged from 2 to 5 days. During the evaluation phase (i.e., when Protocol interviews were conducted) the majority of the studies included regular review sessions and individualized feedback about the interviews conducted. Some of the studies examined the composition of the preparatory phase of the interview, whereas others focused on the substantive phase.

Coding

In all studies, the researchers coded transcripts of the electronic recordings of the interviews to quantify the frequency with which interviewers used different types of utterances and the number of details conveyed in the children's responses, using the techniques and categories described in Chapter 3. In each study, some of the transcripts were independently recoded by another coder to ensure that the utterances were reliably categorized and the details reliably counted.

Orbach et al. (2000): Israel

Orbach et al. conducted the first systematic evaluation of the extent to which use of the Protocol improved interviewer and child communication during forensic interviews. This study compared 55 Protocol-guided forensic interviews of alleged sexual abuse victims with 50 non-Protocol interviews, conducted by the same 6 experienced youth investigators (2 male, 4 female) in Israel. The 55 children (43 girls and 12 boys) in the Protocol group and the 50 children (30 girls and 20 boys) in the non-Protocol group ranged in age from 4 to 13 years and averaged just over 9 years in each group.

The cases included in the Protocol group were drawn from the pool of sex-abuse cases involving 4- to 13-year-old children who were referred to these six investigators during 1995, provided that the interviewers followed the Protocol and that the cases could be matched with comparable cases investigated by the same interviewers before the Protocol was introduced. The cases included in the non-Protocol group were drawn from interviews conducted by the same six investigators in 1993 and 1994, right before they began using the Protocol. All interviews in the Protocol group closely followed the Protocol whereas interviews in the non-Protocol group followed the general interviewing guidelines provided by the Israeli Youth Investigative Service.

Investigators were trained in group and individual sessions. All interviewers first attended a 3-day-long seminar focused on the research literature and the techniques recommended by professional experts. In the monthly group sessions that followed, instructors reviewed the evidence base and conceptual framework for the Protocol. Excerpts of videotaped interviews illustrated both desirable and risky practices, and the trainees then systematically analyzed videotaped and transcribed interviews on an utterance-by-utterance basis before conducting role-play interviews of one another using the structured Protocol. These interviews were reviewed by the other investigators and their instructors, and were used to promote group discussions. Recurring problems prompted rehearsal of more desirable alternatives.

In addition to the monthly group sessions, each interviewer attended monthly individual sessions during which transcripts of each of her/his interviews were analyzed and discussed in detail. The progress of each investigator was monitored and displayed graphically. Letters, faxes, and telephone calls were used to provide feedback outside the individual and group meetings.

Sternberg et al. (2001): The United States

This study examined 100 forensic interviews of alleged sexual abuse victims, conducted by six experienced police officers (four women and two men) in a mid-sized city in the Western United States. The 27 boys and 73 girls interviewed averaged 8 years of age, and ranged from 4 to nearly 13 years. Fifty of the interviews followed the Protocol, whereas a matched sample of 50 interviews, comprising the standard condition, were conducted by the same interviewers immediately before the Protocol was introduced.

Prior to implementation of the structured Protocol, all interviewers participated in an intensive five-day training program. The program included review of the conceptual and empirical support for the Protocol, videotaped illustrations of both appropriate and inappropriate interview techniques, and role-played interviews with confederates. After demonstrating their ability to adhere to the Protocol, interviewers were observed conducting forensic interviews using the Protocol and were given feedback on their techniques. Written feedback was provided on all transcribed field interviews until the study ended. In addition, individual and group training sessions focused on adherence to the Protocol and its adaptation to individual circumstances were conducted every 6 to 8 weeks.

Lamb et al. (2009): The United Kingdom

In the third study, 50 interviews conducted using the Protocol were compared with 50 interviews conducted in accordance with the Memorandum of Good Practice on Video Recorded Interviews with Child Witnesses for Criminal Proceedings (Home Office, 1992). Six police officers (or their colleagues) in a mid-sized constabulary in the British Midlands conducted the Protocol interviews in 1999 and 2000; those in the comparison group were conducted by these and other officers prior to the Protocol training. The 20 boys and 80 girls interviewed ranged in age from 4 to 13 years and averaged just over 9 years of age.

Prior to the implementation of the Protocol, all interviewers participated in an intensive 5-day training program. The program included review of the conceptual and empirical support for the Protocol. Videotaped illustrations of both appropriate and inappropriate interview techniques were shown and participants role-played interviews with confederates. After demonstrating their ability to adhere to the Protocol, interviewers were observed conducting field forensic interviews using the Protocol and were given feedback on their practices and techniques. Written feedback was provided on all transcribed field interviews until the study ended. In addition, individual meetings with the research team every 6 to 8 weeks focused on critical analysis of the interviewers' adherence to the Protocol and its strategies in their recent interviews.

Cyr and Lamb (2009): Canada

In this study, 83 Protocol-guided forensic interviews of French-Canadian alleged sexual abuse victims, interviewed using a French translation of the Protocol, were compared with 83 non-Protocol forensic interviews, conducted by the same 17 experienced police officers and mental health workers before they were trained to use the Protocol. Children were between 3 and 13 years of age and averaged 9 years.

Interviewers completed an intensive five-day training program reviewing current knowledge of memory, suggestibility, and children's developing cognitive and communicative capacities. The Protocol was then explained, with the research literature used to explain its structure and aims. Videotaped and transcribed interviews were used to illustrate both desirable and risky practices, and practice periods each day allowed trainees to use the Protocol when interviewing role-playing "victims" who followed predetermined scripts. These role-plays were filmed for review and analysis with the trainee and with the whole group. Following this week of intensive training, the investigators began interviewing alleged victims using the Protocol and received written feedback on each interview until the study concluded. They also participated in a discussion reviewing practice within 2 weeks of each interview.

Naka (2011): Japan

Naka compared 62 interviews conducted by 32 social workers and psychologists working at Child Guidance Centers in Japan prior to ($n=31$) and following ($n=31$) training about the NICHD Protocol. Interviewers questioned witnesses (ages ranged from 5 to 62 years) about a brief video that the witnesses had viewed (different video clips were watched by witnesses for the pre- and post-training interviews). Interviewers received approximately 24 hours of training on the use of the Protocol.

Cyr, Dion, McDuff, and Trotier-Sylvain (2012): Canada

In this study, 79 interviews conducted with alleged sexual abuse victims by 19 police officers prior to training in use of the Protocol were compared to a matched set of 84 interviews conducted post-training.

The interviews were matched on the basis of child and allegation characteristics, rather than by interviewer. Children were between 3 and 13 years of age with an average age of 8 years. As in the previous Canadian study, interviewers attended a five-day training course that covered relevant theory and knowledge about memory and developmental psychology, along with an introduction and practice using the Protocol. In this study, half of the interviewers received detailed feedback about each interview during the research program whereas the remaining interviewers had no further input after completing the training course.

Yi, Jo, and Lamb (2016): South Korea

Following the introduction of the Protocol in 2010, Yi et al. examined 1 pre- and 1 post-Protocol training interview conducted by each of 18 South Korean police officers. Officers attended a 2-day training course that covered research in child development, the foundation and content of the Protocol, video examples of good practice, and role-plays of interviews with feedback. Written feedback was provided about the pre-training interview submitted. Children were, on average, 9 years old.

SUMMARY OF THE FINDINGS

Interviewer and Child Behavior in the Substantive Phase

Except in the Korean and Japanese studies, Protocol-trained interviewers offered significantly fewer prompts overall than interviewers not using the Protocol. In addition, as predicted, the number and proportion of open-ended free-recall utterances (i.e., invitations) were significantly higher in Protocol interviews than in the non-Protocol interviews during the substantive phase (see Table 6.1) of the interviews. In all but the Korean study, interviewers following the Protocol also posed proportionally fewer directive and option-posing prompts. The proportion of suggestive utterances decreased in four of the studies (United States, Canada (Cyr & Lamb, 2009), Japan (based on mean number of utterances), and Korea).

Overall, Protocol interviews did not elicit more substantive details than non-Protocol interviews. In all of the studies, however, proportionally more of the substantive details provided by children in the Protocol condition were elicited using invitations and proportionally

Table 6.1 Proportion of major utterance types in Protocol and non-Protocol interviews (substantive phase only)

Study	Type of prompt							
	Invitation		Directive		Option-posing		Suggestive	
	Protocol	Comparison	Protocol	Comparison	Protocol	Comparison	Protocol	Comparison
Orbach et al. (2000) Israel	.30 (.14)	.06 (.04) ***	.44 (.11)	.51 (.12) *	.18 (.08)	.32 (.09) **	.07 (.07)	.10 (.06)
Sternberg et al. (2001) United States	.33 (.13)	.10 (.06) ***	.35 (.12)	.43 (.09) ***	.26 (.09)	.36 (.10) ***	.06 (.06)	.11 (.06) ***
Lamb et al. (2009) United Kingdom	.34 (.16)	.07 (.04) ***	.43 (.12)	.28 (.08) ***	.18 (.08)	.27 (.10) ***	.06 (.06)	.08 (.08) (5.22)
Cyr and Lamb (2009) Canada	.48 (.18)	.12 (.08) **	.26 (.13)	.42 (.11) **	.19 (.11)	.36 (.13) **	.07 (.06)	.10 (.07) **
Naka (2011)[a] Japan	.63 (.22)	.18 (.15) ***	.09 (.09)	.27 (.14)	.12 (.10)	.30 (.14) ***	.03 (.05)	.07 (.07)
Cyr et al. (2012) Canada	.31 (.17)	.06 (.05) ***	.30 (.11)	.42 (.14) ***	.21 (.10)	.31 (.10) ***	.05 (.05)	.04 (.05)
Yi et al. (2016) Korea	.11 (.07)	.04 (.05) **	.37 (.08)	.39 (.13)	.35 (.26)	.31 (.12)	.19 (.10)	.25 (.09)

*p < .05 **p < .01 ***p < .001; significance levels refer to differences between the Protocol and non-Protocol conditions
[a] Naka did not examine the proportions of interviewer utterances; the mean numbers of each interviewer utterance type were all significantly different in pre- and post-training interviews.

fewer details were provided by children in response to directive prompts (see Table 6.2). Six of the studies showed a decrease in the proportion of children's details elicited using option-posing prompts, and four showed a reduction in the proportion of details reported in response to suggestive prompts.

Benia, Hauck-Filho, Dillenburg, and Stein (2015): Meta-analysis

Benia and colleagues conducted a meta-analysis of interviewer utterance types and child responsiveness. The analysis included five of the seven studies described above (all but Naka and Yi et al. were included). Benia et al. combined the data from the five studies and compared interviews conducted using the Protocol with those in a comparison group (either a standard interview, or matched interviews conducted prior to the introduction of the Protocol). Their analysis focused on the use of "desirable" (open-ended) and "undesirable" (option-posing and suggestive) prompts and the overall number of details (as well as central details) reported by children. Benia et al. also examined interviewers' prompts and children's responses in interviews of the 3- to 6-year-old children to examine whether young age moderated the findings. Across the five studies, 544 children between 3 and 14 years were interviewed (277 using the Protocol and 267 using another approach), in four countries.

The findings confirmed that the Protocol was highly effective in helping interviewers to employ recommended interviewing practices and to avoid prompt types which are more likely to elicit inaccurate information. In both the entire sample, and the preschool-aged subsample, the analyses showed significant increases in the interviewers' use of invitations (with a large effect size), and a significant decrease in the use of option-posing (with a large effect size) and suggestive (with a moderate effect size) questions when interviewers followed the Protocol.

More variability was evident when examining the children's responsiveness. The analyses confirmed a significant increase in the total number of details children reported in response to invitations, and a decrease in the number of details reported in response to suggestive questions, with effect sizes ranging from moderate to large across the individual studies (because of the variability, no combined effect size could be calculated). Variability in child responsiveness was particularly evident with preschoolers, although, as with older children, more details were reported in response to invitations and fewer in response to suggestive prompts.

Table 6.2 Proportions of the total amount of information reported in response to each type of utterance in Protocol and non-Protocol interviews (substantive phase only)

Study	Type of prompt							
	Invitation		Directive		Option-posing		Suggestive	
	Protocol	Comparison	Protocol	Comparison	Protocol	Comparison	Protocol	Comparison
Orbach et al. (2000) Israel	.51 (.21)	.14 (.15) **	.28 (.16)	.46 (.14) **	.10 (.09)	.26 (.12) **	.10 (.16)	.15 (.14)
Sternberg et al. (2001) United States	.47 (.19)	.18 (.13) **	.28 (.17)	.40 (.12) **	.18 (.11)	.28 (.13) **	.07 (.13)	.14 (.10) **
Lamb et al. (2009) United Kingdom	.55 (.18)	.14 (.12) ***	.25 (.11)	.46 (.13) ***	.10 (.09)	.29 (.16) ***	.06 (.09)	.10 (.08) **
Cyr and Lamb (2009) Canada	.63 (.19)	.16 (.14)	.22 (.15)	.45 (.15) ***	.09 (.08)	.29 (.16) ***	.06 (.09)	.10 (.08) **
Naka (2011)[a] Japan	.72 (.22)	.25 (.24) ***	.08 (.08)	.30 (.18) ***	.09 (.09)	.26 (.16) ***	.01 (.03)	.04 (.05) ***
Cyr et al. (2012) Canada	.46 (.22)	.09 (.09) ***	.31 (.16)	.49 (.18) ***	.13 (.08)	.29 (.14) ***	.04 (.07)	.05 (.06)
Yi et al. (2016) Korea	.27 (.11)	.12 (.15) **	.37 (.10)	.44 (.10) *	.19 (.12)	.23 (.11)	.10 (.07)	.18 (.14)

*p < .05 **p < .01 ***p < .001 ; statistics refer to differences between proportions in the Protocol and non-Protocol conditions.
[a] Naka's paper did not examine the proportions of interviewee responses by prompt type; the mean numbers of details elicited by each utterance type were all significantly different in pre- and post-training interviews.

Inclusion of Elements in the Preparatory (Pre-substantive) Phase

Two of the field studies also examined the frequency with which interviewers included important components during the pre-substantive portions of the interviews. Both Sternberg et al. (2001) and Yi et al. (2016) demonstrated that interviewers were more likely in Protocol interviews to introduce themselves, outline the ground rules for the interview, and provide children with practice in narrating a recent event. In the Korean study, efforts to establish rapport did not differ whether or not interviewers followed the Protocol, whereas Sternberg et al. (2001) showed improvement in this practice. In contrast, Yi et al. documented increases in the numbers of interviewers who explained their roles when the Protocol was used, but Sternberg et al. (2001) did not (see Table 6.3).

Sternberg et al. (2001) also examined the ways in which interviewers attempted to introduce the substantive topic, as well as the proportion of children who responded to various prompts with allegations of sexual abuse. Four of the 50 children in the Protocol condition disclosed before any of the scripted substantive prompts were offered. Of the remaining 46 children, 41 (89%) disclosed in response to an open-ended prompt, whereas 5 of the 46 children (11%) disclosed abuse only after being asked a scripted option-posing (i.e., "Is your mom worried that something may have happened to you?") or suggestive (e.g., "I heard that someone has been bothering you. Tell me everything about the bothering") question. By contrast, when the interviewers formulated their own questions in the standard condition, 18 (36%) of the 50 children disclosed abuse in response to an open-ended question, whereas 29 (58%) disclosed abuse in response to an option-posing or suggestive question.

Table 6.3 Percentage of interviews including preparatory components in Sternberg et al.'s (2001) and Yi et al.'s (2016) studies

Recommended practice	Sternberg et al. (2001)		Yi et al. (2016)	
	Baseline	Protocol	Baseline	Protocol
Interviewer introduces him/herself	58	88	44	94
Interviewer explains purpose of interview	76	90	17	94
Interviewer establishes rapport	52	100	39	44
Interviewer practices discussing neutral topic	2	100	6	61
Interviewer outlines ground rules	34	72	22	72

Notes: All group differences, except for "interviewer explains purpose of the interview" in Sternberg et al.'s (2001) study and "establishes rapport" in Yi et al.'s (2016) study, were statistically significant, $p < .01$.

Examining Children's Accuracy—Laboratory and Field-based Studies

The above field studies examined forensic interviews with children about suspected child sexual abuse. As such, there was no way of directly knowing whether the increased amounts of detail reported by children in response to invitations in the Protocol condition came at the expense of accuracy; the improved accuracy of children's responses was instead inferred from the nature of the questions eliciting them (Brown & Lamb, 2015). Brown and colleagues thus conducted a laboratory-based study to directly evaluate the accuracy of information elicited from children in response to various types of prompts by comparing children's accounts with objective records of a staged event they had experienced. The study also examined whether children reported entirely false events when interviewed using the NICHD Protocol about an event that had not happened.

One hundred and twenty-eight 5- to 7-year-old children took part individually in a staged event (dressing in a costume and having a photograph taken). Children were interviewed about the event 4- to 6-weeks later, using the NICHD Protocol, and were also asked about an event that did not happen (a class trip to the fire station). The interviews were largely comprised of invitations and children provided the majority of their accounts in response to these prompts (see Table 6.4). Cued invitations (invitations that asked children to elaborate upon their previous disclosed contents) were especially productive, eliciting as much information per prompt as invitations and more information than directive and suggestive prompts. The accuracy of the information children reported was uniformly high, regardless of the type of the eliciting prompt. A small number (11%) of children responded to the prompt about the false event, and elaborated upon their initial response when interviewed.

Brown, Lewis, Lamb, and Stephens (2012) examined the quality of information children reported about a known event in a study that included children with intellectual disabilities (CWID). The CWID were between 7 and 12 years old, and were compared with typically developing (TD) children of either the same chronological age (7 to 12 years), or the same mental age (4 to 9 years). Children were interviewed about a staged event (an interactive class presentation about health and safety) 1 week or 6 months later. They were addressed with similar proportions of invitations, directive, and option-posing prompts and with very few suggestive prompts (see Table 6.4). Despite the similar numbers of invitation, directive, and option-posing prompts, children provided most information in response to invitations (Table 6.4) at both time points, highlighting the productivity of such prompts. Children were highly accurate after 1 week (89%), but accuracy declined after the

Table 6.4 Proportion of interviewer prompts of each type posed and proportion and accuracy of children's responses to utterances of each type in laboratory analogue studies

	Brown et al. (2012)		Brown et al. (2013)
	1 week	6 months	
Proportion of prompts posed			
Invitations	.25	.26	.65
Directives	.20	.23	.22
Option-posing	.19	.21	.00
Suggestive	<.01	<.01	.13
Proportion of child's information elicited			
Invitations	.63	.48	.67
Directives	.25	.30	.19
Option-posing	.10	.12	.00
Suggestive	.03	.09	.06
Accuracy of responses			
Invitations	.88	.82	.84
Directives	.82	.64	.81
Option-posing	.76	.56	–
Suggestive	.88	.90	.80

delay (75% at 6 months), as did the total number of reported details. Information reported in response to invitations remained highly accurate after the 6-month delay, whereas responses to directive and option-posing prompts became less accurate. There were differences in the informativeness and accuracy of both CWID and the younger TD children, as discussed further in Chapters 7 and 8.

Comparing Witness and Suspect Accounts—Another Approach to Establishing Accuracy

In field studies, it is rare to know what actually happened during incidents of abuse, and so the emphasis on the value of recalled information is based on the results of the experimental research, described in Chapter 3, showing that information elicited using recall prompts is more likely to be accurate than information elicited using recognition based prompts. We were thus very fortunate to have access to some cases in Israel where it was possible to compare the accounts provided by alleged victims with those provided by young suspects, who admitted the central details of the same alleged incidents (Lamb, Orbach, Hershkowitz, Horowitz et al., 2007). On average, the victims provided nearly 360 details, with about half elicited using invitations or produced spontaneously (i.e., not in response to information requesting prompts), another 33% elicited using directive prompts, 12% elicited using option-posing prompts, and 8% elicited using suggestive prompts.

Each detail reported by the alleged victim was classified as Confirmed, Contradicted, Ambiguous, or Ignored by comparing the victim's statement with that provided by the suspect. Details were deemed to have been confirmed when the suspect reported exactly the same information as the victim, contradicted when the details reported by the alleged victim were incompatible with those reported by the suspect, ambiguous when one suspect reported details that were consistent and another suspect reported details that were inconsistent with those reported by the alleged victim, and ignored when the suspect made no reference to details similar to those reported by the alleged victim. An average of 30 (9%) of the details were contradicted, 73 (24%) were confirmed, 1 (.4%) was ambiguous, and 253 (66%) were ignored by the suspects. Importantly, significantly more details elicited from the victims using open-ended prompts were confirmed by the suspects than those elicited in response to more focused prompts, and there was a non-significant tendency for the proportion of details elicited using open-ended recall prompts to be confirmed more often than those elicited using focused recognition prompts.

These results thus only partially supported the prediction that information retrieved using open-ended recall prompts is more likely to be accurate than information elicited using prompts that triggered recognition processes. However, over 71% of the details reported by the suspects confirmed information reported by the victims and only 28.7% of the suspects' details contradicted information reported by the victims. Details reported by victims were deemed confirmed when the suspects specifically agreed with the victims' reports. Relatively few details—just over 20% of the total number reported, on average—were confirmed in this way, but nearly 30% of those retrieved using invitations were confirmed by the suspects, whereas a third fewer—around 20%—of those elicited using all other types of prompts were confirmed. However, the results did not confirm expectations that the fewest confirmations would be elicited by suggestive prompts, and that option-posing prompts would be less risky (with respect to the accuracy of the information retrieved) than suggestive prompts, though more risky than directive prompts. In fact, even though directive prompts tap recall processes, they did not elicit a higher rate of confirmations than either option-posing or suggestive prompts, both of which depend on recognition memory processes. This suggests that the superiority of invitations rests at least in part on their openness, with the interviewer not narrowing the focus of the informant's retrieval in any way.

The results of the analyses involving contradictions were even more puzzling, inasmuch as the rate of contradiction did not vary depending on the type of prompts used to elicit the information. These unexpected findings may reflect the fact that surprisingly few details reported by the child victims were contradicted by the suspects and this is likely to have reduced the sensitivity of the analyses. The low number of contradictions may be explained by the fact that only cooperative suspects (i.e., those who fully or partially admitted the allegations) were included in the study.

The age differences were also unexpected, although they were not surprising. The proportion of details confirmed decreased substantially with age, presumably because the accounts provided by the younger children were significantly less detailed but perhaps especially rich in the most important and salient details which were, in turn, the details most likely to be confirmed by the other participants. Stated differently, the greater verbosity of the older victims may have led them to include many more specific (even if central) details that were less likely to be mentioned by the suspects describing the same incidents and events.

THE MEANING OF THESE FINDINGS

The studies described above reveal a range of positive outcomes when interviewers follow the Protocol: Interviewers engage in better preparation with children prior to introducing the matter under investigation, and employ more desirable and fewer risky questioning strategies in the course of their interviews. Children provide a greater proportion of their accounts in response to invitations, even when fewer of these are posed. Laboratory-based studies confirm that children's responses to invitations are likely to be highly accurate, even after substantial delays, and that invitations are effective when addressed to younger children and to those who have cognitive impairments.

Although children provided more of the reported information in response to invitations in the various field studies, there was typically no difference in the total number of details reported by children in Protocol than in non-Protocol interviews (but Cyr and Lamb, 2009, showed a difference in favor of Protocol interviews). Because the Protocol trains children in the pre-substantive phase to retrieve detailed information from episodic memory, we expected that children would provide more information about substantive issues when interviewed using the Protocol. This prediction was not confirmed in most of the studies, as children in the two conditions typically provided the same amount of information. We suspect that the interviewers implicitly settled for "enough" information, and that additional detail could often have been elicited had the investigators employed further open-ended prompts. Investigators obviously must engage in a challenging balancing act—obtaining as much information as possible without compromising the quality of the information obtained. Because of their training, interviewers in the Protocol conditions were perhaps especially aware of the risks associated with some interview practices and may thus have chosen not to pursue issues they might formerly have explored in risky ways. Clearly, further research on this issue in both field and laboratory analogue contexts is warranted.

Although implementation of the Protocol fostered 40% to 60% reductions in the number of details elicited using option-posing and suggestive questions, respectively, approximately one quarter of the information was elicited using option-posing and suggestive questions even when the Protocol was used. Because these types of questions are significantly more likely to elicit erroneous information than are open-ended questions, concerns about the accuracy of children's responses to these questions is warranted. Because this research was conducted in the field, of course, we typically do not know which of the reported details were accurate.

Interviewing Young Witnesses

Lamb, Sternberg, Orbach, Hershkowitz et al. (2003) compared the structure and informativeness of forensic interviews with alleged witnesses and alleged victims of similar incidents, matched with respect to factors (such as age or relationship between victim and perpetrator) likely to affect how responsive children were. Because experienced events should be richer and more salient than events that were simply watched, Lamb et al. expected that witnesses would provide fewer details about incidents they had merely observed than would peers describing comparable incidents they had allegedly experienced.

In this study, 26 young witnesses of sexual abuse ($M = 10$ years) who had been interviewed using the Protocol were matched with respect to age, relationship between victim and alleged perpetrator, and type of offense with 26 alleged victims of sexual abuse who had also been interviewed using the Protocol. The same 22 investigators interviewed children in both groups, but the witnesses and victims were not interviewed about the same alleged incidents.

Interviewer utterances. There was no significant effect of age on the types of utterance used by interviewers, but there was a significant effect of role (victim/witness) on the number of invitations posed by interviewers and a significant age X role interaction with respect to suggestive prompts: Whereas a decreasing number of suggestive prompts were addressed to witnesses with increasing age, an increasing number of suggestive prompts were addressed to victims with increasing age. Comparable analyses of the proportions of all utterances that fell into each category showed role differences with respect to invitations and option-posing prompts, but no significant effect of age and no age X role interaction. More invitations were made to witnesses than to victims, whereas more option-posing prompts were offered to victims than to witnesses.

Children's response. The total number of details provided by alleged victims and witnesses did not differ significantly, although children under 9 provided significantly fewer details than children over 11 years of age. Comparable analyses of central and peripheral details yielded similar effects for age and no differences between witnesses and alleged victims, although witnesses tended to provide more peripheral details than victims did. In addition, more details were elicited using invitations from witnesses than from victims, whereas more details were elicited using option-posing prompts from older than from younger children. Suggestive prompts also elicited more central details, on average, from victims than from witnesses.

In general, the findings demonstrated quite conclusively that young witnesses can provide substantial amounts of forensically relevant details, especially when interviewers make extensive use of open-ended prompts. Similarities between the response patterns of witnesses and alleged victims suggested that the same principles should guide forensic interviewers seeking information from victims and witnesses and that the Protocol was a useful guide in both contexts.

The similarities between the performance of alleged victims and witnesses was somewhat surprising. Research in laboratory analogue contexts has shown that children often provide less information about events they have merely observed than about events in which they actually participated (Murachver et al., 1996). Such findings imply that witnesses should recall and recount less information than alleged victims, but this was not the case in Lamb et al.'s field study. Witnesses provided as many details as victims, with a tendency to provide more peripheral details (forensically relevant details about appearance or clothing, etc.) than the alleged victims.

Three possible factors (that are not mutually exclusive) may explain why the alleged victims failed to provide more details than the witnesses. First, victims may have been more stressed by their experiences than the witnesses, and this may have affected the amount of information they encoded. Although plausible, this hypothesis is not buttressed by empirical evidence: There remains considerable controversy about whether or not stress impedes or facilitates encoding and memory, as noted in Chapter 2 (e.g., Deffenbacher, 1983; Goodman & Bottoms et al., 1991; Goodman & Hirschman et al., 1991; Oates & Shrimpton, 1991; Ornstein, Gordon, & Larus, 1992; Peters 1991; Peterson & Bell, 1996; Steward et al., 1996). Second, the victims may have been more ashamed or embarrassed describing their experiences; none of the experimental studies concerned with the differential informativeness of participants and witnesses has involved incidents likely to provoke shame or embarrassment, although there is suggestive evidence and common-sense reason to believe that reporters may sometimes fail to report embarrassing details (Saywitz et al., 1991). Third, the interviewers questioned the victims and witnesses quite differently, even though they were all following the same investigative interview Protocol, and these differences in interviewer style may well have enhanced the overall informativeness of the witnesses while degrading the informativeness of the alleged victims. In particular, interviewers offered witnesses more invitations than they offered victims; invitations typically, as they did in this study, elicit more details than more focused questions do. It is noteworthy that individual invitations elicited the same amounts of information from children in the two groups, so the different interview styles should not be attributed to the reticence or unresponsiveness of the alleged victims. Interviewers nevertheless chose to use riskier probes—prompts more likely to elicit inaccurate information—when interviewing alleged victims and their tendencies to do so increased as the children grew older and thus more capable of providing longer and fuller responses to invitations! Although the reasons are not clear, these findings suggest that these interviewers were more willing to "let witnesses do the talking," while directing the alleged victims' retrieval more forcefully, despite known risks to the accuracy of the information obtained.

Overall, the results of this study demonstrated that the Protocol was as suitable for interviewing witnesses as it is for interviewing young victims. Indeed, the results of the study suggested that young witnesses may be surprisingly informative about incidents they have observed. This finding is important because witnesses to incidents of child abuse (especially in public or group-care settings) or to incidents of domestic violence may often be children whose possible value as informants should not be discounted.

CONCLUSION

The studies on which we have focused in this chapter demonstrate quite conclusively that the Protocol is of considerable value to forensic interviewers. When interviewers use the Protocol, they make much greater use of open-ended questions than do their peers, and are able to obtain considerable amounts of information in this fashion—information that is much more likely to be accurate than information obtained using the "riskier" recognition prompts that tend to predominate in most investigative interviews. That said, it is clear that, even when following the Protocol, interviewers continue to make too much use of those risky prompts, and that there has not yet been sufficient research documenting changes in the quality of interviewing as interviewers have more experience using the Protocol and reviewing the interviews they have conducted.

It is also clear that the techniques incorporated in the Protocol are not only effective for interviewing young victims, but can be effectively employed when interviewing young witnesses as well. This should come as no surprise, because the Protocol draws upon a large body of developmental research about the ways young children behave, think, and remember experiences, rather than being limited to features or characteristics that would apply only to alleged victims.

7
Interviewing Suspected Victims under Six Years of Age

Children's age is one of the best recognized factors influencing how they describe their experiences. Increasing age is typically associated with increases in the amount of information children report, although accuracy (at least in free recall) may remain constant (e.g., Gee & Pipe, 1995; Goodman, Aman, & Hirschman, 1987; Goodman & Reed, 1986; Marin, Holmes, Guth, & Kovac, 1979; Oates & Shrimpton, 1991; Saywitz, 1987). As well as differences across various developmental periods, however, variability within age groups is also common, with age differences evident even among preschoolers (Goodman & Aman, 1990, Leichtman & Ceci, 1995; Leichtman, Ceci, & Morse, 1997; Pipe & Salmon, 2002; Quas, Goodman, Ghetti, & Redlich, 2000; Quas, Qin, Schaaf, & Goodman, 1997; Quas & Schaaf, 2002). Thus, age per se does not provide an accurate index of children's ability to recount personal experiences but rather serves to summarize the influence of a number of variables relating to children's abilities, the effects of which may differ across interview/recall contexts. Nevertheless, the many highly publicized daycare cases, where very young children were at the center of investigations about alleged abuse, prompted researchers to determine whether very young as opposed to older children should be interviewed differently.

Tell Me What Happened: Questioning Children About Abuse, Second Edition.
Michael E. Lamb, Deirdre A. Brown, Irit Hershkowitz, Yael Orbach, and Phillip W. Esplin.
© 2018 John Wiley & Sons Ltd. Published 2018 by John Wiley & Sons Ltd.

Reflecting findings generated by research examining the impact of questioning strategies on children's responding (see Chapter 2), the Protocol places special emphasis on the use of open-ended prompts, building on evidence that freely recalled information is more likely to be accurate than information retrieved in response to recognition memory prompts. It is widely believed, however, that preschoolers (4- and 5-year-olds) provide such brief and incomplete responses to free-recall prompts (e.g. Bourg et al., 1999; Hewitt, 1999; Lyon, 1999; Saywitz & Goodman, 1996; Steward et al., 1996) that alternative strategies may be necessary. In this chapter, we examine closely the alleged and real inadequacies and capacities of preschoolers in forensic interview contexts, drawing especially on an extensive study designed to examine age differences in young children's responses to free-recall prompts.

Clearly, there are important differences between the autobiographical memory retrieval strategies and capacities of preschoolers and older children (Schneider & Bjorklund, 1998). Younger children tend to remember less information and to provide briefer accounts of their experiences than older children do (Baker-Ward, Gordon, Ornstein, Larus, & Clubb, 1993; Lamb, Hershkowitz, Sternberg, Boat et al., 1996; Lamb, Hershkowitz, Sternberg, Esplin et al., 1996; Lamb, Sternberg, & Esplin, 2000; Ornstein, Gordon et al., 1992; Sternberg, Lamb, Hershkowitz, Esplin et al., 1996). In addition, young children, especially preschoolers, are more likely than older children to respond erroneously to suggestive questions about their experiences, as well as to show response biases and select erroneous options when responding to forced-choice and yes/no questions (Bruck, Ceci, Francouer, & Renick, 1995; Ceci & Bruck, 1995; Goodman & Aman, 1990; Oates & Shrimpton, 1991; Poole & Lindsay, 1998; Walker, Lunning, & Eilts, 1996). Some researchers have shown that children of different ages are equivalently accurate when freely recalling experiences (e.g., Brown, Lewis, Lamb, & Stephens, 2012; Flin, Boon, Knox, & Bull, 1992; Goodman & Reed, 1986; Jack, Leov, & Zajac, 2014; Johnson & Foley, 1984; Marin, Holmes, Guth, & Kovac, 1979; Oates & Shrimpton, 1991), whereas others have shown that younger children are less accurate than older children even in response to open-ended questions (e.g., Brown, Lewis, & Lamb, 2015).

Two of the initial field studies described in Chapter 6 (Orbach et al., 2000; Sternberg et al., 2001) showed that children in the two youngest age groups (4- to 6-year-olds and 7- to 8-year-olds) interviewed using the NICHD Protocol did not differ significantly with respect to the average number of details provided per invitation (i.e., open-ended free-recall prompts) and the total number of forensically relevant details provided in response to such invitations (Sternberg, Lamb, Orbach et al., 2001). Half of the information provided by the 16 4- to 6-year-olds studied by Sternberg, Lamb, Orbach et al. (2001) was elicited using open-ended invitations (i.e., free-recall prompts). These findings indicate that young children can respond informatively to open-ended free-recall prompts.

These studies included too few 4- to 6-year-old children, however, to permit close examination of age differences in children's responses to free-recall prompts. To more specifically examine the compentency of young victims when interviewed using the Protocol, Lamb, Sternberg, Orbach, Esplin et al. (2003) examined interviews with 130 4- to 8-year-old child-witnesses (90 girls and 40 boys). The purpose of that study was to examine age differences in the amount and quality of information provided by young children in response to different types of free-recall prompts. Open-ended invitations differ in scope, and it is possible that younger children may have greater difficulty than older children responding informatively to the more general invitations (e.g., "Tell me what happened" or "Tell me more about it") than to the narrower, refocusing cued invitations (e.g., "You said he kissed you; tell me about the kissing"), recommended to users of the Protocol. "Cued invitations" use pre-disclosed details as contextual cues to prompt further free-recall elaboration, with those that refocus on time periods labeled "time-segmenting cues." Time-segmenting cues use pre-disclosed actions as temporal reference points for requesting event information about what happened before or after such reference points, during the time elapsing between two such temporal reference points, or at the same time as a designated act (e.g., "What happened while your mother was in the kitchen?" [pre-disclosed]). One purpose of Lamb, Sternberg, Orbach, Esplin et al.'s (2003) study was to see whether these types of cued invitations could be used effectively when interviewing 4- to 8-year-old children, and whether their effectiveness varied depending on the children's ages.

The study included forensic interviews of suspected victims who were 4, 5, 6, 7, and 8 years old, with the 130 interviews selected from a total of 271 interviews of 4- to 8-year-olds conducted between 1997 and 2001 by participating police officers in three police departments or constabularies, one in the United Kingdom and two in the Western United States, where the Protocol had been introduced. All forensic interviews of alleged victims of sexual abuse conducted by the 16 participating police officers during the study periods, which differed from site to site, were considered for inclusion in the study. Interestingly, 60 of the 141 interviews that were excluded yielded no allegation of abuse, revealing a non-disclosure rate of 22%. This rate was significantly higher than the rate reported in earlier studies, but consistent with the evidence (see Chapter 9) that younger suspected victims are less likely to make allegations when questioned than older children (Hershkowitz et al., 2005; Hershkowitz, Orbach, Lamb, Sternberg, Pipe, & Horowitz, 2007; London et al., 2005, 2007). A total of 134 interviews were excluded: 60 because the interviewers did not use the Protocol, 59 because they yielded allegations of physical rather than sexual abuse, 12 were interviews of witnesses rather than alleged victims, while 3 were second interviews, or involved intermediaries or other possible sources of confusion. No interviews yielded allegations that appeared to be false; indeed, all of the alleged complaints were deemed valid by police investigators although details of the actual incidents were not known. There were no differences between children of each age with respect to the severity of the reported abuse, relationship to the perpetrators, or the reported number of abusive events.

All interviews studied followed the standard NICHD Protocol and all interviewers had received extensive training from researchers at NICHD on the use of the Protocol while conducting simulated and actual forensic interviews during the course of the project. For some analyses, Lamb, Sternberg, Orbach, Esplin, Stewart, and Mitchell (2003) distinguished between general invitations (e.g., "Tell me everything that happened") and cued invitations. Cued invitations were further categorized depending on whether they referenced events, actions, segments of time, or other topics.

Investigators' Behavior

In the substantive portions of the interviews, investigators posed an average of 16 invitations, 17 directive prompts, 13 option-posing prompts, and 3 suggestive prompts, with the average numbers of prompts of each type not varying significantly by age. The investigators asked an average of 8 substantive questions (15% of the total number of substantive prompts) before their first substantive option-posing or suggestive prompt, and this, too, did not vary depending on the children's ages.

The average interview included 5 cued invitations. There was a significant effect for age with respect to the number of cued invitations, with more cued invitations being addressed to 4-, 5-, and 8-year-olds ($Ms = 6$, 6, and 7, respectively) than to 6- and 7-year-olds ($Ms = 4$). With the exception of this one non-linear age difference, these analyses indicate that the interviewers interacted similarly with children of all ages studied.

Children's Responses

Not surprisingly, there were significant age differences in the total number of details elicited as well as in the numbers elicited using each of the different types of prompts (see Table 7.1). Although the proportion of all details elicited using invitations was highest among the 8-year-olds (57%), the second highest percentage was among the 4-year-olds (48%), and there was thus no significant effect for age with respect to the proportion of details elicited using invitations.

There were also significant age differences in the average number of details elicited by each invitation, with means of 3, 4, 5, 6 and 8 details for responses by 4-, 5-, 6-, 7-, and 8-year-olds, respectively. General invitations (as opposed to cued invitations) likewise yielded increasing numbers of details as children grew older. There were no age differences in the number of utterances of each type that elicited one or more details, indicating that children of all ages were equivalently likely to respond informatively to similar types of prompts.

There was also an effect of age on the number of details provided before the first option-posing or suggestive prompt: the older the child, the more details were reported before the first option-posing or suggestive utterance. There was no significant effect with respect to the proportion of the total number of details elicited before the first such prompt, however: despite differences in the total amount of information provided by children of different ages, younger and older children reported similar proportions (out of the total amount of information reported) before the first introduction of interviewer input via the use of option-posing or suggestive prompts.

The results of this study clearly demonstrated that children as young as four years of age can provide substantial amounts of forensically important information about alleged abuse in response to free-recall prompts. On average, almost one-half of the information provided by

Table 7.1 Age differences in the average number of details elicited by each type of prompt

	Utterance types				
Age	Invitations	Directive	Option-posing	Suggestive	Total
4	40.0	21.3	15.8	6.1	83.1
5	54.5	32.8	22.7	6.1	115.6
6	58.1	51.0	30.3	8.8	148.2
7	65.6	43.0	26.5	9.0	144.1
8	139.7	42.1	31.6	7.1	220.4
Overall	68.7	39.2	25.6	7.6	141.1

the children came in response to free-recall prompts. As expected, older children reported more details in total and in their average responses to invitations than the younger children did, but the proportion of details elicited using free-recall prompts did not increase with age. Moreover, even the very youngest children were capable of providing most of the information (Who? What?) needed by forensic investigators in response to free-recall prompts, thereby reducing reliance on the more risky (potentially contaminating) yes/no and forced-choice questions. On average, invitations also elicited more forensically relevant details than did other types of utterances at all ages, as shown in other studies (e.g., Lamb, Hershkowitz, Sternberg, Esplin et al., 1996; Orbach et al., 2000; Sternberg, Lamb, Hershkowitz, Esplin et al., 1996; Sternberg, Lamb, Davies et al., 2001).

Cued Invitations

Because preschoolers are often deemed incapable of providing informative responses to very general prompts (e.g., "Tell me what happened"), we were particularly interested in age differences in response to cued invitations—open-ended prompts in which the interviewer made explicit reference to informative details (e.g., action, object) previously mentioned by the child. An average of 25 details per interview were elicited using cued invitations. Cued invitations thus elicited 18% of the total number of details elicited, and 37% of the total number of details elicited using invitations.

Not surprisingly, both the total number of details and the average number of details per prompt elicited using cued invitations increased with age. Both action and time-segmenting cues elicited more information from 8- than from 4-, 5-, 6-, and 7-year-olds, with action cues eliciting more information from children than did time-segmenting, event-based, and other cue types.

The results of Lamb, Sternberg, Orbach, Esplin et al.'s (2003) study thus illustrated that cued invitations, particularly those that remind children of actions they have previously mentioned, constitute effective ways of triggering the recall of information that is more likely to be accurate than information elicited using forced-choice and yes/no questions from alleged victims as young as 4 years of age. At all ages, furthermore, more information would likely have been elicited if the interviewers had made greater use of cued invitations (the average interview included 5.4 cued invitations), particularly those that made explicit reference to actions (using action-based and time-segmenting cues) mentioned by the child. Cued invitations (e.g., "You said that he touched your vagina. Tell me more about that") are productive and innocuous alternatives to risky yes/no and forced-choice questions (e.g., "So did he put his finger *in* your vagina?") when general invitations (e.g., "And then what happened?") appear to be ineffective. By structuring recall of experienced events, associating them with actions that have been mentioned, and breaking them into smaller units or segments of time, cued invitations enhance the capacity of young children to reconstruct past events and to elaborate upon their narrative accounts, avoiding interviewer contamination during the recall. Interestingly, action-based cues (e.g., "Tell me more about the touching") were consistently more effective than all other types of cues, regardless of age.

Our compelling findings regarding the value of "cued invitations" indicate clearly that forensic interviewers need to provide children of all ages with opportunities to recall information in response to free-recall prompts before assuming that more risky interview techniques are needed. This admonition is especially important in light of repeated demonstrations that younger children are more likely than older children to give inaccurate responses to yes/no questions (Brady, Poole, Warren, & Jones, 1999), to respond affirmatively to misleading questions about non-experienced events (Poole & Lindsay, 1998), and to acquiesce to suggestions (e.g., Cassel et al., 1996; Ceci & Huffman, 1997; Ceci, Ross, & Toglia, 1987a, 1987b; Robinson & Briggs, 1997). Such findings indicate that risky questions are even riskier when addressed to children aged 6 and under, and thus that forensic investigators need to make special efforts to maximize the amounts of information elicited from 4- to 6-year-olds using less risky, free-recall prompts.

In Lamb, Sternberg, Orbach, Esplin et al.'s (2003) study, nearly half of the informative details and 83% of the initial disclosures of sexual abuse were provided by preschoolers in response to free-recall prompts. Such findings suggest that the likely accuracy of information provided by alleged victims is enhanced when interviewers use free-recall prompts exhaustively before turning to more focused prompts. These findings also indicate that cued invitations should be exhausted before "wh" prompts (whether visual or verbal) are introduced because cued invitations foster retrieval of free-recall information without limiting responses to investigator-specified categories (for example, the question "What color was that shirt?" narrowly focuses attention on the color, but not other features, of the shirt that was previously mentioned). Non-suggestive yes/no and forced-choice questions, in which interviewers provide content, should be used only if essential information is still missing after free-recall and directive prompts have been exhausted, because these riskier alternatives are more likely to elicit inaccurate information.

According to Lamb, Sternberg, Orbach, Esplin et al. (2003), non-linear developmental improvements in the effectiveness of cued invitations were especially dramatic with respect to time-segmenting cues, which were quite effective when addressed to 8-year olds (see Table 7.2). At first glance, the developmental trajectory may seem puzzling because action cues and time-segmenting cues both use details about actions mentioned by the child to request additional information, yet responses to action cues steadily improved with age whereas time-segmenting prompts were strikingly more effective with 8-year-olds than with younger children. Perhaps this is because time-segmenting cues differ from action cues with respect to the type of information they request. Whereas action cues seek more information about the action itself, time-segmenting cues solicit information about what happened during a period of time following or preceding the action referenced or during the period of time between two such actions. Thus actions are the focus of the information request in action cues and serve only as temporal reference points in time-segmenting cues. As a result, the cognitive demands of the two types of cued invitations are quite different.

The fact that 8-year-olds responded more informatively to time-segmenting cues than younger children did is consistent with Piaget's (1971) observation that temporal concepts are understood by children later than concepts related to objects and actions. Piaget explained that the comprehension of time is associated with the ability to observe the consequences of actions, to recognize causal relationships in event sequences, and to explain later occurrences in terms of former ones (Gibson, 1991; Piaget, 1964). Whereas action cues require further elaboration about the action itself, time-segmenting cues require a forward projection of events, starting with a given action and continuing sequentially, as well as the capacity to review events in reverse order, going from an effect to an earlier cause. Only when children are able to relate to time operationally are they able to understand and reconstruct time sequences in this

Table 7.2 Age differences in the average number of details in response to each cued invitation

Age	Event cues	Time-segmentation cues	Action cues	Other cue types
4	1.1	1.7	3.7	2.0
5	4.2	1.3	3.1	2.3
6	3.0	2.7	2.3	2.3
7	2.2	0.9	6.2	2.7
8	1.3	4.6	8.6	2.8
Overall	2.5	2.1	5.5	2.4

fashion. Younger children cannot engage in such operational reversibility "whereas 8-year-olds can make use of that power and thus reconstruct the true and irreversible order of events" (Piaget, 1971, p. 6). The development of this capacity at 7 to 8 years of age enables children to deal with event sequences more efficiently, and this may explain the dramatic increase we observed in the amount of information provided in response to time-segmenting cues by 8-year-olds. In addition, although they also request information about events, action cues involve more focused demands for information and are thus less cognitively demanding than time-segmenting cues.

Hershkowitz, Lamb, Orbach, Katz, and Horowitz (2012) later examined preschoolers' responses to different prompt types in forensic interviews about physical and sexual abuse on a larger scale. They examined 299 interviews with children in four age groups (3-, 4-, 5-, and 6-year-olds). Overall, invitations comprised 28% of the prompts posed, directives 33%, option-posing 17%, and suggestive prompts 3% of interviewer utterances during the substantive phase (see Table 7.3). By and large, the usage of each type of prompt changed in relation to the children's ages. The number of invitations posed increased with age. Directives were used less with 4-year-olds than with 3-year-olds, but the usage then increased for 5- and 6-year-olds. Option-posing prompts decreased with age until 5 years, while the use of suggestive prompts was the same, regardless of the children's ages.

Overall, children were responsive to the majority (92%) of prompts (see Table 7.4). Responsivity, the amount of relevant information reported, and the number of new details reported all increased with age. Children were least likely to provide on-task responses to invitations than to the other kinds of prompts and gave more on-task responses to directives than to invitations, with the difference being more marked for 3- and 4-year-olds.

Children provided the fewest new details in response to invitations and there were age-related differences in the number of new details reported that varied depending on the type of prompt used (see Table 7.5). The youngest children (3-year-olds) were least informative in response to all prompts, while 4-year-olds were less informative than 5- and 6-year-olds when responding to invitations and option-posing prompts. When focus shifted to the number of details per prompt, analyses showed that 3- and 4-year-olds provided similar numbers of details per prompt in response to invitations, directives, and suggestive prompts but less in response to option-posing prompts, whereas 5- and 6-year-olds gave more details per prompt in response to invitations, more to directives than to suggestive prompts, and similar numbers to suggestive and option-posing prompts.

Table 7.3 The relative and absolute frequencies with which different prompts were addressed to children of different ages

Age	Types of prompt											Total prompts
	Invitation		Directive		Option-posing		Suggestive		Substantive		Non-substantive	
	Number (SD)	Rate (SD)	Number (SD)	Rate (SD)	Number (SD)	Rate (SD)	Number (SD)	Rate (SD)	Number (SD)	Rate (SD)	Number (SD)	Rate (SD)	Mean (SD)
3	17.50 (13.45)	.21 (.08)	30.56 (23.70)	.34 (.09)	17.23 (9.02)	.23 (.11)	3.32 (4.05)	.03 (.04)	68.63 (43.02)	.83 (.07)	15.69 (13.84)	.16 (.07)	84.32 (55.63)
4	19.89 (12.37)	.27 (.11)	26.76 (21.66)	.32 (.10)	13.17 (8.15)	.19 (.09)	3.18 (3.91)	.04 (.04)	63.02 (37.96)	.84 (.08)	12.30 (10.20)	.15 (.08)	75.32 (45.32)
5	24.93 (12.43)	.31 (.11)	29.65 (19.65)	.34 (.09)	11.97 (7.93)	.14 (.07)	2.90 (3.44)	.03 (.02)	69.47 (36.41)	.83 (.11)	14.94 (21.77)	.16 (.11)	84.42 (43.24)
6	28.37 (16.28)	.29 (.11)	37.33 (22.41)	.34 (.10)	13.28 (8.11)	.14 (.07)	3.49 (3.16)	.03 (.03)	82.49 (38.22)	.82 (.08)	17.96 (13.66)	.17 (.08)	100.45 (46.30)
Average	22.82 (13.89)	.28 (.11)	30.36 (21.74)	.33 (.09)	13.44 (8.35)	.17 (.09)	3.18 (3.64)	.03 (.03)	69.80 (38.77)	.83 (.09)	14.79 (15.95)	.16 (.09)	84.59 (47.20)

Table 7.4 Age differences in the rates at which children made different types of responses to different types of substantive prompts

Age	Rate of responses				Rate of responses to the specific request				Rate of responses providing new details			
	Invitation M (SD)	Directive M (SD)	Option-posing M (SD)	Suggestive M (SD)	Invitation Mean (SD)	Directive Mean (SD)	Option-posing Mean (SD)	Suggestive Mean (SD)	Invitation Mean (SD)	Directive Mean (SD)	Option-posing Mean (SD)	Suggestive Mean (SD)
3	.91 (.15)	.91 (.10)	.83 (.19)	.91 (.17)	.43 (.22)	.59 (.19)	.55 (.21)	.65 (.36)	.26 (.18)	.47 (.18)	.44 (.14)	.56 (.39)
4	.92 (.15)	.93 (.10)	.90 (.16)	.89 (.24)	.47 (.21)	.66 (.21)	.65 (.23)	.61 (.37)	.31 (.17)	.53 (.21)	.52 (.23)	.54 (.37)
5	.95 (.09)	.95 (.10)	.92 (.11)	.97 (.07)	.61 (.20)	.73 (.16)	.78 (.16)	.71 (.32)	.44 (.18)	.60 (.16)	.65 (.22)	.55 (.34)
6	.94 (.07)	.96 (.06)	.93 (.12)	.94 (.14)	.62 (.20)	.72 (.19)	.76 (.16)	.68 (.30)	.45 (.20)	.58 (.19)	.62 (.22)	.58 (.30)
Average	.93 (.12)	.94 (.09)	.90 (.15)	.93 (.17)	.54 (.22)	.68 (.19)	.70 (.21)	.66 (.34)	.37 (.19)	.56 (.19)	.57 (.23)	.55 (.35)

Table 7.5 Age differences in the number of details provided by children in response to different types of substantive prompts

Age	Types of prompt			
	Invitation	Directive	Option-posing	Suggestive
	Mean (SD)	Mean (SD)	Mean (SD)	Mean (SD)
3	1.24 (1.14)	1.43 (.89)	.85 (.42)	1.72 (1.81)
4	1.81 (1.36)	1.85 (1.17)	1.10 (.78)	2.12 (2.64)
5	3.25 (2.35)	2.45 (1.49)	1.85 (1.98)	2.17 (2.28)
6	3.78 (2.81)	2.34 (1.32)	1.74 (1.16)	2.49 (2.99)
Average	2.57 (2.24)	2.07 (1.33)	1.43 (1.37)	2.15 (2.49)

Older children were less likely than younger children to respond non-informatively. Invitations were most likely to elicit noninformative responses, and the tendency for this to occur decreased with age. About one-third of the children's responses were irrelevant or off-track, and even the 6-year-olds responded in this way about 30% of the time, showing that comprehension monitoring and meta-linguistic skills are still developing at this age. On the other hand, about half of all prompts yielded new information, showing that the children continuted to be engaged in retrieving information about their experiences well beyond what they had reported initially.

There are some important differences between the results of this study and that conducted by Lamb, Sternberg, Orbach, Esplin et al. (2003). Preschoolers in Hershkowitz et al.'s study were less responsive and less likely to produce new details in response to broad open-ended invitations than in response to the more narrowly focused directives, or closed-ended option-posing and suggestive prompts. Lamb, Sternberg, Orbach, Esplin et al. (2003) included older children than Hershkowitz et al., with fewer in each age group, so the later findings may be more robust. They suggested that children become more competent responding to very open-ended questions as they mature. While 3-to 4-year-olds can respond informatively to very broad open-ended questions (e.g., "Tell me everything you can remember about that"), children of this age tend to be more responsive to more focused open-ended questions (e.g., "What happened after he touched you?"). Broader open-ended prompts may not provide pre-schoolers with sufficient structure and scaffolding to facilitate comprehension of the questions (Korkman et al., 2006; Melinder & Gilstrap, 2009; Wolfman, Brown, & Jose, 2016b).

Hershkowitz et al.'s results shifted attention to the advantages of directive wh- questions that involve focused recall while providing more concrete retrieval cues signaling the category of information on which to focus. These have been shown to elicit more accurate information from preschoolers than recognition prompts do (Peterson, Dowden, & Tobin, 1999). Directive prompts, although specific, relate to information mentioned by the children and do not introduce any undisclosed information, thereby avoiding the risk of contamination. By using directive prompts, the interviewers studied by Hershkowitz et al. may have afforded even the youngest children the cues they needed to effectively trigger event recall, helping them provide appropriate and informative responses to the interviewers' requests.

Lamb, Sternberg, Orbach, Esplin et al. (2003) reported that cued invitations were especially useful when interviewing young children, particularly when they involved action cues. In fact, because directive prompts use previously disclosed information to focus attention, they may have acted like open-ended cued invitations for the very young preschoolers studied by Hershkowitz and colleagues (2012). Overall, specific prompts appeared less rather than more effective than invitations when the numbers of elicited details were compared, suggesting that directive questions are useful for eliciting responses, especially on-track responses, from young children but that invitations are superior elicitors of elaborated responses. On average, invitations yielded more information than any other type of prompt in Hershkowitz et al.'s study, probably because specific prompts lead children to retrieve targeted details whereas open-ended prompts encourage them to retrieve more elaborate information. As far as the amount of detail was concerned, directives were more productive than invitations for younger children (3- to 4-year-olds) whereas they were less productive than invitations for older children. These findings point to a developmental threshold in the effectiveness of free-recall strategies, with free-recall narrative-eliciting prompts reliably more effective only with children aged 5 and older.

Although experts have previously suggested that recognition prompts are necessary when interviewing young children (Hewitt, 1999; Lyon, 1999) because these children have difficulty with free-recall prompts, Hershkowitz et al.'s (2012) results suggested that focused-recall wh- questions may constitute superior alternatives when questioning preschoolers, because they combine the benefits of focus and recall. Questioners can thus accommodate young children's need for more specific prompts and their own desire to obtain accurate information by relying on specific questions that engage recall processes (i.e., directives) rather than those that involve recognition processes (i.e., option-posing and some suggestive questions) and are thus more likely to prompt inaccurate responses.

Even within the preschool years, it is clear that young children become progressively more adept at responding informatively to open-ended questions, which yield longer and richer responses but still depend on recall rather than recognition processes. There is considerable variation within and across age groups in how informatively children respond to different kinds of prompts, however. In a meta-analysis of studies evaluating the NICHD Protocol, Benia et al. (2015) showed that the degree of variability evident in children's responding was moderated by age, with greater differences in responsivity evident when analyses only involved children of preschool age. This underlines the need for more research on younger children's responses to different types of prompts.

CHILDREN'S REFERENCES TO TEMPORAL ATTRIBUTES

Practitioners working with young children can struggle not only to get enough information to understand what may have happened, but also to determine when it may have happened. In particular, children may struggle to locate events in time and context, especially if they have experienced multiple instances of maltreatment over an extended period of time (Roberts et al., 2015). Children's difficulty in doing so may reflect difficulty understanding and applying abstract concepts such as time, as well as difficulty in recognizing the need to include such information to make their narratives coherent and comprehensible.

In forensic settings, information about such temporal attributes as the date of occurrence, the number of alleged incidents, and the sequence of event components can uniquely define specific incidents (Tulving, 1972, 2002) and help structure narrative accounts of experiences. In the legal context, furthermore, it is often critically important to specify the time at which an alleged criminal offence occurred. In cases of child sexual abuse, it is especially important to obtain such information from alleged victims because corroborative evidence is scarce and in most cases, the victim is the sole witness to the crime other than the suspect.

Even when alibi defenses are unlikely (e.g., because the alleged perpetrator is part of the victim's immediate family and has continuous access to the child or multiple incidents of abuse have been alleged), the value of children's testimony is enhanced when the temporal context of the alleged abuse is specified. Thus references to time of day (e.g., day, night), contiguity with another activity (e.g., "every time my mother works the night shift"), or estimations of when the abuse was initiated (e.g., "it started when I was in first grade"), contribute important forensic information. Moreover, temporal references enhance the retrieval of event-specific narratives and eliminate the non-contextualized lists of actions that are typical of script descriptions. It is much easier to evaluate children's credibility when high-quality interviews yield such narrative accounts, with most information retrieved from recall rather than recognition memory (Hershkowitz, 2001; Hershkowitz, Fisher, Lamb, & Horowitz, 2007; Lamb, Sternberg, Esplin, Hershkowitz, & Orbach, 1997; Raskin & Esplin, 1991a, 1991c; Undeutsch, 1982).

Children as young as 4 years of age can accurately recall the time of day, day of the week, month, and/or seasons associated with events ocurring as much as several months earlier (Friedman, 1991; Friedman, Reese, & Dai, 2011; Jack, Friedman, Reese, & Zajac, 2016; Pathman, Larkina, Burch, & Bauer, 2013), but do they do so in forensic contexts? As mentioned earlier, Orbach and Lamb (2007) examined age-related differences in 4- to 10-year-old children's references to temporal attributes (i.e., sequencing, dating, number of occurrences, duration, and frequency) when describing alleged abuse both spontaneously and in response to temporal requests. Two hundred and fifty children were interviewed using the Protocol, and this made it possible to identify temporal features included in children's accounts. The study explored the relationships among children's ages, the specific temporal attribute referenced, retrieval mode (i.e., spontaneously or in response to requests for temporal information), and the way interviewers formulated their requests for information (i.e., whether tapping recall or recognition memory).

Whereas laboratory studies typically ask participants to focus on single temporal characteristics, the forensic interviews examined by Orbach and Lamb (2007) afforded child witnesses opportunities to describe allegedly experienced events using a range of temporal attributes, both spontaneously and in response to temporal requests. Moreover, whereas the emphasis in laboratory studies is usually on temporal information provided during recognition-based processes, the emphasis in this study was on recall-based processes because freely recalled information is more likely to be accurate than information retrieved in response to recognition memory prompts, although of course the accuracy could not be determined in this field study.

Orbach and Lamb (2007) found age-related increases in the 4- to 10-year olds' appropriate references to temporal attributes, both spontaneously and in response to temporal requests. Children's responsiveness (i.e., the match between their responses and the interviewers' requests) was determined by the appropriateness of the temporal category, the relational terminology, and the temporal scale used.

More references to temporal attributes were elicited from recall than from recognition memory, highlighting spontaneous reporting capabilities. As expected, there were positive correlations between the amount of temporal information (represented by the total number of temporal units in the temporal categories analyzed) and the total amount of forensic information (represented by the total number of details) provided by the children in the course of forensic interviews, as well as between the number of temporal requests by interviewers and the production of temporal references by children. As a result, Orbach and Lamb (2007) controlled for both the total number of details provided and the total number of requests made in many of their analyses.

Sequencing was the most commonly referenced temporal category and occurred at a much earlier age than predicted by Piaget, with linear increases between the ages of 4 and 10 years. As predicted, children made fewer references to backward sequences ("before dinner, I watched TV") than to forward sequences ("after watching TV, I ate dinner") overall, regardless of age. Even after controlling for the total number of details and the number of temporal requests, there were large increases with age in the overall number of references to temporal sequences. This was especially compelling when analyses focused on spontaneous production.

The expected increased use of "temporal location" (representing the time of an event on conventional time scales) around the age of 10 years was not found, however. This was surprising because, in order to associate experienced events with temporal locations, children must be able to represent conventional time patterns and to locate events on long conventional time scales, abilities which are typically acquired between 8 and 9 years of age (Friedman, 1991, 1992). Familiarity with the context in which their memories were embedded (i.e., familiar daily activities) may have enhanced the children's ability to reference nonspecific temporal locations with which even preschoolers are familiar. The simple increase with age that was noted may have reflected the children's ability to link events or event components to short-scale conventional time patterns, like the time of the day or the day of the week (i.e., "non-specific temporal locations"), rather than to long-scale conventional time patterns, like months of the year or calendar dates (i.e., "specific temporal locations").

Overall, the children in this study, like adults, remembered the times of past events by reconstructing their locations relative to time patterns. Adults, however, are capable of using both short- and long-scale time patterns, whereas children mostly referenced short-scale time patterns or anchored their memories to familiar daily activities.

The children studied by Orbach and Lamb (2007) produced a substantial amount of temporal information spontaneously. Of the total number of references to temporal attributes, over 50% were provided spontaneously, i.e., not in response to interviewer requests for temporal information. Moreover, close to 30% of the total number of temporal references were provided by children in response to free-recall prompts and 46% in response to cued-recall prompts, summing to a compelling 74% from "recall" memory. Nearly 72% of the children's spontaneous temporal references involved temporal sequencing, perhaps because the eyewitness accounts examined in the present study involve children's event memories provided in the form of narrative responses to the open-ended invitations emphasized in the Protocol.

Beyond the information they impart, the references to sequence have forensic value because they help structure the investigated events, enabling eyewitnesses to reconstruct their past experiences, report event components in chronological order, and elaborate on what happened prior to a disclosed event component, or if prompted, refer to causally-related event components. By showing that free-recall prompts elicit a large amount of temporal information from children, the study showed that forensic investigators need not rely on the more risky (potentially contaminating) yes/no and forced-choice questions to obtain this information.

Orbach and Lamb (2007) showed that children are capable of providing important temporal information about their experiences. Lamb, Sternberg, Orbach, Esplin et al. (2003) previously showed how the extent to which they may do so rapidly increases during childhood. In their analysis of young children's descriptions of alleged abuse, they demonstrated that children typically included important forensic information about the location and content of events, but information about timing was less commonly provided and was more likely to be given by older children. Preschoolers were considerably less informative with respect to timing than the 7- and 8-year-olds were.

All children responded informatively when asked whether the abuse happened "one time or more than one time." In contrast, children's inclusion of specific temporal location of events was much more infrequent, at least for the preschool children: Rates for 4-, 5-, and 6-year-olds ranged from 50–59%, whereas 83% and 85%, respectively, of the 7- and 8-year-olds indicated when at least one of the incidents took place, either by reference to the calendar (e.g., "last Tuesday") or to a discrete event ("the last time I slept over there"). Similar developmenal changes in young children's ability to provide temporally specific information about repeated events have been shown in laboratory studies (Roberts et al., 2015).

CONCLUSION

It is clear that children as young as 3 years of age can respond to open-ended questions, and that the NICHD Protocol can be used successfully when interviewing these very young children. Regardless of age, it is possible for children to provide a significant proportion of all the information they yield in response to open-ended prompts. It is also clear that there are important differences between interviews with very young and older children, however. Most importantly, the youngest children give very brief responses and need more prompting in order to increase the amounts of information they provide. Cued invitations and directive ("wh-") prompts appear to be a particularly useful technique for helping very young children recall information while avoiding the risks of contamination associated with the use of focused option-posing and suggestive questions. Although young children make many fewer temporal references than older children do, their references to the sequence of event components make it easier to understand the structure of those events, even when the information is provided in a disorganized way.

8

Interviewing Children with Developmental Disabilities

The previous chapter focused on the capacities and limitations of very young witnesses, and how the efficacy of questioning strategies may differ when interviewing very young, as opposed to older children. In this chapter, we consider children who may be especially difficult to interview because they have learning, behavioral, social, or communicative difficulties that might affect how well they can recall and describe their experiences.

POTENTIAL SOURCES OF DIFFICULTY FOR CHILDREN WITH DEVELOPMENTAL DISABILITIES

Children with disabilities (CWDs) face a range of additional challenges relative to their typically developing (TD) peers (Henry, Bettenay, & Carney, 2011). Many developmental disorders are characterized by general or specific deficits in cognitive functioning and information processing that might limit children's ability to understand, attend to, encode, store, retrieve and report maltreatment. For example, slower information processing, poorer comprehension of events, and more specific deficits (particularly in working memory and executive control)

Tell Me What Happened: Questioning Children About Abuse, Second Edition.
Michael E. Lamb, Deirdre A. Brown, Irit Hershkowitz, Yael Orbach, and Phillip W. Esplin.
© 2018 John Wiley & Sons Ltd. Published 2018 by John Wiley & Sons Ltd.

may reduce the amount of information about experiences which is encoded (Henry, 2001; Milne & Bull, 1999; Swanson, 1990; Swanson & Trahan, 1990; Vicari, 2004). Delayed language development (Field, Allen, & Lewis, 2015; Pinborough-Zimmerman et al., 2007) or specific language deficits may make it more difficult for children to understand and respond to questions (Ericson, Perlman, & Isaacs, 1994; Kebbell, Hatton, Johnson, & O'Kelly, 2001).

Additionally, children with developmental disorders may also face social challenges, shaped both by the characteristics of their disorder and their specific social experiences, when interacting with others. For example, parents of children with intellectual disabilities may be less likely to interact with their children in ways that facilitate the development of narrative and autobiographical memory skills (Hatton, 1998). Social demands during the interview or court testimony may make these children more susceptible to suggestive techniques (Sigelman, Budd, Spanhel, & Schoenrock, 1981). Children with developmental disabilities may also struggle to understand the interview context, the implications of the interview, and the expectations held of them. They are often more reliant on others for care than TD children, and their limited knowledge about and understanding of inappropriate behaviors (e.g., sexual interactions) may reduce their ability to recognize others' actions as abusive. Children with disabilities may also be marginalized because others perceive them to be incapable, and this could undermine responses to any disclosure.

It is important to examine the broad array of challenges faced by children with disabilities when engaging in and contributing to forensic interviews because these children are disproportionately likely to be maltreated. Many studies have documented increased rates of abuse in this population (Wissink, Van Vugt, Moonen, Stams, & Hendricks, 2015), with rates as high as 3.4 times that of TD children in some contexts (Sullivan & Knutson, 2000). Eleven percent of the suspected victims in Israel interviewed between 1998 and 2004 were described as having minor disabilities and 1.2% reportedly had severe disabilities (Hershkowitz, Lamb, & Horowitz, 2007). Hershkowitz et al. found that CWDs of all ages tended to be over-represented among suspected victims of sexual abuse and under-represented (especially when the older children were concerned) among victims of physical abuse.

Alleged victims with disabilities also reported more severe forms of sexual abuse than TD children. Specifically, they were more likely to report being repeatedly victimized, victims of more intrusive abuse, and victims of more incidents involving the use of threats and force than were TD children. These findings suggest that CWDs may be used as "safe targets" for sexual abuse because they are less able to avoid or report victimization (Williams, 1995). On most dimensions, in addition, higher levels of disability were associated with increased risks of sexual abuse. Whereas the risks for children with minor disabilities were higher than for TD children, the risks for children with severe disabilities were even higher with respect to the number of incidents reportedly experienced, the severity of the reported sexual acts, the use of force, and the tendency for physical injuries to be inflicted during the abusive incidents.

Compared to TD suspected victims, alleged victims with disabilities disclosed abuse less frequently and delayed disclosure more often (Hershkowitz et al., 2007). Again, children with severe disabilities failed to disclose abuse more frequently and tended to delay disclosure even more often than peers with minor disabilities. Of course, the increased failure to disclose abuse when interviewed may increase the likelihood that CWDs will continue to be abused.

The alleged perpetrators of abuse against CWDs were more likely to be parents or parental figures than were perpetrators of abuse against TD children (Hershkowitz et al., 2007). As discussed in Chapter 9, suspected victims tend to conceal abuse perpetrated by their parents much more often than they conceal abuse by other perpetrators (Hershkowitz et al., 2005; London et al., 2005). Thus, CWDs may delay or avoid disclosing abuse because they are more likely to be dependent psychologically and physically on their abusers. The children with severe disabilities may be especially vulnerable to abuse by their parents; they were suspected of being victimized by their parents almost three times more often than were TD children in Hershkowitz et al.'s (2005) study.

In both Hershkowitz et al.'s (2007) and Kvam's (2000) study, disabled boys appeared to be at greater risk than disabled girls for both sexual and physical abuse, perhaps because boys are more likely than girls to have disabilities. This trend was stronger for children with minor disabilities than for children with severe disabilities, and for children aged 7 to 10 years rather than for older or younger children.

Unfortunately, people with disabilities face other difficulties even after their possible victimization comes to light. Police officers often feel they have insufficient skills, resources, and support when interviewing witnesses with intellectual disabilities, perceiving them as difficult interviewees as a result of behavioral difficulties and cognitive, communicative, and attentional limitations (Aarons & Powell, 2002; Aarons, Powell, & Browne, 2004; Milne, 1999; Sharp, 2001). Relatively few cases involving intellectually disabled children are taken to court (Green, 2001; Gudjonsson, Murphy, & Clare, 2000; Williams, 1995), and few researchers have examined the way legal systems respond to possible victims of crime who are intellectually or communicatively handicapped (Agnew & Powell, 2004; Milne, 1999). Even when cases involving children with developmental or intellectual disabilities (CWID) reach court, procedures and attitudes undermine their ability by seldom acknowledging or accommodating witnesses' intellectual difficulties (Cederborg & Lamb, 2006; Kebbell, Hatton, & Johnson, 2004; O'Kelly, Kebbell, Hatton, & Johnson, 2003a, 2003b). For example, although complex directive and suggestive questions abound, judges tend not to intervene to reduce the potentially harmful impact of such questions on the witnesses' reliability and credibility (Kebbell, Hatton, Johnson, & O'Kelly, 2001).

Cederborg and Lamb (2006) undertook an inductive, qualitative study of 39 Swedish court files, focusing on the ways in which the children's handicaps and their presumed consequences were described and taken into account when the courts were evaluating the children's credibility.

They reported three broad reasons for concerns about the appropriateness of the courts' reactions to these alleged victims. First, in more than half of the cases, the judges argued that credible accounts by CWIDs should have the same clear characteristics as credible accounts by alleged victims who did not have learning disabilities or handicaps. Second, unfortunately, courts seldom (about half the time) received expert guidance that might help them better understand the characteristics of specific witnesses with handicaps. Third, miscommunication between courts and potential sources of expert information about the types of information that would be most helpful diminished the value of the expert testimonies they *were* given. As a result, the courts often made decisions largely in ignorance of the capabilities, behavior, and limitations of vulnerable witnesses.

Despite the considerable obstacles, children with developmental disorders increasingly *do* participate in forensic interviews and court trials in a number of countries (e.g., Cederborg & Lamb, 2008; Cederborg, La Rooy, & Lamb, 2008; Cederborg, Danielsson, LaRooy, & Lamb, 2009; Hanna et al., 2010). Their growing participation may reflect increasing awareness of the prevalence of abuse against children with developmental disabilities, increasing advocacy on their behalf (Collins, Harker, & Antonopolous, 2016); Hepner, Woodward, & Stewart, 2016; Plotnikoff & Woolfson, 2016), and the development of resources to guide professionals interacting with them in this context (e.g., http://www.theadvocatesgateway.org/).

In the following sections, we review the research on how children with developmental or intellectual disabilities (CWID) remember and report their experiences, the impact of different interviewing strategies on their recall, and studies examining the perceived credibility of these children. Relative to TD children, those with disabilities have received scant attention in eyewitness testimony research. Only a handful of studies have examined various aspects of testimony and engagement with legal processes, and when specific disorders are considered, the numbers of studies conducted have been even smaller. Compounding this problem, there is great variability in the cognitive, behavioral, social, emotional, and adaptive function profiles of children with different disorders, meaning that it can be hard to synthesize the findings from the various studies and generalize the conclusions.

The largest body of research has examined the competencies and vulnerabilities of children with intellectual disabilities, so we focus our review primarily on this work, but also describe research focusing specifically on children with other disorders (e.g., Attention Deficit Hyperactivity Disorder, Autism Spectrum Disorder).

RESEARCH ON CWID

Relevant studies examining CWID have almost exclusively been conducted in laboratory analogue contexts, with variations in important aspects of the study methodologies.

Sample. Many of the studies have included children from within a relatively limited age range (typically middle-late childhood). Researchers have used different comparison groups when assessing the relative performance of the CWID: In some studies, researchers have used a group of TD children matched to the chronological ages of the CWID (CA-matches). In such cases, 10-year-old CWIDs would be matched with 10-year-old TD children. In some other studies, researchers have estimated the comparable level of intellectual functioning in children without disabilities to permit mental-age matches (MA-match). In such cases, 10-year-old CWIDs whose intellectual functioning was that of five-year-olds would be matched with TD 5-year-olds. Some researchers have included both CA and MA-matches and many have excluded CWIDs arising from known syndromes (e.g., Down's Syndrome, ASD) to increase the homogeneity of the CWID group and to reduce the impact of specific cognitive or behavioral difficulties associated with other disorders. Some studies have included groups of CWID who have different levels of cognitive and functional impairment (e.g., severe or moderate).

The events under investigation. The events that children have been asked to recall include brief video clips, witnessed interactions, and personally experienced events (including, in field studies, children's reports of alleged maltreatment). Delays since the event occurred have also varied, from immediate recall opportunities to delays of up to 6 months.

The aspect of eyewitness testimony measured. Some studies have exclusively focused on children's suggestibility—either by tracking the integration of misinformation provided after an experience, or by examining responses to leading and misleading questions. Other studies have examined CWID's capacities when they are interviewed in a neutral or supportive manner. Researchers have focused on the quantity of information reported, the accuracy of that information, and/or the coherence of children's narratives about the target events.

Questioning strategy. Some studies have examined CWID's responses to suggestive questions and to questioning strategies that vary with respect to question openness and the types of memory processes (e.g., recall vs recognition) involved. Some studies involve restricted interviewing protocols that become progressively more focused throughout the interview, whereas some have used the NICHD Protocol.

How Well Can CWIDs Recall Events?

Despite widespread perceptions that CWID make less able witnesses, the findings obtained in earlier studies not using the NICHD Protocol are inconsistent and vary depending on question type and the type of competency assessed (e.g., amount of recall vs. suggestibility vs. accuracy). When information is elicited using open questions or during free recall, for example, CWID often provide as much information as TD children —both chronological age- (CA-) matched (Dent, 1986, 1992; Henry & Gudjonsson, 1999, 2003; Agnew & Powell, 2004) and mental age- (MA-) matched (Agnew & Powell, 2004; Gordon, Jens, Hollings, & Watson, 1994; Henry & Gudjonsson, 1999; Jens, Gordon, & Shaddock, 1990; Michel, Gordon, Ornstein, & Simpson, 2000), but in some circumstances provide less information than CA-matched children (Henry & Gudjonsson, 2004, 2007; Michel et al., 2000) or more information than MA-matched children (Henry & Gudjonsson, 2003)! When asked closed or specific questions, CWID provide as much information as MA-matches (Henry & Gudjonsson, 1999; Jens et el., 1990, but see Gordon et al, 1994) and less than CA-matches (Dent, 1986, 1992; Henry & Gudjonsson, 2003, 2004, 2007).

Findings concerning suggestibility are similarly inconsistent, with some studies revealing no differences between CWID and CA- or MA-matched children (Henry & Gudjonsson, 1999, 2004; Jens et al., 1990, Robinson & McGuire, 2006) and others showing heightened suggestibility relative to CA-matches (Henry & Gudjonsson, 1999, 2007; Gudjonsson & Henry, 2003; Michel et al., 2000; Young, Powell, & Dudgeon, 2003).

Almost without exception, however, researchers have shown no differences in the overall accuracy of the accounts provided by CWID and TD children responding to open questions (Agnew & Powell, 2004; Henry & Gudjonsson, 2003). As with TD children, the amount and quality of information elicited from CWID is affected by the way in which they are interviewed (Brown & Lamb, 2015).

The above studies varied with respect to the severity of children's intellectual disability. In the main, children with mild levels of cognitive impairment tended to perform like TD counterparts at the same developmental level (Henry, Bettenay, & Carney, 2011). This is consistent with a developmental delay perspective on intellectual disability (Zigler, 1969; Zigler & Balla, 1982), which proposes that the processes of developmental progression are similar in CWID and TD children, although the rates and end points differ. On some indices, CWID may even be equivalent to TD children of the same age meaning that, at least in some aspects of cognitive functioning, CWID are indistinguishable from TD children (Burack & Zigler, 1990).

The picture was somewhat different for children with more severe levels of cognitive impairment, however. Consistent with a difference model of intellectual disability (Ellis, 1969; Milgram, 1973), these children tend to perform more poorly on most indices of eyewitness competency than TD children matched for developmental level (Brown et al., 2012, 2015; Henry & Gudjonsson, 2003). The difference model proposes that intellectual disability (ID) is characterized by more than simple disparities in developmental rates and end points and that cognitive development is qualitatively different in CWID, with cumulatively increasing deficits relative to TD children.

The NICHD Protocol and CWID

Brown and colleagues (2012, 2015) examined CWID's recall about a staged event, when interviewed first with the NICHD Protocol, and then with a series of suggestive questions (leading and misleading, that were either open-ended or closed). They included two groups of CWID—one with mild levels of cognitive impairment (M (estimated IQ score) = 67; called CWID-Mild), and one with moderate levels of impairment (M (estimated IQ score) = 48; called CWID-Moderate). Two groups of comparison children were included—one group was matched to the two ID groups on the basis of chronological age (CA-matches), whereas the other was matched on the basis of mental-age (MA-matches). Children in the ID and CA-matched groups were 7 to 12 years old, with a mean age of 9 years, while children in the MA-matched group were 4 to 9 years old (mean age of 6 years).

In total, 206 children took part in a 45-minute staged event at school (an interactive lesson about health and safety). Children were interviewed twice (1 week and again 6 months after the event), or after 6 months only. This allowed for comparisons of recall across short and long delays (first interview at 1 week compared to first interview at 6 months, Brown et al., 2012) and for examining the effect of an early interview on later recall (first interview at 6 months compared to second interview at 6 months, Brown et al., 2015), as well as the consistency of information reported across repeated interviews (comparisons of what was reported in their first and second interviews by children interviewed twice, Brown et al., 2015). In all of the analyses, various aspects of testimony were examined: the amount of detail children reported, the effectiveness of different kinds of prompts, the accuracy of children's reports, and their responses to the scripted suggestive questions.

A strikingly consistent pattern emerged in many of the analyses: CA-matched children outperformed the CWID-Mild and MA-matches (who did not differ from each other) who, in turn, outperformed the CWID-Moderate. This was the case for the number of details reported and accuracy when responding to suggestive questions in early and delayed interviews, and in a comparison between the yields of single and repeated interviews. The same pattern was also observed when examining levels of accuracy in early and delayed interviews. When considering all children interviewed at 6 months (those interviewed for the first time and those who had a previous interview) the pattern was slightly different; CWID-Mild were as accurate as the CA-matches, CWID-Moderate were as accurate as the MA-matches, and children in both of the latter groups were less accurate than the CA-matched children.

During early interviews, CWID-Moderate reported proportionally less information in response to cued invitations than TD children. Children in both of the CWID groups reported proportionately more in response to direct and option-posing questions than the TD children. When children were interviewed 6 months after the event, children in the ID groups gave similar proportions of their accounts in response to invitations as children in the MA-matched group; all provided less than children in the CA-matched group. CA-matched children provided proportionally more information in response to cued invitations than children in the CWID-Mild and MA-matched groups (who did not differ), who, in turn reported more than children in the CWID-Moderate group. There were no group differences in how much of the children's accounts were elicited using direct prompts. Children in the CWID-Moderate group gave more information in response to option-posing prompts that those in the CA-matched group.

Children's accuracy in response to different types of prompts declined as specificity and interviewer input increased, regardless of ID or age. Children in the CWID-Mild group and the two TD groups were more likely to report repeated than new details in a second interview nearly 6 months later, whereas the amounts of new and repeated details reported did not differ for children in the CWID-Moderate group. For all children, repeated details were more accurate than those reported for the first time in the second interview.

Dion and Cyr (2008) also examined recall by children with low verbal abilities (as measured by performance on a standardized vocabulary test) interviewed about child sexual abuse. Thirty-four children were interviewed, half using the NICHD Protocol. About 30% of the children in each interview group had low verbal abilities (children's performance was below average although not at a clinically impaired level). As in other studies, more details were reported by Protocol-interviewed children than by those in the comparison group, regardless of verbal ability. Children with low verbal abilities reported fewer details than those with average abilities: Interestingly, children with low verbal abilities interviewed using the Protocol reported as many details as those of average ability interviewed without using the Protocol. Thus a developmentally sensitive interviewing approach appeared to mitigate the adverse effects of low verbal ability on children's informativeness.

Coherence

A disproportionate amount of the research on children's eyewitness testimony has focused on the number and accuracy of details provided, with little examination of the way in which children communicate about their experiences. For testimony to make meaningful forensic contributions, listeners (including investigators and jury members) must be able to understand the narratives that the children construct. The coherence of children's testimony can influence whether their complaints are pursued in court, and how credible they appear (Davis, Hoyano, Keenan, Maitland, & Morgan, 1999; Henry, Ridley, Perry, & Crane, 2011; Pipe, Orbach, Lamb, Abbott, & Stewart, 2013). If jurors and judges are unable to make sense of children's accounts for any reason (i.e., ambiguities, lack of structure or organization, incoherence) the credibility and impact of their evidence may be diminished (Davis et al., 1999; Westcott & Kynan, 2004).

Two studies examining the narrative quality of CWID have shown that their narratives were poorer than those of TD children. Murfett, Powell, and Snow (2008) found that CWID (9 to 12 years old) omitted more story-telling components than did TD children (both mental-age and chronological-age matches) when describing witnessed interactions in response to open-ended prompting. As a result, the clarity and comprehensibility of their accounts was reduced. Similarly, Gentle, Milne, Powell, and Sharman (2013) found that, compared to TD children matched for chronological age, CWID (7- to 10-year-olds) provided fewer story grammar details, contextual details, temporal markers, and logically ordered accounts of discrete episodes observed in a brief video clip a day earlier. All children reported more contextual details, logically ordered sequences, and temporal markers when interviewed using the Cognitive Interview (although there was no effect on inclusion of story grammar elements), suggesting that a supportive interview process may mitigate the difficulties that children have when constructing their accounts.

Brown, Brown, Lewis, and Lamb (2017) examined the narrative quality of the accounts CWID and TD children provided about personally experienced events when they were interviewed using the NICHD Protocol. Markers of narrative coherence were, in the main, frequently included in the children's reports, regardless of group membership. Children in the CWID-Moderate group produced fewer story grammar elements than children in the CWID-Mild, CA- and MA-matched groups, and their accounts included significantly fewer markers of chronology, content, and context. In contrast, children in the CWID-Mild group were equivalent to those in both of the TD groups on all indices of narrative quality.

These findings paint a more positive picture than those reported by Gentle et al. (2013) and Murfett et al. (2008), perhaps reflecting methodological differences between the studies. Whereas Murfett et al. limited the extent to which children were prompted, the NICHD Protocol used by Brown et al. (2017) imposed no such constraints, allowing children to continue responding to such prompts until their recall was exhausted. Gentle et al. (2013) reported that all children interviewed with the CI included more story grammar components than those interviewed using a more constrained structured interview, adding further weight to this argument.

Questioning Strategies
Very few researchers have examined how forensic interviews with CWIDs are conducted. Agnew, Powell, and Snow (2006) compared police officers' and caregivers' interviews with CWIDs about a series of staged activities that had occurred at school. Although police officers used more open questions (e.g., "tell me everything about that") than caregivers, both groups asked many directive (e.g., "wh-") and focused recognition questions. Officers tended to interrupt children's narrative responses by asking specific questions to clarify these responses, showing poor insight

regarding the appropriateness of their techniques and failing to subsequently return to open-ended questioning.

Cederborg and colleagues (Cederborg & Lamb 2008; Cederborg, La Rooy, & Lamb, 2008, Cederborg, Danielsson, La Rooy, & Lamb, 2009; Cederborg, Hultman, & La Rooy, 2012) studied transcripts of forensic interviews in Sweden with alleged abuse victims who had developmental disabilities. The police officers used very few free-recall prompts and the interviews largely comprised directive and option-posing questions. Despite eliciting meaningful information with very broad open-ended prompts, interviewers frequently asked children to elaborate by asking more focused (e.g., "wh-," yes/no, or option-posing) questions, which often led the children to provide inconsistent or contradictory information. When children with intellectual disabilities were given a second chance to provide information about their abuse, however, they further elaborated on the information that they had reported and sometimes provided entirely new information about their experiences (Cederborg et al., 2008).

Brown, Lewis, and Lamb (2017) examined whether interviewers following the NICHD Protocol questioned CWID and TD children about a staged event differently. They examined the transcripts from the study described above, focusing on the interviews conducted 1 week after the staged event, and compared the proportions of different prompt types that comprised the interviews. Even when controlling for the amount of information that the children provided, it was found that children in the ID and TD groups were questioned differently. Interviewers asked more questions overall, more directive questions, and fewer cued invitations of the younger TD participants (MA-matches) and children in both CWID groups than of children in the CA-matched group. Option-posing questions comprised a larger proportion of the interviews with children in both ID groups than with children in the CA-matched group. The few suggestive questions were addressed mostly to children in the CWID-Moderate group, and the children in this group were also asked fewer questions overall than the children in the other groups.

Interviewing strategies were thus influenced by developmental level more than ID status or the children's individual contributions to the interview, thereby highlighting the need to take into account the dynamic nature of exchanges between children and interviewers when evaluating how interviews are conducted.

When questioning CWIDs (at least those whose impairment falls within the mild range), interviewers appear less likely to create optimal recall conditions than when interviewing TD children. Knowledge of disability status may increase the use of less desirable interviewing strategies (e.g., focused and closed questions), perhaps because interviewers assume that CWID require more structure (Aarons & Powell, 2002; Aarons et al., 2004; Ericson et al., 1994; Milne, 1999; Nathanson & Platt, 2005; Phillips, Oxburgh, & Myklebust, 2012; Sharp, 2001). Alternatively, the differences in questioning may reflect differences in the quality of CWID's responses: These children may simply provide sparser responses, suggesting the need for more interviewer guidance and scaffolding, whereas the more intellectually advanced TD children probably provide richer initial accounts, yielding many opportunities for child-provided retrieval cues to be used. The similarities between the performance of children in CWID-Mild and MA-match groups on numerous dimensions, however, suggested that response differences are unlikely to fully account for interviewers' questioning strategies. Perhaps instead, as in Agnew et al.'s (2006) study, interviewers poorly monitor how successfully they are eliciting information from CWID and MA-matched children using open-ended prompts and so adopt more focused interviewing styles as a result. More research is needed to examine whether the strategies that interviewers adopt as interviews unfold reflects children's responses to previous prompts (e.g., Wolfman, Brown, & Jose, 2016b). The research to date suggests that CWID are handicapped, not only by their communicative and cognitive limitations, but also by interviewing approaches that diminish the coherence of their accounts.

NICHD PROTOCOL INVESTIGATIONS OF ADOLESCENTS AND ADULTS WITH ID

A recent study in Israel examined investigative interviews with individuals with mild and moderate ID, and observed both the types of prompts addressed to them and the nature of their responses (Hershkowitz, 2018). The sample comprised 200 alleged victims of sexual and physical abuse, in 4 equal-sized and matched groups: individuals with mild ID and their mental-age (MA) matches, and individuals with moderate ID and their MA-matches. All alleged victims were interviewed by trained investigators following the NICHD Protocol.

Individuals with ID were asked a substantial number of prompts (about 150 prompts on average), with recall prompts (open-ended and directive) predominating. They responded to almost all prompts, providing substantive responses to over two-thirds of the prompts and new details in response to one-third of the prompts, meaning that they tended to respond at lower levels than their TD counterparts. Performance varied depending on the severity of ID, with witnesses in the mild ID group outperforming those in the moderate ID group on all measures. Individuals with ID generally reported fewer details, although all but those in the moderate ID group produced more details in response to recall than to recognition prompts, either because these more disabled witnesses needed more cognitive structuring and focus or because their cognitive functioning was qualitatively different.

Like the other studies described earlier, Hershkowitz's findings challenge the notion that individuals with ID cannot provide forensically useful information or act as witnesses. The data suggest that adolescents and adults with IDs possess the basic communicative and memorial capabilities necessary for providing testimony about their experiences. Awareness of their weakness and strengths is likely to promote informed and effective interviewing, which may yield valuable forensic evidence.

Down Syndrome

Only one study has examined eyewitness testimony in people with Down Syndrome (Collins & Henry, 2016). Down Syndrome is a common genetic disorder, with ID one of its core characteristics. People with Down Syndrome frequently manifest challenging behavior and have unusual and limited language and social skills, all of which may make them vulnerable to abuse, while affecting their ability to recount their experiences.

After showing a short video clip of a petty crime, Collins and Henry compared immediate recall by young adults with Down Syndrome (mean age of 19 years) and TD children of the same mental age (mean age of 6 years). Participants were questioned about the video using open-ended free recall and cued recall prompts, followed by a series of leading and misleading questions, including tag questions, e.g., "The car didn't break down, did it?" (leading); "There was no dog in the car, was there?" (when there was a dog; misleading).

The young adults with Down Syndrome and the MA-matched TD children performed equivalently on all aspects of recall; there were no differences in the amount or accuracy of their responses, or in their levels of suggestibility when responding to the leading and misleading prompts.

Autism Spectrum Disorder

Autism Spectrum Disorder (ASD) is a developmental disorder than includes difficulties in social, language, and behavioral domains. Comorbid difficulties, especially ID, are common. Many people with ASD have a number of memory features that might affect their eyewitness ability, including over-general memory, and deficits in facial recognition, organization of information in memory, source monitoring, and memory for emotional and social features of events (see Maras & Bowler, 2014, for a review).

Studies of autobiographical memory and eyewitness testimony in people with ASD are relatively scarce, and have primarily focused on adults. Evidence from these studies suggests that adults with ASD have impoverished autobiographical memories, typically recalling fewer life events and in sparser detail than adults in TD comparison groups (Chaput et al., 2013; Tanweer et al., 2010). Their accounts often lack indicators of personal involvement and information relating to other people (e.g., names, appearance, reactions). Maras and Bowler (2010, 2012) showed that adults with ASD were more likely to report inaccurate details, especially when describing personal and action-related details, but were able to provide as many details as TD adults.

McCrory, Henry, and Happé (2007) showed that older children and young adolescents with ASD provided fewer free-recall details about staged activities, especially about social features, although their levels of accuracy and suggestibility did not differ from those of TD peers. Bruck et al. (2007) demonstrated that 5- to 10-year-old children with ASD reported fewer details and were less accurate (relative to parents' accounts) than TD children when recalling personal events from their past. They also reported fewer correct details and were more suggestible when recalling staged events. Although they provided less information, children with ASD were as accurate as TD children during free recall, but their accuracy decreased when more specific questions were used.

In two studies, Mattison, Dando, and Ormerod (2015) compared recall of a brief video clip by young adolescents with ASD and TD children matched for mental age. One hour after viewing the video, the young people were interviewed verbally, with mental context reinstatement instructions, or with a sketch-reinstatement of context procedure (participants were instructed to draw as much as they could recall of the video and talk about it while doing so). TD children recalled more correct details than those with ASD and were more accurate, although there were no group differences in the amount of inaccurate information reported. When the young people with ASD were interviewed in the sketch-reinstatement-of-context procedure, they were as accurate as the TD children interviewed in the same way. Similar benefits of the sketch-reinstatement procedure have been shown with adults (Maras, Mulcahy, Memon, Picariello, & Bowler, 2014).

Clearly, although children and young people with ASD have many difficulties recalling and describing their experiences, they are capable of providing meaningful and reliable information. They may omit important contextual and social details from their accounts, which may mean that interviewers need to prompt them for it. One might thus expect that the NICHD Protocol might be very useful when interviewing children (and perhaps adults) with ASD.

In a recent study, Almeida, Lamb, and Weissblat (under review) interviewed 27 6- to 15-year-olds with high-functioning ASD diagnoses about an extended psychological assessment (the ADOS-2) and compared their performance with that of 32 TD peers of the same chronological age. Children in both groups were interviewed about the 40- to 60-minute assessment on two occasions—two weeks and two months after the event—using an adaptation of the NICHD Revised Protocol.

Almeida and her colleagues found that, overall, children with ASD recalled just as many correct details about the experienced event as TD peers and were no more prone to making errors or confabulations. As anticipated, children with ASD recalled fewer details about the experienced event than TD children in response to invitations. But, contrary to predictions, invitations elicited just as many details per prompt from children with ASD as directive prompts. Similarly, the information recalled by children with ASD in response to open-ended invitations was just as accurate as that recalled in response to more specific (directive) questions. Children with ASD were indistinguishable from TD peers with respect to the accuracy of their recall in response to directive questions, but also in response to open-ended invitations. The absence of group differences may imply that children with high-functioning ASD do not necessarily require more specific prompts than TD children to provide meaningful and reliable accounts of experienced events.

Cued invitations, which are a distinctive feature of the NICHD Protocol, were particularly effective when interviewing children with high-functioning autism about their experiences. Although children with ASD recalled fewer details than TD peers in response to cued invitations, the information elicited using such prompts comprised core and highly accurate details about their experiences, even when a substantial amount of time had elapsed between the event and the interview (91% accurate in the 2-week interview and 87% in the 2-month interview). Moreover, when prompted using cued invitations, children with ASD recalled more (and more accurate) information than when prompted using any other type of prompt. It has been argued that more supportive retrieval techniques may aid witnesses with ASD recall more information, because their recall impairments are more related to retrieval than to encoding mechanisms (Maras & Bowler, 2012). Almeida et al.'s findings supported the notion that cued invitations constitute effective ways of triggering the recall of information and enhancing the capacity of children with ASD to elaborate upon their narrative accounts, by structuring recall of experienced events, breaking them into smaller units, and associating them with pre-disclosed actions.

There was no evidence that children with ASD were more likely to confabulate details than TD peers. However, although children reported few confabulated details overall, these were more frequently included in children's responses to recall-based prompts (invitations, cued invitations, and directive prompts). Thus, all those involved in the criminal justice system should be aware that the use of such prompts might elicit extremely valuable information about an event, but might also lead children to include a small amount of incorrect information in their detailed responses.

All types of prompts elicited forensically relevant and accurate information from children, and overall accuracy remained high even when the interviewer used prompts associated with higher error rates, such as option-posing prompts. As predicted, when questioned using prompts tapping recognition memory, children with ASD provided less erroneous information than non-ASD peers, although children in both groups provided more erroneous information when the interviewers used closed (option-posing) prompts, and these were the least productive prompts. Overall accuracy remained high when interviewers asked suggestive questions, with TD children more likely to acquiesce to the suggested input than children with ASD. After a 2-month delay, the accounts provided by children with ASD were less accurate in response to suggestive prompts than after a 2-week delay, but they were no less accurate than those provided by TD children. However, the suggestive questions asked by Almeida et al. did not include highly detrimental questions such as confrontational (e.g., "You are lying, aren't you?"), or tag questions (e.g., "She told you to assemble a puzzle, didn't she?"), which, if used, might have had a more damaging effect on accuracy.

Almeida et al.'s study was the first to explore how well children with ASD could recall a personally experienced event an extended period of time later; it showed that children with and without ASD were similarly affected by delay. As predicted, overall recall was more complete and more accurate, with fewer errors and fewer confabulations, when a shorter amount of time had passed between the event and the interview. The absence of group differences in performance after a lengthier delay suggests that, as with TD children, the most accurate accounts of core information are likely to be obtained soon after an event and, thus, that it is essential to interview children, including those with ASD, as soon as possible.

Children with ASD recalled just as much information about the event as TD children of the same age after a 2-month delay, and were as prone to respond to the interviewers' prompts. Further, as with the TD children, the accuracy of the information recalled about the experienced event did not decrease appreciably with the passage of time: The information reported by children with ASD was 87% accurate after a 2-week delay and 85% accurate after a 2-month delay. Children with ASD and TD children reported similar amounts of repeated and new information after 2 months, and the repeated information was more accurate than the newly reported information for both groups of children. These important findings suggest that children with ASD can be valuable and reliable witnesses even when a substantial amount of time has passed between an event and the interview, and provide a compelling argument for investigators and courts to take their evidence seriously.

Of course, it is possible that the previous supportive interviews played an important role. As noted earlier, Brown et al. (2015) found that children were more informative, more accurate, and less suggestible 6 months after the event when they had been interviewed earlier using the NICHD Protocol than when the first interview took place 6 months after the event. Thus the early interview and the not-too-long delay between interviews in this study may have helped children to consolidate and preserve their memories. Additionally, their previous exposure to the interview setting may have positively contributed to the development of a trusting relationship with the interviewer, making children with ASD feel less anxious and thus more comfortable, which in turn may have promoted further disclosure of relevant information (as with TD children: Carnes, Nelson-Gardell, Wilson, & Orgassa, 2001; Carnes, Wilson, & Nelson-Gardell, 1999; La Rooy, Katz, Malloy, & Lamb, 2010). For all children, the delayed interview yielded a lot (39% of the total) of novel accurate information about the experienced event.

It is possible the narrative practice during the pre-substantive phase and references to the children's own statements to cue further recall may overcome some of the metalinguistic and retrieval difficulties experienced by children with this diagnosis much like the sketch-reinstatement-of-context procedure (Mattison et al., 2015). We need much more research on children with ASD to complement the somewhat larger evidence base for adults with ASD. Investigators need to lean on a strong evidence base delineating the capacities and vulnerabilities of children with ASD and, importantly, how to provide effective interviewing support. However, the data currently available suggest that the NICHD Protocol is well suited for interviews of individuals with ASD.

Attention Deficit Hyperactivity Disorder

Children with Attention Deficit/Hyperactivity Disorder (ADHD) self-report higher levels of sexual abuse and neglect during childhood than do TD children (Ouyang et al., 2008) and are up to seven times more likely to report having been physically abused (Fuller-Thomson et al., 2014). The elevated hyperactivity, impulsivity, and inattention associated with ADHD may elicit high levels of family stress and conflict, and, especially when parents have similar symptoms, families may struggle to appropriately manage the children's behavior (Barkley, 2006; Johnston & Mash, 2001). Given the risk for maltreatment associated with ADHD and the relative prevalence of this disorder (5–7% of the US population; Polanczyk, Willcutt, Salum, Kieling, & Rhode, 2014) it is important to understand the abilities and vulnerabilities of these children when they recount their experiences.

Both the cognitive and behavioral profiles associated with ADHD may lead to differences in what children encode and subsequently recount (Flory et al., 2006). For example, poor attention and impulsivity may influence what children attend to during events they experience, with effects on the amount and type of information they are later able to report. Poor planning and limited working memory capacity may mean that children fail to plan their narratives and may struggle to keep track of what they have reported in interviews and what they have yet to disclose (Freer, Hayden, Lorch, & Milich, 2011; Nigg, 2006). This, combined with excessive talking (Green et al., 2014), may make the children's narratives disjointed and incomplete.

No published research has examined eyewitness testimony capacities in children with ADHD. Research looking at relevant abilities suggests that they may experience a variety of challenges when recalling and describing their experiences. For example, children (4 to 9 years old) with ADHD are just as able to comprehend stories and recall the main themes as TD peers but typically report fewer details and have difficulty sequencing events and creating coherent stories with logical connections (Lorch et al., 2010; Tannock, Purvis, & Schachar, 1993). A different picture emerges, however, when children are asked to recall personally experienced events—then, children with ADHD may actually show superior recall. Parents estimate that children with ADHD recall past experiences better than other family members (Skowronek, Leichtman, & Pillemer, 2008) and, when children's recall is examined quasi-experimentally, children (9 to 14 years of age) with ADHD provide significantly longer and more detailed narratives about special events (Skowronek et al., 2008). Evidence thus suggests that children with ADHD have difficulties with on-line monitoring and organization of their recall, but are just as able to pick out the main themes and important events.

Very few studies have looked at suggestibility in individuals with ADHD. Those that have focused on adults have found that ADHD participants typically do not differ from TD adults, but use significantly more "I don't know" responses (Gudjonsson, Sigurdsson, Bragason, Newton, & Einarsson, 2008; Gudjonsson, Young, & Bramham, 2007). Researchers have, however, examined the association between different aspects of executive function (which is often impaired in children with ADHD) and suggestibility. For example, cognitive control is associated with less yielding to suggestion in 3- to 7-year-olds (Alexander et al., 2002; Roberts & Powell, 2005).

Two studies have examined children with ADHD's recall when interviewed using the NICHD Protocol. McLay, Brown, Palmer, and Beaumont (2016) examined various aspects of eyewitness testimony in 7- to 11-year-old children who had either clinically significant ADHD symptoms (rated by parents and teachers) or average (or lower) levels of symptoms. Children took part in a health and safety event at their school and were interviewed 11 to 18 days later using the NICHD Protocol. Children's accounts were coded for the amount and accuracy of reported details, the coherence of their narratives, and their response to a series of leading and misleading suggestive questions.

No group differences were evident in the overall amount of information children reported, and there were no differences in the children's accuracy, coherence, or suggestibility. Some subtle differences were detected, however: Children with ADHD were more likely to include ambiguous statements in their accounts, which in a forensic setting might necessitate more questioning to clarify their reports, and they were more likely to give irrelevant responses to questions. These children were also less likely to include information about the social context (and in free recall were less likely to include information about outcomes or consequences).

Malloy, Mugno, Pelham, Hawk, and Lamb (2016) also demonstrated how competent children with ADHD can be when interviewed well: Children with clinical diagnoses of ADHD were indistinguishable from TD children when interviewed using the NICHD Protocol about a staged event that included an instance of wrongdoing by the experimenter. Clearly, more research is needed, but emerging evidence suggests that, when supported by a developmentally sensitive and child-led approach to interviewing, children with ADHD can engage well with the interview process and can recount their experiences as well as their TD peers.

Recommendations for Interviewing

Of course, different types of disabilities can influence children's abilities to describe their experiences in diverse ways, although informativeness is likely to vary greatly even when alleged victims have the same diagnosis. It is thus important to recognize the unique characteristics, competencies, and limitations of each child. Even children with poor memory capacity and/or impaired ability to cope with uncertainty or to understand the purposes of the interview are able to answer open-ended questions and give new details about their experiences, especially when directive questions are asked (Brown et al., 2012, 2015; Cederborg & Lamb, 2008b). On the other hand, interviewers also need to recognize that CWIDs indeed have some specific limitations. Children on the Autism Spectrum may, for example, have difficulty understanding the interviewers' perspective and may not understand why some questions are asked. Their abilities to follow and understand lengthy complicated questions may also be impaired. Early identification of developmentally delayed witnesses' abilities, capacities, and behavior may help interviewers understand how to adapt their behavior appropriately (Gordon et al., 1995; Jones, 2003; Milne, 1999; Poole & Lamb, 1998; Westcott, 1993), or work with an intermediary through the interview process (Plotnikoff & Woolfson, 2015). A useful set of evidence-based resources and guidelines for professionals working with adults and children with disabilities in legal settings is publicly available at www.theadvocatesgateway.org, and further recommendations have been outlined by Henry et al. (2011).

When interviewing both TD children and CWIDs, interviewers should start with open-ended questions because those maximize accurate recall even when intellectually impaired witnesses are involved (Brown et al., 2012, 2015; Kasari & Bauminger, 1998). When asked specific, closed questions, people with intellectual disabilities may respond less accurately (Brown et al., 2012, 2015; Henry & Gudjonsson, 2003; Kebbell et al., 2004). Because suggestive questions imply desirable responses, they should be avoided completely. Care should be taken to ensure that option-posing questions are used infrequently, framed neutrally and non-coercively (Brown et al., 2012, 2015; Kebbell et al., 2004; Michel et al., 2000), and followed by open-ended requests for further elaboration whenever possible. In addition to using more open questions, interviewers should take aim to use simple language and shorter sentences, focusing on just one idea or concept in each prompt. Providing lengthy pauses after questions may also allow children who process information more slowly longer to understand questions and formulate responses.

On occasion, it may also be helpful to re-interview children so that they can elaborate on the information that they have already provided, and provide details about topics that have not as yet been discussed. In light of a previous analogue study showing that children with both mild and moderate intellectual disabilities changed their answers in repeated interviews more often than their mental-age-matched peers did (Henry & Gudjonsson, 2003), it is interesting that the new and elaborated information provided by children in Cederborg et al.'s (2007) study did not contradict their previous statements. In fact, the overall number of between-interview contradictions was surprisingly low. However, because poor interviewing techniques predominated, and little was known about the participants' capacities, we cannot assume that the information provided in the repeated interviews was any more accurate than information provided in the first interviews. In Brown et al.'s (2015) study, children with mild levels of impairment provided more repeated than new information 6 months later, with the repeated information being more accurate than details reported for the first time in the later interview. Children with more severe impairment were equally likely to report repeated and new information, and this of course meant that their later accounts were less accurate.

Clearly, it is possible to help CWIDs provide coherent, detailed, and accurate narratives about their experiences, but interviewers need to know and understand the children's levels of functioning. The evidence to date suggests that, for children with intellectual disabilities that fall in the mild range, guidance for TD children of a similar developmental level should be useful. When children have more severe levels of impairment, expectations should be set below those for children of a similar developmental level. Nevertheless, regardless of the degree of impairment, all CWIDs can clearly respond informatively to interviewing techniques that enhance accuracy when given the opportunity. Overcoming prejudice and bias against these children in the judicial system is necessary to promote equity and justice (Cederborg & Gumpert, 2010).

PERCEPTIONS OF CREDIBILITY

Little is known about how children with various disabilities are perceived by juries. As described above, such children perform as well or better then TD children when responding to open questions so there seems to be no good reason to exclude these children from judicial and legal processes, provided developmentally sensitive communication strategies are employed.

Unfortunately, participation in the legal system reflects more than simple capability. At each stage of the investigative process, decisions are made, both formally and informally, that may influence whether or not cases that rely on the testimony of child witnesses with intellectual disabilities proceed. For example, parents, social workers, police officers, investigative interviewers, lawyers, and judges all make judgments about the capacity of child witnesses and their possible contributions to case outcomes, even if the cases never reach court.

Negative perceptions of the reliability and suggestibility of witnesses with intellectual disabilities are widely held by police officers (Aarons & Powell, 2002), and legal professionals (Nathanson & Platt, 2005), meaning that cases are less likely to be investigated thoroughly because successful outcomes (i.e., guilty verdicts) are deemed unlikely (Aarons, Powell, & Browne, 2004). Several studies have also demonstrated a negative juror bias in relation to both adults and children with intellectual disabilities (ID). Stobbs and Kebbell (2003) presented mock jurors with a written transcript that was described as based on an interview with 1) an adult from the general population, 2) an adult with mild ID or 3) an adult with mild ID in addition to expert evidence regarding his abilities. Jurors rated the witness with ID lower on credibility, competency, accuracy, and "good [as] a witness." Furthermore, they gave fewer "guilty" ratings to the perpetrator of the witnessed crime when the witness had an ID.

Peled, Iarocci, and Connolly (2004) then examined perceptions of child witnesses with ID. Mock jurors were asked questions about 1) the general credibility and eyewitness ability of children and adults, and 2) a particular witness's credibility (they were shown a written transcript). The witness was described as either 1) a 15-year-old with a mild ID (mental age of 10); or 2) a 10-year-old TD child. When responding to general questions about eyewitness ability, jurors rated the 15-year-old with an ID as less credible than both a TD 15-year-old and a TD 10-year-old. When evaluating the written transcripts, however, there were no differences between ratings of the CWID's and TD child's testimony. Peled et al. concluded that a general (negative) bias regarding the competency of witnesses with IDs may be ameliorated when jurors are presented with actual testimony.

Nathanson and Platt (2005) examined attorneys' perceptions of witnesses who were CWID and showed that CWID were perceived as less sincere, accurate, or able to make accurate face identifications, and more suggestible and inconsistent than TD children. Finally, Henry, Ridley, Perry, and Crane (2011) examined ratings of the credibility of

CWID's and TD children's recall of a brief video clip depicting a minor crime. Mock jurors were not informed of the cognitive ability of the child whose transcript they were evaluating, yet the transcribed statements by CWIDs were rated as less credible than those by TD children on a number of dimensions.

Recently, Brown and Lewis (2013) asked mock jurors to watch a video excerpt of a child describing an event that had occurred at school. Participants were told the child was either TD and 5 years old, TD and 7 years old, or that he was 7 years old with an ID that meant he was functioning at the level of a 5-year-old. Participants assessed the child described as having an ID as less accurate and less able to recall his experiences than the TD child of the same age, and less able to communicate his experiences than a younger TD child. No differences emerged relative to dimensions of trustworthiness, although raters declared themselves to be less confident when rating the child with an ID than the older TD child. Participants also watched the child answering a series of suggestive questions; When described as having an ID he was rated as less accurate than when he was described as a TD child of the same age.

In sum, evidence suggests that additional intervention may well be required to help juries and court officials overcome negative stereotypes about the eyewitness ability of CWIDs and to emphasize that they typically have the same abilities as children of a similar developmental level. Further research is needed to explore whether jury instructions can ameliorate biases that may diminish the contribution of CWID's testimony. One promising approach may involve using intermediaries during different stages of the forensic process to facilitate appropriate communication between vulnerable witnesses and investigators, lawyers, and judges (Plotnikoff & Woolfson, 2015). Collins et al. (2016) showed that participants who watched a mock cross-examination of a child (4 years old or 13 years old) about a cartoon they had watched rated the child more positively on a number of dimensions when an intermediary facilitated the questioning. The cross-examination was also assessed as more child-centered and appropriate, with the child-lawyer interactions of higher quality when an intermediary was involved. There is thus some evidence that using an intermediary in the cross-examination phase of a trial does not adversely affect juror perceptions of the child.

CONCLUSION

Unfortunately, there is good reason to believe that children suffering from a range of developmental disabilities are disproportionately likely to be victimized and are also disproportionately unlikely to have their complaints and allegations considered as seriously as those made by TD peers. These circumstances underline the need for careful and systematic research on the capacities and limitations of children with developmental disabilities and on the best ways to elicit information from them regarding their experiences.

The research reviewed in this chapter showed that children with mild intellectual disabilities were able to describe their experiences at least as well as TD children of the same mental age; children with more severe disabilities performed somewhat more poorly than their mental-age matches, and further research is needed to determine whether modified questioning strategies might be helpful. Research on children with Down Syndrome, which involves pervasive developmental delays, shows that they can function as well as mental-age-matched-peers.

Children with high-functioning ASDs and ADHD, which are more common that Down Syndrome, appear perfectly capable of describing their experiences and that they, like children with intellectual delays, benefit from the supportive techniques and strategies that are emphasized in the NICHD Protocol.

9

The Revised Protocol: Effectively Supporting Reluctant Witnesses

The original Protocol was primarily targeted at enhancing children's *cognitive processes* during an interview, by increasing the number of retrieval prompts given to them that would lead children to draw upon recall rather than recognition memory, and by encouraging an exhaustive memory search using children's prior recall to form further retrieval cues. Interviewers using the Protocol were also shown how to explain the distinctive "ground rules" so that children would understand how the demands and expectations of the forensic interview differ from those that govern other situations (e.g., the classroom) in which they might be questioned by adults. To overcome children's reticence talking to an unfamiliar adult, the Protocol underlined the importance of establishing rapport, and suggested doing so in ways that allowed children to practice recounting a narrative of a neutral past event, thereby promoting narrative competence.

Beyond this, however, little attention was paid to emotional and motivational factors that might affect the behavior of children when they were being interviewed. Once it had been shown that use of the Protocol indeed allowed interviewers to conduct more informative and

---

Tell Me What Happened: Questioning Children About Abuse, Second Edition.
Michael E. Lamb, Deirdre A. Brown, Irit Hershkowitz, Yael Orbach, and Phillip W. Esplin.
© 2018 John Wiley & Sons Ltd. Published 2018 by John Wiley & Sons Ltd.

uncontaminated investigative interviews, researchers began addressing the *motivational factors* that make some children reluctant to disclose abuse (Pipe, Lamb, Orbach, & Cederborg, 2007). This is an important issue, because, as reported in more detail below, many suspected victims do not report abuse when formally interviewed in forensic contexts, even when there is clear evidence that they were in fact abused. Furthermore, aspects of an interviewer's behavior other than questioning techniques can influence children's participation in an interview. In this chapter, therefore, we discuss our ongoing efforts to develop and evaluate variants of the Protocol that address the special circumstances that attend interviews with such reluctant witnesses.

DISCLOSURE PROCESS

Many alleged victims do not report abuse when formally interviewed, with estimates varying, depending on the context in which the interviews were conducted (London, Bruck, Ceci, & Shuman, 2005, 2007). Of course, children may fail to disclose suspected abuse because none occurred, but they may also fail to disclose abuse that did, in fact, occur (Rush, Lyon, Ahern, & Quas, 2014). In the context of forensic or assessment interviews, allegation rates range widely, with higher rates consistently reported when there is corroborative evidence or when the children have reported abuse prior to the investigation. Allegation rates range from 47% to 62% for non-substantiated cases and from 76% to 96% for substantiated cases (de Voe & Faller, 1999; DiPietro et al., 1997; Dubowitz, Black, & Harrington, 1992; Elliott & Briere, 1994; Keary & Fitzpatrick, 1994; Leach, Powell, Sharman, & Anglim, 2017.

Developmental differences in allegation rates have also been identified, with preschoolers much less likely than older children to report suspected abuse when questioned (DiPietro et al., 1997; Gries et al., 1996; Hershkowitz, Horowitz, & Lamb, 2005, 2007; Keary & Fitzpatrick, 1994; Leach et al., 2017; Pipe et al., 2007; Smith et al., 2000; Wood et al., 1996). This trend might be attributable to a variety of factors, including elevated levels of unwarranted suspicion on the part of adults when young children are involved, as well as cognitive, communicative, and emotional deficits in the ability of young children to understand interviewers and/or to describe experiences of abuse comprehensibly. Some researchers have also shown a decrease in disclosure rates from middle childhood through adolescence (Leach et al., 2016), and gender differences in disclosure rates, with boys more reluctant than girls to report abuse (Ghetti & Goodman, 2001; Gries et al., 1996; Hershkowitz et al., 2005, 2007; Levesque, 1994).

The relationship between suspects and children also appears to be important (Hershkowitz et al., 2005; London et al., 2005, 2007; London,

Bruck, Wright, & Ceci, 2008). Children are particularly hesitant to report abuse by parents and guardians (e.g., DiPietro et al., 1997; Goodman-Brown et al., 2003; Hershkowitz et al., 2005, 2007; Pipe et al., 2007; Sas et al., 1993; Sjöberg & Lindblad, 2002, Ussher & Dewberry, 1995; Wyatt & Newcomb, 1990). Children's expectations of the outcomes that may follow a disclosure also influence when children raise alleged abuse, with concerns about consequences for themselves or another family member associated with delayed disclosure (Hershkowitz, Lanes, & Lamb, 2007; Malloy, Brubacher, & Lamb, 2011), as well as concerns about how others (e.g., parents) would react to the disclosure (Hershkowitz et al., 2007). The type of maltreatment alleged also appears to be associated with reluctance: Some researchers have suggested that reluctance to disclose may be greater among children who are physically rather than sexually abused (Hershkowitz et al., 2007), perhaps because investigations are more likely to be initiated as a result of factors other than the child disclosing (e.g., detection of injury). In such cases, the interview may therefore be the first time the child has an opportunity to talk about the abuse (Rush et al., 2014). Indeed, Rush et al. demonstrated that, in a sample of substantiated physical and sexual abuse cases, children who were physically abused were less likely to have disclosed before being interviewed, and in cases where children had not made a prior disclosure the investigators had more types of evidence (other than the disclosures) to draw upon. Most children made a disclosure during the formal interview, but the number disclosing for the first time in the investigative interview was higher for children who experienced physical rather than sexual abuse.

Children's prior discussions of abuse predict the likelihood of disclosure during formal interviews, with higher rates of disclosure documented when children have previously talked of being abused (74%–93%) than when they have not (25%–65%: de Voe & Faller, 1999; DiPietro et al., 1997; Gries, Goh, & Cavanaugh, 1996; Keary & Fitzpatrick, 1994; Leach et al., 2016), suggesting that an early discussion of the alleged abuse is a strong predictor of children's willingness to make formal allegations. Clearly, it is important to consider disclosure history, as well as the type of abuse and characteristics of the child, when planning for an interview and anticipating whether a child may be reluctant to talk about abuse.

WHO DO CHILDREN DISCLOSE TO?

Because prior disclosure increases the likelihood that children will repeat their disclosures in investigative interviews, Malloy, Brubacher, and Lamb (2013) explored what drove children to disclose informally, and who they chose to disclose to. The Protocol includes a section prompting children to discuss the disclosure process, and so the researchers were able to examine children's responses in 204 transcripts of forensic interviews with 5- to 13-year-old suspected victims of sexual abuse. Their analyses showed that children had commonly told more than one person about the abuse (49.5% disclosed to more than one person), although, as in other research, many children (20%) first described abuse in the formal interview. As in other research, mothers and peers were the most common recipients of disclosures, although preferences varied depending on the children's age (Hershkowitz et al., 2007). Younger children were most likely to tell their mothers, followed by fathers and then other family members. In contrast, older children were most likely to have told peers, followed by mothers, teachers, or other family members.

The fact that many children told more than one person suggests that at least some of the children's early disclosures were "'dead-end'" disclosures (i.e., disclosures that did not lead to official reports). Disclosure to peers may be especially unlikely to lead to intervention, perhaps because peers do not understand how to intervene or because young victims request that peers keep the abuse secret from others. With age, children increasingly value secrecy as a component of friendship (Rotenberg, 1991). Children described a variety of reasons for making disclosures, with the most common being external triggers (e.g., watching a television show with a child sexual abuse theme: 54%), or something specific to the disclosure recipient (24%). Children also reported feeling compelled to (9%) or wanting to protect someone else (9%), whereas disclosure designed to stop the abuse was rarely identified as a trigger (4%). The range of reasons children identified for making disclosures may help us understand why some of them may still be reluctant to talk about their experiences when formally interviewed.

RAPPORT AND EMOTIONAL SUPPORT

Many researchers have highlighted how rapport and an emotionally supportive environment can facilitate children's effective participation in interviews (Ahern et al., 2017; Collins et al., 2014; Hershkowitz, 2009; Saywitz, Larson, Hobbs, & Wells, 2015). Concerns are also often expressed, however, about the extent to which being supportive might appear or be suggestive. For example, the adoption of empathic clinical interviewing styles can be problematic because the supportiveness can easily be seen as suggestive, thereby undermining the value and credibility of the testimony elicited (Saywitz et al., 2015). Similarly, Lyon and his colleagues (Lyon & Dorado, 2008; Lyon, Malloy, Quas, &

Talwar, 2008) have shown, in studies of maltreated children who were coached to conceal forbidden play, that supportive comments may increase false reporting. Although specific reassurance (i.e., "It's okay if you played with the toy house") was associated with fewer false denials, it also resulted in false admissions by some children who had not played with the forbidden toys. In contrast, while general reassurance does not increase false reports, it has relatively limited positive effects on accuracy, at least when children have been exposed to intensive coaching (Lyon et al., 2008). Thus, although researchers recommend that children should be reassured about the consequences of disclosure (Bussey & Grimbeek, 1995; Wagland & Bussey, 2005), it appears that reassurance can be provided safely only when expressed in general terms, with no specific mention of the investigated events/actions. The challenge in forensic interviews is therefore to provide more interviewer support without mentioning any allegation-related details.

Several studies have shown that interviewers behave differently in interviews with reluctant and non-reluctant children (e.g., Hershkowitz, Orbach, Lamb, Sternberg, & Horowitz, 2006; Orbach, Shiloach, & Lamb, 2007). In these studies, the dynamics of interviews with children who were reluctant or failed to disclose abuse were different from those with cooperative children who did disclose from the very outset of the interview. Interviewers posed fewer questions overall but a higher proportion of free-recall prompts during rapport building to disclosers than to non-disclosers (Hershkowitz et al., 2006), and addressed non-reluctant disclosers with more free-recall and fewer recognition prompts, particularly fewer suggestive prompts, than they did reluctant disclosers (Orbach et al., 2007).

In Hershkowitz et al.'s study (2006), children who later failed to disclose abuse seemed to avoid establishing rapport with the interviewers early in the interviews; they were less responsive to interviewers' questions than their disclosing peers and provided fewer personally meaningful details about neutral experiences when invited to do so. Orbach et al. (2007) reported similar differences between non-reluctant disclosers, who disclosed abuse in response to open-ended invitations, and reluctant disclosers, who failed to disclose in response to open-ended prompts but disclosed in response to focused recognition prompts. Non-disclosers were somewhat uncooperative, offered less information, and gave more uninformative responses, even in the pre-substantive rapport-building phase, before the interviewers focused on substantive issues. Although reluctant disclosers did not differ from non-reluctant disclosers with respect to the average number of details provided per prompt in the pre-substantive phase, they provided significantly fewer details on average per invitation, directive, and option-posing prompt in the substantive phase (Orbach et al., 2007).

Hershkowitz and colleagues (2006) have shown that interviews with children who subsequently made a disclosure included more supportive comments by interviewers during rapport building. Hershkowitz et al. (2006) identified a pattern of escalating uncooperativeness and coercion on the part of children and interviewers, respectively, which served only to strengthen the children's reluctance (see also Katz, Hershkowitz et al., 2012). In the pre-substantive rapport-building phase, the non-disclosing children's initial uncooperativeness was clearly challenging for the interviewers, whose response, by way of intrusive questioning, unsupportiveness, and the premature mention of sensitive topics, seemed to make the children even more uncooperative. Hershkowitz et al. concluded that the interviewers' strategies were counter-productive because they did not address the children's emotional needs; they recommended that, in such circumstances, interviewers should make increased efforts to establish meaningful rapport and should avoid shifting the focus to substantive issues until children appear comfortable and cooperative. In short, interviewers should be more, rather than less, supportive of resistant children. Further, because the non-disclosing children had started showing their reluctance early in the rapport-building phase, Hershkowitz et al. stressed the importance of identifying and addressing reluctance at the very beginning of the interview, before negative dynamics had emerged.

Hershkowitz (2009) explored whether pre-substantive interviewer rapport building and support were associated with the amount of forensic information provided by children in the substantive phase, as well as whether these associations differed depending on the children's ages and level of talkativeness. She conducted psycholinguistic analyses of forensic interviews with 71 children (4 to 6 and 7 to 9 years old), suspected of having been victims of sexual abuse and compared the levels of rapport and support in relation to children who were more or less talkative during the pre-substantive phase of the interview.

Interviewers spent longer building rapport with less talkative children and offered them fewer invitations. The proportion of invitations and the length of the rapport-building phase predicted responsivity to invitations in the substantive phase of the interview, especially for the less talkative and older children. The number of supportive comments in the substantive phase did not vary depending on the age or verbosity of the child, but it was modestly associated with measures of how responsive the children were to invitations. When talkativeness was considered separately, the number of supportive comments predicted the responsivity of both less talkative and older children but not the likelihood that talkative or younger children would respond. Hershkowitz thus suggested that, when interviewers adopt a supportive approach from the very outset of the forensic interview they may enhance both children's willingness to disclose abuse and the richness of the information they provide. This may be particularly important for less talkative and for older children.

Child reluctance and interviewer behavior during the substantive phase of the interview also affect how productive or informative children are when talking about abuse. Lewy, Cyr, and Dion (2015) compared (standard) Protocol and non-Protocol interviews with 4- to 13-year-old children and examined instances of child reluctance and interviewer support during the substantive phase. They found that the amount of responsive and non-responsive behavior by the children and the levels of interviewer supportive and non-supportive behavior did not vary as a function of the interviewing approach. After controlling for age and interview type, however, more child reluctance and non-supportive interviewer behavior predicted fewer details reported by the children.

Other research has also shown that interviews with children who do not make a disclosure differ with respect to the children's as well as the interviewers' behavior, not only during the substantive phase, but also from very early in the interview (see above). For example, Katz, Hershkowitz et al. (2012) examined the nonverbal behavior of children who did or did not disclose abuse when interviewed, showing that signs of stress and physical disengagement increased as the interview progressed, while signs of positive emotion decreased. Non-disclosing children demonstrated a higher proportion of behaviors reflecting physical disengagement than children who disclosed in the introductory (i.e., before rapport building began) and substantive phases. Together with Hershkowitz et al.'s (2006) findings, these results suggest that both verbal and nonverbal signs of reluctance can predict the likelihood of disclosure, and that such signs may be evident very early in the interview. It is thus important for interviewers to recognize these signs, which signal the need to develop further rapport to overcome reluctance and enhance children's engagement with the interview.

DEVELOPMENT AND EVALUATION OF THE REVISED PROTOCOL

Because many children made minimal or no disclosures about abuse (e.g., London et al., 2007, 2008; Orbach et al., 2007), even when there was strong evidence to indicate that abuse had occurred (Cederborg, Lamb, & Laurell, 2007; Lawson & Chaffin, 1992), and there was compelling evidence that both interviewer supportiveness and child reluctance were playing a part, we focused on altering the Protocol to more effectively address the socioemotional context of the interview. Field research showed that rapport is best established when 1) children are invited early in the interview to share personally meaningful information in detail and are prompted using open-ended questions to elaborate on it (Brown et al., 2013; Hershkowitz, 2009; Roberts, Lamb, & Sternberg, 2004; Sternberg et al., 1997), 2) interviewers say less and instead encourage children to talk (Teoh & Lamb, 2010), and 3) rapport-building is neither too lengthy nor too cognitively burdensome (Davies, Westcott, & Horan, 2000; Hershkowitz, 2009). Building on these findings, and the research highlighting effective strategies to minimize reluctance, the Protocol was revised to provide interviewers with more guidance about how to 1) behave supportively yet not suggestively and 2) build rapport more effectively with interviewees. The latest version is reproduced in full in this book (see Appendix 1) while Table 9.1 describes the ways interviewers can provide non-suggestive support to alleged victims during forensic interviews.

In an empirical test of a "Revised NICHD Protocol" (RP), Hershkowitz, Lamb, Katz, and Malloy (2015) examined whether more cooperative dynamics could be established during the initial phases of investigative interviews by training interviewers to focus additional attention on their own supportiveness and by then comparing the dynamics of interviewer-child rapport-building interactions in interviews conducted using either the Standard (SP) or Revised (RP) Protocols. All children were suspected of having been abused by family members, and were thus expected to be somewhat uncooperative.

Several changes and additions were made to the Protocol for the purposes of this study. In order to enhance the children's trust and cooperation, the rapport building preceded (rather than followed) explanation of the ground rules and expectations, and additional guidance was provided to interviewers with respect to building and maintaining rapport. In addition to inviting narratives about recent experiences during the rapport-building phase and asking the children to provide more information about personally meaningful topics using free-recall invitations, interviewers were encouraged to address the children by name, welcome them ("I am glad to meet you today, [*child's name*]"), express care ("How are you doing?") and interest in the children's experiences ("I really want to know about things that have happened to you"), and echo the children's feelings ("You say you were [*sad/angry/the feeling mentioned*]"), to acknowledge such feelings ("I see/I understand what you're saying") or to explore them ("Tell me more about [*the feeling*]"), and to ask the children to provide more information about personally meaningful topics using free-recall invitations. The revised

Table 9.1 Supportive non-suggestive techniques and utterances

A. Addressing the Child in a Personal Way
   Address the child in a personal way using his private name. Avoid using nicknames or terms of endearment (e.g., "sweetie").

B. Establishing Rapport
   - Welcoming the child
     "I am glad to meet you today/ to get to know you/ to get to talk." "It's nice to meet you, my name is _____."
   - Expressing personal interest in the child
     "I really want to get to know you/about things that happened to you." "Today is the first time we've met and it is important for me to know you better."
   - Making small gestures of good will
     "Are you warm enough?" "Let me show you the toilets." "Here is a glass of water for you." "Do you want to look at the video camera." "Do you need a short break?"

C. Reinforcement
   - Reinforcement during the interview
     "You are telling me very clearly/in detail and that's important." "You're really helping me understand/ know you." "You corrected me and that's really important." "I understand what you're saying."
     Avoid 'grading' ("you're explaining that very well') or associating reinforcement with specific content ("You told me that you ran away, which was good.").
   - Expressing thanks and appreciation
     "I want to thank you for your help." "I really appreciate that you are talking to me." "I appreciate that you're trying to remember and tell me." "Thank you for sharing with me."
   - Emphasizing the child's discretion
     "It's up to you whether you talk to me or not. I will respect your choice."

D. Using rapport
   - Mentioning and building on trust
     "You've told me a lot about yourself and I feel I know you better." "Now that we know each other better, you can share with me what happened."
   - Expressions of care or concern
     "I'm here for you." "I care about you." "You are important to me." "People are/I am worried that something may have happened to you."
     You can specify the cause for concern (e.g., "The teacher said you were crying this morning.")
   - Portraying the interviewer as someone to disclose to
     "If something happened, I'm here to listen to you." "You can trust me and tell me if something happened." "It's okay to share secrets/problems with me." "I talk to many kids who tell me about things that have happened to them." "It's my job to listen to children who have problems."

E. Emotional Support
   - Generalized comments about the child's perceived difficulties
     "Many children find it difficult to talk/feel ashamed at the beginning but then find it easier." "Many children have secrets."

(*Continued*)

Table 9.1 (Continued)

- Empathy
  "I understand it is difficult for you to tell me." "I know it's been a long interview."
- Checking on the child's feelings
  "How are you doing so far/now that we are done?" "How did you feel before we began/ during our conversation?"
- Exploring emotions
  "Tell me more about your fears." "Tell me what you're afraid of." "Tell me why you're crying." "Tell me why you don't want to tell me." "You said you can't tell me; tell me more about that."
- Open questions about expressed feelings or thoughts
  "You said you were sad/disgusted /wanted to run away. Tell me more about that."
- Echoing emotions
  "You said you were sad/you were crying."
- Acknowledging/Accepting/Recognizing emotions
  "You say that it was very painful. I can understand that/ I see what you are saying."
- Reassurance
  "Don't worry, I won't tell other children." "You won't be late for the bus." "Nobody is going to arrest you." "Sometimes it's possible to help families which/people who have been hurt." "Sometimes it helps children when they tell others and don't have to keep a secret."
- Removing responsibility from the child
  "If something happened/someone hurt you, it is not your fault." "You are not responsible for that." (Or in a generalized way: "When things happen to children, it's not their fault." "Children are not responsible when they are hurt.")
- Exploring unexpressed emotions and conflicts
  "If there is something you are worried about, please tell me."

F. Encouragement
  - Emphasizing that the child is the source of knowledge
    "I'm ask you these questions because I was not there."
  - Legitimating expression
    "You can talk about bad things and good things." "In this office you can tell me everything." "It is okay to tell me about these kinds of things/to say these words bad words." "Many children tell me what happened to them."
  - Expression of confidence/ optimism
    "I think you can explain it well."
  - Offering help
    "I want to make it easier for you. What would help you to talk?" "Would it make it easier if you wrote it down?" "You can start talking and I'll help you by asking questions." "I am here to help."
  - Encouraging non-verbal communication
    "Could you please turn toward me?" "Come on, look at me. I'd like to see your eyes!"
  - Encouraging disclosure
    "It is really important that you tell me if something has happened to you."

instructions advised interviewers to encourage the children verbally and nonverbally (leaning toward the child, smiling, and establishing eye contact) to describe experienced events in both the pre-substantive and substantive portions of the interview. Thanks, appreciation, and positive reinforcement ("thank you for sharing that with me" or "you're really helping me understand") of the children's efforts, but not their specific contents, were recommended. Similarly, expressions of empathy with the children's expressed feelings or difficulties regarding the interview experience ("I know *[it is a long interview / there are many questions / other difficulties the child expressed]*" or "I can see that *[you are tired / it is difficult for you to talk]*"), but not regarding past experiences, were encouraged and supportive interventions such as legitimizing expression ("here you can talk about everything that happened to you" or "here it is okay to say bad words"), generalizing the child's difficulties in the interview (" many children have secrets that they do not talk about. If you have a secret, I am a person who you can trust and share it with"), offering help ("*[child's name]*, if it is difficult for you to talk about it, how can I make it easier for you?") or (" if it is difficult to talk about it, perhaps you could write it down") and reassuring him/her when possible ("don't worry, I won't tell the other children") or expressing optimism ("*[child's name]*, please try explaining that, I think you can") that he/she can overcome the difficulty were also recommended. When children reported abuse, but expressed reluctance about discussing it, containing ("you can trust me and tell me things that have happened to you") or encouraging ("it is really important that you tell me") practices were recommended, as was removing the responsibility from the child ("when somebody hurts a child, it is not the child's fault").

The levels of interviewer support and child reluctance were examined in 199 interviews with 4- to 13-year-old children about alleged intrafamilial abuse. One hundred interviews were conducted using the SP, and 99 using the RP, matched with respect to case characteristics. The allegations were all deemed highly credible by the interviewers, and 66% were substantiated using evidence other than the children's allegations. The SP interviews were conducted before interviewers were trained to use the RP, to avoid diffusion of behavior between the two samples. Experienced interviewers who had already been trained to use the SP attended a 2-day session in which the RP modifications were described and practiced. Interviewers also received monthly supervisions, in groups and individually, about the use of rapport and emotional support in their interviews.

The overall number of prompts that interviewers used in either the SP or RP interviews did not differ in any of the interview phases. The relative proportions of prompts used in the pre-substantive and substantive phases also did not differ, but during the transition phase interviewers used more recall and non-substantive prompts, and fewer recognition prompts when using the RP. During the pre-substantive phase, there were also more comments about positive behavior and fewer instances of negative or unsupportive comments from the interviewers when they were using the RP.

Children interviewed using the RP were less reluctant in the pre-substantive phase, and in particular, responded with fewer omissions ("don't know," "not sure," "that's all," unclear, or no responses). There was no difference in the total number of details children reported when interviewed using either Protocol, but the number of details reported was explained by the children's reluctance (less reluctance was associated with more details), age, and prompt type, whichever Protocol was used.

While interviewers using the RP were clearly more supportive in the pre-substantive and transitional phases than those using the SP, this pattern did not continue into the substantive phase, when allegations were being discussed. RP interviewers apparently attempted to motivate children to disclose abuse, but failed to continue providing higher levels of support while discussing the allegations once they had been made. Interestingly, children in the RP condition showed less reluctance in the substantive phase as well, even though the interviewers were not more supportive during this phase. Thus, reduced reluctance in the substantive part was attributable to the better rapport established early in RP interviews, further emphasizing the role of rapport building in investigative interviews. The findings underlined the importance of exploring how to increase interviewers' supportiveness throughout the interview, and of recognizing and repairing rapport and engagement when they deteriorate (Saywitz et al., 2015).

Hershkowitz et al.'s (2015) study illustrated that increased interviewer support was associated with reduced reluctance during the pre-substantive phase of the interview. To gain a deeper understanding of the specific interplay among the children's reluctance, the interviewers' responses to reluctance, and any impact on the children's subsequent behavior, Ahern, Hershkowitz, Lamb, Blasbalg, and Winstanley (2014) examined the same sample to highlight the specific dynamics unfolding during the pre-substantive phase at a turn-by-turn level. The pre-substantive phase was examined because there were no differences in the interviewers' supportive behavior during the substantive phase, and the early stages of the interview are a critical period for establishing rapport and addressing reluctance. Ahern et al. (2014) identified conversational turns in which reluctance was exhibited in order to examine 1) the likelihood that they would be followed by immediate support from interviewers and 2) whether that support affected the children's behavior in the next conversational turn.

Interviews conducted using the RP included more instances of supportive behavior than those using the SP. The effects were not specifically responsive to the children's behavior, however: children's reluctant utterances were not followed by interviewer support more often in RP than in SP interviews. Reluctance that was followed by support was more likely to promote non-reluctant behavior than was reluctance followed by no support, though only for children interviewed using the RP. Thus, the provision of support during RP interviews appeared to facilitate cooperation but the provision of no support in the RP interviews appeared to decrease children's subsequent cooperation, which suggests possible negative effects.

Negative effects of offering no support were also reported by Lewy et al. (2015), as discussed earlier. The interviewers' failure to respond to reluctance with immediate support may have prevented them from promoting children's cooperation. Perhaps interviewers did not have sufficient opportunities to practice responding to reluctance because reluctant utterances comprised a relatively small portion of the total number of utterances in the pre-substantive portions of these interviews (23%). In addition, interviewers might not have perceived children's omissions (e.g., "I don't know") as indices of reluctance but as factual statements that did not require supportive responses. Children who continued to be reluctant following no support (rather than support) in the RP might also have come to expect support, and thus became less responsive when not provided with it. Some of these children may also have been especially reluctant because they were disclosing in response to the support offered in the RP rather than because they had come to the interview as willing informants (Hershkowitz, Lamb, & Katz, 2014).

In their study, Hershkowitz et al. (2014) examined whether use of the RP was associated with increased rates of allegations made by suspected victims of intra-familial abuse because, as noted above, they are less likely to make allegations when interviewed formally. Interviews were conducted using either the SP or RP, with 426 4- to 13-year-old children. Allegations were coded when the children reported any of a range of abusive physical (hitting, use of objects, injury) or sexual (touch over or under clothes; vaginal, anal or oral penetration) acts. All of the suspected abuse was corroborated by independent evidence.

Over half of the children in the sample made allegations, with more doing so when they were interviewed using the RP (60%) than the SP (50%). Effects varied by interviewer, with the rates of disclosure ranging from 43% to 70% across the seven different interviewers contributing to the study. As in previous research examining children's disclosures, whether children made an allegation or not was correlated with their age, gender, whether or not they had made previous reports, and, importantly, whichever version of the Protocol was used. The positive impact of the Protocol on allegation rates remained when the effects of interviewer, age, gender, and previous reporting were controlled for. The study therefore showed that interviewer behavior was meaningfully associated with the likelihood that children would make valid allegations.

Importantly, the RP was equally effective when interviewing various sub-groups of children, notably those children who are typically least likely to make allegations when interviewed (Ghetti & Goodman, 2001; Gries et al., 1996; Hershkowitz et al., 2009; Levesque, 1994) and may be more susceptible to pressure from familial adults on whom they are dependent (Malloy et al., 2007). Thus, use of the RP appeared to have successfully motivated children known to be particularly reluctant to reveal their victimization.

The increase in allegation rates following use of the RP inevitably raises concerns about the veracity and validity of those allegations. Much research has focused on the risks that children may make false allegations, especially when they are offered potentially suggestive support (Ceci & Bruck, 1995; Lyon et al., 2008). Even though Hershkowitz et al.'s (2014) was a field study, the sample was large enough that it was possible to restrict analyses to cases in which there was clear independent evidence that the children had indeed been abused as they alleged. The study thus showed how the supportive but non-suggestive practices embedded in the RP helped abused children make valid allegations of abuse. The risk of suggestive contamination was also contained because the RP (like the SP) involved carefully structured prompts designed to evoke free-recall (see Appendix 1 for the most recent version of the Revised Protocol and Table 9.1 for descriptions of appropriate non-suggestive support).

By creating more meaningful rapport with children and providing them with emotional support throughout the interview, it is likely that forensic interviewers using the RP better helped children overcome their reluctance to communicate. Best practice recommendations clearly need to underscore the importance of supportive yet non-suggestive practices when investigating possible occurrences of abuse and of using structured protocols for shaping relationships with children effectively (Langer, McLeod, & Weisz, 2011).

FURTHER REVISION OF THE REVISED PROTOCOL

Because the positive impact of the RP on interviewer and child contributions to forensic interviews had been documented in several studies, Hershkowitz et al. (2017) examined the impact of an extended training program on interviewers' responses to non-cooperation when using the latest version of the RP. In addition to encouraging interviewers to provide support, the instructors focused on how to avoid missing opportunities to demonstrate support, especially during the substantive phase of the interview (Ahern et al., 2014; Hershkowitz et al., 2006). Hershkowitz et al. (2017) thus implemented and assessed a training program that addressed the documented needs and difficulties experienced by child investigators in Israel who had been using the RP. The new training program described a broader range of supportive techniques for interviewers to draw upon and included more detailed guidance about how support should be employed in each phase of the interview. The training format used a *train the trainer* approach, with interviewers trained to evaluate their own interviews. This self-review involved identifying instances of support offered, missed opportunities to provide support, as well as instances of inappropriate (or unsupportive) interviewer behavior.

Supervisors were trained for 5 days; the sessions included instructions on how to identify various types of supportive and unsupportive behavior in their own previous interviews, as well as a 1-day workshop on how to deliver training to their teams. Supervisors then trained the interviewers that they typically supervised in eight 1-day workshops. The workshops included a review of theory and research, practice with the various supportive interventions, learning how to code, reviewing recent interviews, and exercises for use throughout the training period. Interviewers also had 2-hour long individual meetings with their supervisor following each workshop.

Hershkowitz et al.'s analyses examined the presence or absence of support and inadequate interviewer responses, as well as the absence of supportive responses when they would have been appropriate, throughout each interview. In all, 321 interviews with 3- to 14-year-old alleged victims were examined; they took place at varying stages of the training program, and were spread across nearly a year (8 training sessions). Results showed that insensitivity (failing to provide support when it was needed) decreased relative to baseline after the second and third training sessions, while support increased at each time point relative to baseline and between the second and third training sessions. Inadequate support decreased relative to baseline following each subsequent training session (see Figures 9.1, 9.2, and 9.3).

More support was also given to younger children while insensitivity was higher for older children (9 years or older). More inadequate responses were made to younger children during the baseline and following the first training session, but age differences were no longer apparent thereafter. The researchers speculated that the interviewers' differential sensitivity to signs of reluctance may have reflected differences in the

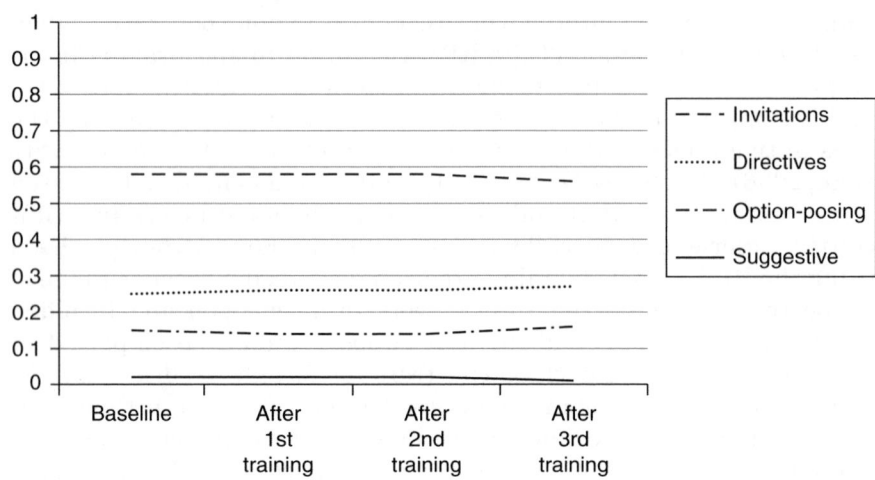

Figure 9.1 Proportion of utterance types used by interviewers through the course of training.

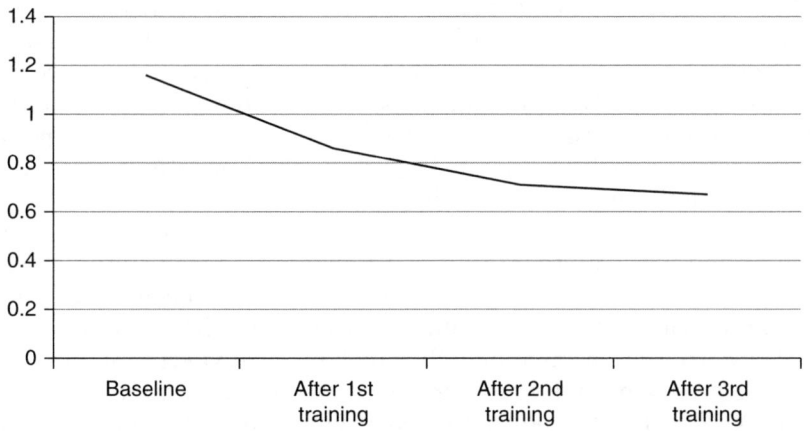

Figure 9.2 Ratio of missed support opportunities to reluctant utterances.

ways in which younger and older children verbalized their reluctance. This would imply that the passive resistance exhibited by older children (pausing; "I don't know") may be more difficult for interviewers to detect and address supportively than active resistance ("I want to go") by younger children. It is also possible that interviewers were more empathic toward younger children because they appeared more immature and vulnerable.

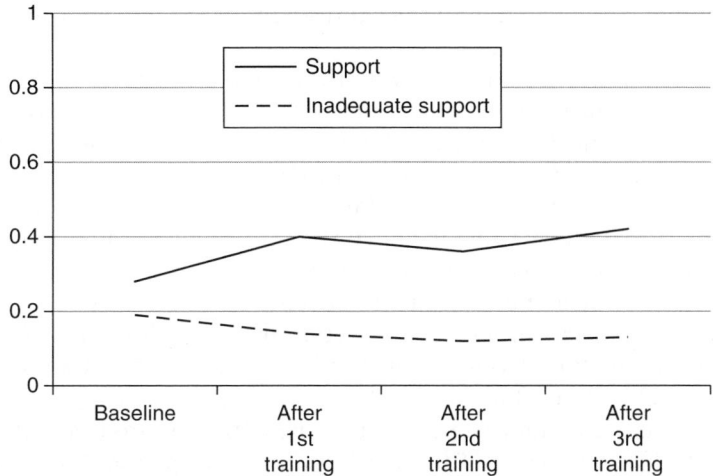

Figure 9.3 Changing levels of appropriate and inappropriate support over the course of the training program.

Clearly, over the course of the training program, interviewers became better able to recognize the need for support and to respond appropriately. Interviewers' increasing insight into their own practice and children's responding may have been helped, at least in part, by a focus in the self-review and supervision sessions on the use of desired behaviors but also by the identification of missed opportunities. Some skills were more easily acquired in the course of training, whereas others took longer to perfect. For example, trainees quickly increased the rates at which they provided support and decreased the rates at which they responded inadequately, whereas sensitivity to signs of reluctance only increased after further training sessions. Similarly, improvements in responding to young children took place later than improvements in patterns of responding to older children. These findings underline how difficult it is both to develop and enhance sensitive interviewing skills and to ensure that the lessons learned are correctly and fully generalized.

Ahern, Hershkowitz, Lamb, Blasbalg, and Karni-Visel (in press) later compared the numbers of supportive statements and various measures of reluctance in each phase of RP and SP interviews with 230 3- to 13-year-olds who alleged that they had been physically abused. Because physical abuse is, by legal definition, perpetrated by parents or guardians, it typically involves considerable reluctance to disclose (Ghetti, Goodman, Eisen, Qin, & Davis, 2002; Hershkowitz et al., 2014; Hershkowitz & Elul, 1999; but see Rush et al., 2014). There was independent evidence that all the children interviewed had been abused by specific family members.

Ahern and her colleagues showed that the RP interviews were characterized by more emotionally supportive statements throughout. When children disclosed physical abuse in the RP interviews, they did so in response to fewer prompts than children in the SP interviews. This finding is significant, particularly because the number of turns in the transitional phase (during which the interviewer transitioned from rapport building to exploring the possibility of abuse) was associated with increased directness and more specific utterance types.

In addition, as in other studies (Hershkowitz, Horowitz, & Lamb, 2005; Pipe et al., 2007), the younger children displayed reluctance more than older children. The older children disclosed abuse in response to earlier, fewer, and more open-ended transitional prompts than the youngest children. These findings highlight the particular challenge interviewers often encounter when striving to avoid using option-posing prompts when speaking to the youngest children and is especially important because their responses to more focused prompts are more likely to be unreliable (e.g., Shrimpton, Oates, & Hayes, 1998).

Blasbalg, Hershkowitz, Lamb, and Karni-Visel (2018a, 2018b) selected interviews conducted after interviewers had been trained how to provide non-suggestive support throughout the entire course of forensic interviews with 200 6- to 13-year-old alleged victims of physical abuse by family members. The cases were validated based on independent evidence, including eyewitnesses' statements, medical evidence, and suspect admissions, or by earlier disclosures to professionals such as teachers or nurses.

Blasbalg et al. (2018a) hypothesized that supportive statements during the substantive phase would be associated with subsequent decreases in the children's reluctance and a corresponding increase in informativeness, with the association between support and increased informativeness mediated by decreases in the children's reluctance. As predicted, regardless of whether interviewers requested information, support predicted declines in reluctance (Blasbalg et al., 2018a). Asking a question attenuated this effect and so did severity of abuse. Support also led to increased informativeness, although requests for information were more influential than support. Overall, informativeness was much greater when reluctance was less.

These studies demonstrated the beneficial effects of support in the substantive phase of interviews, during which reluctance can undermine the value of the testimony itself whereas previous studies had only shown the beneficial effects of support in the pre-substantive and transitional phases of the interview (Hershkowitz, Ahern, Lamb, Blasbalg, &

Karni-Visel, in press; Hershkowitz, Lamb, & Katz, 2014; Hershkowitz, Lamb, Katz, & Malloy, 2013). In addition, most previous studies had examined the effects of support across phases of the interview, whereas Blasbalg et al. (2018a) focused on specific utterance-level sequences. The research thus underlined the importance of supportiveness during the substantive phase of the interview, during which reluctance can diminish the quality of the actual testimony.

A later study using the same sample examined the effects of support on the coherence of children's accounts – that is, the degree to which the account made sense to listeners (Blasbalg et al., 2018b). Three dimensions of coherence were emphasized on the basis of prior research by Reese and her colleagues (2011): (1) context, consisting of information about the spatial and temporal location, (2) chronology, referring to the temporal organization of the event, and (3) theme, reflecting topic unity, elaborative and evaluative information, narrative structure, and resolution. As predicted, Blasbalg and his colleagues found a negative association between reluctance and coherence. Support had positive effects on coherence that were mediated in part by decreased reluctance. The mediation model showed how support and reluctance affected cognitive competency both directly and perhaps (as explained below) by way of enhanced emotion regulation which freed cognitive resources to engage in memory retrieval (Saywitz, Wells, Larson, & Hobbs, 2016).

Blasbalg, Hershkowitz, Lamb, and Karni-Visel (2018c) next compared 88 Standard and 166 Revised Protocol interviews of children whose abuse had been independently substantiated. The RP was associated with better interviewer support and questioning as well as reduced reluctance and increased informativeness on the part of children throughout the interview. Thus, the main goal of the RP, to equip interviewers with skills to reduce children's reluctance and elicit fuller accounts, appeared to have been accomplished.

The Revised Protocol was designed to emphasize supportive interviewing in order to facilitate the development of trust between interviewers and interviewees as well as to help interviewers effectively address and help manage the children's expressions of emotion. In a study comparing RP and SP interviews with alleged victims, Karni-Visel, Hershkowitz, Lamb, and Blasbalg (2018c) showed that alleged victims indeed displayed more and more varied abuse-related emotions when interviewed using the RP, especially when the children were younger.

Karni-Visel, Hershkowitz, Blasbalg, and Lamb (2018a, 2018b) focused on the association between interviewer support, children's emotional expressions when talking about the abuse, and children's informativeness in RP interviews. Cognitive and neurophysiological research indicates that memory for emotional events is superior to that for non-emotional events (LeDoux, 1992). Negative emotions experienced during an event seem to focus attention on the core details and therefore lead to "tunnel memory," enhancing the representation of central details at the expense of peripheral details (Bless, 2001; Bless & Fiedler, 2006; Fiedler, 2001; Fredrickson, 2001; Sorbeck & Clore, 2005). In addition, negative emotions seem to promote specific encoding of threatening elements even when events occur repeatedly, and to facilitate retrieval following long delays (Bahrick, Parker, Fivush, & Levitt, 1998; Brainerd & Reyna, 1996, 2002; Hintzman, 1984; Goodman, Hirschman, Hepps, & Rudy, 1991; Ornstein, Gordon & Larus, 1992; Peterson, 1999). However, children rarely express emotion when they disclose abuse (Katz, Hershkowitz, Malloy, Lamb, Atabaki, & Spindler, 2012; Castelli & Goodman, 2014; Sayfan, Mitchell, Goodman, Eisen, & Qin, 2008, although a few studies have suggested that interviewer support can help children express their emotions (Ahern & Lyon, 2013; Klemfuss, Milojevich, Yim, Rush, & Quas, 2013; Lyon, Scurich, Choi, Handmaker, & Blank, 2012). It was thus hypothesized that reports of negative emotions would positively correlate with the amount of central rather than peripheral details reported, as well as, when the abuse had been repeated, with the amount of specific rather than generic information.

Karni-Visel et al. (2018a) found that the expressions of emotion declined as the interview progressed. The expression of emotion was associated with an increase in informativeness, and this was especially true with respect to the expression of negative emotions. Although children expressed few emotions, their expression predicted the different types of details that children reported. Negative emotions were associated with the production of both central and peripheral details, contrary to the claim that negative emotions lead to tunnel memory and thus limit the encoding of peripheral information (Bless, 2001; Bless & Fiedler, 2006; Fiedler 2001; Fredrickson, 2001; Sorbeck & Clore, 2005). When older children who had been abused repeatedly expressed negative emotions, they provided more specific details and fewer generic details, suggesting that the negative emotions triggered memory mechanisms which enabled top-down scanning processes and assisted the children with the challenging task of retrieving specific episodic details about each event (Hitchcock, Nixon, & Weber, 2014; Moore & Zoellner, 2007).

Abuse severity was positively correlated with informativeness, possibly suggesting that higher levels of stress experienced during the event led to enhanced memory (Bornstein, Liebel, & Scarberry, 1998; Derakshan & Eysenck, 2009; Goodman, Bottoms, Schwartz-Kenney, & Rudy, 1991; Quas, Rush, Yim, & Sumaroka, 2012). Interestingly, girls and older children, who are typically more informative, also displayed more emotions, which may explain their advantage in emotional memory cueing.

Karni-Visel, Hershkowitz, Blasbalg, and Lamb (2018b) explored the effects of interviewer support on the expression of emotions during the substantive phase of RP interviews. As expected, interviewer support in response to expressions of emotion led to further expressions of emotion which in turn led to increased informativeness. Importantly, the association between support and informativeness was fully mediated by the expression of emotions. These data showed that interviewers can enhance informativeness by responding appropriately to expressions of emotion and thereby facilitating children's access to emotion-laden memories (for review see Saywitz, Wells, Larson, & Hobbs, 2016). The indirect pathway between supportiveness and informativeness had not previously been documented.

All of these effects on the interviewer-child dynamics clearly affected the willingness of the suspected victims to make allegations when interviewed. Hershkowitz and Lamb (under review) recently showed that the nationwide implementation of the Revised Protocol in Israel had significantly affected both the likelihood that suspected victims would make allegations and that those allegations would be deemed credible. Their analyses focused on 19,738 4- to 13-year-olds interviewed by any one of the 63 trained interviewers anywhere in Israel between 2013 and 2016 following reported suspicions that the children had been physically ($n = 14,913$) or sexually ($n = 4,828$) abused. Nearly 70% (69.2%) of the children made allegations when interviewed using either the Standard (SP) or Revised (RP) Protocol. As in earlier analyses of similar data (Hershkowitz et al., 2005), older children were more likely to make allegations than younger children. Allegations were more common when sexual rather than physical abuse was suspected, and allegations were more common when non-family members rather than parents were the suspected perpetrators. Some interviewers were more likely than others to elicit allegations, as well. Once such factors were taken into account statistically, however, multilevel analyses revealed that children were 13.3% more likely to make allegations when interviewed using the Revised rather than the Standard Protocol. Furthermore, whereas the plurality of interviews left investigators uncertain whether the children had indeed been abused, they were 9% more likely to deem the allegations credible when the interviews had been conducted using the Revised Protocol.

INTERVIEWING SUSPECTS RATHER THAN VICTIMS

Like victims who are too afraid or embarrassed to disclose abuse, young alleged perpetrators are also reluctant to discuss their behavior, and one early study used some of the principles learned through our work with young victims and witnesses and applied them to interviews of young alleged perpetrators being questioned about the alleged offenses.

Children who are suspected of abusing others might be expected to resist providing information, whether for fear of likely sanctions or shame. When confronting such resistance or apparent deception, interviewers might feel the need to use more focused and even coercive strategies to gain information from youthful alleged perpetrators. Presumably, the eagerness of suspects to be informative is further diminished when interviewers are required by law to warn suspects that their statements may be used against them in criminal or civil proceedings.

Hershkowitz et al. (2004) examined 72 forensic interviews by 13 Israeli youth investigators with 9- to 14-year old alleged perpetrators of child sexual abuse. There were 37 younger suspects who ranged in age from 9 to 12.5 years and 35 older suspects who ranged in age from 12.6 to 14 years. Twenty-one suspects denied the allegations completely, 23 admitted committing all of the offenses alleged by the victims (full admissions), and 28 acknowledged committing some but not all of the alleged offenses (partial admissions). All interviews were conducted using a specially designed investigative interview protocol by interviewers who had already been trained to interview alleged victims using the Standard NICHD Investigative Interview Protocol. The sample was highly representative of the population of youthful suspects interviewed by Israeli youth investigators. All incidents described by the alleged victims and described (or denied) by the suspects were deemed likely to have happened by the investigators but we do not know what actually happened in the incidents described, nor how much of the information provided by the suspects (or victims) was accurate, although most victim accounts were corroborated in at least general terms by witnesses or other suspects.

Interviewers began by explaining the purpose of the interview and warning the suspect, as required by Israeli law, that their statements could be used against them in legal proceedings. Attempts were then made to establish rapport with the suspects before the investigators switched focus to the substantive topic – the alleged abuse. Whereas victim interviews conducted using the Protocol include efforts to entrain narrative responsive style in the pre-substantive portion of the interview and to switch focus to substantive issues in a non-suggestive fashion, neither of these strategies was employed in the suspect interview. Open-ended prompts were encouraged, but pilot research confirmed expectations that most suspects would deny the incidents or fail to provide useful information when first questioned using such prompts. As a result, more directive and even suggestive prompts (guided by reports of the incident by alleged victims or the results of investigative work by the police) were developed. Whenever possible, however, interviewers were instructed to ask for open-ended elaboration of information provided in response to more focused prompts.

Surprisingly, the suspects' ages did not affect the dynamics of the interviewers, but the dynamics were profoundly affected by whether or not the suspects admitted involvement in the incidents under investigation. Interviewers addressed fewer invitations, directives, and option-posing questions to suspects who denied the allegations than to those who fully or partially admitted the allegations, although the means for the full and partial admitters never differed significantly. There were no group differences in the use of suggestive prompts.

Comparable analyses concerned with the proportion of utterances of each type revealed a similar pattern: Interviewers addressed proportionally fewer directive and proportionally more suggestive prompts to deniers than to those who partially or fully admitted their alleged role in the incidents under investigation, and again, it was the deniers who differed from suspects in the other groups.

Examination of the suspect's responses focused only on the 51 children (25 younger, 26 older) who admitted the allegations fully or partially because, by definition, suspects who denied completely provided no forensically relevant details about their involvement in the alleged incidents. Somewhat surprisingly, neither age nor admission affected the suspects' responsiveness significantly. The total number of details provided likewise did not vary depending on the age or admission status of the interviewees.

Interviewers offered fully and partially admitting suspects significantly more suggestive prompts than free-recall invitations. However, contrary to expectations, significantly more details were elicited from partially and fully admitting suspects using invitations rather than option-posing and suggestive prompts. Similarly, partially and fully admitting suspects provided significantly more details per invitation than per option-posing or suggestive utterance. These findings suggest that the investigators may have misjudged the need for suggestive and coercive prompts, because these suspects were considerably more responsive to free-recall prompts than had been expected.

The more advanced age of even the younger suspects, who were 9 to 12 years of age (unlike young child-victims who are 4 to 8 years old), may explain the larger than expected amounts of free-recall information they reported as well as the similarities between older and younger suspects with respect to the amount of free-recall information reported.

As expected, interviewers behaved differently when addressing alleged suspects and victims. Whereas free-recall and suggestive prompts constituted 30% and 7%, respectively, of the average total number of interviewer utterances in victim interviews conducted using the Protocol, and 6% and 10%, respectively, of the total number of utterances in non-Protocol victim interviews (see Chapter 6), 19% and 24%, respectively, of the utterances offered to the suspects were invitations and suggestive prompts. Even though the suspects' responsiveness to free-recall and directive prompts made the expected reliance on option-posing and suggestive prompts unnecessary, over 43% of the utterances addressed by interviewers to young suspects were option-posing and suggestive. As predicted, therefore, it appeared that the interviewers were skeptical of the suspects' responsiveness and thus exerted more pressure on them, using riskier (e.g., suggestive) prompts that may contaminate the information retrieval process, while affording these suspects inadequate opportunities to freely recall their experiences. The extensive reliance on suggestive and coercive prompts increases the risk that interviewers may elicit inaccurate information.

Hershkowitz et al. (2004) also found that interviewers asked fewer questions of suspects who denied involvement in the alleged incidents than of those who fully or partially admitted their role in the alleged abuse. They had expected interviewers to address deniers with fewer invitations and more suggestive utterances, perceiving them as less cooperative than suspects who admit their involvement, but the findings only partially confirmed the predictions. Interviewers indeed addressed fewer invitations to youngsters who denied the allegations but there were no significant differences among suspects in the different admission status groups with respect to the numbers of suggestive prompts, perhaps because the interviewers viewed all suspects with skepticism, regardless of admission status. In addition, examination of the relative rather than absolute number of prompts of each type indicated that, as predicted, interviewers addressed deniers with proportionally more suggestive utterances than they did full or partial admitters, presumably because the interviewers were skeptical of the interviewees' denials. In addition to skepticism or disbelief, the disproportionate use of suggestive prompts when interviewing deniers may reflect the limited amount of information they provided about the alleged events. To varying degrees, non-suggestive prompts of all types build on the information provided, so the absence of information forces interviewers to introduce topics or details not recounted by the interviewee. The latter prompts are, by definition, more likely to be suggestive or coercive. Suspects who fully admitted the alleged incidents thus elaborated more on details they had already disclosed, providing considerably more information in response to "directive" prompts than partially admitting suspects.

Because deniers and younger partially admitting suspects were addressed similarly by interviewers, Hershkowitz et al. expected that both would provide less allegation-related information than children in the "full admission" group. In fact, however, younger partially admitting suspects were treated by interviewers more like deniers than older partially admitting suspects, but the number of details provided in response to invitations by partially and fully admitting suspects did not differ. This may be because children who partially admitted typically denied their role in the incident while providing somewhat detailed information about what they saw other participants do, as well as about the location, time, actions, and participants.

Overall, the findings confirmed that, like alleged victims, youthful suspects can provide considerable amounts of forensically relevant information in response to open-ended prompts, even when they minimize their own involvement and culpability. This information can be compared with accounts provided by other witnesses and alleged victims, and can also yield investigative leads that can be pursued by law enforcement. Pursuing an open-ended style of questioning is also likely to optimize opportunities to detect deception in young suspects. The cognitive-load approach to lie detection suggests that, when the mental effort required by suspects to maintain their lies increases, they are more likely to "slip" (Vrij & Granhag, 2012), because telling and maintaining a lie is cognitively more difficult than telling the truth. Cognitive loading techniques include asking suspects to elaborate upon their accounts, asking unanticipated questions, and asking for recall in unexpected ways (e.g., reversed order). Many of these techniques have begun to amass empirical evidence supporting their efficacy (Vrij & Fisher, 2016; Vrij, Fisher, & Blank, 2015). The extent to which cognitive-load techniques similarly enhance detection of children's false reports is unclear however (e.g., Saykaly, Crossman, Morris, & Talwar, 2016). To the extent that information provided in response to open-ended prompts is more likely to be accurate, it is clear that interviewers might well suspend their skepticism and pursue information as non-coercively as possible, even if later—perhaps in subsequent interviews—it becomes necessary to adopt more suggestive and coercive strategies. Certainly, the risks of coercive interviewing have been well documented in the popular and professional literature (Ceci & Bruck, 1993, 1995; Dwyer, 2002; Dwyer & Saulny, 2002; Lamb & Fauchier, 2001; McFadden & Saulny, 2002; "Excerpts from...," 2002; Malloy, Shulman, & Cauffmann, 2014; Orbach & Lamb, 2001; Orbach et al., 2016; Saulny, 2002; Wilgoren, 2003) making it clear that care is warranted when interviewing both suspects and alleged victims.

Although much less is known about the dynamics of interviews with alleged suspects as opposed to victims, Hershkowitz et al.'s study (2004) yielded some encouraging findings, suggesting that young suspects may be more willing to disclose information in response to open-ended prompts than had been expected. Hence, further research is warranted on providing young suspects with more opportunities to describe their experiences in response to open-ended prompts, while using the information they provide as contextual cues for enhancing further free-recall elaboration.

Building on Hershkowitz et al.'s study (2004) of young suspects, and Hershkowitz's study (2006) of reluctant witnesses, a Revised Suspect Protocol has recently been developed (Hershkowitz, Lamb, & Breitman, under review). It was designed to help elicit more and more accurate forensically relevant information by providing young suspects with more support throughout the interview and thus making them more cooperative.

Because children over 12 years of age are deemed criminally responsible in Israel, the Revised Suspect Protocol (RSP) had to comply with legal provisos and limitations. Accordingly, the new Protocol was extensively discussed with legal professionals, including prosecutors, judges, defense attorneys, and legislators, in addition to senior police and youth probation officers. At the same time, a multi-professional committee updated the precise wording of Israel's "Miranda warning" to make it easier for children to understand.

Child investigators who had previously been trained to use the RP (see above) then attended additional training focused on four practices: 1) communicating Miranda rights in a developmentally appropriate manner, while monitoring children's comprehension, 2) building meaningful rapport with young suspects, 3) providing support to children who showed anxiety, reluctance or negative emotions, and 4) non-suggestive questioning strategies.

Ten interviewers and their supervisors (4) were trained in seven day-long sessions, with intervals of 1–2 months between sessions. The sessions included opportunities to practice using these specific practices as well as discussions of theory and research, coding procedures, recent interviews, and exercises for use outside the training sessions. Interviewers also had two 2-hour long individual meetings with their supervisors in order to evaluate interviews they had recently conducted. Prior to these individual sessions, the interviewer, supervisor and a research assistant coded the interviews, to help interviewers develop their skills recognizing different interview strategies and child responses.

Preliminary analyses showed that Miranda rights were conveyed in more developmentally appropriate ways in RSP interviews, while interviewers made additional efforts to monitor the children's understanding, and to adjust their explanations appropriately when comprehension failed. In addition, interviewers used more prompts, especially supportive prompts, to build rapport with the children. Supportive prompts were more frequent while unsupportive or intimidating comments were less frequent throughout the interviews. Fewer suggestive questions were posed as well.

CONCLUSION

Many child abuse victims do not disclose maltreatment when interviewed, but it seems likely that skillful management of their reluctance by providing social support may help reduce these barriers (Hershkowitz, Lamb, Katz, & Malloy, 2015; Saywitz et al., 2015). There is now substantial evidence that reluctant children may signal their unwillingness to engage by displaying a range of verbal and nonverbal behaviors from the very beginning of the interview. It is thus critical for interviewers to be aware of such signs and be prepared to manage them sensitively and appropriately. Studies in both laboratory and field settings have shown how non-suggestive interviewers' support can help reluctant witnesses describe their experiences more fully. By contrast, interviewers not trained to be supportive often provide less support and behave more coercively in response to reluctance, which in turn can intensify uncooperativeness and minimize the amount of information children provide. Offering children non-suggestive social support during forensic interviews may not only promote their sense of well-being and improve their experience during interviews, but also enhances the richness and accuracy of their testimony. Importantly, non-suggestive support may benefit both young witnesses and suspects.

10

Using Tools and Props to Complement the Protocol

As explained in previous chapters, users of the NICHD Protocol are encouraged to use invitations and cued invitations preferentially throughout the interview, perhaps complemented when necessary by more focused questions paired with follow-up invitations. However, some children may fail to respond to invitations at all (Korkman, Santtila, & Sandnabba, 2006; Korkman, Santtila, Westeråker, & Sandnabba, 2008; Melinder & Gilstrap, 2009; Wolfman et al., 2016), or may not provide forensically important information. In such cases, some interviewers resort to tools, such as body diagrams or dolls, or ask children to draw or to mentally reinstate the context of the event, to facilitate recall and reporting (Hill & Brown, 2017; Poole, Bruck, & Pipe, 2011; Rivard & Schreiber-Compo, 2017; Wolfman, Brown, & Jose, 2017). Some practitioners believe that such tools and techniques help children to overcome linguistic, motivational, or retrieval problems by allowing them to communicate nonverbally (e.g., by pointing, showing, or drawing), or to use external sources to foster the retrieval of information (e.g., by encouraging children to concentrate on particular aspects of an event, such as spatial layout, or sensory experiences). Other experts have warned that the tools and props can be suggestive (e.g., Ceci & Bruck, 1995; Poole & Bruck, 2012) and the competing claims have stimulated research on the efficacy of various visual aids (see, for example, Brown, 2011; Pipe & Salmon, 2009; Poole, Bruck, & Pipe, 2011; Zajac & Brown, 2017 for reviews). Most of the research has focused on the amount and accuracy of children's reports when visual aids are used to elicit information about their experiences. Research examining the efficacy of using aids for other reasons (e.g., to facilitate rapport or engagement, or to minimize emotional distress) is relatively scarce. In this chapter, we summarize research that has examined the use of various aids to complement Protocol strategies when interviewing alleged victims and witnesses.

DOLLS

Dolls are the most studied visual aids, largely because of concerns raised by researchers and the courts about whether they are inherently suggestive or place too many demands on young children's cognitive and social capacities. Most studies have focused on their use with young children (Zajac & Brown, in press). By and large, laboratory-based studies have shown that, when children are interviewed using dolls, they may report or re-enact more details about experiences than children interviewed without dolls, but the number of erroneous details reported also increases, resulting in lower accuracy overall (Bruck, Ceci, Francouer, & Renick, 1995; Goodman et al., 1997; Saywitz et al., 1991). When Salmon, Pipe, Malloy, and Mackay (2012) invited 5- to 7-year-old children during an NICHD Protocol interview to indicate on a doll the location of touches experienced during a staged event, they found no significant effect on the number of correct details, descriptions of touches, or errors, but the proportion of direct questions asked by the interviewers increased (with an accompanying decrease in the proportion of invitations posed).

Field studies of doll use, in which accuracy cannot be assessed, have not revealed increases in the amount of forensically relevant information provided by children (Lamb, Hershkowitz, Sternberg, Boat, & Everson, 1996; Santtila, Korkman, & Sandnabba, 2004). In addition, Thierry, Lamb, Orbach, and Pipe (2005) found that the use of dolls was associated with play, ambiguous enactments, and contradictions, rather than with increases in the amount or quality of information that young alleged victims, in particular, provided.

Studies of young children's symbolic representation skills also suggest that dolls are likely to be particularly inappropriate with young children. Young children have difficulty simultaneously holding in mind the two representations of the doll (i.e., the doll's usual identity as a plaything, and the doll's intended identity as a representation of the child or someone else; DeLoache, 2000, 2004; DeLoache & Marzolf, 1995). As a result, researchers have cautioned that very young children may interact with dolls in a playful manner, with their interactions being mistakenly interpreted as representations of their experiences (Dickinson et al., 2005; Thierry, Lamb, Orbach, & Pipe, 2005).

Despite the problems highlighted by this research, many professional guidance documents still recommend or approvingly describe the use of dolls in forensic contexts (e.g., The Cornerhouse Forensic Interview Protocol: RATAC®, Anderson, 2010; Achieving Best Evidence in Criminal Proceedings, in the UK, Ministry of Justice, 2011; APSAC, 2012; New Zealand Specialist Child Witness Interviewing Model, New Zealand Police and Ministry for Vulnerable Children Oranga Tamaraki, 2017). Because of the findings briefly summarized here, The NICHD Protocol does not recommend using dolls with children of any age.

DRAWINGS

Many interviewers invite children to draw during interviews (Hill & Brown, 2017; Wolfman et al., 2017), either to facilitate rapport and engagement (Katz, Barnetz, & Hershkowitz, 2014; Poole & Dickinson, 2014), or to help children to recall and report more information (Macleod, Gross, & Hayne, 2016). Drawing may achieve these goals by providing a focus other than the interviewers' questions, helping children to generate their own retrieval cues, or prolonging the interview so that children have more time to recall and report what they know.

The most commonly studied form of drawing is the "draw-and-talk" procedure: Interviewers ask children to draw pictures of what happened while talking about their experiences, providing no specific instructions about the content of the drawings. Many laboratory-based studies have demonstrated that children (3- to 12-year-olds) who draw and talk about a variety of events, provide more information about those events than children who do not draw, without reductions in accuracy (e.g., Butler, Gross, & Hayne, 1995; Gross & Hayne, 1998; Patterson & Hayne, 2011; Salmon et al., 2003; Wesson & Salmon, 2001).

Drawing does not always help children recall more information about their experiences, however (Gentle, Powell, & Sharman, 2014; MacLeod et al., 2016; Otgaar, van Ansem, Pauw, & Horselenberg, 2016), and may lead to increases in the number of erroneous details reported (MacLeod et al., 2016; Otgaar et al., 2016), and descriptions of entirely false events (Bruck, Melnyk, & Ceci, 2000). The instructions accompanying the drawing, the type of questioning used alongside them, the kind of event that children are recounting, and the delay since the event all appear to influence the effectiveness of drawing.

One field study and two laboratory-based studies have examined the impact of asking children to draw while being interviewed using the NICHD Protocol. In a field study of children interviewed about alleged sexual abuse ($n = 125$, 4- to 12-year-olds) Katz and Hershkowitz (2010) showed that giving children the opportunity to draw after an initial verbal interview increased the number of details they reported when asked to describe their experiences again, relative to children who had a short play or rest break before the second recall. The positive effects of drawing were not related to the age or gender of the children, nor to the type of abuse or length of the delay. Children who drew reported significantly more new details that were relevant to the investigation, including details about people, actions and the location of the alleged event(s).

Salmon et al. (2012) examined the impact of adding an opportunity to draw after an initial NICHD Protocol interview on children's reports of a staged event. The children (5- to 7-year-olds) were interviewed 7 to 10 days after an event, and were then asked either to make drawings of the event or to complete puzzles, before being re-interviewed about their experiences. Children in both groups reported new information and were less accurate during the second interview; there were no significant effects of drawing on the amount or accuracy of what children reported.

O'Connor, Brown, and Wolfman (under review) examined two different types of drawing instruction – drawing about the event, and drawing a sketchplan of the layout of the event – complementing NICHD Protocol interviews of 11- and 12-year-old children. Neither type of drawing resulted in an increase in the overall number of details reported, although children who drew a sketchplan reported more information about spatial aspects of the event. Both types of drawing instruction did not affect the children's accuracy. Similarly, Brown, McKennie, and Barton (under review) examined whether asking 5- to 6-year-old children, when interviewed using the NICHD Protocol, to draw and talk about an event before they were interviewed, as the interview unfolded, or after their initial recall was exhausted improved the amount of detail they reported about a staged event. There were no differences in the amount or accuracy of children's accounts depending on the timing of the drawing. Further, no form of drawing led children to report more information than they did when simply interviewed verbally.

Taken together, the evidence suggests that drawing may help children to say more about their experiences when they are offered minimal verbal prompting, but any positive effects may be overshadowed when a more elaborative verbal interview protocol (like the NICHD Protocol) is followed. The effectiveness of drawing may also depend on the kind of event that is being recalled; some kinds of events may be easier to draw, and distressing events may be easier to narrate when children have an external focus (like drawing). To more clearly identify when drawing is most (and least) likely to be effective, researchers need to compare the inclusion of drawing with verbal-only interviewing alongside different kinds of interviewing protocols in relation to different events and functions (e.g., drawing for rapport rather than recall support).

BODY DIAGRAMS

Body diagrams may be used to facilitate communication about very specific information. Interviewers may ask children at the beginning of the interview what words they use for various body parts (Anderson, 2010; Pipe & Salmon, 2009; Teoh et al., 2010). The impact of doing so on children's subsequent reporting of touch has yet to be examined (though Poole & Dickinson, 2011, reported preliminary evidence that the use of body diagrams to elicit labels primed children to report more touches, including non-experienced touches, later in the interview). Diagrams may also be used during interviews to elicit further details about touches that have been reported, or to probe for new information (e.g., about suspected touches). Several forensic interviewing protocols (e.g., the guidelines for Video Recorded Forensic Interviews with At-Risk Children and Young People, Child Youth & Family/New Zealand Police, 2007, in New Zealand, and Achieving Best Evidence in Criminal Proceedings, in the UK, Ministry of Justice, 2011) suggest that diagrams might be introduced at the end of the interview to elicit more information about previously reported touches (essentially providing a second retrieval attempt).

The extent to which children are able to use these drawings as "maps" of their own body to accurately communicate their experiences is unclear. Most studies have focused on children under 9 years of age, and so we know even less about whether body maps might be effective with older children (Zajac & Brown, in press). Most studies report increases in the number of details reported by children when body diagrams are presented, but more errors, including false reports of forensically relevant touches, are common as well (Bruck, 2009; Bruck, Kelley, & Poole, 2016; Dickinson & Poole, 2017; Otgaar, Horselenberg, van Kampen, & Lalleman, 2012; Poole & Dickinson, 2011; Steward et al., 1996; Willcock, Morgan, & Hayne, 2006). While we do not yet know which children are most likely to benefit from body diagrams, it seems that they are particularly risky when used with young children (under 5 years of age; Lytle, London, & Bruck, 2015) and with those whose executive function skills are less well developed. Such children are most likely to make multiple false reports when presented with a diagram, perhaps because of thoughtless or impulsive responding (Poole, Dickinson, Brubacher, Liberty, & Kaake, 2014).

HUMAN BODY DIAGRAMS AND THE NICHD PROTOCOL

Aldridge et al. (2004) presented 4- to 13-year-old alleged abuse victims with a human figure drawing, following an exhaustive verbal interview using the NICHD Protocol. Children were asked to show on the drawing where (a "directive" question) previously reported touches had occurred and to provide further information about these touches. Children were then asked a series of "yes/no" (recognition) questions about possible touches on other parts of the body and were prompted (using invitations) to elaborate after any affirmative response. A large amount of new information (an average of 86 new forensically relevant details) was reported during this phase of the interview even though it followed an exhaustive verbal interview. Moreover, the drawings appeared to be particularly helpful for the youngest (4- to 7-year-old) children, who reported 27% of their total information in response to the drawings. Because specific questions predominated, however, Aldridge et al. cautioned that the elicited information may have been unreliable, given that these questions are typically associated with lower accuracy (see Chapter 3).

In a further analysis of the transcripts from the Aldridge et al. study, Teoh et al. (2010) examined whether the additional information reported in response to the introduction of body diagrams was specifically about touch, whether these touches had been previously mentioned, and whether diagrams improved the clarity of the children's accounts. When presented with the body diagrams, children indeed provided new details about touches, especially about body parts. Younger and older children reported similar amounts of touch-related information post-diagram, but the clarity of the information varied by age: Younger children (4- to 7-year-olds) provided more unclear information than older (11- to 13-year-olds) children following the introduction of the diagrams, and all children provided more clarity when responding to recall rather than recognition prompts.

Several laboratory-based studies have examined how well children recall touches that occurred as part of a staged event, when interviewed using the NICHD Protocol and a body diagram. Brown, Pipe, Lewis, Lamb, and Orbach (2007) examined recall by 5- to 7-year-old children following a 4- to 6-week delay. Body diagrams were introduced after a complete verbal interview (for some children following instruction and practice using them) or children were asked questions about touch without a diagram. During the initial recall interview and even when asked very specific recognition questions (e.g., "Did the photographer tickle you on the feet?"), many children failed to report touches that had occurred. Most children (61%) reported new and apparently plausible information about the event following the introduction of the diagrams or questions about touching, but the accuracy of the information was poor. Of concern, the number of incorrect details children reported increased when a body diagram was used. Moreover, children who were interviewed with a body diagram without prior practice were less accurate when responding to recognition questions than children who had had practice.

In a follow-up study, Brown, Pipe, Lewis, Lamb, and Orbach (2012) re-interviewed the children 7 months later in the same way that they had been interviewed originally (verbal questions, diagram with instruction, or diagram only). As in the earlier interview, spontaneous reports of touch were rare. When questioned about touch the majority of children again reported new information: Relative to the earlier interview, children interviewed with a diagram but without instruction reported increased amounts of information, whereas children interviewed without a diagram reported decreased amounts of information. Children interviewed with a body diagram and instruction were less accurate than children interviewed without one when asked open-ended questions about touch (those interviewed with a diagram with no instruction did not differ from children in the other two groups). When asked recognition questions, children interviewed without a diagram were again the most accurate, but for these questions the children in the diagram-without-instruction group were less accurate (those in the diagram-with-instruction group did not differ from children in the other two groups).

Salmon and colleagues (Salmon, Pipe, Malloy, & Mackay, 2012) examined whether body diagrams helped young children (5- to 7-year-olds) to clarify previously reported touches during an interview using the NICHD Protocol. There were no differences in the amount or accuracy of the children's responses, but interviewers asked more direct questions and fewer invitations when using a diagram.

Brown, Higgs, Barton, Lamb, and Pipe (2017) examined whether diagrams might support older children's recall of touch better than photographs of the children or verbal questions alone using the NICHD Protocol. Children (5- to 6-year-olds, and 9- to 12-year-olds) were interviewed two weeks after a staged event. The impact of the interviewing aids varied by age group: Older children reported the same number of touches but more details about them when interviewed with body diagrams or photographs and the accuracy of the information was unaffected. Younger children reported more instances of touching when interviewed using a photograph (but not a diagram), but there were no age differences in the level of detail provided nor the accuracy of the information.

In summary, the results of both field and laboratory studies show that body diagrams may sometimes enhance the amount of detail that children report, but, at least for young children (7 years and younger), the clarity and accuracy of their reports may be compromised. Problems are especially likely when recognition rather than recall questions are posed.

CONTEXTUAL CUES

Drawing from theories of memory and information processing, researchers have also explored the impact of reinstating the context of the event on children's ability to report what occurred. Reinstating the context may involve taking children back to the location where the events in question occurred (physical context reinstatement) or asking children to recreate the context in their mind (Mental Context Reinstatement). Reinstatement of context increases the similarity between the conditions at the time of the event and at the time of recall, which should make information more accessible (Tulving & Thomson, 1973). Contextual cues should thus enhance the completeness and accuracy of memory retrieval because features of a memory trace accessible at the time of retrieval may bring to awareness other features of the to-be-remembered event that are not otherwise accessible (Tulving, 1983; Tulving & Thomson, 1973). The greater the overlap between retrieval cues and encoding features, the more effective cues should be at helping retrieve further details from memory. As specified in Smith's (1988) "outshining hypothesis," contextual cues should be more effective when other retrieval cues are absent, and therefore should ensure greater and more accurate memory retrieval in free recall conditions (in which no information is provided by the interviewer) than in recognition tasks (in which the target information is presented). Contextual cueing may only be effective, however, to the extent that the context is uniquely associated with the event (Nairne, 2002) – and so in cases of maltreatment, where children may experience abuse in highly familiar environments that are also associated with other events, cueing the context may add little value.

There have been a limited number of studies exploring the utility of reinstating the physical context of the event that children experienced, and the findings have been mixed. One study showed no effect of context reinstatement alone relative to a verbal interview (Pipe & Wilson, 1994) (although context reinstatement in conjunction with the presence of real items from the event was associated with increased recall), whereas another showed that children who returned to the place where the event occurred reported more information (Wilkinson, 1988).

Two studies have examined the effects of physical context reinstatement when using the NICHD Protocol. Hershkowitz et al. (1998) interviewed 4- to 13-year-old children at the scene of the alleged abuse, following an initial interview in the investigator's office. Children reported a large number of new details at the scene (23% of their total reports), with the majority of those details (86%) being related to new issues, and the remainder contextualizing previously mentioned information. Because the interview at the scene was a second retrieval attempt, however, the researchers could not attribute the additional retrieval solely to the contextual cueing rather than simply being interviewed again. Orbach, Hershkowitz, Lamb, Sternberg, and Horowitz (2000) thus compared children who were first interviewed in an investigator's office with those taken to the scene of the alleged events after their initial disclosure to continue the interview (thereby removing the confusion of a repeated interview). There was no difference between the numbers of details reported by children in the two groups. The researchers speculated that the context reinstatement was not effective because 1) the retrieval process was disrupted when the interview was paused for travel to the scene, 2) the scene had changed (e.g., variations in layout or activities in shopping malls), and/or 3) the context was not uniquely associated with the event in question (e.g., the child had visited the shopping mall on other non-abuse related occasions).

Mental context reinstatement (MCR) is often viewed as a more practical, safer, and child-led alternative to physical context reinstatement. One advantage of MCR is that it does not require the interviewer to know anything about the event in question, and the child, rather than the interviewer, generates the retrieval cues. MCR instructions typically ask children to think about different sensory features of the event (e.g., what they could hear, see, smell) and different aspects of the event (e.g., what the place looked like) to reconstruct the scene before beginning to verbally recount what they remember.

MCR is one component of the Cognitive Interview (CI; Fisher & Geiselman, 1992; Geiselman, 1988), which can improve recall by adult witnesses (see Memon, Meissner, & Fraser 2010 for a meta-analysis). The CI does not help child witnesses as consistently as it helps adults, but improved recall has been demonstrated in laboratory studies involving children ranging in age from four years (Holliday & Albon, 2004) to middle childhood (Akehurst, Milne, & Köhnken, 2003; Geiselman

& Padilla, 1988; Holliday, 2003; Larsson, Granhag, & Spjut, 2003; Milne & Bull, 2003; Saywitz, Geiselman, & Bornstein, 1992). As with adults, some researchers have reported increases in the numbers of erroneous details reported when the CI is used (Memon, Wark, Bull, & Köhnken, 1997) although the proportion of incorrect to correct information appears to remain constant (McCauley & Fisher, 1995). Other researchers have reported no improvements in recall when children were interviewed using the CI (Memon, Cronin, Eaves, & Bull, 1993).

Laboratory-based studies examining the impact of MCR instructions on children's recall independent of the CI have shown both positive (Bowen & Howie, 2002; Dietze, Powell, & Thomson, 2010, 2012) and non-existent (Dietze, Sharman, Powell, & Thomson, 2013; Gentle, Powell, & Sharman, 2014) effects. Similarly, the effects of MCR on children's suggestibility are also varied. Some studies have shown that use of the CI helps children resist suggestive questioning at the conclusion of an interview (Drohan-Jennings, Roberts, & Powell, 2010; Gentle et al., 2014; Memon, Holley, Wark, Bull, & Köhnken, 1996; Milne & Bull, 2003) and misinformation provided prior to the interview (Holliday, 2003, Experiment 2; Holliday & Albon, 2004), while others showed that children are still vulnerable to post-event misinformation despite use of the CI (Holliday, 2003 (exp 1); Milne, Bull, Köhnken, & Memon, 1995; Hayes & Delamothe, 1997).

Two field studies and one laboratory study have examined the impact of adding MCR instructions to the NICHD Protocol. Hershkowitz, Orbach, Lamb, Sternberg, and Horowitz (2001) compared children interviewed using the standard NICHD Protocol with those who were also given MCR prompts. The 4- to 13-year-old children did not provide more details about the alleged events and their first narrative responses were not richer when MCR instructions were added. Children in the MCR condition did, however, provide proportionally more information about the alleged events in response to invitation prompts (55%) than children who were interviewed using the standard Protocol (46%), and less of their information was elicited using more focused (direct or option-posing) prompts.

Hershkowitz, Orbach, Lamb, Sternberg, and Horowitz (2002) directly compared the impact of PCR-enriched, MCR-enriched, and standard NICHD Protocol interviews. Children (4 to 13 years old) were either taken to the scene of the alleged event once a location was disclosed (only cases where the alleged abuse was extra-familial and the location was therefore outside of the home were included), interviewed in the office with MCR prompts posed during the presubstantive narrative practice and once the children had disclosed, in response to any of the initial questions about why they were there, or interviewed using the standard NICHD Protocol. There were no group differences in the total number of details children reported. Children given MCR instructions reported more information than those interviewed at the scene during their first narrative description and when responding to the main invitation ("tell me everything that happened from the beginning to the end"). Children interviewed with MCR also provided more of their accounts in response to invitations and less in response to direct prompts than did children in the other two groups.

Brown et al. (2017) examined the impact of adding MCR instructions to the NICHD Protocol in a laboratory study in which children (5 to 6 years old) were interviewed about a staged event that had occurred 1 to 2 weeks earlier. Just as in the field studies, Brown et al. found no differences in the overall amount of information children reported, but in contrast, also found no difference in the proportion of information that was elicited using invitations. Children in the two conditions also did not differ with respect to the accuracy of their accounts.

In summary, evidence regarding the utility of physically reinstating the context is equivocal. Abuse frequently occurs in well-known situations or contexts that are familiar to the victims or associated with other events or experiences. As a result, it may be difficult to establish the relevant psychological context (over and above the physical context), and this reduces the effectiveness of the location as a retrieval cue. There is some evidence that MCR may help children, especially those talking about alleged maltreatment, to provide more detailed responses to those prompts that are most likely to elicit accurate information. MCR has the advantage of being child-led and does not require any information to be provided by the interviewer, thus avoiding possible contamination of the children's statements. Because field and laboratory have yielded different findings, however, more research is needed to establish when and how MCR is most likely to support children's recall.

CONCLUSION

In general, studies reviewed in this chapter have often yielded different findings depending on whether they were conducted in the field or in the laboratory. Many of the field studies show no enhancement when aids (e.g., dolls, physical reinstatement of context) are combined with NICHD Protocol interviews whereas laboratory-based analogue studies often show increased risk (e.g., increases in errors, risky questioning, or decreased accuracy) when such approaches are adopted. Some of the field studies show that including a visual aid or complementary technique (e.g., drawing, body diagrams) can enhance either the number of details children report or the richness of children's responses to the kinds of prompts most likely to elicit accurate information (e.g., MCR). In contrast, the laboratory-based evaluations of these approaches have produced varying outcomes – no impact (e.g., drawing, MCR) or detrimental effects on accuracy (e.g., body diagrams).

The contrasting and contradictory findings suggest an interaction between the kind of event under examination and other aspects of the interviewing context (e.g., delay, perpetrator identity, etc.). In all, the empirical evidence shows that there is currently no strong substitute for a good verbal interview, but there is much scope for further research to determine how and when the types of aids discussed here may add value without also compromising children's reliability.

11

Training and Maintaining Good Interviewing Practice

Interviewing children is a challenging task, requiring practitioners to be sensitive to the developmental capacities and vulnerabilities of witnesses, to understand how to facilitate children's effective retrieval and reporting of information, and to set aside the usual dynamics and expectations of how adults and children communicate (Lamb & Brown, 2006). As we discussed in Chapter 4, interviewing evaluations around the world have demonstrated that, despite increased knowledge and consensus about best practice, interviewers typically do not adhere to evidence-based recommendations (Cederborg et al., 2000; Craig et al, 1999; Johnson et al, 2015; Korkman et al., 2008; Lamb, Hershkowitz, Sternberg, Esplin et al., 1996; Luther et al., 2015; Powell & Hughes-Scholes, 2009; Sternberg, Lamb, Hershkowitz, Esplin et al., 1996; Sternberg et al., 2001; Wolfman et al., 2016a; Yi et al., 2015). Early studies of the impact of training showed increases in interviewers' knowledge about what they *ought* to do, without improvements in what they *actually* did when subsequently interviewing children (Aldridge & Cameron, 1999; Warren et al., 1999). Deviations from recommended practice may persist even in the context of increased resources for interviewers, including improved training and specialized child forensic interviewing units (Johnson, Magnussen, Thoresen, Lonnum, Burrell, & Melinder, 2015). Training

---

Tell Me What Happened: Questioning Children About Abuse, Second Edition.
Michael E. Lamb, Deirdre A. Brown, Irit Hershkowitz, Yael Orbach, and Phillip W. Esplin.
© 2018 John Wiley & Sons Ltd. Published 2018 by John Wiley & Sons Ltd.

programs that are based on knowledge transmission models (mostly, classroom style presentations of theory and research about development, memory and interviewing) are unlikely to be effective unless complemented by extensive practice opportunities and regular feedback (Lamb, 2016).

The Protocol was designed to help practitioners apply the evidence-based recommendations that have emerged from research over the past three decades. As noted previously, evaluation studies have demonstrated that the quality of forensic interviewing does improve when interviewers follow the Protocol (e.g., Benia et al., 2015; Cyr & Lamb, 2009; Cyr et al., 2012; Lamb et al., 2009; Naka, 2011; Orbach et al., 2000; Sternberg et al., 2001; Yi et al., 2016).

The incremental value of verbal and written feedback during the course of training has been experimentally demonstrated in individual (Adams, Fields, & Verhave, 1999; Clark, 1971; Frayer & Klausmeier, 1971; Sweet, 1966) and group (Gully, 1998) contexts. However, of the published interview models, only the NICHD training model underlines the importance of providing feedback beyond the training period (i.e., to post-training investigative interviews as well). Because the success of their efforts contrasted with the failures of those whose efforts were limited to intensive but time-limited training seminars, Orbach et al. (2000) and Sternberg, Lamb, Orbach et al. (2001) suggested that both the detailed Protocol and the ongoing supervision and feedback were absolutely crucial. Other researchers have echoed this hypothesis and demonstrated the importance of continuing to provide feedback on interviewing practice beyond the training period in a range of countries and with a range of interviewing models (Benson & Powell, 2015; Krause, Pompedda, Antfolk, Zappala, & Santtila, 2017; Lamb, 2016; Pompedda, Zappala, & Santilla, 2015; Powell, Guadagno, & Benson, 2016; Wolfman et al., 2016).

Studies examining factors that may predict the quality of interviewing have not established any strong associations between interviewer or workplace characteristics and adherence to recommended questioning strategies. Variability in interviewing practice is common, even after training (Lafontaine & Cyr, 2016). Importantly, the amount of interviewing experience does not typically predict the quality of interviewing. Except for one study that found a negative association between years of experience and adherence to the NICHD Protocol (Lafontaine & Cyr, 2017), no association between experience and performance is evident in field studies (e.g., Lafontaine & Cyr, 2016; La Rooy et al., 2011; Powell & Hughes-Scholes, 2009; Wolfman et al., 2016).

Laboratory analogue studies have shown that interviewers who have had more experience interviewing children are less likely to pose open-ended prompts in simulated interviews (Powell, Hughes-Scholes, Smith & Sharman, 2014; Smith, Powell, & Lum, 2009). It would seem that systemic issues such as the quality of training provided, the availability of a structured interviewing model, and provision for continuing professional development, practice-focused supervision, and regular opportunities for objective feedback on interviewing promote good interviewing practice better than how long interviewers have been working.

Two studies have explored whether interviewers' personal characteristics predict interviewing performance after they have been trained to use the NICHD Protocol. Lafontaine and Cyr (2016) examined the association between critical thinking and problem-solving skills, as well as emotional intelligence and personality, and 24 interviewers' performance in mock interviews conducted at the end of a 1-week training course in use of the NICHD Protocol. The interviewers' gender, critical thinking/problem-solving skills, and one aspect of emotional intelligence (stress management) predicted interviewing performance—interestingly, *low* (not high) stress management competencies predicted better interviewing! Three aspects of personality (openness to experience, introversion, and neuroticism) also predicted performance. Interviewing experience was negatively correlated with performance, but did not predict performance in regression analyses. A second, much smaller study (n = 13 interviewers, 114 interviews) examined the association between the same characteristics and features of police officers who interviewed children (3- to 17-year-olds) about alleged sexual abuse (Lafontaine & Cyr, 2017). In this study, emotional intelligence positively predicted adherence to the Protocol, conscientiousness positively predicted the relative prominence of open-ended questions, and critical thinking/problem solving positively predicted the richness of children's responses (number of details per response). These variables accounted for significant amounts of variance even when the age of the child, time since the interviewer's completion of training, and the amount of post-training feedback received were taken into account.

While providing some interesting data regarding interviewer characteristics that might facilitate better interviewing and responsivity to training, both of these studies involved small samples, so findings must be viewed cautiously until replicated. Nevertheless, the results illustrated that we still have much to learn about how to ensure that children are forensically interviewed most effectively.

A key component of training with the NICHD Protocol is the emphasis on continued supervision and feedback about interviewing performance (Lamb, 2016; La Rooy et al., 2015). The importance of continuing quality control and feedback was illustrated in one early study by comparing the effectiveness of four different training models designed to help interviewers implement recommended interviewing practices (Lamb, Sternberg, Orbach, Hershkowitz et al., 2002). In all training conditions, interviewers were first provided with a theoretical framework to help them understand how the recommended practices were consistent with basic research on children's memory, linguistic, communicative, and social development. The first training condition only involved such conceptual training. In the second training condition, interviewers were not only introduced to scientific principles, but were also urged to employ structured modules in the pre-substantive rapport building phase of their investigative interviews, and they practiced using these modules. In the third and fourth training conditions, interviewers were introduced to the scientific principles but were also given copies of the fully structured NICHD Interview Protocol and practiced using it under close supervision.

The third and fourth conditions differed with respect to the amount and type of supervision provided. Interviewers in the third training condition attended intensive training courses, followed by monthly daylong group meetings in which their actual field interviews were analyzed (using video recordings and transcripts of their recent interviews) and desirable and undesirable practices were discussed. In addition, interviewers in the third condition received detailed written and verbal feedback on each of their subsequent field interviews. Interviewers in the fourth condition participated in the monthly meetings alongside those in the third condition but received no individual supervision and feedback on their interviews.

The effects of these forms of training were assessed by examining the extent to which the interviewers, in the course of real-world investigative interviews, employed open-ended as opposed to focused questions, the amount of information elicited using open-ended rather than focused prompts or questions, and the extent to which the interviewers delayed introducing substantive information by using recognition prompts. In all cases, the performance of interviewers who had been trained in one of the four conditions was compared with their own performance during interviews with children of comparable ages and circumstances in the 6 months prior to the training.

As expected, we found that meaningful long-term improvements in the quality of information obtained from young alleged victims of sexual abuse were observed only when well-established principles were operationalized in a clear and concrete fashion and when training was distributed over time, rather than provided in the form of a single initial session, however intensive. Significant differences between the baseline and training conditions we studied were clearly evident only when interviewers were guided by the structured NICHD Investigative Interview Protocol and continued to attend regular intensive training workshops.

The effects were most clearly marked by improvements in the extent to which interviewers tried to elicit information using open-ended prompts, in the amount of information actually elicited from the children's free recall, and in the extent to which the interviewers were able to delay their first recognition (option-posing or suggestive) question which, by definition, involved the introduction of allegation-related information by the interviewer rather than by the child. By contrast, interviewers who received intensive short-term training, but no continuing training, generally performed little better than they had before training. There were no differences between interviews in conditions 3 and 4, however.

In a related study, furthermore, Lamb, Sternberg, Orbach, Esplin, and Mitchell (2002) showed the adverse effects of the termination of supervision and feedback on investigators' performance. Forensic interviews conducted by trained investigative interviewers who received close and continuing supervision and intensive individual feedback were compared with interviews conducted by the same interviewers in the 6 months immediately following the completion of training and the termination of the supervision and feedback. As predicted, the quality of the later interviews was inferior to that of the earlier interviews: interviewers demonstrated a decline in the use of open-ended prompts with a corresponding increase in the reliance on more focused prompts, and introduced recognition prompts earlier in the interview. The expected changes in the interviewers' questioning style were accompanied by decreases in the amount of information elicited using free-recall prompts.

Other researchers have also demonstrated the importance of feedback and supervision for maintaining high-quality interviewing practice. Cederborg and her colleagues (Cederborg, Alm, Da Silva Nises, & Lamb, 2013; Lindholm, Cederborg, & Winerdal, 2016) developed training courses at the Swedish police academy for police officers who investigate crimes against children. This program emphasized key concepts: the explanation of ground rules, rapport building, the elicitation of open narratives about experienced events, and the extensive use of open prompts. Like many of the other training programs discussed here, the courses included systematic and extensive feedback-monitored practice and evaluation of actual forensic interviews over a 5-month period. Trainees were required to demonstrate that their interviews were of an acceptable standard before they passed the course.

In their first study, Cederborg et al. (2013) compared interviews conducted by the trainees before the course started and after it ended. In the post-training interviews, the officers asked three times as many open questions and used two-thirds fewer recognition questions than they had at the beginning, suggesting that the course had been effective. The question, of course, was whether these improvements were maintained after the course ended. In a later study, therefore, Lindholm, Cederborg, and Winerdal (2016) examined interviews conducted both immediately after the course ended as well as at least two months later. As in the previous study, the use of open questions increased and the use of recognition questions declined. Importantly, these differences were still evident in interviews conducted at least 2 months after the end of the course, suggesting some maintenance of skills. Studies focusing on longer-range follow-up interviews are currently being conducted by these Swedish researchers.

Price and Roberts (2011) showed that an 8-month training program, based on the NICHD Protocol, which included a 2-day classroom-based workshop, weekly evaluation and feedback to interviewers, and a refresher training session 2 months after the initial training workshop, improved the quality of interviewing regarding a variety of child maltreatment allegations. Rischke, Roberts, and Price (2011) examined the same data to identify *how* interviewing practice changed over time and *when* interviewers began to demonstrate improvements in recommended practices. Improvements in practice relative to the pre-training baseline interviews were only evident in the months following the refresher training (and not immediately post-training), suggesting that it may take some time for interviewers to consolidate the new information and skills provided in training and then consistently integrate those into their practice. Rischke et al. (2011) also emphasized the importance of spaced learning and refresher training for supporting the consolidation and integration of learning. Wolfman et al. (2016c) similarly showed that interviewers who more frequently engaged in practice-focused supervision activities used proportionately more open-ended questions when interviewing children about sexual abuse.

Collectively, the studies reviewed thus far highlight how critical it is that interviewers are provided with opportunities for evaluation and feedback about their work—without such feedback, interviewers struggle to adhere to best practice even when following evidence-based guidance like the NICHD Protocol.

Recent research makes clear that training does not need to be conducted in classroom formats, and can be delivered over a longer period of time using computer-assisted technologies, which have become increasingly important in a number of economic sectors (education, health care, manufacturing, etc.) because of their diverse advantages. In the first such study, Powell, Guadagno, and Benson (2016) provided trainee interviewers with remote access to computer-based training activities over a period of several months, avoiding the need for interviewers (especially those working in large and geographically remote locations) to meet a trainer in person. The material to be learned was organized into 12 modules, each of which took about 3 hours to master, with regular quizzes and practices facilitating the acquisition and mastery of the material. The modules examined and provided examples related to the nature of "best practice" guidelines, question types, memory and language development, the prioritization of open-ended questions, the use of appropriate questions in the context of interviews, the non-suggestive shift of focus to the topic of concern, the specific interview protocol, self-assessment tools, the exploration of repeated incidents, evidentiary requirements, the value of narrative accounts, cross-cultural issues, and the special circumstances surrounding interviews with children who have communication difficulties. An evaluation of interviews with mock victims showed that there were significant improvements in the quality of interviews performed after training, and that these improvements were maintained over a 6-month period.

In a second study, Benson and Powell (2015) documented the value of training conducted remotely using computer-assisted technology. There were 15 substantive modules, covering the topics outlined above, and trainees were advised to complete a maximum of one module per week. The remote delivery model thus allowed Benson and Powell to provide more detailed conceptual training and the pacing ensured that information was provided in manageable units. Intermediate tests ensured that trainees acquired and implemented fundamental interviewing skills before progressing to more advanced modules. All trainees participated in numerous mock interviews, which were conducted by telephone or Skype with actors trained to play the role of abused children. Detailed, individualized, expert feedback was provided immediately after each of these practice interviews. Clearly, this well-organized and carefully delivered training program facilitated the acquisition of skills, while providing considerable evidence that learning is superior when opportunities to acquire knowledge, practice skills, and consolidate learning are distributed over time (Son & Simon, 2012).

In the first of two studies, Benson and Powell (2015) showed that trainees who completed the 15-modular training sessions conducted better interviews with actors portraying children after they completed the course. The post-training mock interviews included more open questions, were briefer, yielded more of the evidentially important information, and were more compliant with the interview guidance that had been communicated in the modules. Assessments were made shortly after the training was completed, but continued improvement was evident, on at least some dimensions, as long as 12 months after the training ended, albeit only in mock interviews rather than forensic interviews with suspected victims of abuse.

In their second study, Benson and Powell (2015) evaluated the quality of forensic interviews conducted by the trainees both before and after they completed the computer-assisted course described above. As in the first study, there were clear improvements in the quality of the interviews and there was some evidence that these improvements were maintained after the training ended and the interviewers began conducting interviews regularly as part of their professional work.

In two other studies, a team of researchers examined the utility of computer-generated avatars as part of interviewing training. The avatars' responses to interviewer questions were determined by algorithms developed from research regarding children's patterns of responding to different kinds of interviewer prompts. The avatars held pre-defined "memories" that either did or did not include sexual abuse. Use of the avatars thus allowed the interviewers to practice their skills and receive feedback about their questioning styles and the conclusions they reached. Pompedda, Zappala, and Santtila (2015) and Krause, Pompedda, Antfolk, Zappala, and Santtila (2017) showed that untrained interviewers who interviewed the avatars and received feedback about their performance later used more recommended questions and fewer undesirable questions while obtaining more relevant details and fewer inaccurate details than when they had obtained no such feedback. The avatars' response patterns alone (that is, when interviewers did not receive feedback) were not sufficient to reinforce recommended questioning practice. The studies thus showed that technology can make a useful contribution to training and provide beneficial practice opportunities for interviewers, so long as it is accompanied by systematic feedback about performance during the training sessions.

Despite clear evidence of the need for ongoing supervision, practice-focused feedback, and refresher training for the maintenance of high-quality interviewing skills, practitioners often have difficulty accessing appropriately trained and experienced supervisors (La Rooy, Lamb, & Memon, 2011; Powell & Barnett, 2015; Wolfman et al., 2016c), often for either financial or geographical reasons (Wolfman et al., 2016c). In addition, interviewers often report having limited opportunities and time for professional development and supervision activities (Benson & Powell, 2015). Alternative approaches that complement traditional face-to-face supervision may offer a solution to these problems (Krause et al., 2017; Lamb et al., 2002; Pompedda et al., 2015; Powell, Wright, & Clark, 2010).

Interviewers' poor adherence to recommended questioning strategies may also be affected by the difficulties they seem to have accurately monitoring their own practices (Agnew, Powell, & Snow, 2006; Wright & Powell, 2006). Studies suggest that interviewers generally have difficulty recognizing their use of appropriate and inappropriate interviewing strategies, and there is often a discrepancy between subjective perceptions and objective evaluations (Agnew et al., 2006; Wright, Powell, & Ridge, 2007; Yi, Lamb, & Jo, 2015). For example, Agnew et al. (2006) asked police officers to rate the appropriateness of their questions when interviewing children with intellectual disabilities. Their ratings ranged from "Okay" to "Good." However, their self-ratings did not reliably discriminate between uses of open-ended prompts by the best and worst interviewers. In fact, one of the interviewers who rated his performance as "good" also asked the most closed-ended questions.

Learning how to effectively self-review one's interviewing practice (and, by extension, being able to offer guidance to others in peer review) might be achieved by high-quality post-training. Yii, Powell, and Guadagno (2014) found that interviewers' ability to identify different types of questions accurately was associated with increased use of open-ended questions in mock interviews. Thus, developing skill and expertise in accurately identifying different types of questions may influence the use of such questions in interviews. Trainee interviewers also highly valued the process of transcribing and coding their own interviews in training designed to increase adherence to open-ended questioning (Powell & Wright, 2008).

For a guided self-review to be effective, however, it needs to be structured (Wright, Guadagno, & Powell, 2009) and be based on the objective evaluation of interviewing practice rather than global and subjective judgments (e.g., "Good" interviewing practice; Agnew, Powell, & Snow, 2006). Wright et al. (2009), for example, asked forensic interviewers to engage in self-initiated practice without instructions about format, structure, or timing. Interviewers did not consistently adhere to this task, and interviewing performance was not significantly affected. By contrast, Wolfman (2016) trained a small group of interviewers to apply a guided self-review tool to their interviews (coding their questions, tracking the proportions of prompts that were sequenced, and noting the inclusion of recommended components of the local interviewing protocol). Interviews during the self-review period were compared with those conducted before the interviewers had learned how to use the self-review tool.

Whereas during the baseline period, interviewers' subjective ratings of their interviewing quality were not associated with objective measures of recommended practice, during the self-review period the interviewers' subjective ratings predicted their use of open-ended questions. During the self-review period, interviewers used proportionately more invitations and fewer directive prompts, and were more likely to follow up option-posing prompts with invitations than during the baseline period.

The same principles were clearly evident in the heavily-structured training program, developed by Hershkowitz, Ahern et al. (2017), that we described in Chapter 9. Every session in a training program that extended over several months focused on how to deliver each of the supportive interventions emphasized in the RP. Thus, the first session discussed the reasons why the recommended supportive interventions were appropriate, modeled supportive statements, and taught trainees how to code their interviews; the second training session focused on creating, enhancing, and maintaining rapport during the pre-substantive phase; the third on the principles of providing support in the transitional phase; and the fourth on providing support during the substantive phase of investigative interviews. The fifth and sixth sessions were dedicated to the principles of planning and conducting repeated interviews when children were unwilling to disclose possible abuse despite strong suspicions that abuse had occurred (fifth session) or when children required another interview in order to elicit further details about their alleged victimization (sixth session). Session 7 focused on identifying and analyzing nonverbal indicators of reluctance, and session 8 ended the main training program, providing guidance on how to conduct an integrative analysis of a completed investigation. The figures included in Chapter 9 clearly illustrate the slow process of change across the months during which the experienced interviewers were taught how to recognize signs of reluctance and to respond in an appropriately sensitive but non-suggestive way.

Stolzenberg and Lyon (2015) also showed that self-reviewing had positive effects on students' interviewing during a forensic interviewing course. Self-reviewing may thus be a promising complement to independent supervision and feedback which is accessible and cost effective, but replication of these studies is required. Interviewers report that training and professional development activities are often overly time consuming and that managers may not provide enough time in which interviewers could complete such activities (Benson & Powell, 2015; Wolfman et al., 2016c). Thus determining how much and how frequently interviewers should engage in various training tasks is important for future research.

CONCLUSION

The research reviewed in this chapter shows that interview quality *can* be improved, but only when the training moves beyond the classroom, is spaced over time, and involves extensive opportunities to consolidate learning and practice skills in contexts that ensure prompt feedback and guidance. Changes in interviewing practice are most likely to be achieved only in the context of well-structured and extended training.

The research thus has important, although somewhat sobering, implications for those attempting to translate findings from basic research to practice in the real world. Clearly, it is possible to employ our accumulated knowledge of memory and communicative development to improve the quality of information elicited from alleged victims of child abuse, but this benefit is obtained only when extensive efforts are made not only to train interviewers to adopt recommended practices, but to ensure the maintenance of these practices as well.

12

Case-related Outcomes When the Protocol is Used

We have discussed in previous chapters how the adoption of the NICHD Protocol improves both interviewing practice and children's informativeness. In this chapter, we focus on the impact that the use of the Protocol has on broader case-related outcomes. In particular, we consider research examining whether the information elicited from children during Protocol interviews enhances assessments of their credibility and of their testimony more generally, the impact of the Protocol on the availability of investigative leads, its impact on allegation and disclosure rates, and, finally, its impact on the resolution of cases within the criminal justice system.

ASSESSING CREDIBILITY

How testimony is received by others—and critically, whether the audience (e.g., the jury) is likely to find the child's account believable and accurate—is of crucial importance. However, we know relatively little about factors affecting assessments of truthfulness, although factors such as the children's ages, family structure, and characteristics of the alleged maltreatment (e.g., the perpetrator's use of coercion or grooming)

Tell Me What Happened: Questioning Children About Abuse, Second Edition.
Michael E. Lamb, Deirdre A. Brown, Irit Hershkowitz, Yael Orbach, and Phillip W. Esplin.
© 2018 John Wiley & Sons Ltd. Published 2018 by John Wiley & Sons Ltd.

all influence raters' judgments of children's believability (e.g., Melkman, Hershkowitz, & Zur, 2017; Roberts & Lamb, 2010). Nonetheless, when children make disclosures of sexual abuse, a substantial proportion of cases may be deemed insufficiently credible to pursue (42% in Melkman et al.'s 2017 study, for example). Unfortunately, those judgments themselves may be flawed. Studies of adults' ability to accurately identify whether children are telling the truth show that, overall, they are able to do so at a rate only slightly above chance (54%; Gongola, Scurich, & Quas, 2017). Adults are better at correctly identifying truthful (64%) than untruthful (48%) accounts, but even many of these are wrongly categorized (Gongola et al., 2017; Hershkowitz, Fisher, Lamb, & Horowitz, 2007).

In an effort to improve the accuracy and consistency of credibility assessment, researchers developed tools such as Statement Validity Analysis (SVA) and one of its components, Criterion Based Content Analysis (CBCA) (Akehurst, Koehnken, & Hoefer, 2001; Steller, Wellerhaus, & Wolf, 1988; Yuille, 1988) as a means of measuring the likely veracity of statements or testimony. CBCA had its origins in the observation that descriptions of events that really happened differ in content and quality from descriptions of events that were not actually experienced (Undeutsch 1982, 1989). In particular, Undeutsch hypothesized that experienced events are reported in richer detail and with clearer links to other real-world events than events that have been fabricated or imagined. Undeutsch was specifically concerned with the qualitative characteristics of narrative accounts, believing that credibility was reflected in such factors as the extent to which descriptions of the target incidents were placed in temporal and spatial context, logically coherent though marked by digressions, and contained the unique details that appeared to define specific incidents rather than generic descriptions of general situations. Undeutsch did not claim that credible accounts necessarily contained more details than implausible accounts, and even recognized lack of confidence as an index of credibility rather than its absence.

Steller and Koehnken (1989) and Raskin and Esplin (1991a) subsequently developed a list of 19 criteria that could be used to quantify features of children's statements or accounts and thereby systematically evaluate the credibility of children's accounts. They proposed that trained raters should review a verbatim transcript of the child's statement or account, decide whether or not each of the criteria or characteristics was present, and then assign a score indicating how many criteria were present.

Since the original criteria were specified, many studies have examined the extent to which CBCA can 1) be reliably applied (i.e., how well-trained raters can agree on whether a criterion is present or not), and 2) accurately distinguish truthful and non-truthful accounts. A recent meta-analysis provides evidence for good convergence between raters in identifying whether most criteria are present (some criteria, which are more subjective in nature, have lower reliability scores) (Hauch, Sporer, Masip, & Blandon-Gitlin, 2017), consistent with findings from a field study of interviews about child sexual abuse (Horowitz et al., 1997). Hauch et al. also identified that reliability is typically higher in field studies than in laboratory-based studies. Importantly, they cautioned against the use of summary scores, which may include items that are unreliable. With those caveats, however, it appeared that the CBCA system might provide a reliable means of quantitatively evaluating children's credibility.

In determining whether CBCA reliably identifies truthful accounts, however, a major difficulty inevitably arises: How can researchers determine whether or not the alleged incident actually occurred? Because judicial disposition is itself influenced by the child's statement, it does not constitute an independent validation of the child's allegations. For research purposes, it is thus necessary to consider only independent validating information (Wells & Loftus, 1991). Several researchers have recommended that multifaceted procedures should be used to synthesize the results of medical examinations, suspect statement, polygraphic examinations, witness statements, and other circumstantial or physical evidence when determining, with varying degrees of certainty, the probability that the alleged events actually occurred (e.g., Horowitz, Lamb, Esplin, Boychuk, Reiter-Lavery, & Krispin, 1995). Raskin and Esplin (1991c) based their identification of "confirmed" cases on the results of polygraphic and medical examinations, suspects' confessions, and eyewitnesses' accounts; it was obviously much more difficult to obtain independent evidence about doubtful cases. The absence of supporting or corroborative evidence should never be confused with contradictory evidence, however: corroborative evidence is lacking in the majority of cases which is one of the reasons why field research on credibility is both so difficult to conduct and so important to those who would like to see more cases proceed to prosecution.

Lamb, Sternberg, Esplin, Hershkowitz, Orbach, and Hovav (1997) adopted a multifaceted approach to estimating likelihood of abuse in a study in Israel, where the established system made it easier to obtain a representative sample of cases. Because interviews were selected only on the basis of external characteristics, rather than following examination of the interviews themselves, the interviews varied widely in quality and length, with no standardized interview procedures employed. From a pool of 1,187 interviews, Lamb et al. selected 98 for which independent validating information was available and the alleged victims were between 4 and 13 years of age. The interviews were rated by at least two native Hebrew speakers who had been trained to reliably employ the revised CBCA codes and were totally unfamiliar with the independent validating material. Meanwhile, other researchers used all investigative information other than the children's statements to evaluate, on a 6-point scale, the likelihood that the events described by the children indeed occurred: Very Likely, Quite Likely, Questionable, Quite Unlikely, Very Unlikely, and No Judgment Possible.

Very few (just 13) of the cases were rated as either Quite Unlikely or Very Unlikely, but there was a significant association between the plausibility of the allegations and the total CBCA scores, with the highest scores assigned to statements about events deemed Very or Quite Likely to have occurred on the basis of independent case facts. Five of the criteria were significantly more likely to be present in Plausible than in Implausible accounts.

Although the CBCA scores indeed differentiated significantly between more and less credible accounts in this study, the differences between them were much less dramatic than reported by Boychuk (1991) or Raskin and Esplin (1991b, 1991c), and erroneous judgments were too frequent to make forensic application appropriate. The results of another validation study in the United States, using CBCA rating procedures similar to Lamb et al.'s, yielding surprisingly similar findings (Craig et al., 1999). Thus, although CBCA reliably discriminates between "true" and "false" statements, its precision is not good enough for forensic application.

In light of Raskin and Esplin's (1991a) insistence on the need for high-quality interviews to be available before credibility could be assessed reliably, Hershkowitz, Lamb, Sternberg, and Esplin (1997) then sought to determine whether there was a relationship between the interview characteristics empirically associated with the elicitation of greater amounts of information and the presence of the CBCA criteria that ostensibly index credibility. As noted earlier, open-ended invitations elicit longer (more words) and richer (more details) responses than more focused utterances. The superiority and importance of invitational prompts might be further underscored if it could be shown that these prompts were also more likely to elicit responses that contain CBCA criteria. Accordingly, Hershkowitz et al. asked not simply whether the criteria were more likely to be present in truthful accounts but the association between the presence of these criteria and features of the interview process, particularly the types of interviewer utterances known to elicit greater amounts of information from children.

As expected, invitations evoked responses containing significantly more details and CBCA criteria than did all the other types of utterances, including facilitators, and the number of criteria present was significantly correlated with the number of words spoken by and the number of details provided by the child.

In a subsequent study, Hershkowitz (1999) applied the same CBCA analyses to groups of interviews deemed (on the basis of independent information) to constitute either highly plausible or implausible accounts of sexual abuse. In that study, she was especially interested in the dynamics of interviews with children who appeared likely to be fabricating their accounts. Because such accounts are presumably not drawn from memories of the alleged events, it was particularly interesting to determine whether various investigative utterances, including suggestive prompts, elicited qualitatively and quantitatively distinctive responses. The study involved interviews of 24 children ranging in age from 4 to 13 (the average age was just over 8).

The 24 interviews were selected from the 98 included in Lamb et al.'s (1997) CBCA study. For the purposes of the new study, transcripts of 12 interviews describing incidents that were deemed unlikely to have happened were matched on the basis of the children's ages with 12 interviews describing events that appeared likely to have happened. In each case, the plausibility or implausibility of the allegations was based on Lamb et al.'s (1997) evaluation of independent evidence of various types (medical examinations, witness and suspect statements, and physical evidence) rated and integrated using the Independent Case Fact Scales.

There were several important differences between interviews yielding plausible and implausible accounts. In particular, children describing events that probably happened provided longer and richer responses to open-ended prompts than to more focused prompts, just as did children in previous studies (Hershkowitz et al., 1997; Lamb et al., 1997a, 1997b; Sternberg et al., 1996a). Such a pattern of responding is predicted when respondents extract details about experienced events from recall and recognition memories respectively. This pattern was not evident in the interviews yielding accounts of events that probably did not happen, however.

There was an intriguing, albeit non-significant, tendency for suggestive prompts to yield richer responses from children providing implausible accounts. This may have reflected a tendency for children to elaborate upon the interviewers' suggestions in the absence of memories to decode, and is consistent with evidence that, in laboratory analogue studies, children are more susceptible to suggestions when their memories are weaker (Ceci & Bruck, 1997).

Such findings underscore the potential dangers inherent in suggestive investigative prompts and the potential advantage of open-ended prompts and free recall narratives in the distinction between credible and incredible allegations. In the absence of such narratives, it is difficult to evaluate the credibility of children's statements, and thus high-quality interviews that tap recall memory are essential if credibility is to be assessed with validity (e.g., Raskin & Esplin 1991b; Raskin & Yuille 1989). This conclusion was underscored by the results of a study conducted in Israel by Hershkowitz, Fisher, Lamb, and Horowitz (2007).

THE EFFECTS OF THE PROTOCOL ON CREDIBILITY ASSESSMENT

To more directly assess the impact of the quality of interviewing on the validity and reliability of assessments of children's statements, Hershkowitz et al., (2007) examined credible and incredible allegations of sexual abuse provided by children in non-Protocol and Protocol interviews. The study thus constituted the first systematic attempt to see whether introduction of the Protocol affected the ability of youth investigators to judge children's credibility, one of their responsibilities under Israeli law.

Half of the interviews studied by Hershkowitz et al. were supported by clear independent evidence that the allegations were plausible, with the remainder judged implausible. Three independent raters used "ground truth" information such as confessions, witness accounts, physical information (e.g., photographs), and the results of medical examinations (Horowitz, Lamb, Esplin, Boychuk, Krispin, & Reiter-Lavery, 1997; Lamb et al., 1997) to make the plausibility assessments.

Twenty-four interviews were selected for analysis, and were then rated by 42 experienced Israeli youth investigators. Half the plausible allegations (credible statements) and half of the implausible allegations (incredible statements) were obtained in interviews conducted using the Protocol. These cases were individually matched with cases investigated by the same interviewers without the Protocol in the years before the use of the Protocol became mandatory. Cases were matched with respect to the children's ages, the types of allegations, and the strength of the validating evidence before transcripts of the interviews were sought.

Each participating youth investigator was asked to rate four transcribed statements, one from each of these categories, so 7 child investigators independently judged the credibility of each of the transcribed interviews. Participants had no access to the validating information used to assess "ground truth" and thus assessed the statements' credibility based only on the interviews. Participants judged how likely it was that the alleged incidents had really happened using a 4-point scale: "very likely," "quite likely," "quite unlikely," or "very unlikely," or made a "no judgment possible" (NJP) decision. Participants also indicated their confidence in their judgments on a 5-point scale ("very unconfident" to "very confident").

None of the raters selected "very unlikely to have happened" for either plausible or implausible cases. Raters had higher levels of reliability when rating Protocol compared to non-Protocol interviews, whether or not the allegations were plausible. Raters were much more likely to make a "NJP" decision when evaluating non-Protocol than Protocol interviews (52% vs. 17%).

Nearly 60% of the ratings of Protocol interviews, including nearly all of the judgments regarding plausible and a quarter of the judgments regarding implausible statements, were accurate (i.e., allegations correctly judged as either credible or incredible). By contrast, less than a third of the judgments regarding non-Protocol interviews, including nearly 40% of the judgments about plausible allegations and 12% of those about implausible allegations, were accurate. Both plausible and implausible allegations were more likely to be judged accurately when Protocol rather than non-Protocol interviews were being judged.

Raters expressed more confidence when assessing Protocol interviews than when assessing non-Protocol interviews. There were no associations between raters' confidence and the accuracy or their assessments of both non-Protocol interviews and Protocol interviews of implausible cases. When assessing plausible Protocol cases, however, interviewers who were more confident were also more accurate.

Using the Protocol clearly seemed to facilitate judgments of credibility when examining the children's statements. These experienced investigators were twice as likely to judge children's credibility accurately when the interviews were conducted using the Protocol than when they were not similarly structured. This dramatic effect was especially impressive because no other tools have been shown to enhance credibility assessment, leaving professionals frequently incapable of distinguishing between accounts of experienced and non-experienced events (Ceci et al., 1994; Horner et al., 1993a, 1993b; Leichtman & Ceci, 1995).

The Protocol appears to enhance the accuracy of credibility assessments because children's statements are of higher quality when interviewers follow "best practice" professional recommendations and more putative indices of credibility can be observed. As we showed earlier, the ability to identify CBCA criteria in children's statements is enhanced when interviewers elicit narrative responses from alleged victims using open-ended strategies (Hershkowitz et al., 1997). In comparison with focused questions, furthermore, open-ended strategies elicit richer descriptions from children making plausible as opposed to implausible allegations (Hershkowitz, 1999).

Use of the Protocol thus not only enhances the quality of interviewing and of the elicited information, but also facilitates assessments of children's credibility. Although the Protocol was designed to foster adherence to recommended practices that enable children to provide statements of high quality, the broader goal was to help forensic professionals assess children's statements, thereby promoting justice for abused children. The results reported here show that the Protocol is a valuable forensic tool in this regard.

Protocol-guided interviews yielding both plausible and implausible allegations were rated more accurately than non-Protocol interviews. With respect to plausible allegations, the use of the Protocol almost totally eliminated inaccurate judgments, whereas incorrect judgments about implausible statements were still made with alarming frequency. Abused children interviewed using the Protocol were never incorrectly considered to be making implausible allegations, whereas non-abused children fabricating allegations were disconcertingly often perceived as real victims by these experienced professionals.

The high inter-rater reliability achieved when Protocol interviews were assessed reflects the high levels of accuracy but deserves special mention as well. Levels of agreement regarding the Protocol interviews were remarkably high in comparison with both the levels of agreement regarding non-Protocol interviews in this study as well as comparable rates reported in previous studies (Finlayson & Koocher, 1991; Horner et al., 1993a, 1993b; Jackson & Nuttal, 1993; Poole & Lindsay, 1997). High agreement in itself does not necessarily indicate that the judgments are valid because raters can agree about incorrect judgments (as happened frequently in the case of non-Protocol interviews), but the high levels of agreement with respect to correct judgments regarding allegations made in Protocol interviews reveals another advantage of the Protocol.

Evidently, use of the Protocol not only improves the quality of investigative interviews, but also decreases individual differences in both interviewing and credibility assessment, thereby increasing the chances that justice will be served, regardless of who performs the investigation or assessment.

ALLEGATION RATES IN REVISED AND STANDARD PROTOCOL INTERVIEWS

As discussed in Chapter 9, a substantial proportion of alleged victims do not report abuse when formally interviewed, with estimates varying depending on the context in which the interviews were conducted

(London, Bruck, Ceci, & Shuman, 2005, 2007). The presence of corroborating evidence, and a prior disclosure are associated with higher rates of children making an allegation during an interview. The tendency to make allegations is also affected by the child's relationship to the suspect, their age, gender, and the type of abuse suspected (DiPietro et al., 1997; Ghetti & Goodman, 2001; Gries et al., 1996; Hershkowitz et al., 2005; Hershkowitz, Lanes, & Lamb, 2007; Keary & Fitzpatrick, 1994; Levesque, 1994; Pipe et al., 2007; Smith et al., 2000; Wood, Orsak, Murphy, & Cross, 1996).

Although many children are willing to disclose abuse when interviewed appropriately, some children are reluctant to do so, and frequently signal this reluctance in the early (preparatory) phases of the interview (Hershkowitz, Horowitz, & Lamb, 2007; Hershkowitz et al., 2006; Katz et al., 2012; Orbach et al., 2007), as we have noted previously. Interviewers typically do not respond supportively to reluctance and their efforts to elicit a disclosure with these children may result in sparse accounts (Orbach et al., 2007). As we discussed in Chapter 9, interviewers who employed the emotionally supportive techniques that are integrated into the Revised Protocol elicited higher rates of corroborated allegations from children than when they followed the Standard Protocol.

Thus far we have shown that the use of the Protocol influences the likelihood that abused children will disclose abuse during forensic interviews, and the accuracy and reliability of raters' assessments of the credibility of children's accounts when they are talking about abuse. Because many allegations of child maltreatment are deemed either implausible or inadequate bases for intervention because there is not enough information to judge their validity, we next consider research examining whether introduction of the Protocol led to differences in the way allegations were judged, presumably as a result of improvements in interviewing practice and children's informativeness.

CASE OUTCOMES

Pipe, Orbach, Lamb, Abbott, and Stewart (2013) examined whether the adoption of the Protocol was reflected in "downstream effects" on the progress of cases through the criminal justice system, as well as case decisions and outcomes. In particular, the study focused on whether the quality of the investigative interview predicted outcomes such as the filing of criminal charges, prosecution, and guilty pleas or convictions.

Pipe et al. compared outcomes of investigations of child sexual abuse (the children were 3 to 14 years of age) across a six-year period in Salt Lake City, Utah, during the three years prior to the adoption of the NICHD Protocol (350 cases), and the three years following its introduction (410 cases). They showed significant differences between cases conducted prior to and after the introduction of the Protocol at two crucial decision points: the filing of charges by prosecutors and the final judicial disposition, through either plea negotiation or trial. Charges were filed in 48% of the cases. More charges were filed when Protocol interviews had been conducted (meaning they were less likely to have been screened out early by police or prosecutors) than after pre-Protocol interviews. Specifically, charges were filed in 53% of the Protocol interviews but in only 42% of the pre-Protocol interviews. As in previous studies (e.g., Cross et al., 1995, 2003; MacMurray, 1989), the initial screening seemed to be crucial. Many non-prosecuted cases were "declined" during the screening process, and proportionally fewer cases were declined in the Protocol (17.6%) than in the pre-Protocol (28%) periods. As a result, proportionately more Protocol than pre-Protocol cases were prosecuted.

Interview condition (pre- vs post-Protocol) was a significant predictor of the likelihood of charges being filed—this outcome was 1.46 times more likely with Protocol interviews when other aspects of the case were controlled for. The majority (97%) of cases where charges were filed reached disposition with most of those charged pleading guilty. Interview condition was not associated with many of the case outcomes (e.g., charges dismissed, plea reduced). As in earlier research on the outcomes of child sexual abuse cases (see Cross et al., 2003, for review) few cases went to trial (n = 23) but Protocol cases were more likely to result in guilty verdicts than pre-Protocol cases (10/11 compared to 6/12).

Improvements in the quality of victim statements are likely to have accounted for increases in the proportion of cases in which charges were filed, although other factors may have been important, too. For example, Darvish, Hershkowitz, Lamb, and Orbach (2005) found that forensic interviews conducted using the Protocol yielded more investigative leads (i.e., information suggesting new avenues for investigation) as well as more central, stronger, and more verifiable leads than those produced in non-Protocol interviews, and the availability of such leads may have facilitated more thorough and productive investigations of the alleged crimes.

Although few cases went to trial, the high rate of convictions in trials following introduction of the Protocol is nonetheless striking. Whereas previous studies have reported trial conviction rates between 50% and 75% (see Cross et al., 1995), trial conviction rate for Protocol cases in the present study amounted to 91%. Only one of the 11 Protocol cases (9%) tried yielded an acquittal in contrast to six of the 12 pre-Protocol cases (50%). Cross et al. (2003) pointed out that, although only a small number of cases go to trial, they are important because of their potential impact on both children who must testify (see, for example, Goodman, Batterman-Faunce, & Kenney, 1992), and on future decisions by prosecutors and defendants (and their attorneys), potentially influencing the much larger category of plea negotiations.

Evidence that charges are more likely to be filed and that suspects are more likely to be convicted at trial provides strong endorsement indeed of a best-practice approach to interviewing, with potentially important implications for policy and practice regarding child victims. It is clear that improvements in the quality of investigative interviewing are critical for ensuring children can provide detailed and accurate accounts of their experiences, and also for optimising the likelihood that substantiated allegations of sexual abuse are addressed in the criminal justice system (Cross & Hershkowitz, 2017).

CONCLUSION

The research described in this chapter has demonstrated how use of the Protocol can improve case evaluation, progression, and disposition. Although errors in distinguishing credible from implausible allegations still remain unacceptably high in assessments of children's allegations, more reliable and accurate decisions are made when children are interviewed using the Protocol. Whether the use of the Protocol similarly increases juror perceptions of children's credibility has yet to be tested: Other researchers have shown that the quality of the interview can significantly influence how credible children are to be perceived by prospective jurors (Castelli, Goodman, & Ghetti, 2005; Johnson & Shelley, 2014) and so it is likely that accounts elicited using the Protocol are viewed more positively. Higher rates of (plausible) allegations are obtained when children are interviewed using the Protocol without inflating the numbers of false allegations elicited. Cases are more likely to progress through the criminal justice system and are more likely to produce guilty pleas or convictions when the Protocol is employed.

There are thus a number of ways in which use of the Protocol has a positive impact on the investigation of child abuse and the implementation of appropriate interventions. By improving the quality of forensic interviews, children are not only helped to provide testimony about maltreatment, but their well-being is promoted by the increased access to justice.

13

Progress to Date and the Challenges Ahead

In this book, we have summarized a remarkably successful program of research, informed by decades of scholarship by developmental scientists, clinicians, and practitioners, on the most effective ways of eliciting accurate and detailed information from alleged victims of child abuse. In the first edition of the book, our goal was to identify the challenges faced by children and interviewers interacting during a forensic interview, and to describe the development and evaluation of an interviewing Protocol designed to facilitate evidence-based and developmentally sensitive interviewing with children in forensic contexts. In this second edition, we have added discussion of subsequent research relating to children's development, interviewing strategies, and importantly, have introduced a revised version of the Protocol which addresses the socioemotional needs of children describing instances of maltreatment they have experienced.

In Chapter 2, we outlined some of the characteristics of children which together affect their ability to talk coherently and informatively about their experiences. We discussed how age may serve as a proxy indicator of performance in an array of domains which influence recall and reporting of events. Research to date indicates that children report more details about their experiences as they get older, but the influence of age on the accuracy of children's accounts varies depending on the types of questions used to elicit that information. Language, cognitive ability, knowledge, and various aspects of information processing (e.g., Theory of Mind, source monitoring, memory, attention, strategy use) are all likely to influence children's testimony, and there is some evidence that other individual differences (e.g., fantasy, attachment and temperament) may also be implicated in children's accounts of their experiences.

We also reviewed evidence about the characteristics of the events being recalled that may affect children's testimony about or accounts of those events. Recall of events declines as the delay between the event and the interview increases. The number of instances of an event may also influence recall, particularly through the formation of representations of what typically occurs or is consistent across episodes, and this may make describing any particular instance of the event challenging, especially for young children. Children's ability to give testimony may also be influenced by their degree of involvement in the events in question, with experienced events typically better recalled than those that were only witnessed.

While there remains much to learn about the impact on recall of stress experienced either at the time of the event (encoding) or at the time of retrieval, it is apparent that memories for highly emotional and salient events are still subject to the same kinds of memory processes as other experiences—and thus may be forgotten as well as both incompletely and/or erroneously recalled in much the same way as more neutral or positive experiences.

In Chapter 3, we examined the interview context and how it may influence children's testimony. The research reviewed there highlighted how the ways in which children are prepared for an interview, and then questioned about their experiences, affect what they recount, whether (and when) children have made disclosures, as well as the nature of any discussions triggered by those disclosures, before formal interviews need to be considered when planning for an interview and evaluating children's testimony. So too is the number of times children are interviewed (and importantly, the way in which those interviews were conducted). We discussed how establishing and maintaining rapport promotes accurate recall and buffers the negative effects of any potentially suggestive influences that may be present. We examined research evaluating the efficacy of establishing ground rules for the interview at the outset, and concluded that, while there is some evidence showing the value of some of the rules, more research is needed to identify the most effective and developmentally sensitive ways of presenting and reinforcing these rules to increase the likelihood that children will follow them and thus provide more detailed and accurate accounts to interviewers.

We also highlighted the benefits of giving children the opportunity to practice both narrating a recent event and responding to the kinds of questions interviewers are likely to ask about the alleged maltreatment; such practice enhances children's responsiveness during the later substantive phase of forensic interviews. Such preparation helps overcome the challenges posed by the contrasting expectations and dynamics of forensic interviews as opposed to more typical adult-child conversational interactions. Most importantly, we reviewed research examining the impact of different types of questions on the richness and accuracy of the responses they elicit, noting extensive evidence that broadly open-ended questioning enhances the amount and quality of information obtained.

In Chapter 4, we showed how typical interviewing practices around the world tend to deviate from such evidence-based recommendations. Evaluations of forensic practice in a number of countries have consistently demonstrated how common it is for interviewers to omit various strategies that support child witnesses (e.g., presenting a range of ground rules, conducting a practice narrative). Of particular concern, the proportions of recommended question types (e.g., broad open-ended invitations) relative to those known to have detrimental effect on children's reliability (e.g., closed or suggestive questions) tend to be disappointing, with recommended questions tending to be asked only in the early stages of the interview, if at all. The difficulties interviewers have adhering to recommended practice are evident in many countries, suggesting that the challenges are independent of jurisdiction, interviewing models, and cultures.

In Chapter 5 we described the structure and content of the NICHD Investigative Interviewing Protocol, and in Chapter 6 presented evidence from a range of field and laboratory studies showing the positive impact its use has on both how interviewers question children and how informatively the latter respond. A meta-analysis demonstrated moderate to large effects of Protocol usage on both interviewer questioning and child responding.

The needs of very young victims who must be interviewed about their experiences of maltreatment were discussed in Chapter 7: Studies with these children demonstrate that they are able to provide some useful information in response to invitation prompts, but that with 3 to 4 year olds, directive prompts can be the most productive. Cued invitations, which use previously mentioned details as prompts for further elaboration, also seem particularly effective with young children, especially when they focus on action related information. Benia et al. (2015)

noted in their meta-analysis a higher level of variability in findings with pre-schoolers, and highlighted the need for more research with this group, who have been the focus of substantial speculation but limited research.

We next (Chapter 8) considered evidence concerning the testimonial capacities of children with developmental disabilities, who are disproportionately likely to be maltreated and yet may be denied the opportunities (e.g., to provide testimony) available to typically developing children. Both laboratory and field research has contributed to an emerging evidence base documenting the capacities of children with intellectual disabilities. These findings challenge the negative perceptions held of children with intellectual disabilities by lawyers, jury members, and investigators and suggest that the same approaches to interviewing are appropriate for typically developing children and children with intellectual disabilities, although children with more severe cognitive impairments may (as with very young typically developing children) require more structured questioning to ensure that they provide sufficiently detailed information.

Children with mild levels of intellectual disability tend to perform across many domains of testimonial ability much like typically developing children matched for mental age (developmental level). Interviewers would benefit from having clear information about children's levels of functioning before interviewing them; this would allow interviewers to determine how children with intellectual disabilities might best be supported while being interviewed.

In Chapter 9, we described a revision to the Protocol that addresses motivational factors that may influence whether or not children disclose being abused and how much information they provide about those experiences. While rates of disclosure during Protocol interviews are impressively high, many victims are reluctant to disclose or discuss their maltreatment. These children often signal this reluctance in the very early stages of forensic interviews, and yet interviewers typically do not respond in ways that change the dynamics of the interaction by increasing the children's cooperativeness. The Revised Protocol incorporates a range of non-suggestive strategies that interviewers can employ to offer social and emotional support to reluctant children. The strategies included in the Revised Protocol have not yet been tested in isolation, and interviewers are advised to use them flexibly as required in individual cases, so we do not know how important and effective the various techniques are.

Evaluations of interviews conducted using the Revised Protocol show that it fosters detailed disclosures from those children who are the most likely to be reticent (e.g., victims of intra-familial abuse), without increasing the numbers of false reports. It is possible to manage children's well-being during interviews and enhance their experience of the process, without compromising the reliability of the information elicited.

In Chapter 10, we discussed research examining the impact of using visual aids (dolls, drawings, diagrams) on children's testimony. There is mixed evidence regarding the values and risks associated with the various types of aids. We do not yet have a clear understanding of when aids might help, hinder, or make no difference to children's reports, but the kinds of questions used alongside them, the types of event children are asked to recall, and other aspects of the event (delay, perpetrator etc.) are certainly important considerations. Because there is no compelling evidence that their use is beneficial, the Protocol does not recommend the use of dolls, and evidence for the efficacy of other tools is weak. The effects of free drawing are often overshadowed when it is paired with effective verbal prompting in Protocol interviews. The use of body diagrams may compromise accuracy and clarity, and physical context reinstatement is not especially helpful. Taken together, there is no persuasive evidence that aids increase the quality of statements made by children when interviewed using the Protocol, and this is especially true in relation to the younger children who are most likely to be presented with aids.

In Chapter 11, we discussed what we have learned about training programs designed to enhance the quality of forensic interviews with children. Although we have learned a great deal about what constitutes best-practice techniques, widespread training has had a limited impact on the actual quality of interviews conducted in the field. Recent studies using both in-person and computer-assisted delivery mechanisms to provide information in modular fashion over an extended period of time have shown that training can enhance the acquisition of complex interviewing skills, making it possible for interviewers to create conditions that motivate and guide alleged victims to provide richly detailed accounts of experienced events.

Importantly, it is clear that effective training must move beyond the classroom, provide opportunities for spaced learning, and continued consolidation of learning and skills in context. The evidence for the critical importance of prompt feedback for interviewers is convincing and thus poses a challenge for managers and agencies: To ensure the maintenance of high-quality interviewing, workloads must be adjusted to ensure that continued professional development and evaluation is possible.

The impact of interviewing quality on case evaluation, progression, and outcomes was discussed in Chapter 12. We saw there that, in addition to improvements in interviewing and resultant testimonial quality, the introduction of the Protocol has had a broader impact on the way allegations of child maltreatment are managed and resolved. When children are interviewed using the Protocol, formal assessments of credibility are more reliable and accurate (although still not precise enough to be used as diagnostic tools). When the Protocol is used charges are more likely to be filed and suspects are more likely to plead guilty or be convicted at trial. By improving the quality of forensic interviews children are not only helped to provide testimony about their maltreatment, but their well-being and safety is promoted by their enhanced access to justice.

THE INTERVIEW IS ONLY PART OF THE INVESTIGATION

Before considering issues that would benefit from the attention of researchers in the future, it is important to emphasize that forensic interviews need to be recognized as only a part of the investigative process. As Raskin and Esplin (1991c) argued nearly three decades ago, any information obtained by interviewing alleged victims' needs to be viewed in the context of fuller investigations which incorporate other information that allows the children's statements to be evaluated more comprehensively, guides the interviewers, and is in turn informed and guided by information provided by the young interviewees. It is perhaps a truism to note that witnesses or informants, whatever their age, do not always provide accurate or credible information, and the competent investigator must always be attentive to the existence or absence of factors that may affect the accuracy of the witness' statement.

As we have emphasized repeatedly, for example, delay typically degrades the quality and richness of an informant's account, so investigators need to consider this factor when evaluating the information provided in any interview. Degradation in the quality of memory attributable to delay also makes informants' memories more susceptible to contamination, so vigilant investigators need to consider not only the potential for contamination, but also the existence of circumstances that may increase the likelihood that others might want to contaminate the child's memory or might unwittingly do so. The existence of a custody dispute, for example, should prompt the investigator to consider the possibility of intended or unintended contamination when evaluating the child's statement.

Similarly, investigators need to consider whether alleged victims might have reasons to fabricate allegations, perhaps to achieve some secondary gains. In our research on false allegations (Lamb et al., 1997a, 1997b), for example, we encountered several cases in which children alleged victimization in order to avoid punishment for returning home later than their parents had allowed. Of course, factors such as these (potential for contamination, motivation to be deceptive) do not in themselves signal that the allegations should be dismissed; many credible allegation arise when the parents are separating, for example, or when children have good reason to fear their parents' punishment for violating curfews (again). Nevertheless, good investigators identify such circumstances and attempt to seek information that would help clarify the circumstances.

By the time witnesses are formally interviewed, they have often retrieved and described their experience more than once, perhaps too concerned family members or friends (Ceci, Kulkofsy, Sweeney, Klemfuss, & Bruck, 2007). We do not know how well children can recall and describe the content and structure of those disclosure conversations. Memories for conversations are generally poor: Although people can typically remember the general gist of conversations, they are not very good at accurately remembering who said what in the conversation, whether information was provided spontaneously or in response to questions, and what kinds of questions were used to get the information (Bruck, Ceci, & Francoeur, 1999).

When cases are prosecuted, conversations that children have had with others about their disclosure may be viewed as potential sources of contamination, so it may be especially important for children to be asked about the disclosure process early in the investigative process. The NICHD Protocol includes a section focused on children's recall of the disclosure process. Ahern and Lamb (2017) showed that children provided more information about the disclosure, and did so in response to more open prompts, in Protocol than in Memorandum of Good Practice interviews in the UK. Of course, it is important to determine how accurate such recollections are, especially in light of recent studies demonstrating that children poorly recall the content and structure of conversations with unfamiliar adults (Lawson & London, 2015, 2017), and so we hope that future research will examine how well use of the Protocol facilitates children's recall of such content.

The broader characteristics and components of forensic investigation are not explored in this book, but remain worthy of close study. Because the forensic interviews of alleged victims are part of broader investigations, they should typically take place after preliminary investigations have provided some hypotheses about what might have happened. One key goal of the interview is to obtain information that allows evaluation of these hypotheses, while perhaps suggesting others. Following the interviews, of course, investigation often continues, aided in part by the increased understanding obtained by interviewing the alleged victims. Interviews are often the source of investigative leads that can direct investigators to seek independent corroborative information that can further clarify both the child's allegations and the alleged incidents. In many cases, further investigation will bring to light details or questions that were not addressed in the initial interviews and may necessitate re-interviewing, albeit with a narrower focus than in the original interview.

Policies designed to reduce the number of interviews should not preclude re-interviewing when necessary. Similarly, interviewers should expect, not be surprised, that subsequent interviews elicit new information. This is entirely predictable, both because second and first interviews often have a different focus, and also because the retrieval of information is almost never exhaustive. Considerably more research on second (or later) interviews is needed to further clarify the benefits and risks of repeated interviewing, but we know enough already to assert that blanket "one-interview only" rules do not serve the best interests of either child victims or justice (La Rooy, Katz, Malloy, & Lamb, 2010; La Rooy, Lamb, & Pipe, 2009).

FUTURE DIRECTIONS

Over the past 20 years, many studies have been conducted using the Protocol, as we have described throughout this book, but several issues remain relatively unexplored.

Ground Rules

Over the past 50 years, developmental psychologists have shown that children may interpret and respond to adult questions in unexpected ways (Brubacher, Poole, & Dickinson, 2015; Donaldson, 1978; Hughes & Grieve, 1980; Rose & Blank, 1974; Waterman, Blades, & Spencer, 2000). When children are interviewed about past events, they rarely acknowledge when they do not understand questions and instead comply by answering (Waterman, Blades, & Spencer, 2004). Children often respond to unanswerable questions (Waterman et al., 2004; Danby, Brubacher, Sharman, & Powell, 2015; Dickinson, Brubacher, & Poole, 2015), acquiesce to questions that imply a particular response (Saywitz, Lyon, & Goodman, 2017), and leave inaccurate statements by their conversational partners uncorrected (Roberts & Lamb, 1999). Children do this particularly when there is an imbalance of knowledge (e.g., when children must take on the unfamiliar role of an expert, Lamb & Brown, 2006) and power (i.e., children defer to adults' higher status (Lamb &

Brown, 2006) or when adults direct the conversation (Principe, DiPuppo, & Gammel, 2013; Kelly & Bailey, 2013; Fivush, Haden, & Reese, 1996)).

As we discussed earlier in the book, forensic interviewers have been encouraged to establish ground rules at the beginning of the interview (e.g., encourage children to say "I don't know" (Earhart, La Rooy, Brubacher, & Lamb, 2014; Gee, Gregory, & Pipe, 1999; Mulder & Vrij, 1996), "I don't understand" (Lyon, 2010; Saywitz & Camparo, 2013), and to correct interviewers if they make mistakes (Ellis, Powell, Thomson, & Jones, 2003; Geddie, Beer, Bartosik, & Wuensch, 2001; Krackow & Lynn, 2010; Saywitz & Moan-Hardie, 1994). We know surprisingly little, however, about how well children of different ages can learn the various rules, and how best to train them to effectively follow those rules. Currently, interviewers may introduce the ground rules in a standard way, regardless of the children's developmental level and competency with some potentially important prerequisite skills (Brubacher et al., 2015). For example, to effectively follow the instruction to say "I don't know," children must be able to monitor their own knowledge. To correct an interviewer's misunderstanding, children must be able to recognize that someone else can hold a false belief. To learn and hold a rule in mind during an interview implicates working memory. Research identifying developmental changes in children's comprehension of individual ground rules and the role that potential prerequisite skills play in children's understanding and use of them should thus be of great value to developmentally sensitive forensic interviewers.

Although the NICHD Protocol outlines some examples to test children's understanding of the ground rules once they have been introduced, the "test" questions bear little resemblance to the questions and content that children may encounter during the interview (Brubacher et al., 2015; Earhart et al., 2014). For example, an interviewer might say to a girl, "If I said you were a boy called Henry what should you say to me?" when "testing" the "correct the interviewer" rule. Such practices are unlikely to capture the range of questions about personal experiences that might require children to correct interviewers (Brown & Lamb, 2017). Research examining children's learning in domains such as problem solving, language, categories, and numeracy has shown that the degree of similarity between practice examples and test problems affects how well children transfer learning to new problems (Day & Goldstone, 2012). Providing multiple and varied practice examples following initial instruction can also enhance learning, as can using visual cues to support instruction (Braithwaite & Godlstone, 2015; Gentner, Loewenstein, & Hung, 2007; Moreno & Mayer, 1999; Sweller, Van Merrienboer, & Paas, 1998; Thompson & Opfer, 2010).

There is clearly much to learn about how best to train children of various ages to follow the ground rules when recounting their experiences, and we still need to determine how useful the presentation of ground rules really is.

Rapport

The development of the Revised Protocol is an important step towards addressing some of the challenges that arise as forensic interviewers strive to establish and maintain rapport with reluctant or distressed children. The research to date shows that use of the Revised Protocol mitigates some of the reluctance shown by some children and promotes increased responding from them in response to the interviewers' greater sensitivity. Researchers have yet to examine children's perceptions of the interview process and of the extent to which they felt that rapport had been established. We also do not know how the changed dynamics might be perceived by those required to assess the reliability of the evidence in court. Historically, much attention has been given to how easily children are influenced by adults, so it is possible that jurors, lawyers, and judges might (mistakenly) perceive the strategies employed by interviewers following the Revised Protocol as examples of suggestive behavior. Alternatively, the use of an interview protocol that is both cognitively and emotionally supportive may enhance jurors' perceptions of children's credibility (Castelli et al., 2005; Johnson & Shelley, 2014).

Coherence

When children testify about maltreatment, the extent to which they can effectively communicate influences whether their complaints are deemed credible and worthy of further action (Davis, Hoyano, Keenan, Maitland, & Morgan, 1999; Henry, Ridley, Perry, & Crane, 2011; Pipe, Orbach, Lamb, Abbott, & Stewart, 2013). Listeners (including investigators and jury members) must be able to understand children's responses to questions, especially when video recordings are played in court. If they are unable to make sense of children's accounts for any reason (i.e., ambiguities, lack of structure or organization, incoherence) the credibility and impact of their evidence may be diminished (Davis et al., 1999; Westcott & Kynan, 2004). Children's coherence also plays a role in how well they remember events. The narrative quality of children's accounts is associated with increases in the amount, accuracy, and retention of their reports (Chae, Kulkofsky, Debaran, Wang, & Hart, 2016; Kleinknecht & Beike, 2004; Kulkofsky, Wang, & Ceci, 2008; Morris, Baker-Ward, & Bauer, 2010; Peterson, Morris, Baker-Ward, &

Flynn, 2014; Wang, Bui, & Song, 2015). Research on the Protocol has, to date, predominantly focused on the number of details children have reported, rather than the way in which their accounts have been structured; examining whether use of the Protocol helps elicit more coherent and organized accounts from children is thus important.

Maintaining Good Practice

We have highlighted throughout the book how the uptake of evidence-based best-practice guidelines has been insufficient. It is important to understand, therefore, why so many agencies and practitioners have failed to align their practices with best-practice guidelines. The failure to invest in adequate and appropriate training and quality assurance is significant, and illustrates the difficulty researchers and policymakers face when attempting to translate robust findings into policies and practices in the field. Earlier, we discussed the positive impact that various forms of review (individualized, group-based, self-directed) can have on interviewers' questioning strategies (Lamb, Sternberg, Orbach, Hershkowitz et al., 2002; Yii et al., 2014; Wolfman, 2016). With this evidence in mind, researchers should seek to identify the necessary and sufficient "dose" of review that is both sustainable and effective. For example, it will be important to identify how frequently interviewers should participate in review-based activities to sustain and exceed post-training levels of interviewing, and whether complete interviews must be evaluated, or whether similar benefits can be achieved by reviewing random (shorter) segments.

Using the Protocol with Other Groups and in Other Contexts

Children's experiences are relevant in a number of contexts, and it is possible that the approach embodied within the Protocol might be effective in other settings. For example, it is possible that some of the elements of the Protocol (e.g., establishing ground rules, staging brief practice in child-directed elaborative conversation, use of invitations) might be useful when clinicians and other practitioners assess children's health and well-being. Mental state examinations and clinical assessments have very different purposes and outcomes than the information-gathering focus of forensic interviews. We believe that the Protocol will be helpful whenever it is necessary to gain detailed information about experienced events, but there is no evidence that it can or should be used when assessing psychological status or emotional states. Whether the protocol may be useful in other judicial contexts, such as in family court, remains unknown.

Further work is also needed to determine whether the Protocol for young suspects is as effective as the versions tested for young victims and witnesses. There is some promising evidence that the Protocol is suitable for children with intellectual disabilities as well as for children with other developmental disorders (e.g., Attention Deficit Disorder, Autism Spectrum Disorder) but further research on these children as well as those with conditions that may precipitate or arise from maltreatment (e.g., Traumatic Brain Injury, Post Traumatic Stress Disorder) is urgently needed.

Because common memory mechanisms underlie remembering across the lifespan, it is possible that the Protocol would also serve adult witnesses well. Adopting a common approach to interviewing victims and witnesses of all ages would offer the advantage of standardized training and supervision systems within agencies, which may enhance the quality of interviewing by all investigators. Fluidity in the workforce not only makes it difficult currently for individuals to develop and hone specialized skills, but also vastly inflates the numbers of individuals who are given modest (and often ineffective) training and increases the risk that developmentally inappropriate techniques will be used when interviewing children.

The effectiveness of the Protocol has now been examined in a number of countries. The impact of culture on children's testimony and responding within forensic interviews has received very little attention, however. The importance of culture, and how individuals interact within a cultural context has been increasingly recognized (Alea & Wang, 2015; Wang, 2016) but this level of analysis has yet to be applied to the forensic interviewing of children. Relatedly, the extent to which intermediaries and interpreters are able to translate the principles embedded within the Protocol when catering to children's communicative needs remains to be determined.

The Protocol as Part of a Broader Process

As we discussed earlier, a forensic interview is just part of the broader process of investigating and responding to allegations of child maltreatment (Cross & Hershkowitz, 2017). Most research on children's testimony has focused on the investigative interview in isolation, however. Importantly, there is much to learn about the broader systems within which maltreated children are nested: How well do parents and other adults recognize possible signs of abuse? How would they broach initial concerns with their children? How do they respond to disclosure, and how can investigators understand and elucidate possible pre-interview experiences (e.g., lack of support from families or disclosure recipients, coaching or intimidation)? Considerable delays often occur between forensic interviews and trials, and the types of questions that children are asked in the courtroom are typically not those that facilitate detailed and accurate responding (Andrews & Lamb, 2014, 2016, 2017a, 2017b; Andrews, Lamb, & Lyon, 2015; Fogliati & Bussey, 2014; Zajac, O'Neill, & Hayne, 2012; Zajac, Westera, & Kaladelfos, 2017). It is questionable whether an initial developmentally sensitive interview that addresses both the cognitive and emotional needs of child witnesses can protect children from some of the negative impacts of the extended investigative process and the questioning styles that predominate in the courtroom also merits further research.

Independent Evaluation

Most research on the NICHD Protocol has involved at least one of its original developers. The Protocol is freely available (http://nichdprotocol.com/) and many resources to facilitate training and access to related research are also available on the website. Benia et al. (2015) called for more independent research in a range of countries, and we echo this call.

CONCLUSION

The research reviewed in this book demonstrates how much we have learned about children's communicative and memory retrieval capacities and how this information can be used by investigators to maximize the value of their interviews with alleged victims of abuse. The Protocol described in this book translates the principles about which there has been clear expert professional consensus into practice. Use of the Protocol dramatically improves the performance of investigative interviewers by helping them to elicit information that is more likely to be accurate because it is recalled by the child freely rather than in response to information and probes provided by the interviewer. In addition, interviewers are better able to judge whether victims are telling the truth when the interviews are conducted using the Protocol, and cases are more likely to progress to court and to achieve convictions. The Revised Protocol provides guidance about how to build rapport with alleged victims and overcome reluctance to disclose abuse. The Protocol can be used effectively with very young children and with children with intellectual disabilities, although the dynamics of those interviews may differ from those with older and typically developing children.

We have shown how interactive and spaced learning opportunities are important for the acquisition of interviewing skills, and the critical importance of continued practice-focused feedback for maintaining high-quality interviewing. Ensuring these practices are implemented by the institutions that employ forensic interviewers is an important challenge for the future.

In all, although we believe that development of the Protocol has permitted considerable progress in the way in which children are interviewed forensically, we have outlined in this chapter how much more work is needed before we can feel confident that vulnerable children are being protected from further abuse while innocent adults are not being accused following poor investigative interviewing. Obviously, the Protocol remains a "work-in-progress" and will continue to develop while accommodating the results of new research.

Revised Investigative Interview Protocol: Version 2018

A. INTRODUCTION

My name is [name]. Today's date is [date], and it is now [time]. I'm interviewing [child's name] at [location].

Verify that the recorder is on.

Hello, [child's name], I am glad to meet you today. How are you?

My name is _____ and my job is to talk to children about things that have happened to them. As you can see, we have a video-camera here. It will record us talking so I can remember everything you tell me.

In the introduction, gestures of goodwill are appropriate:
Are you comfortable?
Can I do anything to make you more comfortable?

B. RAPPORT BUILDING AND NARRATIVE TRAINING

B.1 Now, [child's name], I want to get to know you better. Tell me about things you like to do.
Wait for child to respond.

Tell Me What Happened: Questioning Children About Abuse, Second Edition.
Michael E. Lamb, Deirdre A. Brown, Irit Hershkowitz, Yael Orbach, and Phillip W. Esplin.
© 2018 John Wiley & Sons Ltd. Published 2018 by John Wiley & Sons Ltd.

If the child responds, express appreciation and reinforcement:
Thank you for sharing that with me, it helps me get to know you.
I am glad I am starting to get to know more about you.
Then skip to B.3, if you think the child should go directly into narrative training from here.

If the child does not answer, gives a short answer, or gets stuck, you can say:
I know this is the first time we have met and I really want to know about you.
I am glad I can talk to you today, [Child's name].
Skip to B.2, if you think more rapport building is necessary.

If the child displays nonverbal cues of avoidance or resistance (e.g., gaze aversion), address it right away:
[Child's name], let me see your eyes.
[Child's name], go ahead and sit closer to me.
[Child's name], I can see you're [crying, quiet], tell me what is happening so I can help.
[Child's name], thanks for letting me listen to you today. Please tell me about what you're going through.

B.2 I really want to know you better, [child's name]. I would like you to tell me about things you like to do at school, during recess, after school].

Wait for an answer.
If the child continues showing avoidance or resistance:
Invite him/her to talk about a neutral topic chosen before the interview began (e.g., child's caregiver may have been asked to report about activities the child enjoys):
I heard you like [activity, hobby]. Tell me about [activity, hobby].

Ask about distinctive items (e.g., of clothing):
I can see you are wearing [a unique item, e.g., soccer team T-shirt]. Tell me about [that item].

Offer the child the opportunity to draw:[1]
[Child's name], would you like to draw a picture of something [you like to do, something fun that happened]? Here are some crayons and paper for you.

---

[1] Note that this activity is designed to promote the child's comfort, not to learn about the abuse. Do not attempt to interpret what the child draws or ask the child to draw anything related to the suspicions that led to the interview.

B.3   Now, [child's name], Tell me more about [activity the child already mentioned].
Avoid TV shows, videos, or fantasy.
Wait for an answer.

B.4   [Child's name], Tell me about something fun that has happened to you [at school, kindergarten]?

B.5   Tell me about [something the child mentioned]. Use various invitations to ask about different topics; one of those invitations should focus on internal contents: thoughts, feelings, sensations, or emotions.

B.6   You told me about something [happy, pleasant, fun] that has happened to you. Now, tell me about something unpleasant that has happened to you [at school, kindergarten].
Important: Do not mention the location in which the alleged abuse may have taken place.

B.7   Please tell me about [something the child has mentioned]. Ask various invitations to elicit richer information about a variety of topics; one invitation should focus on internal contents: thoughts, feelings, sensations, or emotions.

If the child reveals distressing information, please explore that briefly while making supportive statements. You may want to check whether the child has previously reported it: You told me about [the distressing incident]. Have you told an adult about that?

If the child says no, say: Would you like me to help you tell someone?

B.8   [child's name], you told me about [pleasant event already described] and about [unpleasant event already described], and shared your [emotions, thoughts] with me (if s/he did). Thank you for letting me know. It's important that you know you can talk to me about anything, both good things and bad things.

C. EXPLAINING AND PRACTICING GROUND RULES

Adjust the questions according to the child's developmental level.

C.1   [Child's name], I'm interested in you and I'll be asking you all kinds of questions today.

If I ask a question that you don't understand, just say, "[interviewer's name], I don't understand." Okay, [child's name]?
Pause
If I ask a question, and you don't know the answer, just tell me, "I don't know." So, [child's name], if I ask you [e.g. what did I have for breakfast today], what would you say?
Wait for an answer.
If the child says "I don't know," say: Right. You don't know, [child's name], do you?
If the child offers a guess, say: No, [child's name], you don't know me and [e.g., you weren't with me when I had my breakfast this morning], so you don't know. When you don't know the answer, please don't guess; just say that you don't know.
Pause
But if you do know or do remember, it is very important that you tell me, okay, [child's name]?

C.2 And if I say things that are wrong, you should tell me. Okay, [child's name]?
Wait for an answer.
So if I said that you are a 2-year-old girl [when interviewing a 5-year-old boy, etc.], what would you say?

If the child only denies and does not correct you, say: You're right! You're not a 2-year-old girl. What would be right?
Wait for an answer.

Reinforce the child if s/he gives the right answer: That's right, [child's name]. Now you know you should tell me if I make a mistake or say something that is not right.
Pause
Correct a wrong answer: No, [child's name], you are not [wrong age], you are [real age].
So if I said you were standing up, what would you say?
Wait for an answer.
Okay.
[Child's name], now you understand that if I say something incorrect, you need to correct me and tell me what is right.

C.3 Part of my job is to talk to [children, teenagers] about things that have happened to them. I meet with lots of [children, teenagers] so that they can tell me the truth about things that have happened to them. [child's name], it is very important that you tell me the truth today about things that have happened to you.

D. FURTHER RAPPORT BUILDING AND EPISODIC MEMORY TRAINING

Prior to the interview, please identify a recent, short, positive and meaningful event in which the child actively participated. If possible, choose an event that took place at about the same time as the alleged or suspected abuse. If the alleged abuse took place during a specific day or event, ask about a different event.

I am glad to meet with you today, [child's name], and I would like to get to know you even better.

D.1 *Main invitation*
A few [days, weeks] ago was [a holiday, birthday party, other event]. Tell me everything that happened [during the event], from the beginning to the end, as best as you can.

In case an event wasn't identified previously, ask: Did you do something special recently, like did you get to go somewhere or go to a birthday party?

If the child doesn't identify a suitable event, say: So, I want you to tell me everything that happened [today, yesterday], from the time you woke up.

D.2 *Follow-up invitations*
Please repeat the first action that started the event. Then ask:
And then what happened, [child's name]?
Use this question as often as needed throughout this section until you have been given a full account of the event.
Thank you, [child's name], you have told me many things (if s/he did). I want to ask you some more questions about what just you told me.

D.3 *Time segmenting invitations*
Try to use 3 time segmenting invitations, although you may adjust the quantity and type of invitations to the child's capabilities and reactions.
[Child's name], I would like you to tell me everything about [the event]. Please tell me everything that happened from the moment [an activity the child mentioned] to the moment [a subsequent mentioned activity].

If the child has difficulty understanding delineated segments, say:
Please tell me everything that happened from the moment [an activity the child mentioned] began.

Thank you, [child's name], for telling me that. What you say is very clear and that helps me understand what you mean.

D.4 *Cued invitations*
Try to use three cued invitations, but you may adjust the number depending on the child's capabilities and reactions. Please focus on thoughts and feelings as well.

Cued invitations can be used in one of two formats:
Tell me more about [activity, object, thought, feeling].
Earlier you spoke about [activity, object, thought, feeling]. Tell me more about that.

D.5 [Child's name], thank you for telling me about [title of the event]. When we talk today, it is very important that you tell me everything about things that have really happened to you.

D.6 [Child's name], how are you feeling so far in our conversation?

> *If during the pre-substantive phase, the child is not cooperative and remains reluctant, end the interview now. Skip to section G in order to end the interview and schedule an additional interview for continued rapport building.*

E. SUBSTANTIVE PHASE

E.1 *Transition to substantive issues*
Important: If the child expresses explicit verbal resistance without denying the abuse at any point, skip to section E.1.a, "support for managing overt refusals," and deal with the resistance without using additional transitional prompts.

Now that I know you a little better, I want to talk about why [you are, I am] here today.

At any stage, if the child makes an allegation, skip to section E.2.

If the child reports an irrelevant event, say: I hear what you are saying to me, [child's name]. If you want, we can talk about that later. Right now, though, I want to know about something else that may have happened to you.

1. I understand that something may have happened to you. Tell me everything that happened from the beginning to the end.
2. As I told you, my job is to talk to children about things that might have happened to them. It is very important that you tell me why you think [your mum, dad, grandmother] [brought you here today, I came to talk to you today].
3. *If the child doesn't make an allegation and looks avoidant or resistant, you may address him/her with general supportive statements which do not refer specifically to him/her and do not mention abuse:*

> a. [Child's name], my job is to listen to children about things that happened to them.
> b. [Child's name], I really want to know when something happens to children. That's what I am here for.
> c. [Child's name], here kids can talk about good things and bad things that have happened to them.

4. I've heard that you talked to [a doctor, teacher, social worker, other professional] at [time, location]. Please tell me what you talked about.
5. I [saw, heard] that you have/had [documented injuries, bruises] on your [body part]. Tell me everything about [those, that].
6. [Child's name], has anything happened to you at [location, time of alleged incident]?

If the child doesn't make an allegation and looks avoidant or resistant, you may use some of the supportive statements above (a–c) or one of the following statements, which refer specifically to the child, but still do not mention abuse:

> d. You have told me a lot about yourself. I feel I know you better and you can tell me more [about things, about both good things and bad things] that have happened to you.
> e. You have told me a lot about yourself, thank you for letting me know. When you talk to me today please go on and tell me about other things that have happened to you.
> f. [Child's name], if there is anything you want to tell me, [I want to know/listen, It's important for me to know/listen].

> **If there is no allegation or a denial: Evaluate and plan your next steps.**
>
> *You may use the child's verbal and nonverbal indications of reluctance to evaluate the situation and decide whether or not to proceed. Consider ending the interview (skip to E.1.b) and planning an additional interview if you believe that the child is resisting or avoiding cooperation and that an additional session of rapport building might be beneficial.*
>
> *Proceed through the transitional prompts gradually when you suspect that:*
>
> – Abuse may not have occurred.
> – The child doesn't recognize the aim of the interview.
> – The child is resisting your efforts or avoiding cooperation but there is serious concern about his/her welfare or the investigation so delay might leave the child unsafe.

7. [child's name], has anybody been bothering you?
8. [child's name], did someone do something to you that you don't think was right?
9. [child's name], did someone [briefly summarize allegations or suspicions without specifying name of the alleged perpetrator or providing too many details]?

If the child doesn't make an allegation but looks avoidant or resistant and there is independent evidence arousing suspicion, you may use the above supportive statements (a–f) or one of the following:

> g. [Child's name], [I am, people] are worried about you and I want to know if something may have happened to you.
> h. [Child's name], if something has happened to you and you want it to stop, you can tell me about it.
>   i-1. [Child's name], if it is hard for you to tell, what makes it so hard?
>   i-2. [Child's name], is there anything you are concerned about?
>   i-3. [Child's name], what would happen if you told me?
>   i-4. [Child's name], has someone told you not to tell?
> j. Sometimes children think that if something happened to them, it's their fault, but children are not responsible if things happen to them.
> k. It's your choice if you want to tell me and it is my job to let you choose.

10. [child's name], I understand [you, someone] [reported, saw] [briefly summarize allegations or suspicions without specifying the name of the alleged perpetrator or providing too many details]. I want to find out if something may have happened to you.

E.1.a Supportive statements to help manage overt refusals.

If the child has explicitly expressed difficulty or reluctance to disclose but hasn't denied the abuse, you may use the supportive statements above (a–k) and the following statements dealing with overt refusals to engage:

---

l. [Child's name], I understand you are [difficulty the child mentioned, e.g., embarrassed]. Let's start talking and I'll try to help you with it.
m. Many children are [difficulty the child mentioned] and I try to help them.
n. I understand you are [difficulty the child mentioned], tell me more about that.
o. *If the child expressed lack of confidence:* I'm sure you can talk about it well.
p. *If the child said s/he was worried about something specific and the reassurance you can give is true:* Do not worry, I will [not tell the other children/make sure you are not late for the bus].
q. It's your choice whether to tell and I will go with your choice.

E.1.b *Ending the interview without an allegation.*
If at any point while exploring whether abuse might have occurred you believe that the child is resistant or uncooperative and that rapport building will benefit from an additional meeting, end the interview and plan an additional one. Skip to section G if you want to end the interview.

E.2 *Exploring the incidents*
Throughout the entire substantive part it is important to preserve and enhance the rapport established with the child, continue providing supportive statements, and address expressed inhibitions, distress and conflicts.

E.2.a *Free recall invitations*
10.a *Invitation for a first narrative about the incidents.*

If the child mentions a specific incident:
[Child's name], you told me that [briefly summarize the allegation the child has made]. Tell me everything from the beginning to the end as best you can.

If the child mentions a number of incidents:
[Child's name], you told me that [a brief summary of the allegation the child has made]. Tell me everything about [the last/first time/at place/ at time/specific incident] from the beginning to the end.

If the child gives a generic description and you cannot determine the number of incidents:
[Child's name], you told me that [briefly summarize the allegation the child has made]. Did that happen one time or more than one time? *Depending on the answer please invite a first narrative (10.a).*

If the description is still generic, please say:
[Child's name], you told me that [briefly summarize the generic description]. Tell me everything from the beginning to the end.

10.b *Follow-up invitations*
Please repeat the child's description of the action/occurrence that started the event. Then ask
And then what happened?
Use this question as often as needed until you have a complete description of the alleged incident.

10.c *Time segmenting invitations*
You have told me many things and helped me understand what happened. Now, [child's name], I want to ask you more questions about [incident title].

[child's name], Think back to that time [day, night] and please tell me everything that happened from the moment [an activity the child mentioned] to the moment [a subsequent activity the child mentioned].

10.d *Cued invitations*
Cued invitations can have two formats:

- Tell me more about [activity, object, feeling, thought].
- [Child's name], you mentioned [activity, object, feeling, thought]. Tell me more about that.

Use this question as often as needed throughout this section.

Important! Free-recall invitations should be exhausted before proceeding to directive questions.

E.2.b *Directive questions*
If some central details of the allegation are still missing or unclear after the exhaustive use of open-ended questions, use directive questions.

11. [Child's name], you said that/mentioned [activity, object, feeling, thought]. [How, when, where, who, what, which, how many, what did you mean]?
    It is important to pair open-ended invitations with directive questions whenever possible:
    Tell me more about that.

E.2.c *Exploring multiple incidents*
If in reply to question 11 the child mentions a single incident:

12. [Child's name], what you just told me, did that happen one time or more than one time?

If the child has said that such incidents happened more than one time, go back to question 10.a and explore additional incidents. It is often best to explore the last, first, or best remembered incident.

E.2.d Break
[Child's name], now I want to make sure I have understood everything you said and see if there's anything else I need to ask. I will take a couple of minutes to think about what you told me/go over my notes.

>   *During the break time, review the information you have received, see if there is any missing information, and plan the rest of the interview. Be sure to formulate option-posing questions in writing and consider replacing them with open-ended or directive prompts.*

E.2.e *Option-posing questions—eliciting information that has not been mentioned by the child.*

>   *You should ask these focused questions only if you have already tried other approaches and you realize that some forensically important information is still missing. It is very important to pair option-posing questions with open invitations ("Tell me all about that") whenever possible.*

In case of multiple incidents, you should direct the child to the relevant incidents in his own words.

13. [child's name], when you told me about [specific incident embedded in time and place] you mentioned [activity, object, feeling, thought]. [Did, have, has, is, are] [a detail for child to confirm or deny]? *Example: Sarah, when you told me about being in the kitchen with Lewis, were there other people with you?*

Whenever appropriate, follow with an invitation:
Tell me everything about that [activity, object, feeling, thought].

Before you move to the next incident, make sure you have obtained all the missing details about each specific incident.

F. DISCLOSURE INFORMATION

You've told me why you came to talk to me today. You've given me [lots of] information and that really helps me to understand what happened.

If the child has mentioned telling someone about the incident(s), you may say:

Now I want to understand how other people found out about [last incident].

If he has not mentioned telling anyone, probe about possible disclosure by saying: Does anybody else know what happened?

Then explore the disclosure process, addressing the disclosure time, circumstances, recipients, potential discussions of the event, and reactions to disclosure by both the child and recipients. Use open-ended questions whenever possible.

G. ENDING THE INTERVIEW

[Child's name], what are you going to do after we finish talking?

Talk to the child for a couple of minutes about a neutral topic.

References

Aarons, N. M., Powell, M. B., & Browne, J. (2004). Police perceptions of interviews involving children with intellectual disabilities: A qualitative inquiry. *Policing and Society, 14*(3), 269–278.

Ackerman, B. P. (1981). Encoding specificity in the recall of pictures and words in children and adults. *Journal of Experimental Child Psychology, 31*, 193–211.

Ackil, J. K., & Zaragoza, M. S. (1995). Developmental differences in suggestibility and memory for source. *Journal of Experimental Child Psychology, 60*, 57–83.

Adams, B. J., Field, L., & Verhave, T. (1999). Effects of unreinforced conditional selection training, multiple negative comparison training, and feedback on equivalence class formation. *Psychological Record, 49*, 685–702.

Ageton, S. S. (1983). The dynamics of female delinquency, 1976–1980. *Criminology: An Interdisciplinary Journal, 21*, 555–584.

Agnew, S. E., & Powell, M. B. (2004). The effect of intellectual disability on children's recall of an event across different question types. *Law and Human Behavior, 28*, 273–294.

Agnew, S. E., Powell, M. B., & Snow, P. C. (2006). An examination of the questioning styles of police officers and caregivers when interviewing children with intellectual disabilities. *Legal and Criminological Psychology, 11*(1), 35–53.

Ahern, B., Hershkowitz, I., Lamb, M. E, Blasbalg, U., & Karni-Visel, Y. (in press). Examining reluctance and emotional support in forensic interviews with substantiated victims of physical abuse. *Applied Developmental Science*.

Ahern, E. C., Hershkowitz, I., Lamb, M. E., Blasbalg, U., & Winstanley, A. (2014). Support and reluctance in the pre-substantive phase of alleged child abuse victim investigative interviews: Revised versus standard NICHD protocols. *Behavioral Sciences & the Law, 32*(6), 762–774.

Ahern, E. C., & Lamb, M. E. (2017). Children's reports of disclosure recipient reactions in forensic interviews: Comparing the NICHD and MoGP Protocols. *Journal of Police and Criminal Psychology, 32,* 85–93.

Ahern, E. C., & Lyon, T. D. (2013). Facilitating maltreated children's use of emotional language. *Journal of Forensic Social Work, 3*(2), 176–203.

Ahern, E. C., Sadler, L. A., Lamb, M. E., & Gariglietti, G. M. (2017). Practitioner perspectives on child sexual exploitation: Rapport building with young people. *Journal of Child Sexual Abuse, 26,* 78–91.

Akehurst, L., Koehnken, G., & Hoefer, E. (2001). Content credibility of accounts derived from live and video presentations. *Legal and Criminological Psychology, 6,* 65–83.

Akehurst, L., Milne, R., & Koehnken, G. (2003). The effects of children's age and delay on recall in a cognitive or structured interview. *Psychology, Crime & Law, 9,* 97–107.

Alaggia, R., & Turton, J. V. (2005). Against the odds: The impact of woman abuse on maternal response to disclosure of child sexual abuse. *Journal of Child Sexual Abuse, 14,* 95–113.

Aldridge, J., & Cameron, S. (1999). Interviewing child witnesses: Questioning techniques and the role of training. *Applied Developmental Science, 3,* 136–147.

Aldridge, J., Lamb, M. E., Sternberg, K. J., Orbach, Y., Esplin, P. W., & Bowler, L. (2004). Using a human figure drawing to elicit information from alleged victims of child abuse. *Journal of Consulting and Clinical Psychology, 72,* 304–316.

Alea, N., & Wang, Q. (2015). Going global: The functions of autobiographical memory in cultural context. *Memory, 23,* 1–10.

Alexander, K. W., Goodman, G. S., Schaaf, J. M., Edelstein, R. S., Quas, J. A., & Shaver, P. R. (2002). The role of attachment and cognitive inhibition in children's memory and suggestibility for a stressful event. *Journal of Experimental Child Psychology, 83,* 262–290.

Almeida, T. S., Lamb, M. E., & Weissblat, E. (under review). Assessing the effectiveness of the revised NICHD Protocol when interviewing children with Autism Spectrum Disorder about a live personally experienced event.

Almerigogna, J., Ost, J., Bull, R., & Akehurst, L. (2007). A state of high anxiety: How non-supportive interviewers can increase the suggestibility of child witnesses. *Applied Cognitive Psychology, 21,* 963–974.

Alonzo-Proulx, A., & Cyr, M. (2016). Factors predicting central details in alleged child sexual abuse victims' disclosure. *Journal of Forensic Psychology Practice, 16,* 129–150.

American Professional Society on the Abuse of Children (APSAC). (1990/1997). *Guidelines for psychosocial evaluation of suspected sexual abuse in young children.* Chicago, IL: Author.

American Professional Society on the Abuse of Children (APSAC). (1995). *Use of anatomical dolls in child sexual abuse assessments.* Chicago, IL: Author.

American Professional Society on the Abuse of Children (APSAC). (2002). *Practice guidelines: Investigative interviewing in cases of alleged child abuse.* Chicago, IL: Author.

American Professional Society on the Abuse of Children (APSAC). (2012). *Practice guidelines: Investigative interviewing in cases of alleged child abuse.* Chicago, IL: Author.

Anderson, D. E., DePaulo, B. M., Ansfield, M. E., Tickle, J. J., & Green, E. (1999). Beliefs about cues to deception: Mindless stereotypes or untapped wisdom? *Journal of Nonverbal Behavior, 23,* 67–89.

References

Anderson, G. D., Anderson, J. N., & Gilgun, J. F. (2014). The influence of narrative practice techniques on child behaviors in forensic interviews. *Journal of Child Sexual Abuse, 23*(6), 615–634.

Anderson, J. (2010). Cornerhouse Forensic Interviewing Protocol: RATAC. *Thomas M. Cooley Journal of Practical and Clinical Law, 12*, 193–331.

Andrews, S. J., & Lamb, M. E. (2014). The effects of age and delay on responses to repeated questions in forensic interviews with children alleging sexual abuse. *Law and Human Behavior,38*, 171–180.

Andrews, S. J., & Lamb, M. E. (2016). How do lawyers examine and cross-examine children in Scotland? *Applied Cognitive Psychology, 30*(6), 953–971.

Andrews, S. J., & Lamb, M. E. (2017). The structural linguistic complexity of lawyers' questions and children's responses in Scottish criminal courts. *Child Abuse & Neglect, 65*, 182–193.

Andrews, S. J., Lamb, M. E., & Lyon, T. D. (2015a). The effects of question repetition on responses in direct- and cross-examinations of children alleging sexual abuse in court. *Law and Human Behavior, 39*(6), 559–570.

Andrews, S. J., Lamb, M. E., & Lyon, T. D. (2015b). Question types, responsiveness and self-contradictions when prosecutors and defense attorneys question alleged victims of child sexual abuse. *Applied Cognitive Psychology, 29*(2), 253–261.

Aslan, A., & Bäuml, K. H. T. (2010). Retrieval-induced forgetting in young children. *Psychonomic Bulletin & Review, 17*(5), 704–709.

Azad, A., Christianson, S.-A., & Selenius, H. (2014). Children's reporting patterns after witnessing homicidal violence—the effect of repeated experience and repeated interviews. *Psychology, Crime & Law, 20*, 407–429.

Bahrick, L., Parker, J., Fivush, R., & Levitt, M. (1998). The effects of stress on young children's memory for a natural disaster. *Journal of Experimental Psychology: Applied, 4*, 308–331.

Baker-Ward, L., Burgwyn, E. O., Ornstein, P. A., & Gordon, B. N. (1995, April). *Children's reports of a minor medical emergency procedure*. Paper presented at the biennial meeting of the Society for Research in Child Development, Indianapolis, IN.

Baker-Ward, L., Gordon, B. N., Ornstein, P. A., Larus, D. M., & Clubb, P. A. (1993). Young children's long-term retention of a pediatric examination. *Child Development, 64*, 1519–1533.

Baker-Ward, L., Hess, T. M., & Flannagan, D. A. (1990). The effects of involvement on children's memory for events. *Cognitive development, 5*(1), 55–69.

Baker-Ward, L., Ornstein, P. A., & Principe, G. F. A. (1997). Revealing the representation: Evidence from children's reports of events. In P. W. Van Den Broek, P. J. Bauer, & T. Bourg (Eds.), *Developmental spans in event comprehension and representation: Bridging fictional and actual events* (pp. 79–107). Mahwah, NJ: Erlbaum.

Barkley, R. A. (2006). *Attention-deficit hyperactivity disorder: A handbook for diagnosis*. New York, NY: Guilford Press.

Bauer, P. J. (2015). A complementary processes account of the development of childhood amnesia and a personal past. *Psychological review, 122*(2), 204–231.

Bauer, P., & Fivush, R. (1992). Constructing event representations: Building on a foundation of variation and enabling relations. *Cognitive Development, 7*, 381–401.

Bauer, P. J., & Larkina, M. (2014a). The onset of childhood amnesia in childhood: A prospective investigation of the course and determinants of forgetting of early-life events. *Memory, 22*, 907–924.

Bauer, P. J., & Larkina, M. (2014b). Childhood amnesia in the making: Different distributions of autobiographical memories in children and adults. *Journal of Experimental Psychology. General*, *143*, 597–611.

Bauer, P. J., & Larkina, M. (2015). Predicting remembering and forgetting of autobiographical memories in children and adults: A 4-year prospective study. *Memory*, 1–24.

Bauer, P., Van Abbema, D., Wiebe, S., Cary, M., Phill, C., & Burch, M. (2004). Props, not pictures, are worth a thousand words: Verbal accessibility of early memories under different conditions of contextual support. *Applied Cognitive Psychology*, *18*, 373–392.

Bauer, P. J., & Wewerka, S. S. (1997). Saying is revealing: Verbal expression of event memory in the transition from infancy to early childhood. In P. W. Van Den Broek, P. J. Bauer, & T. Bourg (Eds.), *Developmental spans in event comprehension and representation: Bridging fictional and actual events* (pp. 139–168). Mahwah, NJ: Erlbaum.

Baugerud, G. A., Magnussen, S., & Melinder, A. (2014). High accuracy but low consistency in children's long-term recall of a real-life stressful event. *Journal of Experimental Child Psychology*, *126*, 357–368.

Baugerud, G. A., & Melinder, A. (2012), Maltreated children's memory of stressful removals from their biological parents. *Applied Cognitive Psychology*, *26*, 261–270.

Bekerian, D. A., & Dennet, J. L. (1993). The cognitive interview technique: Reviving the issue. *Applied Cognitive Psychology*, *7*, 275–297.

Bekerian, D. A., & Dennet, J. L. (1995). Assessing the truth in children's statements. In T. Ney (Ed.), *True and false allegations of child sexual abuse: Assessment and case management* (pp. 163–175). Philadelphia, PA: Brunner/Mazel.

Bekerian, D. A., Dennet, J. L., Hill, K., & Hitchcock, R. (1990). *Effects of detailed imagery on simulated witness recall*. Paper presented at the Second European Conference on Law and Psychology, Nuremberg, Germany.

Bell, G. E. (1984). Developmental differences in preschoolers' comprehension of wh- questions. *Dissertation Abstracts International*, *45*(6-A), 1634.

Belli, R. F., Lindsay, D. S., Gales, M. S., & McCarthy, T. T. (1994). Memory impairment and source misattribution in postevent misinformation experiments with short retention intervals. *Memory and Cognition*, *21*, 40–54.

Belsky, J., Spritz, B., & Crnic, K. (1996). Infant attachment security and affective-cognitive information processing at age 3. *Psychological Science*, *7*, 111–114.

Benia, L. R., Hauck-Filho, N., Dillenburg, M., & Stein, L. M. (2015). The NICHD Investigative Interview Protocol: A meta-analytic review. *Journal of Child Sexual Abuse*, *24*, 259–279.

Benson, M. S., & Powell, M. B. (2015a). Australian prosecutors' perceptions of the utility of child investigative interview protocols. *International Journal of Police Science & Management*, *17*(4), 216–229.

Benson, M. S., & Powell, M. B. (2015b). Evaluation of a comprehensive interactive training system for investigative interviewers of children. *Psychology, Public Policy, and Law*, *21*, 309.

Bettenay, C., Ridley, A. M., Henry, L. A., & Crane, L. (2015). Changed responses under cross-examination: The role of anxiety and individual differences in child witnesses. *Applied Cognitive Psychology*, *29*, 485–491.

Bjorklund, D. F. (1987). How age changes in knowledge base contribute to the development of children's memory: An interpretive review. *Developmental Review, 7*, 93–130.

Bjorklund, D. F., Bjorklund, B., Brown, R., & Cassel, W. (1998). Children's susceptibility to repeated questions: How misinformation changes children's answers and their minds. *Applied Developmental Science, 2*, 99–111.

Bjorklund, D. F., & Thompson, B. E. (1983). Category typicality effects in children's memory performance: Qualitative and quantitative differences in the processing of category information. *Journal of Experimental Child Psychology, 35*, 329–344.

Bjorklund, D. F., & Zeman, B. R. (1982). Children's organization and metamemory awareness in their recall of familiar information. *Child Development, 53*, 799–810.

Billings, F. J., Taylor, T., Burns, J., Corey, D. L., Garven, S., & Wood, J. M. (2007). Can reinforcement induce children to falsely incriminate themselves? *Law and Human Behavior, 31*, 125–139.

Blahauvietz, S. (2005, January). *Forensic use of anatomical dolls*. Paper presented at the meeting of the American Professional Society on Child Abuse, San Diego, CA.

Blasbalg, U., Hershkowitz, I., & Karni-Visel, Y. (2018). Support, reluctance and production in child abuse investigations. Manuscript under review.

Blasbalg, U., Hershkowitz, I., Karni-Visel, Y. & Lamb, M. E. (March, 2018a). *The associations among interviewer support, child reluctance, and informativeness in forensic interviews with alleged victims of intra-familial abuse*. Paper presented at the American Psychology–Law Society conference, Memphis, TN.

Blasbalg, U., Hershkowitz, I., Karni-Visel, Y. & Lamb, M. E (March, 2018b). *The associations among socio-emotional factors and the coherence of the statement in forensic interviews with alleged victims of intra-familial abuse*. Paper presented at the American Psychology–Law Society conference, Memphis, TN.

Blasbalg, U., Hershkowitz, I., Lamb, M.E., & Karni-Visel, Y. (July, 2018c). *Support, reluctance and informativeness in the substantive phase of investigative interviews with alleged victims of child abuse: Comparing the Revised and Standard NICHD Protocols*. Paper presented at the 11th annual IIIRG conference, Porto, Portugal.

Bless, H. (2001). Mood and the use of general knowledge structures. In L. L. Martin & G. L. Clore (Eds.), *Theories of mood and cognition: A user's guide* (pp. 9–26). Mahwah, NJ: Erlbaum.

Bless, H., Fiedler, K., & Forgas, J. P. (2006). Mood and the regulation of information processing and behavior. *Affect in social thinking and behavior*, 65–84.

Boat, B. W., & Everson, M. D. (1994). Exploration of anatomical dolls by nonreferred preschool-aged children: Comparisons by age, gender, race, and socioeconomic status. *Child Abuse & Neglect,* 139–153.

Boat, B. W., & Everson, M. D. (1996). Concerning practices of interviewers when using anatomical dolls in child protective services investigations. *Child Maltreatment, 1*, 96–104.

Boggs, S. R., & Eyberg, S. (1990). Interview techniques and establishing rapport. In A. M. La Greca (Ed.), *Through the eyes of the child: Obtaining self-reports from children and adolescents* (pp. 85–108). Boston, MA: Allyn & Bacon.

Borkowski, J. G., Milstead, M., & Hale, C. (1988). Components of children's metamemory: Implications for strategy generalization. In F. E. Weinert & M. Perlmutter (Eds.), *Memory development: Universal changes and individual differences* (pp. 73–100). Hillsdale, NJ: Erlbaum.

Bornstein, B. H., Liebel, L. M., & Scarberry, N. C. (1998). Repeated testing in eyewitness memory: A means to improve recall of a negative emotional event. *Faculty Publications, Department of Psychology*, 177.

Bourg, W., Broderick, R., Flagor, R., Kelly, D. M., Ervin, D. L., & Butler, J. (1999). *A child interviewer's guidebook*. Thousand Oaks, CA: Sage.

Boychuk, T. D. (1991). *Criteria-based content analysis of children's statements about sexual abuse: A field-based validation study*. Unpublished doctoral dissertation. Arizona State University, Tempe, AZ.

Bowen, C. J., & Howie, P. M. (2002). Context and cue cards in young children's testimony: A comparison of brief narrative elaboration and context reinstatement. *Journal of Applied Psychology, 87*, 1077–1085.

Bradley, A. R., & Wood, J. M. (1996). How do children tell? The disclosure process in child sexual abuse. *Child Abuse & Neglect. 20*, 881–891.

Brady, M., Poole, D. A., Warren, A., & Jones, D. (1999). Young children's responses to yes-or-no questions: Patterns and problems. *Applied Developmental Science, 3*, 47–57.

Brainerd, C. J., & Ornstein, P. A. (1991). Children's memory for witnessed events: The developmental backdrop. In J. Doris (Ed.), *The suggestibility of children's recollections* (pp. 10–20). Washington, DC: American Psychological Association.

Brainerd, C. J., & Reyna, V. F. (1990). Gist is the grist: Fuzzy-trace theory and the new intuitionism. *Developmental Review, 10*, 3–47.

Brainerd, C. J., & Reyna, V. F. (1996). Mere testing creates false memories in children. *Developmental Psychology, 32*, 467–476.

Brainerd, C. J., & Reyna, V. F. (2002). Recollection rejection: How children edit their false memories. *Developmental Psychology, 38*, 156–172.

Brainerd, C. J., & Reyna, V. F. (2005). *The science of false memory*. Oxford, UK: Oxford University Press.

Brainerd, C. J., & Reyna, V. F. (2012). Reliability of children's testimony in the era of developmental reversals. *Developmental Review, 32*, 224–267.

Brainerd, C. J., Reyna, V. F., Howe, M. L., & Kingma, J. (1990). The development of forgetting and reminiscence. *Monographs of the Society for Research in Child Development, 55*(3/4), 94–109.

Braithwaite, D. W., & Goldstone, R. L. (2015). Effects of variation and prior knowledge on abstract concept learning. *Cognition and Instruction, 33*, 226–256.

Brennan, M., & Brennan, R. E. (1988). *Strange language: Child victims under cross examination* (3rd ed.). Wagga Wagga, NSW, Australia: Riverina Literacy Centre.

Brewer, W. F., & Nakamura, G. V. (1984). The nature and functions of schemas. In R. S. Wyer & T. K. Srull (Eds.), *Handbook of social cognition* (Vol. 1, pp. 119–160). Hillsdale, NJ: Erlbaum.

Brown, D. A. (2011). The use of supplementary techniques in forensic interviews with children. In M. E. Lamb, D. LaRooy, C. Katz, & L. Malloy (Eds.), *Children's testimony: A handbook of psychological research and forensic practice* (2nd ed., pp. 217–249). Chichester, UK: Wiley.

Brown, D. A., Brown, E.-J., Lewis, C. N., & Lamb, M. E. (in press). Narrative skill and testimonial accuracy in typically developing children and those with intellectual disabilities. *Applied Cognitive Psychology.*

Brown, D. A., Higgs, W., Barton, R., Lamb, M. E., & Pipe, M.-E. (2017). The influence of visual aids on the detail and accuracy of children's reports about touch. Manuscript under review.

Brown, D. A., & Lamb, M. E. (2015). Can children be useful witnesses? It depends how they are questioned. *Child Development Perspectives, 9*, 250–255.

Brown, D. A., & Lamb, M. E. (2017). A contextually and developmentally sensitive view of children's memory development: Between the laboratory and the field. In A. S. Dick and U. Müller (Eds). *Advancing developmental science: Philosophy, theory, and method* (pp. 119–132). New York, NY: Routledge.

Brown, D. A., Lamb, M. E., Lewis, C. N., Pipe, M.-E., Orbach, Y., & Wolfman, M. (2013). Evaluating the NICHD Investigative Interview Protocol: A laboratory study. *Journal of Experimental Psychology: Applied, 19*, 367–382.

Brown, D. A., & Lewis, C. N. (2013): Competence is in the eye of the beholder: Perceptions of intellectually disabled child witnesses. *International Journal of Disability, Development and Education, 60*, 3–17.

Brown, D. A., Lewis, C. N., & Lamb, M. E. (2015). Preserving the past: An early interview improves delayed event memory in children with intellectual disabilities. *Child Development, 86*, 1031–1047.

Brown, D. A., Lewis, C. N., Lamb, M. E., Gwynne, J., Kitto, O., & Stairmand, M. (2016). Developmental differences in children's learning and use of ground rules during an interview about an experienced event. Manuscript under review.

Brown, D. A., Lewis, C. N., Lamb, M. E., & Stephens, E. (2007). Facilitating eyewitness testimony in children with learning disabilities. *Final report to the Economic and Social Research Council (ESRC).* Swindon, UK: ESRC.

Brown, D. A., Lewis, C. N., Lamb, M. E., & Stephens, E. (2012). The influences of delay and severity of intellectual disability on event memory in children. *Journal of Consulting and Clinical Psychology, 80*, 829–841.

Brown, D., Lewis, C., Stephens, E. & Lamb, M. (2017). Interviewers' approaches to questioning vulnerable child witnesses: The influences of developmental level versus intellectual disability status. *Legal and Criminological Psychology, 22*, 332–349.

Brown, D. A., McKennie, S., & Barton, R. (2018). Supplementary techniques do not enhance children's recall when added to a best-practice interviewing protocol. Manuscript under preparation.

Brown, D. A., & Pipe, M.-E. (2003a). Individual differences in children's event memory reports and the narrative elaboration technique. *Journal of Applied Psychology, 88*, 195–206.

Brown, D. A., & Pipe, M.-E. (2003b). Variations on a technique: Enhancing children's recall using narrative elaboration training. *Applied Cognitive Psychology, 17*, 377–399.

Brown, D. A., Pipe, M.-E., Lewis, C., Lamb, M. E., & Orbach, Y. (2007). Supportive or suggestive: Do human figure drawings help 5- to 7-year-old children to report touch? *Journal of Consulting and Clinical Psychology, 75*, 33–42.

Brown, D., Pipe, M.-E., Lewis, C., Lamb, M. E., & Orbach, Y. (2012). How do body diagrams affect the accuracy and consistency of children's reports of bodily touch across repeated interviews? *Applied Cognitive Psychology, 26*, 174–181.

Brown, D. A., Salmon, K., Pipe, M.-E., Rutter, M., Craw, S., & Taylor, B. (1999). Children's recall of medical experiences: The impact of stress. *Child Abuse & Neglect*, *23*, 209–216.

Brown, R. (1973). *A first language*. Cambridge, MA: Harvard University Press.

Browne, A., & Finkelhor, D. (1986). Impact of child sexual abuse: A review of the research. *Psychological Bulletin*, *99*, 66–77.

Brubacher, S. P., Glisic, U., Roberts, K. P., & Powell, M. (2011). Children's ability to recall unique aspects of one occurrence of a repeated event. *Applied Cognitive Psychology*, *25*, 351–358.

Brubacher, S. P., Malloy, L. C., Lamb, M. E., & Roberts, K. P. (2013). How do interviewers and children discuss individual occurrences of alleged repeated abuse in forensic interviews?. *Applied Cognitive Psychology*, *27*, 443–450.

Brubacher, S. P., Poole, D. A., & Dickinson, J. J. (2015). The use of ground rules in investigative interviews with children: A synthesis and call for research. *Developmental Review*, *36*, 15–33.

Brubacher, S. P., Roberts, K. P., & Powell, M. (2011). Effects of practicing episodic versus scripted recall on children's subsequent narratives of a repeated event. *Psychology, Public Policy & Law*, *17*, 286–314.

Brubacher, S. P., Roberts, K. P., & Powell, M. (2012). Retrieval of episodic versus generic information: Does the order of recall affect the amount and accuracy of details reported by children about repeated events? *Developmental Psychology*, *48*, 111–122.

Bruck, M. (1999). A summary of an affidavit prepared for Commonwealth of Massachusetts v. Cheryl Amirault LeFave. *Applied Developmental Science*, *3*, 110–127.

Bruck, M. (2009). Human figure drawings and children's recall of touching. *Journal of Experimental Psychology: Applied*, *15*, 361–374.

Bruck, M., & Ceci, S. J. (1995). Amicus Brief for the case of State of New Jersey v. Michaels presented by Committee of Concerned Social Scientists. *Psychology, Public Policy, and The Law*, *1*, 272–322.

Bruck, M., & Ceci, S. J. (1996). Issues in the scientific validation of interviews with young children. *Monographs of the Society for Research in Child Development*, *61*, 204–214.

Bruck, M., & Ceci, S. (2004). Forensic developmental psychology unveiling four common misconceptions. *Current Directions in Psychological Science*, *13*, 229–232.

Bruck, M., Ceci, S. J., & Francoeur, E. (1999). The accuracy of mothers' memories of conversations with their preschool children. *Journal of Experimental Psychology: Applied*, *5*, 89–106.

Bruck, M., Ceci, S. J., Francoeur, E., & Renick, A. (1995a). Anatomically detailed dolls do not facilitate preschoolers' reports of a pediatric examination involving genital touching. *Journal of Experimental Psychology: Applied*, *1*, 95–109.

Bruck, M., Ceci, S. J., Francouer, E., & Barr, R. (1995b). "I hardly cried when I got my shot!" Influencing children's reports about a visit to their pediatrician. *Child Development*, *66*, 193–208.

Bruck, M., Ceci, S. J., & Hembrooke, H. (1998). Reliability and credibility of young children's reports: From research to policy and practice. *American Psychologist*, *53*, 136–151.

Bruck, M., Hembrooke, H., & Ceci, S. J. (1997). Children's reports of pleasant and unpleasant events. In D. Read & S. Lindsay (Eds.), *Recollections of trauma: Scientific research and clinical practice* (pp. 199–219). New York, NY: Plenum.

Bruck, M., Kelley, K., & Poole, D. A. (2016). Children's reports of body touching in medical examinations: The benefits and risks of using body diagrams. *Psychology, Public Policy, and Law, 22*, 1–11.

Bruck, M., London, K., Landa, R., & Goodman, J. (2007). Autobiographical memory and suggestibility in children with autism spectrum disorder. *Development and Psychopathology, 19*, 73–95.

Bruck, M., Melnyk, L., & Ceci, S. J. (2000). Draw it again Sam: The effect of drawing on children's suggestibility and source monitoring ability. *Journal of Experimental Child Psychology, 77*, 169–196.

Bugental, D. B., Blue, J., Cortez, V., Fleck, K., & Rodriguez (1992). Influences of witnessed affect on information processing in children. *Child Development, 63*, 774–786.

Burack, J. A., & Zigler, E. (1990). Intentional and incidental memory in organically mentally retarded, familial retarded, and nonretarded individuals. *American Journal on Mental Retardation, 94*, 532–540.

Burgess, A. W., & Holmstrom, L. L. (1978). Recovery from rape and prior life stress. *Research in Nursing & Health, 1*, 165–174.

Burgwyn-Bailes, E., Baker-Ward, L., Gordon, B. N., & Ornstein, P. A. (2001). Children's memory for emergency medical treatment after one year: The impact of individual difference variables on recall and suggestibility. *Applied Cognitive Psychology, 15*, S25–S48.

Bussey, K., & Grimbeek, E. J. (1995). Disclosure processes: Issues for child sexual abuse victims. In K. J. Rotenberg (Ed.), *Disclosure processes in children and adolescents* (pp. 166–203). Cambridge UK: Cambridge University Press. https://doi.org/10.1017/CBO9780511527746.009.

Butler, S., Gross, J., & Hayne, H. (1995). The effect of drawing on memory performance in young children. *Developmental Psychology, 31*, 597–608.

Butterfield, E. C., & Ferretti, R. F. (1987). Toward a theoretical integration of cognitive hypothesis about intellectual differences among children. In J. B. Borkowski & J. D. Day (Eds.), *Cognition in special children: Comparative approaches to retardation, learning disabilities and giftedness* (pp. 195–233). Norwood, NJ: Ablex.

Bybee, D., & Mowbray, C. T. (1993). An analysis of allegations of sexual abuse in a multi-victim day care center case. *Child Abuse & Neglect, 17*, 767–783.

Camparo, L. B., Wagner, J. T., & Saywitz, K. J. (2001). Interviewing children about real and fictitious events: Revisiting the narrative elaboration procedure. *Law and Human Behavior, 25*, 63–80.

Cantlon, J., Payne, G., & Erbaugh, C. (1996). Outcome-based practice: Disclosure rates of child sexual abuse comparing allegation blind and allegation informed structured interviews. *Child Abuse & Neglect, 20*, 1113–1120.

Carnes, C. N. (2000). *Forensic evaluation of children when sexual abuse is suspected* (2nd ed.). Huntsville, AL: National Children's Advocacy Center.

Carnes, C. N., Nelson-Gardell, D., Wilson, C., & Orgassa, U. C. (2001). Extended forensic evaluation when sexual abuse is suspected: A multisite field study. *Child Maltreatment, 6*, 230–242.

Carnes, C. N., Wilson, C., & Nelson-Gardell, D. (1999). Extended forensic evaluation when sexual abuse is suspected: A model and preliminary data. *Child Maltreatment, 4*, 242–254.

Carrick, N., & Quas, J. A. (2006). Effects of discrete emotions on young children's ability to discern fantasy and reality. *Developmental Psychology, 42*, 1278–1288.

Carrick, N., Rush, E., & Quas, J. A. (2013). Suggestibility and imagination in early childhood. In M. Taylor (Ed.). *The Oxford handbook of the development of imagination* (pp. 113–125). Oxford, UK: Oxford University Press.

Carter, C. A., Bottoms, B. L., & Levine, M. (1996). Linguistic and socioemotional influences in the accuracy of children's reports. *Law and Human Behavior, 20,* 335–358.

Cassel, W. S., & Bjorklund, D. F. (1995). Developmental patterns of eyewitness memory and suggestibility: An ecologically based short-term longitudinal study. *Law and Human Behavior, 19,* 507–532.

Cassel, W. S., Roebers, C. E. M., & Bjorklund, D. F. (1996). Developmental patterns of eyewitness responses to repeated and increasingly suggestive questions. *Journal of Experimental Child Psychology, 61,* 116–133.

Castelli, P., & Goodman, G. S. (2014). Children's perceived emotional behavior at disclosure and prosecutors' evaluations. *Child Abuse and Neglect, 38,* 1521–1532.

Castelli, P., Goodman, G. S., & Ghetti, S. (2005). Effects of interview style and witness age on perceptions of children's credibility in sexual abuse cases. *Journal of Applied Social Psychology, 35,* 297–317.

Cauchi, R. T., Powell, M., & Hughes-Scholes, C. H. (2010). A controlled analysis of professionals' contemporaneous notes of interviews about alleged child abuse. *Child Abuse and Neglect, 34,* 318–323.

Ceci, S. J., & Bruck, M. (1993). Suggestibility of the child witness: A historical review and synthesis. *Psychological Bulletin, 113,* 403–439.

Ceci, S. J., & Bruck, M. (1995). *Jeopardy in the courtroom: A scientific analysis of children's testimony.* Washington, DC: American Psychological Association.

Ceci, S. J., & Friedman, R. D. (2000). The suggestibility of children: Scientific research and legal implications. *Cornell Law Review, 86,* 34–108.

Ceci, S. J., Hritz, A., & Royer, C. (2015). Understanding suggestibility. In W. T. O'Donohue & M. Fanetti (Eds.), *Forensic interviews regarding sexual abuse: A guide to evidence-based practice* (pp. 141–153). New York, NY: Springer International.

Ceci, S. J., & Huffman, M. L. C. (1997). How suggestible are preschool children? Cognitive and social factors. *Journal of the American Academy of Child & Adolescent Psychiatry, 36,* 948–958.

Ceci, S. J., Huffman, M. L. C., Smith, E., & Loftus, E. F. (1994). Repeatedly thinking about a non-event: Source misattributions among preschoolers. *Consciousness and Cognition, 3,* 388–407.

Ceci, S. J., Huffman, M. L. C., Smith, E., & Loftus, E. F. (1996). Repeatedly thinking about a non-event: Source misattributions among preschoolers. In W. P. Banks & K. Pezdek (Eds.), *The recovered memory/false memory debate* (pp. 225–244). San Diego, CA: Academic Press.

Ceci, S. J., Kulkofsky, S., Klemfuss, J. Z., Sweeney, C. D., & Bruck, M. (2007). Unwarranted assumptions about children's testimonial accuracy. *Annual Review of Clinical Psychology, 3,* 311–328.

Ceci, S. J., Leichtman, M. D., & Bruck, M. (1995). The suggestibility of children's eyewitness reports: Methodological issues. In F. E. Weinert & W. Schneider (Eds.), *Memory performance and competencies: Issues in growth and development* (pp. 323–347). Mahwah, NJ: Erlbaum.

Ceci, S. J., Loftus, E. F., Leichtman, M. D., & Bruck, M. (1994). The possible role of source misattributions in the creation of false beliefs among preschoolers. *International Journal of Clinical and Experimental Hypnosis, 42,* 304–320.

Ceci, S. J., Powell, M. B., & Principe, G. F. (2002). The scientific status of children's memory and testimony. In D. L. Faigman, D. H. Kaye, M. J. Saks, &

J. Sanders (Eds.), *Modern scientific evidence: The law and science of expert testimony* (Vol. 2, pp. 144–205). St Paul, MN: West Publishing Co.

Ceci, S. J., Ross, D. F., & Toglia, M. P. (1987a). Suggestibility of children's memory: Psycholegal issues. *Journal of Experimental Psychology: General, 116,* 38–49.

Ceci, S. J., Ross, D. F., & Toglia, M. P. (1987b). Age differences in suggestibility: Narrowing the uncertainties. In S. J. Ceci, M. P. Toglia, & D. F. Ross (Eds.), *Children's eyewitness memory* (pp. 79–91). New York, NY: Springer.

Ceci, S., Toglia, M., & Ross, D. (1988). On remembering more or less: A trace strength interpretation of developmental differences in suggestibility. *Journal of Experimental Psychology: General, 117,* 201–203.

Cederborg, A.-C., Alm, C., Lima da Silva Nises, D., & Lamb, M. E. (2013). Investigative interviewing of alleged child abuse victims: An evaluation of a new training programme for investigative interviewers. *Police Practice and Research, 14,* 242–254.

Cederborg, A.-C., Danielsson, H., La Rooy, D., & Lamb, M. E. (2009). Repetition of contaminating question types when children and youths with intellectual disabilities are interviewed. *Journal of Intellectual Disability Research, 53,* 440–449.

Cederborg, A.-C., & Gumpert, C. H. (2010). The challenge of assessing credibility when children with intellectual disabilities are alleged victims of abuse. *Scandinavian Journal of Disability Research, 12,* 125–140.

Cederborg, A.-C., Hultman, E., & La Rooy, D. (2012). The quality of details when children and youths with intellectual disabilities are interviewed about their abuse experiences. *Scandinavian Journal of Disability Research, 14,* 113–125.

Cederborg, A.-C., & Lamb, M.E. (2006). How does the legal system respond when disabled children are victimized? *Child Abuse & Neglect, 30,* 537–547.

Cederborg, A.-C., & Lamb, M. (2008a). Interviewing alleged victims with intellectual disabilities. *Journal of Intellectual Disability Research, 52,* 49–58.

Cederborg, A.-C., & Lamb, M. E. (2008b). The need for systematic and intensive training of forensic interviewers. In T. I. Richardson and M. V. Williams (Eds.), *Child abuse and its impact* (pp. 1–17). New York, NY: Nova Science Publishers.

Cederborg, A.-C., Lamb, M. E., & Laurell, O. (2007). Delay of disclosure, minimization, and denial when the evidence is unambiguous: A multi-victim case. In Y. Orbach, A.-C. Cederborg, M.-E. Pipe & M. E. Lamb (Eds.), *Child sexual abuse: Disclosure, delay, and denial* (pp. 159–173). Mahwah, NJ: Erlbaum.

Cederborg, A.-C., La Rooy, D., & Lamb, M. E. (2008). Repeated interviews with children who have intellectual disabilities. *Journal of Applied Research in Intellectual Disabilities, 21,* 103–113.

Cederborg, A.-C., Orbach, Y., Sternberg, K. J., & Lamb, M. E. (2000). Investigative interviews of child witnesses in Sweden. *Child Abuse & Neglect, 24,* 1355–1361.

Chae, Y., Goodman, G. S., & Edelstein, R. S. (2010). Autobiographical memory development from an attachment perspective: The special role of negative events. *Advances in Child Development and Behavior, 40,* 1–49.

Chae, Y., Kulkofsky, S., Debaran, F., Wang, Q., & Hart, S. L. (2016). Low-SES preschool children's eyewitness memory: The role of narrative skill. *Behavioral Sciences & The Law, 34,* 55–73.

Chae, Y., Ogle, C. M., & Goodman, G. S. (2009). Remembering traumatic childhood events: An attachment theory perspective. In J. A. Quas & R. Fivush (Eds.), *Emotion and memory development* (pp. 3–27). New York, NY: Oxford University Press.

Chahal, K., & Cassidy, T. (1995). Deception and its detection in children: A study of adult accuracy. *Psychology, Crime & Law, 1*, 237–245.

Chaput, V., Amsellem, F., Urdapilleta, I., Chaste, P., Leboyer, M., Delorme, R., & Goussé, V. (2013). Episodic memory and self-awareness in Asperger Syndrome: Analysis of memory narratives. *Research in Autism Spectrum Disorders, 7*, 1062–1067.

Cheung, K. M. (1997). Developing the interview protocol for video-recorded child sexual abuse investigations: A training experience with police officers, social workers, and clinical psychologists in Hong Kong. *Child Abuse & Neglect, 21*, 273–284.

Chi, M. T. H. (1978). Knowledge structures and memory development. In R. S. Siegler (Ed.), *Children's thinking: What develops?* (pp. 73–96). New York, NY: Wiley.

Chi, M. T. H., & Ceci, S. J. (1987). Content knowledge: Its role, representation, and restructuring in memory development. In H. W. Reese (Ed.), *Advances in child development and behavior* (Vol. 20, pp. 91–142). New York, NY: Academic Press.

Chi, M. T., & Koeske, R. D. (1983). Network representation of a child's dinosaur knowledge. *Developmental Psychology, 19*, 29–39.

Children's Bureau (2003). *12 years of reporting child maltreatment 2001*. Washington, DC: U.S. Department of Health and Human Services, Administration on Children, Youth, and Families.

Christianson, S. (1992). Emotional stress and eyewitness memory: A critical review. *Psychological Bulletin, 112*, 284–309.

Clare, I. (2001). Witnesses with learning disabilities. *British Journal of Learning Disabilities, 29*, 79–80.

Clark, D. C. (1971). Teaching concepts in the classroom: A set of prescriptions derived from experimental research. *Journal of Educational Psychology Monograph, 62*, 253–278.

Clerc, J., Miller, P. H., & Cosnefroy, L. (2014). Young children's transfer of strategies: Utilization deficiencies, executive function, and metacognition. *Developmental Review, 34*, 378–393.

Cleveland, K. C., Quas, J., & Lyon, T. D. (2016). Valence, implicated actor, and children's acquiescence to false suggestions. *Journal of Applied Developmental Psychology, 43*, 1–7.

Clubb, P. A., Nida, R. E.., Merritt, K., & Ornstein, P. A. (1993). Visiting the doctor: Children's knowledge and memory. *Cognitive Development, 8*, 361–372.

Cole, C. B., & Loftus, E. F. (1987). The memory of children. In S. J. Ceci, M. P. Toglia, & D. F. Ross (Eds.), *Children's eyewitness testimony* (pp. 178–208). New York, NY: Springer.

Collins, K., Doherty-Sneddon, G., Doherty, G. J. (2014). Practitioner perspectives on rapport building during child investigative interviews, *Psychology, Crime & Law, 20*, 884–901.

Collins, K., Harker, N., & Antonopoulos, G. A. (2017). The impact of the Registered Intermediary on adults' perceptions of child witnesses: Evidence from a mock cross examination. *European Journal on Criminal Policy and Research, 23*, 211–225.

Collins, D., & Henry, L. (2016). Eyewitness recall and suggestibility in individuals with Down syndrome. *Journal of Intellectual Disability Research, 60*, 1227–1231.

Connolly, D. A., & Gordon, H. M. (2014). Can order of general and specific memory prompts help children to recall an instance of a repeated event that was different from the others? *Psychology, Crime & Law, 20*, 852–864.

Connolly, D. A., Gordon, H. M., Woiwod, D. M., & Price, H. L. (2016). What children recall about a repeated event when one instance is different from the others. *Developmental Psychology, 52*, 1038–1051.

Connolly, D. A., & Lindsay, D. S. (2001). The influence of suggestions on children's reports of a unique experience versus an instance of a repeated experience. *Applied Cognitive Psychology, 15*, 205–223.

Conte, J. R., Sorenson, E., Fogarty, L., & Dalla Rosa, D. (1991). Evaluating children's reports of sexual abuse: Results from a survey of professionals. *American Journal of Orthopsychiatry, 61*, 428–437.

Cordón, I. M., Pipe, M.-E., Sayfan, L., Melinder, A., & Goodman, G. S. (2004). Memory for traumatic experiences in early childhood. *Developmental Review, 24*, 101–132.

Cowan, N., & Davidson, G. (1984). Salient childhood memories. *Journal of Genetic Psychology, 145*, 101–107.

Craig, R. A., Scheibe, R., Kircher. J., Raskin, D. C., & Dodd, D. (1999). Interviewer questions and content analysis of children's statements of sexual abuse. *Applied Developmental Science, 3*, 77–85.

Criminal Justice System. (2007). Sections 2.13, 2.117, 2.188.

Cronin, O., Memon, A., Eaves, R., Kupper, B., & Bull, R. (1992). *The cognitive interview with child witnesses: A child centered approach?* Paper presented at NATO Advanced Study Institute: The Child Witness in Context, Marateo, Italy.

Cross, T. P., & Hershkowitz, I. (2017). Psychology and child protection: Promoting widespread improvement in practice. *Psychology, Public Policy, and Law, 23*(4), 503.

Cross, T. P., Walsh, W. A., Simone, M., & Jones, L. M. (2003). Prosecution of child abuse: A meta-analysis of rates of criminal justice decisions. *Trauma, Violence, & Abuse, 4*, 323–340.

Cross, T. P., Whitcomb, D., & De Vos, E. (1995). Criminal justice outcomes of prosecution of child sexual abuse: A case flow analysis. *Child Abuse & Neglect, 19*, 1431–1442.

Crosse, S. B., Kaye, E., & Ratnofsky, A. C. (1993). *A report on the maltreatment of children with disabilities*. Washington, DC: National Center of Child Abuse and Neglect.

Cutler, B. L., & Penrod, S. D. (1988). Context reinstatement and eyewitness identification. In G. M. Davies & D. M. Thomas (Eds.), *Memory in context: Context in memory* (pp. 231–244). New York, NY: Wiley.

Cutler, B. L., Penrod, S. D., & Martens, T. K. (1987). Improving the reliability of eyewitness identification: Putting context into context. *Journal of Applied Psychology, 72*, 629–637.

Cutler, B. L., Penrod, S. D., O'Rourke, T. E., & Martens, T. K. (1986). Unconfounding the effects of contextual cues on eyewitness identification accuracy. *Social Behaviour, 1*, 113–134.

Cyr, M., Dion, J., McDuff, P., & Trotier-Sylvain, K. (2012). Transfer of skills in the context of non-suggestive investigative interviews: Impact of structured interview protocol and feedback. *Applied Cognitive Psychology, 26*, 516–524.

Cyr, M., & Lamb, M. E. (2009). Assessing the effectiveness of the NICHD investigative interview protocol when interviewing French-speaking alleged victims of child sexual abuse in Quebec. *Child Abuse & Neglect, 33*, 257–268.

Cyr, M., Lamb, M. E., Pelletier, J., Leduc, P., & Perron, A. (2006, July). *Assessing the effectiveness of the NICHD investigative interview protocol in Francophone Quebec*. Paper presented at the Second International Investigative Interviewing Conference, University of Portsmouth, UK.

Daehler, M. W., & Greco, C. (1985) Memory in very young children. In M. Pressley & C. J. Brainerd (Eds.), *Cognitive learning and memory in children: Progress in cognitive development research*. New York, NY: Springer.

Dahl, J. J., Kingo, O. S., & Krøjgaard, P. (2015). The magic shrinking machine revisited: The presence of props at recall facilitates memory in 3-year-olds. *Developmental Psychology, 51*, 1704–1716.

Danby, M. C., Brubacher, S. P., Sharman, S. J., Powell, M. B., & Roberts, K. P. (2017). Children's reasoning about which episode of a repeated event is best remembered. *Applied Cognitive Psychology, 31*(1), 99–108.

Dale, P. S. (1976). *Language development: Structure and function*. New York, NY: Holt, Rinehart, & Winston.

Dale, P. S., Loftus, E. F., & Rathbun, L. (1978). The influence of the form of the question on the eyewitness testimony of preschool children. *Journal of Psycholinguistic Research, 7*, 269–277.

Danby, M. C., Brubacher, S. P., Sharman, S. J., & Powell, M. B. (2015). The effects of practice on children's ability to apply ground rules in a narrative interview. *Behavioral Sciences & the Law, 33*, 446–458.

Darvish, T., Hershkowitz, I., Lamb, M. E., & Orbach, Y. (2005, January). *The effect of the NICHD Interview Protocol on the elicitation of investigative leads in child sexual abuse investigations.* Paper presented to the Society for Applied Research on Memory and Cognition, Victoria, NZ.

Davidson, D., & Hoe, S. (1993). Children's recall and recognition memory for typical and atypical actions in script-based stories. *Journal of Experimental Child Psychology, 55*, 104–126.

Davies, G. M., Westcott, H. L., & Horan, N. (2000). The impact of questioning style on the content of investigative interviews with respected child sexual abuse victims. *Psychology, Crime, and the Law, 6*, 81–97.

Davies, G. M., Tarrant, A., & Flin, R. (1989). Close encounters of the witness kind: Children's memory for a simulated health inspection. *British Journal of Psychology, 80*, 415–429.

Davis, G., Hoyano, L., Keenan, C., Maitland, L., & Morgan, R. (1999). *The admissibility and sufficiency of evidence in child abuse prosecutions*. London, UK: Home Office, Research, Development and Statistics Directorate.

Davis, S. L., & Bottoms, B. L. (2002a). Effects of social support on children's eyewitness reports: A test of the underlying mechanism. *Law & Human Behavior, 26*, 185–215.

Davis, S. L., & Bottoms, B. L. (2002b). The effects of social support on the accuracy of children's reports: Implications for the forensic interview. In I. B. Weiner (Ed.), *Personality and clinical psychology series* (pp. 437–457). Chichester, UK: Wiley.

Day, S. B., & Goldstone, R. L. (2012). The import of knowledge export: Connecting findings and theories of transfer of learning. *Educational Psychologist, 47*, 153–176.

Deffenbacher, K. A. (1983). The influence of arousal on reliability of testimony. In S. M. A. Lloyd-Bostock & B. R. Clifford (Eds.), *Handbook of Neuropsychology* (Vol. 9). Amsterdam: Elsevier.

DeLoache, J. S. (1990). Young children's understanding of scale models. In R. Fivush & J. Hudson (Eds.), *Knowing and remembering in young children* (pp. 94–126). New York, NY: Cambridge University Press.

DeLoache, J. S. (2000). Dual representation and young children's use of scale models. *Child Development, 71*, 329–338.

DeLoache, J. S. (2004). Becoming symbol minded. *Trends in Cognitive Sciences*, *8*, 66–70.

DeLoache, J. S., & Marzolf, D. P. (1992). When a picture is not worth a thousand words: Young children's understanding of pictures and models. *Cognitive Development*, *7*, 317–329.

DeLoache, J. S., & Marzolf, D. P. (1995). The use of dolls to interview young children: Issues of symbolic representation. *Journal of Experimental Child Psychology*, *60*, 155–173.

DeMarie-Dreblow, D. (1991). Relation between knowledge and memory: A reminder that correlation does not imply causality. *Child Development*, *62*, 484–498.

De Villiers, J., & De Villiers, P. (1999). Language development. In M. H. Bornstein & M. E. Lamb (Eds.), *Developmental psychology: An advanced textbook* (4th ed., pp. 313–373). Mahwah, NJ: Erlbaum.

Dent, H. R. (1982). The effects of interviewing strategies on the results of interviews with child witnesses. In A. Trankell (Ed.), *Reconstructing the past: The role of psychologists in criminal trials* (pp. 279–297). Stockholm, Sweden: Norstedt.

Dent, H. R. (1986). An experimental study of the effectiveness of different techniques of questioning mentally-handicapped child witnesses. *British Journal of Clinical Psychology*, *25*, 13–17.

Dent, H. R. (1992). The effects of age and intelligence on eyewitnessing ability. In H. Dent & R. Flin (Eds.), *Children as witnesses* (pp. 1–13). Oxford, England: John Wiley & Sons.

Dent, H. R., & Stephenson, G. M. (1979). An experimental study of the effectiveness of different techniques of questioning child witnesses. *British Journal of Social and Clinical Psychology*, *18*, 41–51.

DePaulo, B. M., Charlton, K., Cooper. H., Lindsay, J. L., & Muhlenbruck, L. (1997). The accuracy-confidence correlation in the detection of deception. *Personality and Social Psychology Review*, *1*, 346–357.

Derakshan, N., & Eysenck, M. W. (2009). Anxiety, processing efficiency, and cognitive performance: New developments from attentional control theory. *European Psychologist*, *14*(2), 168–176.

DeVoe, E. R., & Faller, K. C. (1999). The characteristics of disclosure among children who may have been sexually abused. *Child Maltreatment*, *4*, 217–227.

Dickinson, J. J., Brubacher, S. P., & Poole, D. A. (2015). Children's performance on ground rules: Implications for forensic interviewing. *Law and Human Behavior*, *39*, 87–97.

Dickinson, J. J., & Poole, D. A. (2017). The influence of disclosure history and body diagrams on children's reports of inappropriate touching: Evidence from a new analog paradigm. *Law and Human Behavior*, *41*, 1–12.

Dickinson, J. J., Poole, D. A., & Bruck, M. (2005). Back to the future: A comment on the use of anatomical dolls in forensic interviews. *Journal of Forensic Psychology Practice*, *5*, 63–74.

Dietze, P. M., Powell, M. B., & Thomson, D. M. (2010). Mental reinstatement of context with child witnesses: Does it matter whether context is reinstated "out loud"? *Psychology, Crime & Law*, *16*, 439–448.

Dietze, P. M., Powell, M. B., & Thomson, D. M. (2012). Examination of the effect of mental reinstatement of context across developmental level, retention interval and type of mnemonic instruction. *Psychiatry, Psychology and Law*, *19*, 89–103.

Dietze, P. M., Sharman, S. J., Powell, M. B., & Thomson, D. M. (2013). Does free recall moderate the effect of mental context reinstatement instructions on children's cued recall? *Psychology, Crime & Law, 19*, 881–891.

Dietze, P. M., & Thompson, D. M. (1993). Mental reinstatement of context: A technique for interviewing child witnesses. *Applied Cognitive Psychology, 7*, 97–108.

Dion, J., & Cyr, M. (2008). The use of the NICHD Protocol to enhance the quantity of details obtained from children with low verbal abilities in investigative interviews: A pilot study. *Journal of Child Sexual Abuse, 17*, 144–162.

DiPetro, E. K., Runyan, D. K., & Fredrickson, D. D. (1997). Predictors of disclosure during medical evaluation for suspected sexual abuse. *Journal of Sexual Abuse, 6*, 133–142.

Distel, N. E. (1999). Disclosure of childhood sexual abuse: Links to emotion expression and adult attachment. *Dissertation Abstracts: Section B: The Sciences and Engineering, 60* (6-B), 2938.

Dodd, D. H., & Bradshaw, J. M. (1980). Leading questions and memory: Pragmatic constraints. *Journal of Verbal Learning and Verbal Behavior, 19*, 695–704.

Donaldson, M. (1978). *Children's minds*. London: Croom Helm.

Dorado, J. S., & Saywitz, K. J. (2001). Interviewing preschoolers from low- and middle-SES communities: A test of the Narrative Elaboration Recall Improvement technique. *Journal of Clinical Child Psychology, 30*, 568–580.

Doris, J. (Ed.) (1991). *The suggestibility of children's recollections: Implications for eyewitness testimony*. Washington, DC: American Psychological Association.

Douglas, R., Park, C., Bjorklund, B., Gache, J., Sanders, L., Nelson, L., Cassel, W., & Bjorklund, D. (1997, April). *Social demand characteristics in children's eyewitness memory and suggestibility: The effects of different interviewers*. Paper presented to the Society for Research in Child Development, Washington, DC.

Drohan-Jennings, D. M., Roberts, K. P., & Powell, M. B. (2010). Mental context reinstatement increases resistance to false suggestions after children have experienced a repeated event. *Psychiatry, Psychology and Law, 17*, 594–606.

Drummey, A. B., & Newcombe, N. S. (1995). Remembering versus knowing the past: Children's explicit and implicit memories for pictures. *Journal of Experimental Child Psychology, 59*, 549–565.

Dubowitz, H., Black, M., & Harrington, D. (1992). The diagnosis of child sexual abuse. *American Journal of Diseases of Children, 146*, 668–693.

Dwyer, J. (2002, December 24). Man cleared in jogger case goes free at the age of 28 [Electronic version]. *The New York Times*.

Dwyer, J., & Saulny, S. (2002, December 19). Judge vacates convictions in central park jogger case [Electronic version]. *The New York Times*.

Earhart, B., La Rooy, D. J., Brubacher, S. P., & Lamb, M. E. (2014). An examination of "don't know" responses in forensic interviews with children. *Behavioral Sciences & The Law, 32*, 746–761.

Eigsti, I. M., & Cicchetti, D. (2004). The impact of child maltreatment on expressive syntax at 60 months. *Developmental Science, 7*, 88–102.

Elischberger, H. B., & Roebers, C. M. (2001). Improving young children's free narratives about an observed event: The effects of nonspecific verbal prompts. *International Journal of Behavioral Development, 25*, 160–166.

Elliott, D. M., & Briere, J. (1994). Forensic sexual abuse evaluations of older children: Disclosures and symptomatology. *Behavioral Sciences and the Law, 12*, 261–277.

Ellis, N. R. (1969). A behavioural research strategy in mental retardation: Defence and critique. *American Journal of Mental Deficiency, 73*, 557–567.

Ellis, L. M., Powell, M. B., Thomson, D. M., & Jones, C. (2003). Do simple "ground rules" reduce preschoolers' suggestibility about experienced and nonexperienced events? *Psychiatry, Psychology and Law, 10*, 334–345.

Endres, J., Poggenpohl, C., & Erneb, C. (1999). Repetitions, warnings and video: Cognitive and motivational components in preschool children's suggestibility. *Legal and Criminological Psychology, 4*, 129–146.

Erdelyi, M. H. (1996). *The recovery of unconscious memories: Hypermnesia and reminiscence*. Chicago, IL: University of Chicago Press.

Ericson, K., Perlman, N., & Isaacs, B. (1994). Witness competency, communication issues and people with developmental disabilities. *Developmental Disabilities Bulletin, 22*, 101–109.

Estes, D., Wellman, H. M., & Woolley, J. D. (1989). Children's understanding of mental phenomena. *Advances in Child Development and Behavior, 22*, 41–87.

Evans, A. D., & Lee, K. (2010). Promising to tell the truth makes 8- to 16-year olds more honest. *Behavioral Sciences & the Law, 28*, 801–811.

Evans, A. D., Roberts, K. P., Price, H. L., & Stefek, C. P. (2010). The use of paraphrasing in investigative interviews. *Child Abuse & Neglect, 34*, 585–592.

Evans, A. D., Stolzenberg, S. N., Lee, K., & Lyon, T. D. (2014). Young children's difficulty with indirect speech acts: Implications for questioning child witnesses. *Behavioral Sciences & The Law, 32*, 775–788.

Evans, A. D., Stolzenberg, S. N., & Lyon, T. D. (2015). Pragmatic failure and referential ambiguity when attorneys ask child witnesses "do you know/remember" questions. *Psychology, Public Policy, and Law, 23*, 191–199.

Everson, M. D., & Boat, B. W. (1994). Putting the anatomical doll controversy in perspective: An examination of the major uses and criticisms of the dolls in child sexual abuse evaluations. *Child Abuse & Neglect, 18*, 113–129.

Everson, M. D., & Boat, B. W. (2002). The utility of anatomical dolls and drawing in child forensic interviews. In M. L. Eisen, J. A. Quas, & G. S. Goodman (Eds.), *Memory and suggestibility in the forensic interview* (pp. 383–408). Mahwah, NJ: Erlbaum.

Everson, M. D., Hunter, W. M., Runyon, D. K., Edelsohn, G. A., & Coulter, M. L. (1989). Maternal support following disclosure of incest. *American Journal of Orthopsychiatry, 59*, 197–207.

Excerpts from District Attorney's report on re-examination of jogger case [Electronic version]. (2002, December 6). *The New York Times*.

Farrar, M. J., & Goodman, G. S. (1990). Developmental differences in the relation between scripts and episodic memory: Do they exist? In R. Fivush & J. A. Hudson (Eds.), *Knowing and remembering in young children. Emory symposia in cognition* (Vol. 3, pp. 30–64). New York, NY: Cambridge University Press.

Farrar, M. J., & Goodman, G. S. (1992). Developmental changes in event memory. *Child Development, 63*, 173–187.

Fasig, L. (1999, April). *The influence of script memory on children's suggestibility*. Paper presented at the biennial meeting of the Society of Research in Child Development, Albuquerque, NM.

Feltis, B. B., Powell, M. B., Snow, P. C., & Hughes-Scholes, C. H. (2010). An examination of the association between interviewer question type and story-grammar detail in child witness interviews about abuse. *Child Abuse & Neglect, 34*, 407–413.

Field, C., Allen, M. L., & Lewis, C. (2016). Attentional learning helps language acquisition take shape for atypically developing children, not just children with autism spectrum disorders. *Journal of Autism and Developmental Disorders, 46*, 3195–3206.

Finkelhor, D., Hotaling, G., Lewis, I. A., & Smith, C. (1990). Sexual abuse in a national survey of adult men and women: Prevalence, characteristics, and risk factors. *Child Abuse & Neglect*, *14*, 19–28.

Finlayson, L. M., & Koocher, G. P. (1991). Professional judgment and child abuse reporting in sexual abuse cases. *Professional Psychology: Research and Practice*, *22*, 464–472.

Fisher, R. P., Brennan, K. H., & McCauley, M. R. (2002). The cognitive interview method to enhance eyewitness recall. In G. S. Goodman, M. L. Eisen, & J. A., Quas (Eds.), *Memory and suggestibility in the forensic interview* (pp. 265–286). Mahwah, NJ: Erlbaum.

Fisher, R. P., & Geiselman, R. E. (1992). *Memory-enhancing techniques for investigative interviewing: The cognitive interview*. Springfield, IL: Charles C. Thomas.

Fisher, R. P., Geiselman, R. E., Raymond, D. S., Jurkevich, L. M., & Warhaftig, M. L. (1987). Enhancing enhanced eyewitness memory: Refining the cognitive interview. *Journal of Police Science and Administration*, *15*, 291–297.

Fisher, R. P., Ross, S. J., & Cahill, B. S. (2010). Interviewing witnesses and victims. In P. A. Granhag (Ed.), *Forensic psychology in context: Nordic and international approaches* (pp. 56–74). Cullompton, UK: Willan Publishing.

Fivush, R. (1997). Event memory in early childhood. In C. A. Nelson (Ed.), *The development of memory in childhood. Studies in developmental psychology* (pp. 139–161). Hove, UK: Psychology Press.

Fivush, R. (1998a). Children's recollections of traumatic and nontraumatic events. Trauma, memory, and suggestibility in children. *Development and Psychopathology*, *10*, 699–716.

Fivush, R. (1998b). Gendered narratives: Elaboration, structure, and emotion in parent-child reminiscing across the preschool years. In C. P. Thompson, D. J. Herrmann, D. Bruce, J. D. Read, D. G. Payne, & M. P. Toglia (Eds.), *Autobiographical memory: Theoretical and applied perspectives* (pp. 79–103). Mahwah, NJ: Erlbaum.

Fivush, R. (2002). Scripts, schemas, and memory of trauma. In N. L. Stein, P. J. Bauer, & M. Rabinowitch (Eds.), *Representation, memory, and development: Essays in honor of Jean Mandler* (pp. 53–74). Mahwah, NJ: Erlbaum.

Fivush, R. (2004a). The silenced self: Constructing self from memories spoken and unspoken. In D. Beike, J. Lampinen, & D. Behrand (Eds.), *The self and memory* (pp. 75–94). Hove, UK: Psychology Press.

Fivush, R. (2004b). Voice and silence: A feminist model of autobiographical memory. In J. Lucariello, J., Hudson, A., Fivush, R., & Bauer, P. J. (Eds.), *The mediated mind: Essays in honor of Katherine Nelson* (pp. 79–100). Mahwah, NJ: Erlbaum.

Fivush, R. (2011). The development of autobiographical memory. *Annual Review of Psychology*, *62*, 559–582.

Fivush, R., Haden, C., & Adam, S. (1995). Structure and coherence of preschoolers' personal narratives over time: Implications for childhood amnesia. *Journal of Experimental Child Psychology*, *60*, 32–56.

Fivush, R., Haden, C., & Reese, E. (1996). Remembering, recounting, and reminiscing: The development of autobiographical memory in social context. In D. C. Rubin (Ed.), *Remembering our past: Studies in autobiographical memory* (pp. 341–359). Cambridge, UK: Cambridge University Press.

Fivush, R., & Hamond, N. B. (1990). Autobiographical memory across the preschool years: Toward reconceptualizing childhood amnesia. In R. Fivush & J. A.

Hudson (Eds.), *Knowing and remembering in young children. Emory symposia in cognition* (Vol. *3*, pp. 223–248). New York, NY: Cambridge University Press.

Fivush, R., Hazzard, A., Sales, J. M., Sarfati, D., & Brown, T. (2003). Creating coherence out of chaos? Children's narratives of emotionally positive and negative events. *Applied Cognitive Psychology, 17*, 1–19.

Fivush, R., & Hudson, J. A. (Eds). (1990). *Knowing and remembering in young children*. New York, NY: Cambridge University Press.

Fivush, R., Hudson, J., & Nelson, K. (1984). Children's long-term memory for a novel event: An exploratory study. *Merrill-Palmer Quarterly, 30*, 303–316.

Fivush, R., Kuebli, J., & Clubb, P. A. (1992). The structure of events and event representations: A developmental analysis. *Child Development, 63*, 188–201.

Fivush, R., Peterson, C., & Schwarzmueller, A. (2002). Questions and answers: The credibility of child witnesses in the context of specific questioning techniques. In M. L. Eisen, J. A. Quas, & G. S. Goodman (Eds.), *Memory and suggestibility in the forensic interview* (pp. 331–354). Mahwah, NJ: Erlbaum.

Fivush, R., Pipe, M.-E., Murachver, T., & Reese, E. (1997). Events spoken and unspoken: Implications of language and memory development for the recovered memory debate. In M. A. Conway (Ed.), *Recovered memories and false memories. Debates in psychology* (pp. 34–62). Oxford: Oxford University Press.

Fivush, R., Sales, J. M., Goldberg, A., Bahrick, L., & Parker, J. (2004). Weathering the storm: Children's long-term recall of Hurricane Andrew. *Memory, 12*, 104–118.

Fivush, R., & Schwarzmueller, A. (1998). Children remember childhood: Implications for childhood amnesia. *Applied Cognitive Psychology, 12*, 455–473.

Fivush, R., & Shukat, J. R. (1995). Content, consistency, and coherence of early autobiographical recall. In M. S. Zaragoza, J. R. Graham, G. C. N. Hall, R. Hirschman, & Y. S. Ben-Porath (Eds.), *Memory and testimony in the child witness* (Vol. *1*, pp. 5–23). Thousand Oaks, CA: Sage.

Flavell, J. (1970). Developmental studies of mediated memory. In H. Reese & L. Lipsitt (Eds.), *Advances in child development and behavior* (pp. 181–211). New York, NY: Academic Press.

Flavell, J. H., Flavell, E. R., & Green, F. L. (1987). Young children's knowledge about the apparent-real and pretend-real distinctions. *Developmental Psychology, 23*, 816–822.

Flavell, J. H., Miller, P. H., & Miller, S. A. (1993). *Cognitive development* (3rd ed.). Upper Saddle River, NJ: Prentice-Hall.

Flin, R., Boon, J., Knox, A., & Bull, R. (1992). The effect of a five month delay on children's and adults' eyewitness memory. *British Journal of Psychology, 83*, 323–336.

Flory, K., Milich, R., Lorch, E. P., Hayden, A. N., Strange, C., & Welsh, R. (2006). Online story comprehension among children with ADHD: Which core deficits are involved? *Journal of Abnormal Child Psychology, 34*, 850–862.

Fogliati, R., & Bussey, K. (2014). The effects of cross-examination on children's reports of neutral and transgressive events. *Legal and Criminological Psychology, 19*, 296–315.

Foley, M. A., & Johnson, M. K. (1985). Confusions between memories for performed and imagined actions: A developmental comparison. *Child Development, 56*, 1145–1155.

Frayer, D. A., & Klausmeier, H. J. (1971). *Variables on concept learning: Task variables* (No. 28). Madison, WI: Wisconsin Research and Development Center for Cognitive Learning, Theoretical paper.

Fredrickson, B. L. (2001). The role of positive emotions in positive psychology: The broaden-and-build theory of positive emotions. *American Psychologist, 56*(3), 218.

Freeman, K. A., & Morris, T. L. (1999). Investigative interviewing with children: Evaluation of the effectiveness of a training program for child protective service workers. *Child Abuse & Neglect, 23*, 701–713.

Freer, B. D., Hayden, A., Lorch, E. P., & Milich, R. (2011). The stories they tell: Story production difficulties of children with ADHD. *School Psychology Review, 40*, 352–366.

Friedman, W. J. (1990). Children's representations of the pattern of daily activities. *Child Development, 61*, 1399–1412.

Friedman, W. J. (1991). The development of children's memory for the time of past events. *Child Development, 62*, 139–155.

Friedman, W. J. (1992). Children's time memory: The development of a differentiated past. *Cognitive Development, 7*, 171–187.

Friedman, W. J. (1993). Memory for the time of past events. *Psychological Bulletin, 113*, 44–66.

Friedman, W. J. (2000). The development of children's knowledge of the times of future events. *Child Development, 71*, 913–932.

Friedman, W. J., & Lyon, T. D. (2005). Development of temporal-reconstructive abilities. *Child Development, 76*, 1202–1216.

Friedman, W. J., Reese, E., & Dai, X. (2011). Children's memory for the times of events from the past years. *Applied Cognitive Psychology, 25*, 156–165.

Fuller-Thomson, E., Mehta, R., & Valeo, A. (2014). Establishing a link between attention deficit disorder/attention deficit hyperactivity disorder and childhood physical abuse. *Journal of Aggression, Maltreatment & Trauma, 23*, 188–198.

Gagnon, K., & Cyr, M. (2017). Sexual abuse and preschoolers: Forensic details in regard of question types. *Child Abuse and Neglect, 67*, 109–118.

Garry, M., Manning, C. G., Loftus, E. F., & Sherman, S. J. (1996). Imagination inflation: Imagining a childhood event inflates confidence that it occurred. *Psychonomic Bulletin and Review, 3*, 208–214.

Garven, S., Wood, J. M., & Malpass, R. S. (2000). Allegations of wrongdoing: The effects of reinforcement on children's mundane and fantastic claims. *Journal of Applied Psychology, 85*, 38–49.

Garven, S., Wood, J. M., Malpass, R. S., & Shaw, J. S. (1998). More than suggestion: The effect of interviewing techniques from the McMartin Preschool case. *Journal of Applied Psychology, 83*, 347–359.

Geddie, L. F., Beer, J., Bartosik, S., & Wuensch, K. L. (2001). The relationship between interview characteristics and accuracy of recall in young children: Do individual differences matter?. *Child Maltreatment, 6*, 59–68.

Geddie, L., Fradin, S., & Beer, J. (2000). Child characteristics which impact accuracy of recall and suggestibility in preschoolers: Is age the best predictor? *Child Abuse & Neglect, 24*, 223–235.

Gee, S., Gregory, M., & Pipe, M.-E. (1999). "What colour is your pet dinosaur?" The impact of pre-interview training and question type on children's answers. *Legal and Criminological Psychology, 4*, 111–128.

Gee, S. & Pipe, M.-E. (1995). Helping children to remember: The influence of object cues on children's accounts of a real event. *Developmental Psychology, 31*, 746–758.

Geiselman, R. E. (1988). Improving eyewitness memory through mental reinstatement of context. In G. M. Davies & D. M. Thomson (Eds.), *Memory in context: Context in memory* (pp. 245–266). Chichester, UK: Wiley.
Geiselman, R. E., Fisher, R. P., Firstenberg, I., Hutton, L. A., Sullivan, S. J., Avetissian, I. V., & Prosk, A. L. (1984). Enhancement of eyewitness memory: An empirical evaluation of the Cognitive Interview. *Journal of Police Science and Administration, 12*, 74–80.
Geiselman, R. E., Fisher, R. P., MacKinnon, D. P., & Holland, H. L. (1985). Eyewitness memory enhancement in the police interview: Cognitive retrieval mnemonics versus hypnosis. *Journal of Applied Psychology, 70*, 401–412.
Geiselman, R. E., Fisher, R. P., MacKinnon, D. P., & Holland, H. L. (1986). Enhancing of eyewitness memory with the cognitive interview. *American Journal of Psychology, 99*, 385–401.
Geiselman, R. E., & Padilla, J. (1988). Cognitive interviewing with child witnesses. *Journal of Police Science & Administration, 16*, 236–242.
Geiselman, R. E., Saywitz, K. J., & Bornstein, G. K. (1993). Effects of cognitive questioning techniques on children's recall performance. In G. S. Goodman & B. L. Bottoms (Eds.), *Child victims, child witnesses: Understanding and improving testimony* (pp. 71–93). New York, NY: Guilford.
Gentle, M., Milne, R., Powell, M. B., & Sharman, S. J. (2013). Does the cognitive interview promote the coherence of narrative accounts in children with and without an intellectual disability? *International Journal of Disability, Development and Education, 60*, 30–43.
Gentle, M., Powell, M. B., & Sharman, S. J. (2014). Mental context reinstatement or drawing: Which better enhances children's recall of witnessed events and protects against suggestive questions?. *Australian Journal of Psychology, 66*, 158–167.
Gentner, D., Loewenstein, J., & Hung, B. (2007). Comparison facilitates children's learning of names for parts. *Journal of Cognition and Development, 8*, 285–307.
George, R. C., & Clifford, B. R. (1996). The cognitive interview: Does it work? In G. Davies, S. Lloyd-Bostock, M. McMurran, & C. Wilson (Eds.), *Psychology, law and criminal justice* (pp. 146–154). New York, NY: Walter de Gruyter.
Ghetti, S., & Goodman, G. S. (2001). Resisting distortion? *Psychologist, 14*, 592–595.
Ghetti, S., Goodman, G. S., Eisen, M. L., Qin, J., & Davis, S. L. (2002). Consistency in children's reports of sexual and physical abuse. *Child Abuse and Neglect, 26*, 977–995.
Gibling, F., & Davies, G. (1988). Reinstatement of context following exposure to post-event information. *British Journal of Psychology, 79*, 129–141.
Gibson, E. J. (1991). *An odyssey in learning and perception*. Cambridge, MA: MIT Press.
Gilstrap, L. (2004). A missing link in suggestibility research: What is known about the behavior of field interviewers in unstructured interviews with young children? *Journal of Experimental Psychology: Applied, 10*, 13–24.
Gobbo, C., Mega, C., & Pipe, M.-E. (2002). Does the nature of the experience influence children's suggestibility? A study of children's event memory. *Journal of Experimental Child Psychology, 81*, 502–530.
Gongola, J., Scurich, N., & Quas, J. A. (2017). Detecting deception in children: A meta-analysis. *Law and Human Behavior, 41*, 44–54.

Gonzalez, L. S., Waterman, J., Kelly, R., McCord, J., & Oliveri, K. (1993). Children's patterns of disclosures and recantations of sexual and ritualistic abuse allegations in psychotherapy. *Child Abuse & Neglect, 17*, 281–289.

Goodman, G. S., & Aman, C. (1990). Children's use of anatomically detailed dolls to recount an event. *Child Development, 61*, 1859–1871.

Goodman, G. S., Aman, C., & Hirschman, J. (1987). Child sexual and physical abuse: Children's testimony. In S. J. Ceci, M. P. Toglia, & D. F. Ross (Eds.), *Children's eyewitness memory* (pp. 1–23). New York, NY: Springer.

Goodman, G. S., Batterman-Faunce, J. M., & Kenney, R. (1992). Optimizing children's testimony: Research and social policy issues concerning allegations of child sexual abuse. In D. Cicchetti & S. Toth (Eds.), *Child abuse, child development, and social policy* (pp.139–166). Norwood, NJ: Ablex.

Goodman, G. S., Batterman-Faunce, J. M., Schaaf, J. M., & Kenney, R. (2002). Nearly 4 years after an event: Children's eyewitness memory and adults' perceptions of children's accuracy. *Child Abuse & Neglect, 26*, 849–884.

Goodman, G. S., Bottoms, B. L., Schwartz-Kenney, B. M., & Rudy, L. (1991). Children's testimony about a stressful event: Improving children's reports. *Journal of Narrative and Life History, 1*, 69–99.

Goodman, G. S., Hirschman, J. E., Hepps, D., & Rudy, L. (1991) Children's memory for stressful events. *Merill-Palmer Quarterly, 37*, 109–157.

Goodman, G. S., & Quas, J. A. (2008). Repeated interviews and children's memory: It's more than just how many. *Current Directions in Psychological Science, 17*, 386–390.

Goodman, G. S., Quas, J. A., Batterman-Faunce, J. M., Riddlesberger, M. M., & Kuhn, J. (1994). Predictors of accurate and inaccurate memories of traumatic events experienced in childhood. *Consciousness and Cognition, 3*, 269–294.

Goodman, G. S., Quas, J. A., Batterman-Faunce, J. M., Riddlesberger, M. M., & Kuhn, J. (1997). Children's reactions to and memory for a stressful event: Influences of age, anatomical dolls, knowledge, and parental attachment. *Applied Developmental Science, 1*, 54–75.

Goodman, G. S., & Reed, D. S. (1986). Age differences in eyewitness testimony. *Law and Human Behavior, 10*, 317–332.

Goodman, G. S., Rudy, L., Bottoms, B. L., & Aman, C. (1990). Children's concerns and memory: Issues of ecological validity on the study of children's eyewitness testimony. In R. Fivush & J. Hudson (Eds.), *Knowing and remembering in young children* (pp. 249–284). New York, NY: Cambridge University Press.

Goodman, G. S., & Schwartz-Kenney, B. M. (1992). Why knowing a child's age is not enough: Influences of cognitive, social, and emotional factors on children's testimony. In H. Dent & R. Flin. (Eds.), *Children as witnesses* (pp. 15–32). Chichester, UK: Wiley.

Goodman, G. S., Taub, E. P., Jones, D. P. H., England, P., Port, L. K., Rudy, L., & Prado, L. (1992). Testifying in criminal court. *Monographs of the Society for Research in Child Development, 57*(5, Serial no. 229), 42–163.

Goodman, G. S., Wilson, M. E., Hazan, C., & Reed, R. S. (1989, April). *Children's testimony nearly four years after an event*. Paper presented to the Eastern Psychological Association, Boston, MA.

Goodman-Brown, T. B., Edelstein, R. S., Goodman, G. S., Jones, D. P. H., & Gordon, D. S. (2003). Why children tell: A model of children's disclosure of sexual abuse. *Child Abuse & Neglect, 27*, 525–540.

Gordon, B. N., Baker-Ward, L., & Ornstein, P. A. (2001). Children's testimony: A review of research on memory for past experiences. *Clinical Child and Family Psychological Review, 4*, 157–181.

Gordon, B. N., Jens, K. G., Hollings, R., & Watson, T. E. (1994). Remembering activities performed versus those imagined: Implications for testimony of children with mental retardation. *Journal of Clinical Child Psychology, 23,* 239–248.

Gordon, B. N., Ornstein, P. A., Nida, R. E., Follmer, A., Crenshaw, M. C., & Albert, G. (1993). Does the use of dolls facilitate children's memory of visits to the doctor? *Applied Cognitive Psychology, 7,* 459–474.

Gordon, B. N., Schroeder, C. S., Ornstein, P. A., & Baker-Ward, L. E. (1995). Clinical implications of research on memory development. In T. Ney (Ed.), *True and false allegations of child sexual abuse: Assessment and case management* (pp. 99–124). Philadelphia, PA: Brunner/Mazel.

Gordon, S., & Jaudes, P. K. (1996). Sexual abuse evaluation in the emergency department: Is the history reliable? *Child Abuse & Neglect, 20,* 315–322.

Green, B. C., Johnson, K. A., & Bretherton, L. (2014). Pragmatic language difficulties in children with hyperactivity and attention problems: An integrated review. *International Journal of Language & Communication Disorders, 49,* 15–29.

Green, G. (2001). Vulnerability of witnesses with learning disabilities: Preparing to give evidence against a perpetrator of sexual abuse. *British Journal of Learning Disabilities, 29,* 103–109.

Greenhoot, A. F. (2000). Remembering and understanding: The effects of changes in underlying knowledge on children's recollections. *Child Development, 71,* 1309–1328.

Greenhoot, A. F., Ornstein, P. A., Gordon, B. N., & Baker-Ward, L. (1999). Acting out the details of a pediatric check-up: The impact of interview condition and behavioral style on children's memory report. *Child Development, 70,* 363–380.

Greenstock, J., & Pipe, M.-E. (1996). Interviewing children about past events: The influence of peer support and misleading questions. *Child Abuse & Neglect, 20,* 69–80.

Gries, L. T., Goh, D. S., & Cavanaugh, J. (1996). Factors associated with disclosure during child sexual abuse assessment. *Journal of Child Sexual Abuse, 5,* 1–20.

Gries, L. T., Goh, D. S., Andrews, M. B., Gilbert, J., Praver, F., & Stelzer, D. N. (2000). Positive reaction to disclosure and recovery from child sexual abuse. *Journal of Child Sexual Abuse, 9,* 29–51.

Gross, J., & Hayne, H. (1998). Drawing facilitates children's verbal reports of emotionally laden events. *Journal of Experimental Psychology: Applied, 4,* 163–179.

Gross, J., & Hayne, H. (1999a). Young children's recognition and description of their own and others' drawings. *Developmental Science, 4,* 476–489.

Gross, J., & Hayne, H. (1999b). Drawing facilitates children's verbal reports after long delays. *Journal of Experimental Psychology: Applied, 5,* 265–283.

Gross, J., Hayne, H., & Poole, A. (2008). The use of drawing in interviews with children: A potential pitfall. In *Child Psychology* (pp. 119–144). New York, NY: Nova Publishers.

Gudjonsson, G. H. (2003). Psychology brings justice: The science of forensic psychology. *Criminal Behavior and Mental Health, 13,* 159–167.

Gudjonsson, G. H., & Henry, L. (2003). Child and adult witnesses with intellectual disability: The importance of suggestibility. *Legal, 8,* 241–252.

Gudjonsson, G. H., Murphy, G. H., & Clare, I. C. H. (2000). Assessing the capacity of people with intellectual disabilities to be witnesses in court. *Psychological Medicine, 30,* 307–314.

Gudjonsson, G. H., Sigurdsson, J. F., Bragason, O. O., Newton, A. K., & Einarsson, E. (2008). Interrogative suggestibility, compliance and false confessions among prisoners and their relationship with attention deficit hyperactivity disorder (ADHD) symptoms. *Psychological Medicine, 38*, 1037–1044.

Gudjonsson, G. H., Young, S., & Bramham, J. (2007). Interrogative suggestibility in adults diagnosed with attention-deficit hyperactivity disorder (ADHD). A potential vulnerability during police questioning. *Personality and Individual Differences, 43*, 737–745.

Gully, S. M. (1998). The influences of self-regulation processes on learning and performance in a team training context. *Dissertation Abstracts International: Section B: the Sciences & Engineering, 58*(9-B), 5175.

Haden, C. A. (2013.) Interactions of knowledge and memory in the development of skilled remembering. In P. J. Bauer and R. Fivush (Eds.), *The Wiley handbook on the development of children's memory* (Vol. I; pp. 807–835). Chichester, UK: Wiley.

Haden, C. A., & Fivush, R. (1996). Contextual variation in maternal conversational styles. *Merrill-Palmer Quarterly, 42*, 200–227.

Haden, C., Ornstein, P., Eckerman, C., & Didow, S. (2001). Mother-child conversational interactions as events unfold: Linkages to subsequent remembering. *Child Development, 72*, 1016–1031.

Hamond, N. R., & Fivush, R. (1991). Memories of Mickey Mouse: Young children recount their trip to Disney World. *Cognitive Development, 6*, 433–448.

Hanna, K. M., Davies, E., Henderson, E., Crothers, C., & Rotherham, C. (2010). *Child witnesses in the New Zealand criminal courts: A review of practice and implications for policy*. Wellington, NZ: New Zealand Law Foundation.

Hardy, C. L., & Van Leeuwen, S. A. (2004). Interviewing young children: Effects of probe structures and focus of rapport-building talk on the qualities of young children's eyewitness statements. *Canadian Journal of Behavioural Science / Revue Canadienne des Sciences du Comportement, 36*, 155–165.

Harner, L. (1975). Yesterday and tomorrow: Development of early understanding of the terms. *Developmental Psychology, 11*, 864–865.

Hatton, C. (1998). Pragmatic language skills in people with intellectual disabilities: A review. *Journal of Intellectual and Developmental Disability, 23*, 79–100.

Hauch, V., Sporer, S. L., Masip, J., & Blandón-Gitlin, I. (2017). Can credibility criteria be assessed reliably? A meta-analysis of criteria-based content analysis. *Psychological Assessment, 29*, 819–834.

Hayes, B. K., & Delamothe, K. (1997). Cognitive interviewing procedures and suggestibility in children's recall. *Journal of Applied Psychology, 82*, 562–577.

Hayne, H. (2004). Infant memory development: Implications for childhood amnesia. *Developmental Review, 24*, 33–73.

Hayne, H., & Rovee-Collier, C. (1995). The organization of reactivated memory in infancy. *Child Development, 66*, 893–906.

Heflin, A. H., Deblinger, E., & Fisher, C. D. (2000). Child sexual abuse. In A. Freeman & F. M. Dattilio (Eds.), *Cognitive behavioral strategies in crisis intervention* (2nd ed., pp. 166–195). New York, NY: Guilford Press.

Henkel, L. A. (2004). Erroneous memories arising from repeated attempts to remember. *Journal of Memory and Language, 50*, 26–46.

Henry, L. A. (2001). How does the severity of a learning disability affect working memory performance? *Memory, 9*, 233–247.

Henry, L. A., Bettaney, C., & Carney, D. (2011). Children with intellectual disabilities and developmental disorders. In M. E. Lamb, D. J. LaRooy, L. C.

Malloy, & Katz, C. (Eds.), *Children's testimony: A handbook of psychological research and forensic practice* (2nd ed., pp. 251–283). Chichester, UK: Wiley.

Henry, L. A., & Gudjonsson, G. H. (1999). Eyewitness memory and suggestibility in children with mental retardation. *American Journal on Mental Retardation, 104*, 491–508.

Henry, L. A., & Gudjonsson, G. H. (2003). Eyewitness memory, suggestibility and repeated recall sessions in children with mild and moderate intellectual disabilities. *Law and Human Behavior, 27*, 481–505.

Henry, L. A., & Gudjonsson, G. H. (2004). The effects of memory trace strength on eyewitness recall in children with and without intellectual disabilities. *Journal of Experimental Child Psychology, 89*, 53–71.

Henry, L. A., & Gudjonsson, G. H. (2007). Individual and developmental differences in eyewitness recall and suggestibility in children with intellectual disabilities. *Applied Cognitive Psychology, 21*, 361–381.

Henry, L. A., Ridley, A., Perry, J., & Crane, L. (2011). Perceived credibility and eyewitness testimony of children with intellectual disabilities. *Journal of Intellectual Disability Research, 55*, 385–391.

Hepner, I., Woodward, M. N., & Stewart, J. (2015). Giving the vulnerable a voice in the criminal justice system: The use of intermediaries with individuals with intellectual disability. *Psychiatry, Psychology and Law, 22*, 453–464.

Hershkowitz, I. (1999). The dynamics of interviews involving plausible and implausible allegations of sexual abuse. *Applied Developmental Science, 3*, 86–91.

Hershkowitz, I. (2001). Children's responses to open-ended utterances in investigative interviews. *Legal and Criminological Psychology, 6*, 49–63.

Hershkowitz, I. (2009). Socioemotional factors in child sexual abuse investigations. *Child Maltreatment, 14*, 172–181.

Hershkowitz, I. (in press). NICHD-protocol investigations of individuals with intellectual disability: A descriptive analysis. *Psychology, Public Policy, and Law*.

Hershkowitz, I., Ahern, E. C., Lamb, M. E. Blasbalg, U., Karniel-Visel, Y., & Breitman, M. (2017). Changes in interviewers' use of supportive techniques during the Revised Protocol Training. *Applied Cognitive Psychology, 31*, 340–350.

Hershkowitz, I., & Elul, A. (1999). The effects of investigative utterances on Israeli children's reports of physical abuse. *Applied Developmental Science, 3*, 28–33.

Hershkowitz, I., Fisher, S., Lamb, M. E., & Horowitz, D. (2007). Improving credibility assessment in child sexual abuse allegations: The role of the NICHD investigative interview protocol. *Child Abuse & Neglect, 31*, 99–110.

Hershkowitz, I., Horowitz, D., & Lamb, M. E. (2005). Trends in children's disclosure of abuse in Israel: A national study. *Child Abuse & Neglect, 29*, 1203–1214.

Hershkowitz, I., Horowitz, D., & Lamb, M. E. (2007). Individual and family variables associated with disclosure and non-disclosure of child abuse in Israel. In M.-E. Pipe, M. E. Lamb, Y. Orbach, & A.-C. Cederborg (Eds.), *Child sexual abuse: Disclosure, delay, and denial* (pp. 63–76). Mahwah, NJ: Erlbaum.

Hershkowitz, I., Horowitz, D., Lamb, M. E., Orbach, Y., & Sternberg, K. J. (2004). Interviewing youthful suspects in alleged sex crimes: A descriptive analysis. *Child Abuse & Neglect, 28*, 423–438.

Hershkowitz, I., & Lamb, M. E. (2018). Allegation rates and credibility assessment in forensic child abuse investigations: Comparing the Revised and Standard NICHD Protocols. Manuscript under review.

Hershkowitz, I., Lamb, M. E., & Breitman, M. (2018). A revision of the NICHD investigative protocol for use with young suspects of sexual abuse. Manuscript under review.

Hershkowitz, I., Lamb, M. E., & Horowitz, D. (2007). Victimization of children with disabilities. *American Journal of Orthopsychiatry*, 77, 629–635.

Hershkowitz, I., Lamb, M. E., & Katz, C. (2014). Allegation rates in forensic child abuse investigations: Comparing the revised and standard NICHD protocols. *Psychology, Public Policy, and Law*, 20, 336.

Hershkowitz, I., Lamb, M. E., Katz, C., & Malloy, L. C. (2015). Does enhanced rapport-building alter the dynamics of investigative interviews with suspected victims of intra-familial abuse? *Journal of Police and Criminal Psychology*, 30, 6–14.

Hershkowitz, I., Lamb, M. E., Orbach, Y., Katz, C., & Horowitz, D. (2012). The development of communicative and narrative skills among preschoolers: Lessons from forensic interviews about child abuse. *Child Development*, 83, 611–622.

Hershkowitz, I., Lamb, M. E., Sternberg, K. J., & Esplin, P. W. (1997). The relationships among interviewer utterance type, CBCA scores, and the richness of children's responses. *Legal and Criminological Psychology*, 2, 169–176.

Hershkowitz, I., Lanes, O., & Lamb, M. E. (2007). Exploring the disclosure of child sexual abuse with alleged victims and their parents. *Child Abuse & Neglect*, 31, 111–123.

Hershkowitz, I., Orbach, Y., Lamb, M. E., Pipe, M.-E., Sternberg, K. J., & Horowitz, D. (2006). Dynamics of forensic interviews with suspected abuse victims who do not disclose abuse. *Child Abuse & Neglect*, 30, 753–769.

Hershkowitz, I., Orbach, Y., Lamb, M. E., Sternberg, K. J., & Horowitz, D. (2002). A comparison of mental and physical reinstatement of the context in child sexual abuse investigations. *Applied Cognitive Psychology*, 16, 429–441.

Hershkowitz, I., Orbach, Y., Lamb, M. E., Sternberg, K. J., & Horowitz, D. (2001). The effects of mental context reinstatement on children's accounts of sexual abuse. *Applied Cognitive Psychology*, 15, 235–248.

Hershkowitz, I., Orbach, Y., Lamb, M. E., Sternberg, K. J., & Horowitz, D. (2002). A comparison of mental and physical context reinstatement in forensic interviews with alleged victims of sexual abuse. *Applied Cognitive Psychology*, 16, 429–441.

Hershkowitz, I., Orbach, Y., Lamb, M. E., Sternberg, K. J., Horowitz, D., & Hovav, M. (1998). Visiting the scene of the crime: Effects on children's recall of alleged abuse. *Legal and Criminological Psychology*, 3, 195–207.

Hershkowitz, I., Orbach, Y., Lamb, M. E., Sternberg, K. J., Pipe, M.-E., & Horowitz, D. (2007). Suspected victims of abuse who do not make allegations: An analysis of their interactions with forensic interviewers. In M.-E. Pipe, M. E. Lamb, Y. Orbach, & A. C. Cederborg (Eds.), *Child sexual abuse: Disclosure, delay, and denial* (pp. 77–96). Mahwah, NJ: Erlbaum.

Hershkowitz, I., Pud, E., & Kaabia, E. (2018). Non-verbal indicators of reluctance in child abuse investigations: The effects of gender and abuse type. Unpublished manuscript.

Hewitt, S. D. (1999). *Assessing allegations of sexual abuse in preschool children*. Thousand Oaks, CA: Sage.

Hildreth, K., Sweeny, B., & Rovee-Collier, C. (2003). Differential memory-preserving effects of reminders at 6 months. *Journal of Experimental Child Psychology*, 84, 41–62.

Hill, A., & Brown, D. A. (2017). *Dolls, diagrams and drawings: Interviewers' perspectives on visual aids in child witness interviews* (Unpublished master's thesis, Victoria University of Wellington). Retrieved from http://hdl.handle.net/10063/6392

Hintzman, D. L. (1984). MINERVA 2: A simulation model of human memory. *Behavior Research Methods, Instruments, & Computers, 16*(2), 96–101.

Hitchcock, C., Nixon, R. D., & Weber, N. (2014). A review of overgeneral memory in child psychopathology. *British Journal of Clinical Psychology, 53*(2), 170–193.

Hlavka, H. R., Olinger, S. D., & Lashley, J. L. (2010). The use of anatomical dolls as a demonstration aid in child sexual abuse interviews: A study of forensic interviewers' perceptions. *Journal of Child Sexual Abuse, 19*, 519–553.

Holliday, R. E. (2003). Reducing misinformation effects in children with cognitive interviews: Dissociating recollection and familiarity. *Child Development, 74*, 728–751.

Holliday, R. E., & Albon, A. J. (2004). Minimising misinformation effects in young children with cognitive interview mnemonics. *Applied Cognitive Psychology, 18*, 263–281.

Home Office (1992). *Memorandum of good practice on video recorded interviews with child witnesses for criminal proceedings*. London: Author, with Department of Health.

Home Office (2002). *Achieving best evidence in criminal proceedings: Guidance for vulnerable and intimidated witnesses, including children*. London: Author.

Home Office (2007). *Achieving best evidence in criminal proceedings (Revised)*. London: Author.

Home Office. (2011). *Achieving best evidence in criminal proceedings: Guidance on interviewing victims and witnesses, and guidance on using special measures*. London: Author.

Horner, T. M., Guyer, M. J., & Kalter, N. M. (1993a). Clinical expertise and the assessment of child sexual abuse. *Journal of the American Academy of Child and Adolescent Psychiatry, 32*, 925–931.

Horner, T. M., Guyer, M. J., & Kalter, N. M. (1993b). The biases of child sexual abuse experts: Believing is seeing. *Bulletin of the American Academy of Psychiatry and the Law, 21*, 281–292.

Horowitz, S. W., Lamb, M. E., Esplin, P. W., Boychuk, T. D., Krispin, O., & Reiter-Lavery, L. (1997). Reliability of criteria-based content analysis of child witness statements. *Legal and Criminological Psychology, 2*, 11–21.

Horowitz, S. W., Lamb, M. E., Esplin, P. W., Reiter-Lavery, L., & Krispin, C. (1995). Establishing ground truth in studies of child sexual abuse. *Expert Evidence, 4*, 42–51.

Howe, M. L. (1997). Children's memory for traumatic experiences. *Learning & Individual Differences, 9*, 153–174.

Howe, M. L. (2000). *The fate of early memories: Developmental science and the retention of childhood experiences*. Washington, DC: American Psychological Association.

Howe, M. L. (2014). The co-emergence of the self and autobiographical memory: An adaptive view of early memory. In P. J. Bauer & R. Fivush (Eds.), *The Wiley handbook on the development of children's memory* (Vols *I* and *II*, pp. 545–567). Chichester, UK: Wiley.

Howe, M. L., & Courage, M. L. (1993). On resolving the enigma of infantile amnesia. *Psychological Bulletin, 113*, 305–326.

Howe, M. L., & Courage, M. L. (2004). Demystifying the beginnings of memory. *Developmental Review, 24*, 1–5.

Howe, M., Courage, M., & Bryant-Brown, L. (1993). Reinstating preschoolers' memories. *Developmental Psychology, 29*, 854–869.

Howe, M. L., Courage, M. L., & Peterson, C. (1994). How can I remember when "I" wasn't there: Long-term retention of traumatic experiences and emergence of the cognitive self. *Consciousness & Cognition, 3*, 327–355.

Howe, M. L., Courage, M. L., & Edison, S. C. (2003). When autobiographical memory begins. *Developmental Review, 23*, 471–494.

Howe, M. L., Courage, M.L., & Peterson, C. (1995). Intrusions in preschoolers' recall of traumatic childhood events. *Psychonomic Bulletin & Review, 2*, 130–134.

Howie, P., Nash, L., Kurukulasuriya, N., & Bowman, A. (2012). Children's event reports: Factors affecting responses to repeated questions in vignette scenarios and event recall interviews. *Journal of Developmental Psychology, 30*, 550–568.

Hubbard, K., Saykaly, C., Lee, K., Lindsay, R. C. L., Bala, N., & Talwar, V. (2016). Children's recall accuracy for repeated events over multiple interviews: Comparing information types. *Psychology, Psychiatry & Law, 23*, 849–862.

Hudson, J. A. (1986). Memories are made of this: General event knowledge and the development of autobiographical memory. In K. Nelson (Eds.), *Knowledge structure and function in development* (pp. 97–118). Hillsdale, NJ: Erlbaum.

Hudson, J. A. (1988). Children's memory for atypical actions in script-based stories: Evidence for a disruption effect. *Journal of Experimental Child Psychology, 46*, 159–173.

Hudson, J. A. (1990a). Constructive processing in children's event memory. *Developmental Psychology, 26*, 180–187.

Hudson, J. A. (1990b). The emergence of autobiographical memory in mother-child conversation. In R. Fivush & J. A. Hudson (Eds.), *Knowing and remembering in young children* (pp. 166–196). New York, NY: Cambridge University Press.

Hudson, J. A., & Fivush, R. (1991). As time goes by: Sixth graders remember a kindergarten experience. *Applied Cognitive Psychology, 5*, 347–360.

Hudson, J. A., Fivush, R., & Kuebli, J. (1992). Scripts and episodes: The development of event memory [Special issue]. *Applied Cognitive Psychology, 6*, 483–505.

Hudson, J. A., & Mayhew, E. M. (2009). The development of memory for recurring events. In M. Courage & N. Cowan (Eds.), *The development of memory in infancy and childhood* (2nd ed., pp. 69–91). New York, NY: Psychology Press.

Hudson, J. A., & Nelson, K. (1986). Repeated encounters of a similar kind: Effects of familiarity on children's autobiographic memory. *Cognitive Development, 1*, 253–271.

Huffman, M. L.C. (1997). *Can criterion-based context analysis discriminate between accurate and false reports of preschoolers? A validation attempt [Unpublished manuscript]*. Cornell University, Ithaca, NY.

Hughes, M., & Grieve, R. (1980). On asking children bizarre questions. *First Language, 1*, 149–160.

Hunt, J. S., & Borgida, E. (1998, March). *Beyond leading questions: Modifications in eyewitness interviews*. Paper presented at the American Psychology-Law Society, Convention, Redondo Beach, CA.

Hunt, J. S., & Borgida, E. (2001). Is that what I said? Witnesses' responses to interviewer modifications. *Law and Human Behavior, 25*, 583–603.

Hutcheson, G. D., Baxter, J. S., Telfer, K., & Warden, D. (1995). Child witness statement quality: Question type and error of omission. *Law and Human Behavior, 19*, 631–648.

Hyman, I. A., Husband, T. H., & Billings, J. F. (1995). False memories of childhood experiences. *Applied Cognitive Psychology, 9*, 181–197.

Iarocci, C., & Burack, J. A. (1998). Understanding the development of attention in persons with mental retardation: Challenging the myths. In E. Zigler, J. A. Burack., & R. M. Hodapp (Eds.), *Handbook of mental retardation and development* (pp. 349–381). New York, NY: Cambridge University Press.

Imhoff, M. C., & Baker-Ward, L. (1999). Preschoolers' suggestibility: Effects of developmentally appropriate language and interviewer supportiveness. *Journal of Applied Developmental Psychology, 20*, 407–429.

Jack, F., Friedman, W., Reese, E., & Zajac, R. (2016). Age-related differences in memory for time, temporal reconstruction, and the availability and use of temporal landmarks. *Cognitive Development, 37*, 53–66.

Jack, F., Leov, J., & Zajac, R. (2014). Age-related differences in the free-recall accounts of child, adolescent, and adult witnesses. *Applied Cognitive Psychology, 28*, 30–38.

Jack, F., MacDonald, S., Reese, E., & Hayne, H. (2009). Maternal reminiscing style during early childhood predicts the age of adolescents' earliest memories. *Child Development, 80*, 496–505.

Jack, F., Martyn, E., & Zajac, R. (2015). Getting the picture: Effects of sketch plans and photographs on children's, adolescents' and adults' eyewitness recall. *Applied Cognitive Psychology, 29*, 723–734.

Jack, F., Simcock, G., & Hayne, H. (2012). Magic memories: Young children's verbal recall after a 6-year delay. *Child Development, 83*, 159–172.

Jackson, H., & Nuttall, R. (1993). Clinician responses to sexual abuse allegations. *Child Abuse & Neglect, 17*, 127–143.

Jackson, J. L. (1996). *Truth or fantasy: The ability of barristers and laypersons to detect deception in children's testimony.* Paper presented to the American Psychology-Law Society conference, Hilton Head Island, South Carolina.

Jehu, D. (1989). Sexual dysfunctions among women clients who were sexually abused in childhood. *Behavioural Psychotherapy, 17*, 53–70.

Jens, K. G., Gordon, B. N., and Shaddock, A. J. (1990). Remembering activities performed versus imagined: A comparison of children with mental retardation and children with normal intelligence. *International Journal of Disability, Development, and Education, 37*, 201–213.

Johnson, J. L., & Shelley, A. E. (2014). Effects of child interview tactics on prospective jurors' decisions. *Behavioral Sciences & The Law, 32*, 846–866.

Johnson, M. K., & Foley, M. A. (1984). Differentiating fact from fantasy: The reliability of children's memory. *Journal of Social Issues, 40*, 33–50.

Johnson, M. K., Hashtroudi, S., & Lindsay, D. S. (1993). Source monitoring. *Psychological Bulletin, 114*, 3–28.

Johnson, M., Magnussen, S., Thoresen, C., Lønnum, K., Burrell, L. V., & Melinder, A. (2015). Best practice recommendations still fail to result in action: A national 10-year follow-up study of investigative interviews in CSA cases. *Applied Cognitive Psychology, 29*, 661–668.

Johnston, C., & Mash, E. J. (2001). Families of children with attention-deficit/hyperactivity disorder: Review and recommendations for future research. *Clinical Child and Family Psychology Review, 4*, 183–207.

Jones, C. H., & Pipe, M.-E. (2002). How quickly do children forget events? A systematic study of children's event reports as a function of delay. *Applied Cognitive Psychology, 16,* 755–768.

Jones, D. C., Swift, D. J., & Johnson, M. A. (1988). Nondeliberate memory for a novel event among preschoolers. *Developmental Psychology, 24,* 641–645.

Jones, D. P. H. (2003). *Communicating with vulnerable children.* London: Gaskell and Royal College of Psychiatrists.

Karni-Visel, Y., Hershkowitz, I., Blasbalg, U. & Lamb, M. E. (March, 2018a). *Emotional expression and children's reports of intra-familial abuse.* Paper presented at the American Psychology–Law Society conference, Memphis, TN.

Karni-Visel, Y., Hershkowitz, I., Blasbalg, U. & Lamb, M. E. (March, 2018b).*The association between emotional expression and children's reports of intra-familial abuse: The facilitating role of emotional support.* Paper presented at the American Psychology–Law Society conference, Memphis, TN.

Karni-Visel, Y., Hershkowitz, I., Lamb, M. E., & Blasbalg, U. (July, 2018c). *Facilitating emotional expressions by alleged victims of child abuse during investigative Interviews using the Revised NICHD Protocol.* Paper presented at the 11th annual IIIRG conference, Porto, Portugal.

Katz, C., Barnetz, Z., & Hershkowitz, I. (2014). The effect of drawing on children's experiences of investigations following alleged child abuse. *Child Abuse & Neglect, 38,* 858–867.

Katz, C., & Hershkowitz, I. (2010). The effects of drawing on children's accounts of sexual abuse. *Child Maltreatment, 15,* 171–179.

Katz, C., & Hershkowitz, I. (2013). Repeated interviews with children who are the alleged victims of sexual abuse. *Research on Social Work Practice, 23,* 210–218.

Katz, C., Hershkowitz, I., Malloy, L. C., Lamb, M. E., Atabaki, A., & Spindler, S. (2012). Non-verbal behavior of children who disclose or do not disclose child abuse in investigative interviews. *Child Abuse & Neglect, 36,* 12–20.

Kasari, C., & Bauminger, N. (1998). Social and emotional development in children with mental retardation. In E. F. Zigler, J. A. Burack., & R. M. Hodapp (Eds.), *Handbook of mental retardation and development* (pp. 411–433). New York, NY: Cambridge University Press.

Kaufman, J., Jones, B., Stieglitz, E., Vitulano, L., & Mannarino, A. P. (1994). The use of multiple informants to assess children's maltreatment experiences. *Journal of Family Violence, 9,* 227–248.

Keary, K., & Fitzpatrick, C. (1994). Children's disclosure of sexual abuse during formal investigation. *Child Abuse & Neglect, 18,* 543–548.

Kebbell, M. R., Hatton, C., & Johnson, S. D. (2004). Witnesses with intellectual disabilities in court: What questions are asked and what influence do they have? *Legal and Criminological Psychology, 9,* 23–35.

Kebbell, M. R., Hatton, C., Johnson, S. D., & O'Kelly, C. M. E. (2001). People with learning disabilities as witnesses in court: What questions should lawyers ask? *British Journal of Learning Disabilities, 29,* 98–102.

Kelley, S. J. (1996). Ritualistic abuse of children. In J. Briere, L. Berliner, J. Bulkley, C. Jenny, & T. Reid (Eds.), *The APSAC handbook on child maltreatment* (pp. 90–99). Thousand Oaks, CA: Sage.

Kelly, K. R., & Bailey, A. L. (2013). Dual development of conversational and narrative discourse: Mother and child interactions during narrative co-construction. *Merrill-Palmer Quarterly, 59,* 426–460.

Kempe, C. H., Silverman, F. N., Steck, B. R., Droegemuller, W., & Silver, H. R. (1962). The battered child syndrome. *Journal of the American Medical Association, 181,* 17–24.

King, M. A., & Yuille, J. C. (1987). Suggestibility and the child witness. In S. J. Ceci, D. F. Ross, & M. P. Toglia (Eds.), *Children's eyewitness memory* (pp. 24–35). New York, NY: Springer.

Kleinknecht, E. (2001). Emerging autobiographies: The role of social-cognition in the development of event memory skills. *Dissertation Abstracts International: Section B: the Sciences & Engineering, 61*, 5019.

Kleinknecht, E., & Beike, D. R. (2004). How knowing and doing inform an autobiography: Relations among preschoolers' theory of mind, narrative, and event memory skills. *Applied Cognitive Psychology, 18*, 745–764.

Klemfuss, J. Z. (2015). Differential contributions of language skills to children's episodic recall. *Journal of Cognition and Development, 16*, 608–620.

Klemfuss, J. Z., Milojevich, H. M., Yim, I. S., Rush, E. B., & Quas, J. A. (2013). Stress at encoding, context at retrieval, and children's narrative content. *Journal of Experimental Child Psychology, 116*, 693–706.

Klemfuss, J. Z., Quas, J. A., & Lyon, T. D. (2014). Attorneys' questions and children's productivity in child sexual abuse criminal trials. *Applied Cognitive Psychology, 28*, 780–788.

Köhnken, G., Finger, M., Nitshe, N., Höfer, E., & Ascherman, E. (1992, March). *Does a cognitive interview interfere with a subsequent statement validity analysis?* Paper presented at the American Psychology and Law Society meeting, San Diego, CA.

Köhnken, G., Milne, R., Memon, A., & Bull, R. (1999). The cognitive interview: A meta-analysis. *Psychology, Crime and Law, 5*, 3–27.

Korkman, J., Juusola, A., & Santtila, P. (2014). Who made the disclosure? Recorded discussions between children and caretakers suspecting child abuse. *Psychology, Crime & Law, 20*, 994–1004.

Korkman, J., Laajasalo, T., Juusola, A., Uusivuori, L., & Santtila, P. (2015). What did the child tell? The accuracy of parents' reports of a child's statements when suspecting child sexual abuse. *Journal of Forensic Psychology Practice, 15*, 93–113.

Korkman, J., Santtila, P., & Sandnabba, N. K. (2006). Dynamics of verbal interaction between interviewer and child in interviews with alleged victims of child sexual abuse. *Scandinavian Journal of Psychology, 47*, 109–119.

Korkman, J., Santtila, P., Westeraker, & Sandnabba, N. K (2008). Interviewing techniques and follow-up questions in child sexual abuse interviews. *European Journal of Developmental Psychology, 5*, 108–128.

Krackow, E., & Lynn, S. J. (2003). Is there touch in the game of Twister®? The effects of innocuous touch and suggestive questions on children's eyewitness memory. *Law and Human Behavior, 27*, 589–604.

Krackow, E., & Lynn, S. J. (2010). Event report training: An examination of the efficacy of a new intervention to improve children's eyewitness reports. *Applied Cognitive Psychology, 24*, 868–884.

Krafka, C., & Penrod, S. (1985). Reinstatement of context in a field experiment on eyewitness identification. *Journal of Personality and Social Psychology, 49*, 58–69.

Krause, N., Pompedda, F., Antfolk, J., Zappalá, A., & Santtila, P. (2017). The effects of feedback and reflection on the questioning style of untrained interviewers in simulated child sexual abuse interviews. *Applied Cognitive Psychology, 31*, 187–198.

Kuehnle, K. (1996). *Assessing allegations of child sexual abuse*. Sarasota, FL: Professional Resource Exchange.

Kuehnle, K., & Connell, M. (Eds.) (2008). *The evaluation of child sexual abuse allegations: A comprehensive guide to assessment and testimony.* Hoboken, NJ: Wiley.

Kulkofsky, S. (2010). The effects of verbal labels and vocabulary skill on memory and suggestibility. *Journal of Applied Developmental Psychology, 31,* 460–466.

Kulkofsky, S., Wang, Q., & Ceci, S. J. (2008). Do better stories make better memories? Narrative quality and memory accuracy in preschool children. *Applied Cognitive Psychology, 22,* 21–38.

Kurtz, B. E., & Borkowski, J. G. (1984). Children's metacognition: Exploring relations among knowledge, process, and motivational variables. *Journal of Experimental Child Psychology, 37,* 335–354.

Kvam, M. H. (2000). Is sexual abuse of children with disabilities disclosed? A retrospective analysis of child disability and the likelihood of sexual abuse among those attending Norwegian hospitals. *Child Abuse and Neglect, 24,* 1073–1084.

Lafontaine, J., & Cyr, M. (2016). A study of the relationship between investigators' Personal characteristics and adherence to interview best practices in training. *Psychiatry, Psychology and Law, 23,* 782–797.

Lafontaine, J., & Cyr, M. (2017). The relation between interviewers' personal characteristics and investigative interview performance in a child sexual abuse context. *Police Practice and Research, 18,* 106–118.

Lamb, M. E. (1994). The investigation of child sexual abuse: An interdisciplinary consensus statement. *Child Abuse & Neglect, 18,* 1021–1028.

Lamb, M. E. (2016). Difficulties translating research on forensic interview practices to practitioners: Finding water, leading horses, but can we get them to drink? *American Psychologist, 71,* 710–718.

Lamb, M. E., & Brown, D. A. (2006). Conversational apprentices: Helping children become competent informants about their own experiences. *British Journal of Developmental Psychology, 24,* 215–234.

Lamb, M. E., & Brown, D. A. (2017). Children's memory development: From the lab to the field. In A. S. Dick and U. Müller (Eds.), *Advancing developmental science: Philosophy, theory, and method* (pp 119–133). New York, NY: Routledge.

Lamb, M. E., & Fauchier, A. (2001). The effects of question type on self-contradiction by children in the course of forensic interviews. *Applied Cognitive Psychology, 15,* 1–9.

Lamb, M. E., Hershkowitz, I., Orbach, Y., & Esplin, P. W. (2008). *Tell me what happened: Structured investigative interviews of child victims and witnesses.* Hoboken, NJ: Wiley-Blackwell.

Lamb, M. E., Hershkowitz, I., Sternberg, K. J., Boat, B., & Everson, M. D. (1996a). Investigative interviews of alleged sexual abuse victims with and without anatomical dolls. *Child Abuse & Neglect, 20,* 1251–1259.

Lamb, M. E., Hershkowitz, I., Sternberg, K. J., Esplin, P. W., Hovav, M., Manor, T., & Yudilevitch, L. (1996b) Effects of investigative utterance types on Israeli children's responses. *International Journal of Behavioural Development, 19,* 627–637.

Lamb, M. E., La Rooy, D. J., Malloy, L. C., & Katz, C. (Eds.). (2011). *Children's testimony: A handbook of psychological research and forensic practice* (2nd ed.). Chichester, UK: Wiley.

Lamb, M. E., Malloy, L. C., Hershkowitz, I., & La Rooy, D. (2015). Children and the law. In R. M. Lerner & M. E. Lamb (Eds.), *Handbook of child psychology* and *developmental science (7th ed.): Vol. 3. Social, emotional and personality development* (pp. 464–512). Hoboken, NJ: Wiley.

Lamb, M. E., Orbach, Y., Hershkowitz, I., Esplin, P., & Horowitz, D. (2007). Structured forensic interview protocols improve the quality and informativeness of investigative interviews with children. *Child Abuse & Neglect, 31,* 1201–1231.

Lamb, M. E., Orbach, Y., Hershkowitz, I., Horowitz, D., & Abbott, C. B. (2007). Does the type of prompt affect the accuracy of information provided by alleged victims of abuse in forensic interviews? *Applied Cognitive Psychology, 21,* 1117–1130.

Lamb, M. E., Orbach, Y., Sternberg, K. J., Aldridge, J., Pearson, S., Stewart, H. L., & Bowler, L. (2009). Use of a structured investigative protocol enhances the quality of investigative interviews with alleged victims of child sexual abuse in Britain. *Applied Cognitive Psychology, 23,* 449–467.

Lamb, M. E., Orbach, Y., Sternberg, K. J., Esplin, P. W., & Hershkowitz, I. (2002). The effects of forensic interview practices on the quality of information provided by alleged victims of child abuse. In H. L. Westcott, G. M. Davies, & R. Bull (Eds.), *Children's testimony: A handbook of psychological research and forensic practice* (pp. 131–145). Chichester, UK: Wiley.

Lamb, M. E., Orbach, Y., Sternberg, K. J., Hershkowitz, I., & Horowitz, D. (2000). Accuracy of investigators' verbatim notes of their forensic interviews with alleged child abuse victims. *Law and Human Behavior, 24,* 699–707.

Lamb, M. E., Orbach, Y., Warren, A. R., Esplin, P. W., & Hershkowitz, I. (2007). Getting the most out of children: Factors affecting the informativeness of young witnesses. In M. P. Toglia, J. D. Read, D. F. Ross, & R. C. L. Lindsay (Eds.), *Handbook of eyewitness psychology. Vol 1: Memory for events.* Mahwah, NJ: Erlbaum.

Lamb, M. E., Sternberg, K. J., & Esplin, P. W. (1995). Making children into competent witnesses: Reactions to the amicus brief In re Michaels. *Psychology, Public Policy, and Law, 1,* 438–449.

Lamb, M. E., Sternberg, K. J., & Esplin, P. W. (1998). Conducting investigative interviews of alleged sexual abuse victims. *Child Abuse & Neglect, 22,* 813–823.

Lamb, M. E., Sternberg, K. J., & Esplin, P. W. (2000). Effects of age and delay on the amount of information provided by alleged sex abuse victims in investigative interviews. *Child Development, 71,* 1586–1596.

Lamb, M. E., Sternberg, K. J., Esplin, P. W., Hershkowitz, I., & Orbach, Y. (1997a). Assessing the credibility of children's allegations of sexual abuse: A survey of recent research. *Learning and Individual Differences, 9,* 175–194.

Lamb, M. E., Sternberg, K. J., Esplin, P. W., Hershkowitz, I., Orbach, Y., & Hovav, M. (1997b). Criterion-based content analysis: A field validation study. *Child Abuse & Neglect, 21,* 255–264.

Lamb, M. E., Sternberg, K. J., Orbach, Y., Aldridge, J., Bowler, L., Pearson, S., & Esplin, P. W. (2006, July). *Enhancing the quality of investigative interviews by British police officers.* Paper presented at the Second International Investigative Interviewing Conference, University of Portsmouth, UK.

Lamb, M. E., Sternberg, K. J., Orbach, Y., Esplin, P. W., & Mitchell, S. (2002). Is ongoing feedback necessary to maintain the quality of investigative interviews with allegedly abused children? *Applied Developmental Science, 6,* 35–41.

Lamb, M. E., Sternberg, K. J., Orbach, Y., Esplin, P. W., Stewart, H., & Mitchell, S. (2003). Age differences in young children's responses to open-ended invitations in the course of forensic interviews. *Journal of Consulting and Clinical Psychology, 71*, 926–934.

Lamb, M. E., Sternberg, K. J., Orbach, Y., Hershkowitz, I., & Esplin, P. W. (1999). Forensic interviews of children. In A. Memon & R. Bull (Eds.), *Handbook of the psychology of interviewing* (pp. 253–277). New York, NY: Wiley.

Lamb, M. E., Sternberg, K. J., Orbach, Y., Hershkowitz, I., & Horowitz, D. (2003). Differences between accounts provided by witnesses and alleged victims of child sexual abuse. *Child Abuse & Neglect, 27*, 1019–1031.

Lamb, M. E., Sternberg, K. J., Orbach, Y., Hershkowitz, I., Horowitz, D., & Esplin, P. W. (2002). The effects of intensive training and ongoing supervision on the quality of investigative interviews with alleged sex abuse victims. *Applied Developmental Science, 6*, 114–125.

Lamb, M. E., & Thierry, K. L. (2005). Understanding children's testimony regarding their alleged abuse: Contributions of field and laboratory analog research. In D. M. Teti (Ed.), *Handbook of research methods in developmental psychology* (pp. 489–508). Malden, MA: Blackwell.

Landis, T. Y. (1982). Interaction between text and prior knowledge in children's memory for prose. *Child Development, 53*, 811–814.

Langer, D. A., McLeod, B. D., & Weisz, J. R. (2011). Do treatment manuals undermine youth–therapist alliance in community clinical practice? *Journal of Consulting and Clinical Psychology, 79*, 427–432.

La Rooy, D., Brubacher, S. P., Aromäki-Stratos, A., Cyr, M., Hershkowitz, I., Korkman, J., ... & Stewart, H. (2015). The NICHD Protocol: A review of an internationally-used evidence-based tool for training child forensic interviewers. *Journal of Criminological Research, Policy and Practice, 1*, 76–89.

La Rooy, D., Katz, C., Malloy, L. C., & Lamb, M. E. (2010). Do we need to rethink guidance on repeated interviews? *Psychology, Public Policy, and Law, 16*, 373–392.

La Rooy, D., Lamb, M. E., & Memon, A. (2011). Forensic interviews with children in Scotland: A survey of interview practices among police. *Journal of Police and Criminal Psychology, 26*, 26–34.

La Rooy, D. J., Lamb, M. E., & Pipe, M.-E. (2009). Repeated interviewing: A critical evaluation of the risks and potential benefits. In K. Kuehnle & M. Connell (Eds.). *The evaluation of child sexual abuse allegations: A comprehensive guide to assessment and testimony* (pp. 327–361). Hoboken, NJ: Wiley.

La Rooy, D., Pipe, M.-E., & Murray, J. E. (2005). Reminiscence and hypermnesia in children's eyewitness memory. *Journal of Experimental Child Psychology, 90*, 235–254.

Larsson, A. S., Anders Granhag, P., & Spjut, E. (2003). Children's recall and the cognitive interview: Do the positive effects hold over time? *Applied Cognitive Psychology, 17*, 203–214.

Larsson, A. S., Teoh, Y.-S., Lamb, M. E., Orbach, Y., & Hershkowitz, I. (2007, July). *Effects of physical and mental context reinstatement on children's reports about extra-familial child sexual abuse*. Paper presented to the Second International Investigative Interviewing Conference, University of Portsmouth, UK.

Lawson, L., & Chaffin, M. (1992). False negatives in sexual abuse disclosure interviews: Incidence and influences of caretaker's belief in abuse in cases of accidental abuse discovery by diagnosis of STD. *Journal of Interpersonal Violence, 7*, 532–542.

Lawson, M., & London, K. (2015). Tell me everything you discussed: Children's memory for dyadic conversations after a 1-week or a 3-week delay. *Behavioral Sciences & The Law, 33*, 429–445.

Lawson, M., & London, K. (2017). Children's memory for conversations after a 1-year delay. *Journal of Applied Research in Memory and Cognition, 6*, 328–336.

Leach, C., Powell, M. B., Sharman, S. J., & Anglim, J. (2017). The relationship between children's age and disclosures of sexual abuse during forensic interviews. *Child Maltreatment, 22*(1), 79–88.

LeDoux, J. E. (1992). "Brain mechanisms of emotion and emotional learning." *Current Opinion in Neurobiology, 2*(2), 191–197.

Lee, J. K., Wendelken, C., Bunge, S. A., & Ghetti, S. (2016). A time and place for everything: Developmental differences in the building blocks of episodic memory. *Child Development, 87*, 194–210.

Leichtman, M. D., & Ceci, S. J. (1995). The effects of stereotypes and suggestion on preschoolers' reports. *Developmental Psychology, 31*, 568–578.

Leichtman, M. D., Ceci, S. J., & Morse, M. B. (1997). The nature and development of children's event memory. In P. S. Applebaum & L. A. Uyehara (Eds.), *Trauma and memory: Clinical and legal controversies* (pp. 158–187). New York, NY: Oxford University Press.

Leichtman, M. D., Morse, M. B., Dixon, A., & Spiegel, R. (2000). Source monitoring and suggestibility: An individual differences approach. In K. P. Roberts & M. Blades (Eds.), *Children's source monitoring* (pp. 257–288). Mahwah, NJ: Lawrence Erlbaum.

Leippe, M. R., Romanczyk, A., & Manion, A.P. (1991). Eyewitness memory for a touching experience: Accuracy differences between child and adult witnesses. *Journal of Applied Psychology, 76*, 367–379.

Leonard, B. J., Hellerstedt, W. L., & Josten, L. (1997). Association of maternal psychological functioning to pathology in child sexual abuse victims. *Issues in Mental Health Nursing, 18*, 587–601.

Leventhal, J. M., Hamilton, J., Rededal, S., Tebano-Micci, A., & Eyster, C. (1989). Anatomically correct dolls used in interviews of young children suspected of having been sexually abused. *Pediatrics, 84*, 900–906.

Levesque, J. R. (1994). Sex differences in the experience of child sexual victimization. *Journal of Family Violence, 9*, 357–369.

Lewis, M. (1993). The development of deception. In M. Lewis & C. Saarni (Eds.), *Lying and deception in everyday life* (pp. 90–105). New York, NY: Guilford Press.

Lewis, M., Stanger, C., & Sullivan, M. W. (1989). Deception in 3-year-olds. *Developmental Psychology, 25*, 439–443.

Lewy, J., Cyr, M., & Dion, J. (2015). Impact of interviewers' supportive comments and children's reluctance to cooperate during sexual abuse disclosure. *Child Abuse & Neglect, 43*, 112–122.

Ligiezinska, M., Firestone, P., Manion, I. G., McIntyre, J., Ensom, R., & Wells, G. (1996). Children's emotional and behavioral reactions following the disclosure of extra familial sexual abuse: Initial effects. *Child Abuse & Neglect, 20*, 111–125.

Lindberg, M. A. (1980). Is knowledge base development a necessary and sufficient condition for memory development? *Journal of Experimental Child Psychology, 30*, 401–410.

Lindberg, M. A., Jones, S., Collard, L., & Thomas, S. W. (2001). Similarities and differences in eyewitness testimonies of children who directly versus vicariously experience stress. *Journal of Genetic Psychology, 162*, 314–333.

Lindholm, J., Cederborg, A.-C., & Winerdal, U. (2016, March). *An evaluation of the training programme for investigative interviewers in Sweden.* Paper presented to the American Psychology-Law Society Annual Conference, Atlanta, GA.

Lindsay, D. S. (1990). Misleading suggestions can impair eyewitness's ability to remember event details. *Journal of Experimental Psychology: Learning, Memory, and Cognition, 16*, 1077–1083.

Lindsay, D. S., & Johnson, M. K. (1987). Reality monitoring and suggestibility. In S. J. Ceci, M. P. Toglia, & D. F. Ross (Eds.), *Children's eyewitness testimony* (pp. 79–91). New York, NY: Springer.

Lindsay, D. S., & Johnson, M. K. (1989). The eyewitness suggestibility effect and memory for source. *Memory & Cognition, 17*, 349–358.

Lindsay, D. S., Johnson, M., & Kwon, P. (1991). Developmental changes in memory source monitoring. *Journal of Experimental Child Psychology, 52*, 297–318.

Loftus, E. F., & Pickrell, J. E. (1995). The formation of false memories. *Psychiatric Annals, 25*, 720–725.

London, K., Bruck, M., Ceci, S. J., & Shuman, D. W. (2005). Disclosure of child sexual abuse: What does the research tell us about the ways that children tell? *Psychology, Public Policy, and the Law, 11*, 194–226.

London, K., Bruck, M., Ceci, S. J., Shuman, D. W. (2007). Disclosure of child sexual abuse: A review of the contemporary empirical literature. In M.-E. Pipe, M. E. Lamb, Y. Orbach, & A. C. Cederborg (Eds.), *Child sexual abuse: Disclosure, delay and denial* (pp. 11–40). Mahwah, NJ: Erlbaum.

London, K., Bruck, M., Wright, D. B., & Ceci, S. J. (2008). Review of the contemporary literature on how children report sexual abuse to others: Findings, methodological issues, and implications for forensic interviewers. *Memory, 16*, 29–47.

London, K., Hall, A. K., & Lytle, N. E. (2017). Does it help, hurt, or something else? The effect of a something else response alternative on children's performance on forced-choice questions. *Psychology, Public Policy, and Law, 23*, 281–289.

Lorch, E. P., Milich, R., Flake, R. A., Ohlendorf, J., & Little, S. (2010). A developmental examination of story recall and coherence among children with ADHD. *Journal of Abnormal Child Psychology, 38*, 291–301.

Luther, K., Snook, B., Barron, T., & Lamb, M. E. (2015). Child interviewing practices in Canada: A box score from field observations. *Journal of Police and Criminal Psychology, 30*, 204–212.

Lyon, T. D. (1999). The new wave in children's suggestibility research: A critique. *Cornell Law Review, 84*, 1004–1087.

Lyon, T. D. (2002a). Expert testimony on the suggestibility of children: Does it fit? In B. L. Bottoms, M. B. Kovera, & B. D. McAuliff (Eds.), *Children and the law: Social science and policy* (pp. 378–411). New York, NY: Cambridge University Press.

Lyon, T. D. (2002b). Scientific support for expert testimony on child sexual abuse accommodation. In J. R. Conte (Ed.), *Critical issues in child sexual abuse* (pp. 107–138). Newbury Park, CA: Sage.

Lyon, T. D. (2007). False denials: Overcoming methodological biases in abuse disclosure research. In M.-E. Pipe, M. E. Lamb, Y. Orbach, & A. C. Cederborg (Eds.), *Child sexual abuse: Disclosure, delay, and denial* (pp. 41–62). Mahwah, NJ: Erlbaum.

Lyon, T. D. (2010). Investigative interviewing of the child. In D. N. Duquette & A. M. Haralambie (Eds.), *Child Welfare Law and Practice* (2nd ed., pp. 87–109). Denver, CO: Bradford.

Lyon, T. D. (2014). Interviewing children. *Annual Review of Law and Social Science, 10*, 73–89.

Lyon, T. D., & Dorado, J. S. (2008). Truth induction in young maltreated children: The effects of oath-taking and reassurance on true and false disclosures. *Child Abuse & Neglect, 32*, 738–748.

Lyon, T. D., Malloy, L. C., Quas, J. A., & Talwar, V. A. (2008). Coaching, truth induction, and young maltreated children's false allegations and false denials. *Child Development, 79*, 914–929.

Lyon, T. D., & Saywitz, K. J. (1999). Maltreated children's competence to take the oath. *Applied Developmental Science, 3*, 16–27.

Lyon, T. D., Scurich, N., Choi, K., Handmaker, S., & Blank, R. (2012). "How did you feel?": Increasing child sexual abuse witnesses' production of evaluative information. *Law and Human Behavior, 36*(5), 448.

Lytle, N., London, K., & Bruck, M. (2015). Young children's ability to use two-dimensional and three-dimensional symbols to show placements of body touches and hidden objects. *Journal of Experimental Child Psychology, 134*, 30–42.

Macleod, E., Gross, J., & Hayne, H. (2016). Drawing conclusions: The effect of instructions on children's confabulation and fantasy errors. *Memory, 24*, 21–31.

MacMurray, B. K. (1989). Criminal determination for child sexual abuse: Prosecutor case-screening judgments. *Journal of Interpersonal Violence, 4*, 233–244.

Madsen, H. B., & Kim, J. H. (2016) Ontogeny of memory: An update on 40 years of work on infantile amnesia. *Behavioural Brain Research, 298*, 4–14.

Malloy, L. C., Brubacher, S. P., & Lamb, M. E. (2011). Expected consequences of disclosure revealed in investigative interviews with suspected victims of child sexual abuse. *Applied Developmental Science, 15*, 8–19.

Malloy, L. C., Brubacher, S. P., & Lamb, M. E. (2013). "Because she's one who listens": Children discuss disclosure recipients in forensic interviews. *Child Maltreatment, 18*, 245–251.

Malloy, L. C., Brubacher, S. P., Lamb, M. E., & Benton, P (2012, March). *How many and how often: Children's use of number words and frequency estimations in forensic interviews*. Paper presented at the American Psychology-Law Society Conference, Puerto Rico.

Malloy, L. C., Katz, C., Lamb, M. E., & Mugno, A. P. (2015). Children's requests for clarification in investigative interviews about suspected sexual abuse. *Applied Cognitive Psychology, 29*, 323–333.

Malloy, L. C., Lyon, T. D., & Quas, J. A. (2007). Filial dependency and recantation of child sexual abuse allegations. *Journal of the American Academy of Child & Adolescent Psychiatry, 46*, 162–170.

Malloy, L. C., Mugno, A. P., Pelham, W. E., Hawk, L. W., & Lamb, M. E. (2016, June) *Memory and secret-keeping among children with Attention Deficit Hyperactivity Disorder*. Paper presented at the 9th Annual Meeting of the International Investigative Interviewing Research Group, London, UK.

Malloy, L. C., & Quas, J. A. (2009). Children's suggestibility: Areas of consensus and controversy. In K. Kuehnle & M. Connell (Eds.), *The evaluation of child sexual abuse allegations: A comprehensive guide to assessment and testimony*. Hoboken, NJ: Wiley.

Malloy, L. C., Shulman, E. P., & Cauffman, E. (2014). Interrogations, confessions, and guilty pleas among serious adolescent offenders. *Law and Human Behavior, 38*(2), 181.

Malpass, R. S. (1996). Enhancing eyewitness memory. In S. L. Sporer, R. S. Malpass, & G. Köhnken (Eds.), *Psychological issues in eyewitness identification* (pp. 177–204). Mahwah, NJ: Erlbaum.

Malpass, R., & Devine, P. (1981). Guided memory in eyewitness identification. *Journal of Applied Psychology, 66*, 343–350.

Maras, K. L., & Bowler, D. M. (2010). The cognitive interview for eyewitnesses with autism spectrum disorder. *Journal of Autism and Developmental Disorders, 40,* 1350–1360.

Maras, K. L., & Bowler, D. M. (2012). Context reinstatement effects on eyewitness memory in autism spectrum disorder. *British Journal of Psychology, 103*(3), 330–342.

Maras, K. L., & Bowler, D. M. (2014). Eyewitness testimony in autism spectrum disorder: A review. *Journal of Autism and Developmental Disorders, 44,* 2682–2697.

Maras, K. L., Mulcahy, S., Memon, A., Picariello, F., & Bowler, D. M. (2014). Evaluating the effectiveness of the self-administered interview© for witnesses with Autism Spectrum Disorder. *Applied Cognitive Psychology, 28,* 693–701.

Marin, B. V., Holmes, D. L., Guth, M., & Kovac, P. (1979). The potential of children as eyewitnesses: A comparison of children and adults on eyewitness tasks. *Law and Human Behavior, 3,* 295–306.

Martin, C. L., & Halverson, C. F. (1983). The effects of sex-typing schemas on young children's memory. *Child Development, 54,* 563–574.

Martin, M. (1988). Individual differences in everyday memory. In M. M. Gruneberg, P. E. Morris, & R. N. Sykes (Eds.), *Practical aspects of memory: Current research and issues: Vol. 1. Memory in everyday life* (pp. 466–471). Oxford, UK: Wiley.

Mattison, M. L., Dando, C. J., & Ormerod, T. C. (2015). Sketching to remember: Episodic free recall task support for child witnesses and victims with autism spectrum disorder. *Journal of Autism and Developmental Disorders, 45,* 1751–1765.

McAuliff, B. D., Kovera, M. B., & Viswesvaran, C. (1998, March). *Methodological issues in child suggestibility research: A meta-analysis.* Paper presented to the American Psychology-Law Society Convention, Redondo Beach, CA.

McCartney, K., & Nelson, K. (1981). Children's use of scripts in story recall. *Discourse Processes, 4,* 59–70.

McCauley, M. R., & Fisher, R. P. (1995). Facilitating children's eyewitness recall with the revised cognitive interview. *Journal of Applied Psychology, 80,* 510–516.

McCauley, M. R., & Fisher, R. P. (1996). Enhancing children's eyewitness testimony with the Cognitive Interview. In G. Davies, S. Lloyd-Bostock, M. McMurran, & C. Wilson (Eds.), *Psychology, law, and criminal justice: International developments in research and practice* (pp. 127–134). Berlin: Walter de Gruyter.

McCrory, E., Henry, L. A., & Happé, F. (2007). Eye-witness memory and suggestibility in children with Asperger syndrome. *Journal of Child Psychology and Psychiatry, 48,* 482–489.

McFadden, R., & Saulny, S. (2002, September 6). DNA in central park jogger case spurs call for new review [Electronic version]. *The New York Times.*

McGee, R. A., Wolfe, D. A., Yuen, S. A., Wilson, S. K., & Carnmochan, J. (1995). The measurement of maltreatment: a comparison of approaches. *Child Abuse & Neglect, 19,* 233–249.

McGough, L. (1994). *Child witnesses.* New Haven, CT: Yale University Press.

McGuigan, F., & Salmon, K. (2004). Time to talk: The influence of the timing of adult-child talk on children's event memory. *Child Development, 75,* 669–686.

McLay, L., Brown, D. A., Palmer, L., & Beaumont, S. (2016). Event memory, coherence and suggestibility in children with ADHD symptoms. Manuscript in preparation.

McNally, R. J. (1998). Measures of children's reactions to stressful life events. In T. W. Miller (Ed.), *Children of trauma: Stressful life events and their effects on children and adolescents*. Madison, CT: International Universities Press.

McNichol, S., Shute, R., & Tucker, A. (1999). Children's eyewitness memory for a repeated event. *Child Abuse & Neglect, 23*, 1127–1139.

McSpadden, M. D., Schooler, J. W., & Loftus, E. F. (1988). Here today, gone tomorrow: The appearance and disappearance of context effects. In G. M. Davies & D. M. Thomson (Eds.), *Memory in context: Context in memory* (pp. 215–229). New York, NY: Wiley.

McWilliams, K., Lyon, T. D., & Quas, J. A. (2016, April). Maltreated children's ability to make temporal judgements using a recurring landmark event. *Journal of Interpersonal Violence*.

Maras, K. L., & Bowler, D. M. (2012). Context reinstatement effects on eyewitness memory in autism spectrum disorder. *British Journal of Psychology, 103*, 330–342.

Maras, K. L., & Bowler, D. M. (2014). Eyewitness testimony in Autism Spectrum Disorder: A review. *Journal of Autism and Developmental Disorders, 44*, 2682–2697.

Maras, K. L., & Bowler, D. M. (2016). The cognitive interview for witnesses with autism spectrum disorder. *Journal of Autism and Developmental Disorders, 40*, 1350–1360.

Maras K. L., Mulcahy S., Memon A., Picariello F., and Bowler D. M. (2014). Evaluating the effectiveness of the Self-Administered Interview© for witnesses with Autism Spectrum Disorder. *Applied Cognitive Psychology, 28*, 693–701.

Mattison, M. L., Dando, C. J. & Ormerod, T. C. (2016). Sketching to remember: Episodic free recall task support for child witnesses and victims with Autism Spectrum Disorder. *Journal of Autism and Developmental Disorders, 45*, 1751–1765.

Melinder, A., Alexander, K., Cho, Y. I., Goodman, G. S., Thoresen, C., Lonnum, K., & Magnussen, S. (2010). Children's eyewitness memory: A comparison of two interviewing strategies as realized by forensic professionals. *Journal of Experimental Child Psychology, 105*, 156–177.

Melinder, A., & Gilstrap, L. L. (2009). The relationships between child and forensic interviewer behaviours and individual differences in interviews about a medical examination. *European Journal of Developmental Psychology, 6*, 365–395.

Melkman, E. P., Hershkowitz, I., & Zur, R. (2017). Credibility assessment in child sexual abuse investigations: A descriptive analysis. *Child Abuse & Neglect, 67*, 76–85.

Memon, A., & Bull, R. (1991). The cognitive interview: Its origins, empirical support, evaluation and practical implications. *Journal of Community & Applied Social Psychology, 1*, 291–307.

Memon, A., & Bull, R. (Eds.). (1999). *Handbook of the psychology of interviewing*. New York, NY: Wiley.

Memon, A., Cronin, O., Eaves, R., & Bull, R. (1993). The cognitive interview and child witnesses. *Issues in Criminological and Legal Psychology, 20*, 3–9.

Memon, A., Cronin, O., Eaves, R., & Bull, R. (1996). An empirical test of the mnemonic components of the cognitive interview. In G. Davies, S. Lloyd-Bostock, M. McMurran, & C. Wilson (Eds.), *Psychology, law, and criminal justice: International developments in research and practice* (pp. 135–145). Berlin: Walter de Gruyter.

Memon, A., Holley, A., Milne, R., Köhnken, G., & Bull, R. (1994). Towards understanding the effects of interviewer training in evaluating the cognitive interview. *Applied Cognitive Psychology, 8*, 641–659.

Memon, A., Holley, A., Wark, L., Bull, R., & Koehnken, G. (1996). Reducing suggestibility in child witness interviews. *Applied Cognitive Psychology, 10*, 503–518.

Memon, A., Meissner, C. A., & Fraser, J. (2010). The cognitive interview: A meta-analytic review and study space analysis of the past 25 years. *Psychology, public policy, and law, 16*(4), 340.

Memon, A., & Vartoukian, R. (1996). The effect of repeated questioning on young children's eyewitness testimony. *British Journal of Psychology, 87*, 403–415.

Memon, A., Wark, L., Bull, R., & Köhnken, G. (1997a). Isolating the effects of the cognitive interview techniques. *British Journal of Psychology, 88*, 179–197.

Memon, A., Wark. L., Holley, A., Bull, R., & Köhnken, G. (1996a). Interviewer behavior in investigative interviews. *Psychology, Crime, & Law, 2*, 135–155.

Memon, A., Wark. L., Holley, A., Bull, R., & Köhnken, G. (1996b). Reducing suggestibility in child witness interviews. *Applied Cognitive Psychology, 10*, 503–518.

Memorandum of Good Practice (1992). London, England: Her Majesty's Stationery Office.

Merritt, K. A., Ornstein, P. A., & Spicker, B. (1994). Children's memory for a salient medical procedure: Implications for testimony. *Pediatrics, 94*, 17–23.

Mian, M., Wehrspann, W., Klajner-Diamond, H., Lebaron, D., & Winder, C. (1986). Review of 125 children 6 years of age and under who were sexually abused. *Child Abuse & Neglect, 10*, 223–229.

Michaels, S. (1981). "Sharing time": Children's narrative styles and different access to literacy. *Language in Society, 10*, 423–442.

Michel, M. K., Gordon, B. N., Ornstein, P. A., & Simpson, M. A. (2000). The abilities of children with mental retardation to remember personal experiences: Implications for testimony. *Journal of Clinical Child Psychology, 29*, 453–463.

Milgram, N. A. (1973). Cognition and language in mental retardation: Distinctions and implications. In D. K. Routh, (Ed.), *The experimental psychology of mental retardation*. (pp. 186–212). Oxford, UK: Aldine.

Miller, P. H. (1990). The development of strategies of selective attention. In D. F. Bjorklund (Ed.), *Children's strategies: Contemporary views of cognitive development* (pp. 157–184). Hillsdale NJ: Erlbaum.

Milne, R. (1999). Interviewing children with learning disabilities. In A. Memon & R. Bull (Eds.), *Handbook of the psychology of interviewing* (pp. 165–180). Chichester, UK: Wiley.

Milne, R., & Bull, R. (1996). Interviewing children with mild learning disability with the cognitive interview. In N. K. Clark, & G. M. Stephenson (Eds.), *Investigative and forensic decision making: Issues in criminological psychology: No. 26* (pp. 44–51). Leicester: British Psychological Society.

Milne, B., & Bull, R. (1999). *Investigative interviewing: Psychology and practice*. Chichester, UK: Wiley.

Milne, R., & Bull, R. (2001). Interviewing witnesses with learning disabilities for legal purposes. *British Journal of Learning Disabilities, 29*, 93–97.

Milne, R., & Bull, R. (2003). Does the cognitive interview help children to resist the effects of suggestive questioning? *Legal and Criminological Psychology, 8*, 21–38.

Milne, R., Bull, R., Köhnken, G., & Memon, A. (1995). The cognitive interview and suggestibility. In G. M. Stephenson & N. K. Clark (Eds.), *Criminal behavior, perception, attributions, and rationality* (pp. 21–27). Leicester, UK: British Psychological Society.
Ministry of Justice (2011). *Achieving best evidence in criminal proceedings.* London, UK: Ministry of Justice.
Mitchell, K. J., & Zaragoza, M. S. (1996). Repeated exposure to suggestion and false memory: The role of contextual variability. *Journal of Memory and Language*, *35*, 246–260.
Moore, S. A., & Zoellner, L. A. (2007). Overgeneral autobiographical memory and traumatic events: An evaluative review. *Psychological Bulletin*, *133*(3), 419.
Moreno, R., & Mayer, R. E. (1999). Cognitive principles of multimedia learning: The role of modality and contiguity. *Journal of Educational Psychology*, *91*, 358.
Morris, G., Baker-Ward, L., & Bauer, P. J. (2010). What remains of that day: The survival of children's autobiographical memories across time. *Applied Cognitive Psychology*, *24*, 527–544.
Muir-Broaddus, J. E. (1997, April). *The effects of social influence and psychological reactance on children's responses to repeated questions.* Paper presented to Society for Research in Child Development Convention, Washington, DC.
Mulder, M. R., & Vrij, A. (1996). Explaining conversation rules to children: An intervention study to facilitate children's accurate responses. *Child Abuse & Neglect*, *20*, 623–631.
Murachver, T., Pipe, M.-E., Gordon, R., Fivush, R., & Owens, J. L. (1996). Do, show, and tell: Children's event memories acquired through direct experience, observation, and stories. *Child Development*, *67*, 3029–3044.
Murayama, K., Miyatsu, T., Buchli, D., & Storm, B. C. (2014). Forgetting as a consequence of retrieval: A meta-analytic review of retrieval-induced forgetting. *Psychological Bulletin*, *140*, 1383–1409.
Murfett, R., Powell, M. B., & Snow, P. C. (2008). The effect of intellectual disability on the adherence of child witnesses to a "story grammar" framework. *Journal of Intellectual and Developmental Disability*, *33*, 2–11.
Murphy, W. J. (2001). The victim advocacy and research group: Serving a growing need to provide rape victims with personal legal representation to protect privacy rights and to fight gender bias in the criminal justice system. *Journal of Social Distress and the Homeless*, *10*, 123–138.
Myers, J., Gramzow, E., Ornstein, P. A., Wagner, L., Gordon, B. N., & Baker-Ward, L. (2003). Children's memory of a physical examination: A comparison of recall and recognition assessment protocols. *International Journal of Behavioral Development*, *27*, 66–73.
Myers, N. A., Perris, E. E., & Speaker, C. J. (1994). Fifty months of memory: A longitudinal study in early childhood. In R. Fivush (Ed.), *Long-term retention of infant memories* (pp. 383–415). Hove, UK: Erlbaum.
Myles-Worsley, M., Cromer, C., & Dodd, D. (1986). Children's preschool script reconstruction: Reliance on general knowledge as memory fades. *Developmental Psychology*, *22*, 2–30.
Nairne, J. S. (2002). The myth of the encoding-retrieval match. *Memory*, *10*, 389–395.
Naka, M. (2011). The effect of forensic interview training based on the NICHD structured protocol. *Japanese Journal of Child Abuse and Neglect*, *13*, 316–325.
Nathan, D., & Snedeker, M. (1995). *Satan's silence.* New York, NY: Basic Books.

Nathanson, R., & Platt, M. D. (2005). Attorneys' perceptions of child witnesses with mental retardation. *The Journal of Psychiatry & Law, 33*(1), 5–42.

Nathanson, R., & Saywitz, K. J. (2003). The effects of courtroom context on children's memory and anxiety. *Journal of Psychiatry & Law, 31,* 67–98.

Neisser, U. (2004). Memory development: New questions and old. *Developmental Review, 24,* 154–158.

Nelson, K. (1986). *Event knowledge: Structure and function in development.* Hillsdale, NJ: Erlbaum.

Nelson, K. (1989). Remembering: A functional developmental perspective. In P. R. Solomon, G. R. Goethals, C. M. Kelley, & B. R. Stephens (Eds.), *Memory: Interdisciplinary approaches* (pp. 127–150). New York, NY: Springer.

Nelson, K. (1993a). Events, narratives, memory: What develops? In C. A. Nelson (Ed.), *Memory and affect in development. The Minnesota Symposia on Child Psychology* (Vol. *26,* pp. 1–24). Hillsdale, NJ: Erlbaum.

Nelson, K. (1993b). The psychological and social origins of autobiographical memory. *Psychological Science, 4,* 85–92.

Nelson, K. (1996a). *Language in cognitive development: The emergence of the mediated mind.* New York, NY: Cambridge University Press.

Nelson, K. (1996b). Memory development from 4 to 7 years. The five to seven year shift: The age of reason and responsibility. In A. J. Sameroff & M. M. Haith (Eds.), *The five to seven year shift* (pp. 141–160). Chicago, IL: University of Chicago Press.

Nelson, K. (2014). Sociocultural theories of memory development. In P. J. Bauer & R. Fivush (Eds.). *The Wiley handbook on the development of children's memory* (Vols. *I and II*; pp. 87–116). Chichester, UK: Wiley.

Nelson, K., & Fivush, R. (2004). The emergence of autobiographical memory: A social cultural developmental model. *Psychological Review, 111,* 486–511.

Nelson, K., & Gruendel, J. (1981). Generalized event representations: Basic building blocks of cognitive development. In M. E. Lamb & A. L. Brown (Eds.), *Advances in development psychology* (Vol. *1,* pp. 131–158). Hillsdale, NJ: Erlbaum.

Nelson, K., & Gruendel, J. (1986). Children's scripts. In K. Nelson (Ed.), *Event knowledge: Structure and function in development* (pp. 21–46). Hillsdale, NJ: Erlbaum.

New Zealand Law Commission. (1997). *Section 97.* Wellington, NZ: Author.

New Zealand Police and Ministry for Vulnerable Children Oranga Tamariki. (2017). *New Zealand specialist child witness interviewing model.* Wellington, NZ: Author.

Nigg, J. T. (2006). *What causes ADHD?: Understanding what goes wrong and why.* New York, NY: Guilford Press.

Oates, K., & Shrimpton, S. (1991) Children's memories for stressful and non-stressful events. *Medical Science and Law, 31,* 4–10.

O'Callaghan, G., & D'Arcy, H. (1989). Use of props in questioning preschool witnesses. *Australian Journal of Psychology, 41,* 187–195.

O'Connor, P., Brown, D. A., & Wolfman, M. Mapping memories: Sketchplans do not facilitate adolescents' recall of a past event. Manuscript under review.

Odegard, T. N., Cooper, C. M., Lampinen, J. M., Reyna, V. F., & Brainerd, C. J. (2009), Children's eyewitness memory for multiple real-life events. *Child Development, 80,* 1877–1890.

O'Kelly, C. M., Kebbell, M. R., Hatton, C., & Johnson, S. D. (2003a). Judicial intervention in court cases involving witnesses with and without learning disabilities. *Legal and Criminological Psychology, 8,* 229–240.

O'Kelly, C., Kebbell, M., Hatton, C., & Johnson, S. D. (2003b). When do judges intervene in cases involving people with learning disabilities. *Legal and Criminal Psychology, 8*, 229–240.

Orbach, Y., Hershkowitz, I., Lamb, M. E., Sternberg, K. J., Esplin, P. W., & Horowitz, D. (2000). Assessing the value of structured protocols for forensic interviews of alleged abuse victims. *Child Abuse & Neglect, 24*, 733–752.

Orbach, Y., Hershkowitz, I., Lamb, M. E., Sternberg, K. J., & Horowitz, D. (2000). Interviewing at the scene of the crime: Effects on children's recall of alleged abuse. *Legal and Criminological Psychology, 5*, 135–147.

Orbach, Y., & Lamb, M. E. (2001). The relationship between within-interview contradictions and eliciting interview utterances. *Child Abuse & Neglect, 25*, 323–333.

Orbach, Y., & Lamb, M. E. (2007). Young children's references to temporal attributes of allegedly experienced events in the course of forensic interviews. *Child Development, 78*, 1100–1120.

Orbach, Y., Lamb, M. E., Abbott, C., Hershkowitz, I., & Pipe, M.-E. (2016). Do allegedly abused children's responses to suggestion differ depending on the type of eliciting suggestions? Unpublished manuscript.

Orbach, Y., Lamb, M. E., La Rooy, D., & Pipe, M.-E. (2012). A case study of witness consistency and memory recovery across multiple investigative interviews. *Applied Cognitive Psychololgy, 26*, 118–129.

Orbach, Y., Lamb, M. E., Sternberg, K. J., Vickerman, K. A., Pelaez, M. T., Sleeth-Keppler, E., & Norris, J. (2003, April). *Developmental differences in young children's reports of temporal information in the course of forensic interviews*. A poster presented at the Biennial Meeting of the Society for Research in Child Development (SRCD) in Tampa, FL.

Orbach, Y., Lamb, M. E., Sternberg, K. J., Williams, J. M. G., & Dawud-Noursi, S. (2001). The effect of being a victim or witness of family violence on the retrieval of autobiographical memories. *Child Abuse & Neglect, 24*, 1427–1437.

Orbach, Y., Shiloach, H., & Lamb, M. E. (2007). Reluctant disclosers of child sexual abuse. In M.-E. Pipe, M. E. Lamb, Y. Orbach, & A.-C. Cederborg (Eds.), *Child sexual abuse: Disclosure, delay, and denial* (pp. 115–134). Mahwah, NJ: Erlbaum.

Ornstein, P. A. (1995). Children's long-term retention of salient personal experiences. *Journal of Traumatic Stress, 8*, 581–605.

Ornstein, P. A., Baker-Ward, L., Gordon, B. N., Merritt, K. A. (1997). Children's memory for medical experiences: Implications for testimony. *Applied Cognitive Psychology, 11*, 87–104.

Ornstein, P. A., Gordon, B. N., & Larus, D. M. (1992). Children's memory for a personally experienced event: Implications for testimony. *Applied Cognitive Psychology, 6*, 49–60.

Ornstein, P. A., Haden, C. A., & Hedrick, A. M. (2004). Learning to remember: Social-communicative exchanges and the development of children's memory skills. *Developmental Review, 24*, 374–395.

Ornstein, P. A., Larus, D. M., & Clubb, P. A. (1992). Understanding children's testimony: Implications of the research on children's memory. In R. Vasta (Ed.), *Annals of child development* (Vol. 8, pp. 147–176). London, UK: Jessica Kingsley.

Ornstein, P. A., Merritt, K. A., Baker-Ward, L., Furtado, E., Gordon, B. N., & Principe, G. (1998). Children's knowledge, expectation, and long-term retention. *Applied Cognitive Psychology, 12*, 387–405.

Ornstein, P. A., Principe, G., Hudson, A. E., Gordon, B. N., & Merritt, K. (1997, April). *Procedural information and stress as mediators of children's long-term recall*. Paper presented at the meeting of the Society for Research in Child Development, Albequerque, NM.

Ornstein, P. A., Shapiro, L. R., Clubb, P. A., Follmer, A., & Baker-Ward, L. (1997). The influence of prior knowledge on children's memory for salient medical experiences. In N. Stein, P. A. Ornstein, B. Tversky, & C. J. Brainerd (Eds.), *Memory for everyday and emotional events* (pp. 83–112). Hillsdale, NJ: Erlbaum.

Otgaar, H., Candel, I., Scoboria, A., & Merckelbach, H. (2010). Script knowledge enhances the development of children's false memories. *Acta Psychologica, 133*, 57–63.

Otgaar, H., Horselenberg, R., van Kampen, R., & Lalleman, K. (2012). Clothed and unclothed human figure drawings lead to more correct and incorrect reports of touch in children. *Psychology, Crime & Law, 18*, 641–653.

Otgaar, H., Smeets, T., & Peters, M. (2012). Children's implanted false memories and additional script knowledge. *Applied Cognitive Psychology, 26*, 709–715.

Otgaar, H., van Ansem, R., Pauw, C., & Horselenberg, R. (2016). Improving children's interviewing methods? The effects of drawing and practice on children's memories for an event. *Journal of Police and Criminal Psychology, 31*, 279–287.

Ouyang, L., Fang, X., Mercy, J., Perou, R., & Grosse, S. D. (2008). Attention-deficit/hyperactivity disorder symptoms and child maltreatment: A population-based study. *The Journal of Pediatrics, 153*, 851–856.

Palmer, S. E., Brown, R. A., Rae-Grant, N. I., & Loughlin, M. J. (1999). Responding to children's disclosure of familial abuse: What survivors tell us. *Child Welfare, 78*, 259–282.

Parker, J. F., Bahrick, L., Lundy, B., Fivush, R., & Levitt, M. (1998). Effects of stress on children's memory for a natural disaster. In C. P. Thompson, D. G. Payne, M. P. Toglia, J. D. Read, & D. Bruce (Eds.), *Eyewitness memory: Theoretical and applied perspectives* (pp. 31–54). Mahwah, NJ: Erlbaum.

Pathman, T., Doydum, A., & Bauer, P. J. (2013). Bringing order to life events: Memory for the temporal order of autobiographical events over an extended period in school-aged children and adults. *Journal of Experimental Child Psychology, 115*, 309–325.

Pathman, T., Larkina, M., Burch, M. M., & Bauer, P. J. (2013). Young children's memory for the times of personal past events. *Journal of Cognition and Development, 14*, 120–140.

Pathman, T., Samson, Z., Dugas, K., Cabeza, R., & Bauer, P. J. (2011). A "snapshot" of declarative memory: Differing developmental trajectories in episodic and autobiographical memory. *Memory, 19*, 825–835.

Patterson, T., & Hayne, H. (2011). Does drawing facilitate older children's reports of emotionally laden events? *Applied Cognitive Psychology, 25*, 119–126.

Paz-Alonso, P. M., & Goodman, G. S. (2016). Developmental differences across middle childhood in memory and suggestibility for negative and positive events. *Behavioral Sciences & The Law, 34*, 30–54.

Pea, R. D. (1980). The development of negation in early child language. In D. R. Olson (Ed.), *The social foundations of language and thought* (pp. 156–186). New York, NY: Norton.

Peled, M., Iarocci, G., & Connolly, D. A. (2004). Eyewitness testimony and perceived credibility of youth with mild intellectual disability. *Journal of Intellectual Disability Research, 48*, 699–703.

Perlman, N. B., Ericson, K. I., Esses, V. M., & Isaacs, B. J. (1994). The developmentally handicapped witness: Competency as a function of question format. *Law and Human Behavior, 18*, 171–187.

Perner, J. (2000). Memory and theory of mind. In E. Tulving & F. I. M. Craik (Eds.), *The Oxford handbook of memory* (pp. 297–312). Oxford, UK: Oxford University Press.

Perry, N. W., McAuliff, B. D., Tam, P., Claycomb, L., Dostal, C., & Flanagan, C. (1995). When lawyers question children: Is justice served? *Law and Human Behavior, 19*, 609–629.

Perry, N. W., & Wrightsman, L. S. (1991). *The child witness: Legal issues and dilemmas*. Newbery Park, CA: Sage.

Peters, D. P. (1987). The impact of naturally occurring stress on children's memory. In S. J. Ceci, M. P. Toglia, & D. F. Ross (Eds.), *Children's eyewitness testimony* (pp. 122–141). New York, NY: Springer.

Peters, D. P. (1991). The influence of stress and arousal on the child witness. In J. L. Doris (Ed.), *The suggestibility of children's recollections* (pp. 60–76). Washington, DC: American Psychological Association.

Peterson, C. (1999). Children's memory for medical emergencies: 2 years later. *Developmental Psychology, 35*, 1493–1506.

Peterson, C. (2011). Children's memory reports over time: Getting both better and worse. *Journal of Experimental Child Psychology, 109*, 275–293.

Peterson, C. (2012). Children's autobiographical memories across the years: Forensic implications of childhood amnesia and eyewitness memory for stressful events. *Developmental Review, 32*, 287–306.

Peterson, C. (2015). A decade later: Adolescents' memory for medical emergencies. *Applied Cognitive Psychology, 29*, 826–834.

Peterson, C., & Bell, M. (1996) Children's memory for traumatic injury. *Child Development, 67*, 3045–3070.

Peterson, C., & Biggs, M. (1997). Interviewing children about trauma: Problems with "specific" questions. *Journal of Traumatic Stress, 10*, 279–290.

Peterson, C., Dowden, C., & Tobin, J. (1999). Interviewing preschoolers: Comparisons of Yes/No and Wh- questions. *Law and Human Behavior, 23*, 539–555.

Peterson, C., Moores, L., & White, G. (2001). Recounting the same events again and again: Children's consistency across multiple interviews. *Applied Cognitive Psychology, 15*, 353–371.

Peterson, C., Morris, G., Baker-Ward, L., & Flynn, S. (2014). Predicting which childhood memories persist: Contributions of memory characteristics. *Developmental Psychology, 50*, 439–448.

Peterson, C., & Noel, M. (2012). "I was just screeching!": Comparing child and parent derived measures of distress. *Stress and Health, 28*, 279–288.

Peterson, C., & Rideout, R. (1998). Memory for medical emergencies experienced by 1- and 2-year-olds. *Developmental Psychology, 34*, 1059–1072.

Peterson, C., Wang, Q., & Hou, Y. (2009). "When I was little": Childhood recollections in Chinese and European Canadian grade school children. *Child Development, 80*, 506–518.

Peterson, C., & Warren, K.L. (2009). Injuries, emergency rooms and children's memory: Factors contributing to individual differences. In J. Quas & R. Fivush (Eds.), *Emotion in memory and development: Biological, cognitive, and social considerations* (pp. 60–85). Oxford, UK: Oxford University Press.

Peterson, C., Warren, K. L., & Short, M. M. (2011). Infantile amnesia across the years: A 2-year follow-up of children's earliest memories. *Child Development, 82*, 1092–1105.

Peterson, C., & Whalen, N. (2001). Five years later: Children's memory for medical emergencies. *Applied Cognitive Psychology, 15*, S7–S24.

Pezdek, K., & Roe, C. (1997). The suggestibility of children's memory for being touched: Planting, erasing, and changing memories. *Law and Human Behavior, 21*, 95–106.

Phillips, E., Oxburgh, G., & Myklebust, T. (2012). Investigative interviews with victims of child sexual abuse: The relationship between question type and investigation relevant information. *Journal of Police and Criminal Psychology, 27*, 45–54.

Piaget, J. (1927/1971). *The child's conception of time* (A. J. Pomerans, trans.). New York, NY: Ballantine Books.

Piaget, J. (1964). Part I: Cognitive development in children: Piaget, development, and learning. *Journal of Research in Science Teaching, 2*, 176–186.

Pillemer, D. B. (1993). Preschool children's memories of personal circumstances: The fire alarm study. In E. Winograd & U. Neisser (Eds.), *Affect and accuracy in recall: Studies of "flashbulb" memories. Emory symposia in cognition* (Vol. 4, pp. 121–137). New York, NY: Cambridge University Press.

Pillemer, D. B., Picariello, M. L., & Pruett, J.C. (1994). Very long-term memories of a salient preschool event. *Applied Cognitive Psychology, 8*, 95–106.

Pillemer, D. B., & White, S. H. (1989). Childhood events recalled by children and adults. In H. W. Reese (Ed.), *Advances in child development and behavior* (Vol. 21, pp. 297–340). New York, NY: Academic Press.

Pinborough-Zimmerman, J., Satterfield, R., Miller, J., Bilder, D., Hossain, S., & McMahon, W. (2007). Communication disorders: Prevalence and comorbid intellectual disability, autism, and emotional/behavioral disorders. *American Journal of Speech-Language Pathology, 16*, 359–367.

Pipe, M.-E., Gee, S., & Wilson, C. (1993). Cues, props and context: Do they facilitate children's events reports? In G. S. Goodman & B. L. Bottoms (Eds.), *Child victims, child witnesses* (pp. 25–45). New York, NY: Guilford.

Pipe, M.-E., & Goodman, G. (1991). Elements of secrecy: Implications for children's testimony. *Behavioral Sciences and the Law, 9*, 33–41.

Pipe, M.-E., Lamb, M. E., Orbach, Y., & Cederborg, A. C. (Eds.). (2007). *Child sexual abuse: Disclosure, delay and denial*. Mahwah, NJ: Erlbaum.

Pipe, M.-E., Lamb, M. E., Orbach, Y., & Esplin, P. W. (2004). Recent research on children's testimony about experienced and witnessed events. *Developmental Review, 24*, 440–468.

Pipe, M.-E., Lamb, M. E., Orbach, O., Stewart, H. L., Sternberg, K. J., & Esplin, P. W. (2007). Factors associated with non-disclosure of suspected abuse during forensic interviews. In M.-E. Pipe, M. E. Lamb, Y. Orbach, & A.-C. Cederborg (Eds.), *Child sexual abuse: Disclosure, delay, and denial* (pp. 77–96). Mahwah, NJ: Erlbaum.

Pipe, M.-E., Orbach, Y., Lamb, M. E., Abbott, C. B., & Stewart, H. (2013). Do case outcomes change when investigative interviewing practices change? *Psychology, Public Policy, and Law, 19*, 179.

Pipe, M.-E., Orbach, Y., Lamb, M. E., & Cederborg, A. C. (2007). Seeking resolution in the disclosure wars: An overview. In Y. Orbach, A.-C. Cederborg, M.-E. Pipe, M. E. Lamb (Eds.), *Child sexual abuse: Disclosure, delay, and denial* (pp. 3–10). Mahwah NJ: Erlbaum.

Pipe, M.-E. & Salmon, K. (2002). What children bring to the interview context: Individual differences in children's event reports. In M. L. Eisen, J. A. Quas, & G. S. Goodman (Eds.), *Memory and suggestibility in the forensic interview* (pp. 235–261). Mahwah, NJ: Erlbaum.

Pipe, M.-E., & Salmon, K. (2009). Dolls, drawing, body diagrams, and other props: Role of props in investigative interviews. In K. Kuehnle & M. Connell (Eds.), *The evaluation of child sexual abuse allegations: A comprehensive guide to assessment and testimony* (pp. 365–395). Hoboken, NJ: Wiley, 2009.

Pipe, M.-E., Stewart, H. L., Sternberg, K. J., Lamb, M. E., & Esplin, P. W. (2003, August). *Non-disclosures and alleged abuse in forensic interviews.* Paper presented at a conference on Non-disclosure and delayed disclosure of child sexual abuse, Satra Bruk, Sweden.

Pipe, M.-E., & Wilson, J. C. (1994) Cues and secrets: Influences on children's event reports. *Developmental Psychology*, *30*, 515–525.

Plotnikoff, J., & Woolfson, R. (1998). *Preparing young witnesses for court: A handbook for child witness supporters.* London, UK: National Society for the Prevention of Cruelty to Children.

Plotnikoff, J., & Woolfson, R. (2009). *Measuring up? Evaluating implementation of government commitments to young witnesses in criminal proceedings: July 2009: Executive Summary.* London, UK: NSPCC.

Plotnikoff, J., & Woolfson, R. (2015). *Intermediaries in the criminal justice system: Improving communication for vulnerable witnesses and defendants.* Bristol, UK: Policy Press.

Polanczyk, G. V., Willcutt, E. G., Salum, G. A., Kieling, C., & Rohde, L. A. (2014). ADHD prevalence estimates across three decades: An updated systematic review and meta-regression analysis. *International Journal of Epidemiology*, *43*, 434–442.

Pompedda, F., Zappalà, A., & Santtila, P. (2015). Simulations of child sexual abuse interviews using avatars paired with feedback improves interview quality. *Psychology, Crime & Law*, *21*, 28–52.

Poole, D. A. (2016). *Interviewing children: The science of conversation in forensic contexts.* Washington, DC: American Psychological Association.

Poole, D. A., & Bruck, M. (2012). Divining testimony? The impact of interviewing props on children's reports of touching. *Developmental Review*, *32*(3), 165–180.

Poole, D. A., Bruck, M., & Pipe, M. E. (2011). Forensic interviewing aids: Do props help children answer questions about touching? *Current Directions in Psychological Science*, *20*, 11–15.

Poole, D. A., & Dickinson, J. J. (2011). Evidence supporting restrictions on uses of body diagrams in forensic interviews. *Child Abuse & Neglect*, *35*, 659–669.

Poole, D. A., & Dickinson, J. J. (2014). Comfort drawing during investigative interviews: Evidence of the safety of a popular practice. *Child Abuse & Neglect*, *38*, 192–201.

Poole, D. A., Dickinson, J. J., Brubacher, S. P., Liberty, A. E., & Kaake, A. M. (2014). Deficient cognitive control fuels children's exuberant false allegations. *Journal of Experimental Child Psychology*, *118*, 101–109.

Poole, D. A., & Lamb, M. E. (1998). *Investigative interviews of children: A guide for helping professionals.* Washington, DC: American Psychological Association.

Poole, D. A., & Lindsay, D. S. (1995). Interviewing preschoolers: Effects of non-suggestive techniques, parental coaching, and leading questions on reports of nonexperienced events. *Journal of Experimental Child Psychology*, *60*, 129–154.

Poole, D. A., & Lindsay, D. S. (1997, April). *Misinformation from parents and children's source monitoring: Implications for testimony.* Paper presented to the Society for Research in Child Development, Washington, DC.

Poole, D. A., & Lindsay, D. S. (1998). Assessing the accuracy of young children's reports: Lessons from the investigation of child sexual abuse. *Applied and Preventive Psychology, 7,* 1–26.

Poole, D. A., & Lindsay, D. S. (2002). Reducing child witnesses' false reports of misinformation from parents. *Journal of Experimental Child Psychology, 81,* 117–140.

Poole, D. A., & White, L. T. (1991). Effects of question repetition on the eyewitness testimony of children and adults. *Developmental Psychology, 27,* 975–986.

Poole, D. A., & White, L. T. (1993). Two years later: Effect of question repetition and retention interval on the eyewitness testimony of children and adults. *Developmental Psychology, 29,* 844–853.

Poole, D. A., & White, L. T. (1995). Tell me again and again: Stability and change in the repeated testimonies of children and adults. In M. S. Zaragoza, J. R. Graham, G. C. N. Hall, R. Hirschman, & Y. S. Ben Porath (Eds.), *Memory and testimony in the child witness* (pp. 24–43). Thousand Oaks, CA: Sage Publications.

Powell, M. B., & Barnett, M. (2015). Elements underpinning successful implementation of a national best-practice child investigative interviewing framework. *Psychiatry, Psychology and Law, 22,* 368–377.

Powell, M. B., Guadagno, B., & Benson, M. (2016). Improving child investigative interviewer performance through computer-based learning activities. *Policing and Society, 26,* 365–374.

Powell, M. B., & Hughes-Scholes, C. H. (2009). Evaluation of the questions used to elicit evidence about abuse from child witnesses: An Australian study. *Psychiatry, Psychology and Law, 16,* 369–378.

Powell, M. B., Hughes-Scholes, C. H., Smith, R., & Sharman, S. J. (2014). The relationship between investigative interviewing experience and open-ended question usage. *Police Practice and Research, 15*(4), 283–292.

Powell, M. B., Roberts, K. P., Ceci, S. J., & Hembrooke, H. H. (1999). The effects of repeated experience on children's suggestibility. *Developmental Psychology, 35,* 1462–1477.

Powell, M. B., Roberts, K. P., & Guadagno, B. (2007). Particularisation of child abuse offences: Common problems when questioning child witnesses. *Current Issues in Criminal Justice, 19,* 64–74.

Powell, M. B., Roberts, K. P., & Thompson, D. M. (2000). The effect of a suggestive interview on children's memory of a repeated event: Does it matter whether suggestions are linked to a particular incident? *Psychiatry, Psychology, & Law, 7,* 182–191.

Powell, M. B., & Thomson, D. M. (1994). Children's eyewitness-memory research: Implications for practice. *Families in Society, 75,* 204–216.

Powell, M. B., & Thomson, D. M. (1996). Children's memory of an occurrence of a repeated event: Effects of age, repetition, and retention interval across three question types. *Child Development, 67,* 1988–2004.

Powell, M. B., & Thomson, D. M. (1997). Contrasting memory for temporal-source and memory for content in children's discrimination of repeated events. *Applied Cognitive Psychology, 11,* 339–360.

Powell, M. B., & Thomson, D. M. (2003). Improving children's recall of an occurrence of a repeated event: It is a matter of helping them to generate options? *Law & Human Behavior, 27,* 365–384.

Powell, M. B., Thomson, D. M., & Ceci, S. J. (2003). Children's memory of recurring events: is the first event always the best remembered? *Applied Cognitive Psychology, 17,* 127–146.

Powell, M. B., & Wright, R. (2008). Investigative interviewers' perceptions of the value of different training tasks on their adherence to open-ended questions with children. *Psychiatry, Psychology and Law, 15,* 272–283.

Powell, M. B., Wright, R., & Clark, S. (2010). Improving the competency of police officers in conducting investigative interviews with children. *Police Practice and Research, 11,* 211–226.

Prebble, S. C., Addis, D. R., & Tippett, L. J. (2013). Autobiographical memory and sense of self. *Psychological Bulletin, 139,* 815–840.

Pressley, M., Forrest-Pressley, D., & Elliott-Faust, D. J. (1985). What is strategy instructional enrichment and how to study it: Illustrations from research on children's prose memory and comprehension. In F. E. Weinert & M. Perlmutter (Eds.), *Memory development: Universal changes and individual differences* (pp. 101–130). Hillsdale, NJ: Erlbaum.

Price, E. A., Ahern, E. C., & Lamb, M. E. (2016). Rapport-building in investigative interviews of alleged child sexual abuse victims. *Applied Cognitive Psychology, 30,* 743–749.

Price, D. W. W., & Goodman, G. S. (1990). Visiting the wizard: Children's memory of a recurring event. *Child Development, 61,* 664–680.

Price, H. L., Connolly, D. A., & Gordon, H. M. (2016). Children who experienced a repeated event only appear less accurate in a second interview than those who experienced a unique event. *Law and Human Behavior, 40,* 362–373.

Price, H. L., & Roberts, K. P. (2011). The effects of an intensive training and feedback program on police and social workers' investigative interviews of children. *Canadian Journal of Behavioural Science/Revue Canadienne des Sciences du Comportement, 43,* 235–244.

Price, H. L., Roberts, K. P., & Collins, A. (2013). The quality of children's allegations of abuse in investigative interviews containing practice narratives. *Journal of Applied Research in Memory and Cognition, 2,* 1–6.

Principe, G. F., DiPuppo, J., & Gammel, J. (2013). Effects of mothers' conversation style and receipt of misinformation on children's event reports. *Cognitive Development, 28,* 260–271.

Principe, G. F., & Schindewolf, E. (2012). Natural conversations as a source of false memories in children: Implications for the testimony of young witnesses. *Developmental Review, 32,* 205–223.

Quas, J. A. (1998). *Children's memory of experienced and nonexperienced events across repeated interviews* (Unpublished doctoral dissertation). University of California, Davis.

Quas, J. A., Goodman, G. S., Bidrose, S., Pipe, M.-E., Craw, S., & Ablin, D. S. (1999). Emotion and memory: Children's long-term remembering, forgetting, and suggestibility. *Journal of Experimental Child Psychology, 72,* 235–270.

Quas, J. A., Goodman, G. S., Ghetti, S., & Redlich, A. D. (2000). Questioning the child witness: What can we conclude from the research thus far? *Trauma, Violence & Abuse, 1,* 223–249.

Quas, J. A., & Lench, H. C. (2007). Arousal at encoding, arousal at retrieval, interviewer support, and children's memory for a mild stressor. *Applied Cognitive Psychology, 21,* 289–305.

Quas, J. A., Malloy, L. C., Melinder, A., Goodman, G. S., D'Mello, M., & Schaaf, J. M. (2007). Developmental differences in the effects of repeated interviews and interviewer bias on young children's event memory and false reports. *Developmental Psychology, 43*, 823–837.

Quas, J. A., Qin, J. J., Schaaf, J. M., Goodman, G. S. (1997). Individual differences in children's and adults' suggestibility and false event memory. *Learning and Individual Differences, 9*, 359–390.

Quas, J. A., Rush, E. B., Yim, I. S., & Nikolayev, M. (2014). Effects of stress on memory in children and adolescents: Testing causal connections. *Memory, 22*, 616–632.

Quas, J. A., & Schaaf, J. M. (2002). Children's memories of experienced and nonexperienced events following repeated interviews. *Journal of Experimental Child Psychology, 83*, 304–338.

Quas, J. A., Schaaf, J. M., Alexander, K. W., & Goodman, G. S. (2000). Do you really remember it happening or do you only remember being asked about it happening? Children's source monitoring in forensic contexts. In K. P. Roberts & M. Blades (Eds.), *Children's source monitoring* (pp. 197–226). Mahwah, NJ: Erlbaum.

Quas, J. A., Yim, I. S., Rush, E., & Sumaroka, M. (2012). Hypothalamic pituitary adrenal axis and sympathetic activation: Joint predictors of memory in children, adolescents, and adults. *Biological Psychology, 89*(2), 335–341.

Rand Corporation. (1975). *The criminal investigation process (Vols. 1–3). Rand Corporation Technical Report* (F-1776-DOJ, R-1777-DOJ). Santa Monica, CA: Rand.

Raskin, D. C., & Esplin, P. W. (1991a). Assessment of children's statements of sexual abuse. In J. Doris (Ed.), *The suggestibility of children's recollections* (pp. 153–164). Washington, DC: American Psychological Association.

Raskin, D. C., & Esplin, P. W. (1991b). Commentary: Response to Wells, Loftus, and McGough. In J. Doris (Ed.), *The suggestibility of children's recollections* (pp. 172–176). Washington, DC: American Psychological Association.

Raskin, D. C., & Esplin, P. W. (1991c). Statement validity assessments: Interview procedures and content analyses of children's statements of sexual abuse. *Behavioral Assessment, 13*, 265–291.

Raskin, D. C., & Yuille, J. (1989). Problems of evaluating interviews of children in sexual abuse cases. In S. J. Ceci, M. P. Toglia, & D. F. Ross (Eds.), *Perspectives on children's testimony* (pp. 184–207). New York, NY: Springer.

Rischke, A. E., Roberts, K. P., & Price, H. L. (2011). Using spaced learning principles to translate knowledge into behavior: Evidence from investigative interviews of alleged child abuse victims. *Journal of Police and Criminal Psychology, 26*, 58–67.

Ratner, H. H. (1984). Memory demands and the development of young children's memory. *Child Development, 55*, 2173–2191.

Reese, E. (2002). Social factors in the development of autobiographical memory: The state of the art. *Social Development, 11*, 124–142.

Reese, E., Haden, C. A., Baker-Ward, L., Bauer, P., Fivush, R., & Ornstein, P. A. (2011). Coherence of personal narratives across the lifespan: A multidimensional model and coding method. *Journal of Cognition and Development, 12*, 424–462.

Reese, E., Haden, C. A., & Fivush, R. (1993). Mother-child conversations about the past: Relationships of style and memory over time. *Cognitive Development, 8*, 403–430.

Reich, P. A. (1986). *Language development*. Englewood Cliffs, NJ: Prentice-Hall.
Reinhold, R. (1990, January 25). How lawyers and media turned the McMartin case into a tragic media circus. *The New York Times*, p. 1D.
Reyna, V. F., & Brainerd, C. J. (1997). Fuzzy-trace theory: An interim synthesis. *Learning and Individual Differences*, 7, 1–75.
Ricci, C. M., & Beal, C. R. (1998). Child witnesses: Effect of event knowledge on memory and suggestibility. *Journal of Applied Developmental Psychology*, 19, 305–317.
Rivard, J. R., & Schreiber Compo, N. (2017). Self-reported current practices in child forensic interviewing: Training, tools, and pre-interview preparation. *Behavioral Sciences & the Law*, 35, 253–268.
Roberts, K. P. (2000). An overview of theory and research on children's source monitoring. In K. P. Roberts & M. Blades (Eds.), *Children's source monitoring* (pp. 11–57). Mahwah, NJ: Erlbaum.
Roberts, K. P. (2002). Children's ability to distinguish between memories from multiple sources: Implications for the quality and accuracy of eyewitness statements. *Developmental Review*, 22, 403–435.
Roberts, K. P., & Blades, M. (1995). Children's discriminations of memories for actual and pretend actions in a hiding task. *British Journal of Developmental Psychology*, 13, 321–333.
Roberts, K. P., & Blades, M. (1999). Children's memory and source monitoring of real-life and televised events. *Journal of Applied Developmental Psychology*, 20, 575–596.
Roberts, K. P., & Blades, M. (2000a). *Children's source monitoring*. Mahwah, NJ: Erlbaum.
Roberts, K. P., & Blades, M. (2000b). Discriminating between memories of television and real-life. In K. P. Roberts & M. Blades (Eds.), *Children's source monitoring* (pp. 147–170). Mahwah, NJ: Erlbaum.
Roberts, K. P., Brubacher, S., Drohan-Jennings, Glisic, U., Powell, M. B., & Friedman, W. J. (2015). Developmental differences in the ability to provide temporal information about repeated events. *Applied Cognitive Psychology*, 29, 407–417.
Roberts, K. P., Brubacher, S. P., Powell, M. B., & Price, H. L. (2011). Practice narratives. In M. E. Lamb, D. J. La Rooy, L. C. Malloy, & C. Katz, (Eds.). *Children's testimony: A handbook of psychological research and forensic practice* (pp. 129–145). Chichester, UK: Wiley.
Roberts, K. P., & Lamb, M. E. (1999). Children's responses when interviewers distort details during investigative interviews. *Legal and Criminological Psychology*, 4, 23–31.
Roberts, K. P., & Lamb, M. E. (2010). Reality-monitoring characteristics in confirmed and doubtful allegations of child sexual abuse. *Applied Cognitive Psychology*, 24, 1049–1079.
Roberts, K. P., Lamb, M. E., & Sternberg, K. J. (2004). The effects of rapport-building style on children's reports of a staged event. *Applied Cognitive Psychology*, 18, 189–202.
Roberts, K. P., & Powell, M. B. (2001). Describing individual incidents of sexual abuse: A review of research on the effects of multiple sources of information on children's reports. *Child Abuse & Neglect*, 25, 1643–1659.
Roberts, K. P., & Powell, M. B. (2005). The relation between inhibitory control and children's eyewitness memory. *Applied Cognitive Psychology*, 19, 1003–1018.

Roberts, K. P., & Powell, M. B. (2007). The roles of prior experience and the timing of misinformation presentation on young children's event memories. *Child Development, 78*, 1137–1152.

Robinson, J., & Briggs, P. (1997). Age trends and eye-witness suggestibility and compliance. *Psychology, Crime and Law, 3*, 187–202.

Robinson, J., & McGuire, J. (2006). Suggestibility and children with mild learning disabilities: The use of the cognitive interview. *Psychology, Crime & Law, 12*(5), 537–556.

Rocha, E. M., Marche, T. A., & Briere, J. L. (2013). The effect of forced-choice questions on children's suggestibility: A comparison of multiple-choice and yes/no questions. *Canadian Journal of Behavioural Science, 45*, 1–11.

Roebers, C. M., & Schneider, W. (2001). Individual differences in children's eyewitness recall: The influence of intelligence and shyness. *Applied Developmental Science, 5*, 9–30.

Roediger, H. L., McDermott, K. B., Pisoni, D. B., & Gallo, D. A. (2004). Illusory recollection of voices. *Memory, 12*, 586–602.

Roesler, T. A., & Wind, T. W. (1994). Telling the secret: Adult women describe their disclosures of incest. *Journal of Interpersonal Violence, 9*, 327–338.

Rose, S. A., & Blank, M. (1974). The potency of context in children's cognition: An illustration through conservation. *Child Development, 45*, 499–502.

Rotenberg, K. J. (1991). *Children's interpersonal trust: Sensitivity to lying, deception and promise violations*. New York, NY: Springer.

Rovee-Collier, C., Greco-Vigorito, C., & Hayne, H. (1993). The time-window hypothesis: Implications for categorization and memory modification. *Infant Behavior and Development, 16*, 149–176.

Rovee-Collier, C., Hartshorn, K., & DiRubbo, M. (1999). Long-term maintenance of infant memory. *Developmental Psychology, 35*, 91–102.

Rovee-Collier, C., & Hayne, H. (2000). Memory in infancy and early childhood. In E. Tulving & F. I. M. Craik (Eds.), *The Oxford handbook of memory* (pp. 267–282). Oxford, UK: Oxford University Press.

Rudy, L., & Goodman, G. S. (1991). Effects of participation on children's reports: Implications for children's testimony. *Developmental Psychology, 27*, 527–538.

Rush, E. B., Lyon, T. D., Ahern, E. C., & Quas, J. A. (2014). Disclosure suspicion bias and abuse disclosure: Comparisons between sexual and physical abuse. *Child Maltreatment, 19*, 113–118.

Rush, E. B., Quas, J. A., Yim, I. S., Nikolayev, M., Clark, S. E., & Larson, R. P. (2014). Stress, interviewer support, and children's eyewitness identification accuracy. *Child Development, 85*, 1292–1305.

Sales, J. M., Goldberg, A., & Parker, J. F. (2001, April). *Children's recall of a stressful event after a six-year-delay*. Poster presented at the biennial meeting of the Society for Research in Child Development, Minneapolis, Minnesota.

Salmon, K. (2001). Remembering and reporting by children: The influence of cues and props. *Clinical Psychology Review, 21*, 267–300.

Salmon, K., Bidrose, S., & Pipe, M.-E. (1995). Providing props to facilitate children's event reports: A comparison of toys and real items. *Journal of Experimental Child Psychology, 60*, 174–194.

Salmon, K., Champion, F., Pipe, M.-E., Mewton, L., & McDonald, S. (2008). The child in time: The influence of parent–child discussion about a future experience on how it is remembered. *Memory, 16*, 485–499.

Salmon, K., Mewton, L., Pipe, M.-E., & McDonald, S. (2011). Asking parents to prepare children for an event: Altering parental instructions influences children's recall. *Journal of Cognition and Development, 12*, 80–102.

Salmon, K., & Pipe, M.-E. (1997). Props and children's event reports: The impact of a 1-year delay. *Journal of Experimental Child Psychology, 65*, 261–292.

Salmon, K., & Pipe, M.-E. (2000). Recalling an event one year later: The impact of props, drawing and a prior interview. *Applied Cognitive Psychology, 14*, 99–120.

Salmon, K., Pipe, M.-E., Malloy, A., & Mackay, K. (2012). Do non-verbal aids increase the effectiveness of 'best practice' verbal interview techniques? An experimental study. *Applied Cognitive Psychology, 26*, 370–380.

Salmon, K., Price, M., & Pereira, J. K. (2002). Factors associated with young children's long-term recall of an invasive medical procedure: A preliminary investigation. *Journal of Developmental and Behavioral Pediatrics, 23*, 347–352.

Salmon, K., & Reese, E. (2015). Talking (or not talking) about the past: The influence of parent–child conversation about negative experiences on children's memories. *Applied Cognitive Psychology, 29*, 791–801.

Salmon, K., & Reese, E. (2016). The benefits of reminiscing with young children. *Current Directions in Psychological Science, 25*, 233–238.

Salmon, K., Roncolato, W., & Gleitzman, M. (2003). Children's report of emotionally laden events: Adapting the interview to the child. *Applied Cognitive Psychology, 17*, 65–80.

Santtila, P., Korkman, J., & Sandnabba, K. N. (2004). Effects of interview phase, repeated interviewing, presence of a support person, and anatomically detailed dolls on child sexual abuse interviews. *Psychology, Crime and Law, 10*, 21–35.

Sas, L., Hurley, P., Hatch, A., Malla, S., & Dick, T. (1993). *Three years after the verdict.* Ontario, Canada: London Family Court Clinic.

Sattler, J. (1998). *Clinical and forensic interviewing of children and families: Guidelines for the mental health, education, pediatric, and child maltreatment fields.* San Diego, CA: Author.

Saulny, S. (2002, December 8). Why confess to what you didn't do? [Electronic version]. *New York Times.*

Sauzier, M. (1989). Disclosure of child sexual abuse: For better or for worse. *Psychiatric Clinics of North America, 12*, 455–469.

Sayfan, L., Mitchell, E. B., Goodman, G. S., Eisen, M. L., & Qin, J. (2008). Children's expressed emotions when disclosing maltreatment. *Child Abuse & Neglect, 32*, 1026–1036.

Saykaly, C., Crossman, A., Morris, M., & Talwar, V. (2016). Question type and its effect on children's maintenance and accuracy during courtroom testimony. *Journal of Forensic Practice, 18*, 104–117.

Saywitz, K. J. (1987). Children's testimony: Age-related patterns of memory errors. In S. J. Ceci, M. P. Toglia, & D. F. Ross (Eds.), *Children's eyewitness testimony* (pp. 36–52). New York, NY: Springer.

Saywitz, K. J. (1988). The credibility of the child witness. *Family Advocate, 10*, 38.

Saywitz, K. J., & Camparo, L. (1998) Interviewing child witnesses: A developmental perspective. *Child Abuse & Neglect, 22*, 825–843.

Saywitz, K. J., & Camparo, L. B. (2013). *Evidence-based child forensic interviewing: The developmental narrative elaboration interview.* Oxford, UK: Oxford University Press.

Saywitz, K. J., & Geiselman, E. (1998). Interviewing the child witness: Maximizing completeness and minimizing error. In K. M. McConkey & S. J. Lynn (Eds.), *Truth in memory* (pp. 190–223). New York, NY: Guilford Press.

Saywitz, K. J., Geiselman, E., & Bornstein, G. (1992). Effects of cognitive interviewing, and practice on children's recall performance. *Journal of Applied Psychology, 77*, 744–756.

Saywitz, K. J., & Goodman, G. S. (1996). Interviewing children in and out of court: Current research and practice implications. In J. Briere, L. Berliner, J. A. Bulkley, C. Jenny, & T. Reid (Eds.), *The APSAC handbook on child maltreatment* (pp. 297–318). Thousand Oaks, CA: Sage Publications.

Saywitz, K. J., Goodman, G. S., Nicholas, E., & Moan, S. F. (1991). Children's memories of a physical examination involving genital touch: Implication for reports of child sexual abuse. *Journal of Consulting and Clinical Psychology, 59,* 682–691.

Saywitz, K. J., Larson, R. P., Hobbs, S. D., & Wells, C. R. (2015). Developing rapport with children in forensic interviews: Systematic review of experimental research. *Behavioral Sciences & the Law, 33,* 372–389.

Saywitz, K. J., & Lyon, T. D. (2002). Coming to grips with children's suggestibility. In M. L. Eisen, J. A. Quas, & G. S. Goodman (Eds.), *Memory and suggestibility in the forensic interview* (pp. 85–113). Mahwah, NJ: Erlbaum.

Saywitz, K. J., Lyon, T. D., & Goodman, G. S. (2011). Interviewing children. In J. E. Myers (Ed.), *APSAC Handbook on Child Maltreatment* (3rd ed., pp. 337–360). Thousand Oaks, CA: Sage.

Saywitz, K. J., Lyon, T. D., & Goodman, G. S. (2017). Interviewing children. In J. Conte & B. Klika (Eds.), *APSAC Handbook on Child Maltreatment* (4th ed., pp. 310–329). Newbury Park, CA: Sage.

Saywitz, K. J., & Moan-Hardie, S. (1994). Reducing the potential for distortion of childhood memories. *Consciousness & Cognition, 3,* 408–425.

Saywitz, K., & Nathanson, R. (1993). Children's testimony and their perceptions of stress in and out of the courtroom. *Child Abuse & Neglect, 17,* 613–622.

Saywitz, K. J., Nathanson, R., & Snyder, L. S. (1993). Credibility of child witnesses: The role of communicative competence. *Topics of Language Disorders, 13,* 59–78.

Saywitz, K., Nathanson, R., Snyder, L., & Lamphear, V. (1993). *Preparing children for the investigative and judicial process: Improving communication, memory and emotional resiliency*. Los Angeles, CA: National Center on Child Abuse and Neglect.

Saywitz, K. J., & Snyder, L. (1993). Improving children's testimony with preparation. In G. S. Goodman & B. L. Bottoms (Eds.), *Child victims, child witnesses: Understanding and improving testimony* (pp. 117–146). New York, NY: Guilford.

Saywitz, K. J., & Snyder, L. (1996). Narrative elaboration: Test of a new procedure for interviewing children. *Journal of Consulting & Clinical Psychology, 64,* 1347–1357.

Saywitz, K. J., Snyder, L., & Lamphear, V. (1996). Helping children tell what happened: A follow-up study of the narrative elaboration procedure. *Child Maltreatment, 1,* 200–212.

Saywitz, K. J., & Snyder, L., & Nathanson, R. (1999). Facilitating the communicative competence of child witness. *Applied Developmental Science, 3,* 58–68.

Saywitz, K. J., Wells, C. R., Larson, R. P., & Hobbs, S. D. (2016). Effects of interviewer support on children's memory and suggestibility: Systematic review and meta-analyses of experimental research. *Trauma, Violence, & Abuse,* 1–18. DOI: 10.1177/1524838016683457

Schaaf, J. M., Bederian-Gardner, D., & Goodman, G. S. (2015). Gating out misinformation: Can young children follow instructions to ignore false information? *Behavioral Sciences & the Law, 33,* 390–406.

Schneider, W., & Bjorklund, D. F. (1998). Memory. In W. Damon, D. Kuhn, & R. S. Siegler (Eds.), *Handbook of child psychology: Cognition, perception, and language* (5th ed., Vol. 2, pp. 467–521). New York, NY: Wiley.

Schneider, W., & Bjorklund, D. F. (2003). Memory and knowledge development. In J. Valsiner & K. Connolly (Eds.), *Handbook of developmental psychology* (pp. 370–403). London: Sage.

Schneider, W., & Pressley, M. (1997). *Memory development between two and twenty* (2nd ed.). Mahwah, NJ: Erlbaum.

Schreiber, N., Wentura, D., & Bilsky, W. (2001). "What else could he have done?" Creating false answers in child witnesses by inviting speculation. *Journal of Applied Psychology, 86*, 525–532.

Schwenck, C., Bjorklund, D. F., & Schneider, W. (2009). Developmental and individual differences in young children's use and maintenance of a selective memory strategy. *Developmental Psychology, 45*, 1034–1050.

Scoboria, A., & Fisico, S. (2013). Encouraging and clarifying "don't know" responses enhances interview quality. *Journal of Experimental Psychology. Applied, 19*, 72–82.

Scottish Executive. (2003). Section 30. Edinburgh, UK: Scottish Government.

Scottish Executive. (2007). Sections 7, 155. Edinburgh, UK: Scottish Government.

Sharman, S. J., & Powell, M. B. (2012). A comparison of adult witnesses' suggestibility across various types of leading questions. *Applied Cognitive Psychology, 26*, 48–53.

Sharman, S. J., Powell, M. B., & Roberts, K. P. (2011). Children's ability to estimate the frequency of single and repeated events, *International Journal of Police Science & Management, 13*, 234–242.

Sharp, H. (2001). Steps towards justice for people with learning disabilities as victims of crime: The important role of the police. *British Journal of Learning Disabilities, 29*, 88–92.

Shrimpton, S., Oates, K., & Hayes, S. (1998). Children's memory of events: Effects of stress, age, time delay and location of interview. *Applied Cognitive Psychology, 12*(2), 133–143.

Sigelman, C. K., Budd, E. C., Spanhel, C. L., & Schoenrock, C. J. (1981). When in doubt, say yes: Acquiescence in interviews with mentally retarded persons. *Mental Retardation, 19*, 53–58.

Simcock, G., & Hayne, H. (2002). Breaking the barrier? Children fail to translate their preverbal memories into language. *Psychological Science, 13*, 225–231.

Sinclair, B. B. (1999). Predicting the impact of child sexual abuse: A model of attachment, coping, and disclosure. *Dissertation Abstracts International: Section B: The Sciences and Engineering, 60*(3-B), 1316.

Sjöberg, R. L., & Lindblad, F. (2002). Delayed disclosure and disrupted communication during forensic investigation of child sexual abuse: A study of 47 corroborated cases. *Acta Paediatrica, 91*, 1391–1396.

Skowronek, J. S., Leichtman, M. D., & Pillemer, D. B. (2008). Long-term episodic memory in children with Attention-Deficit/Hyperactivity Disorder. *Learning Disabilities Research & Practice, 23*, 25–35.

Slackman, E., & Nelson, K. (1984). Acquisition of an unfamiliar script in story form by young children. *Child Development, 55*, 329–340.

Smith, R. M., Powell, M. B., & Lum, J. (2009). The relationship between job status, interviewing experience, gender, and police officers, adherence to open-ended questions. *Legal and Criminological Psychology, 14*, 51–63.

Smith, B. S., Ratner, H. H., & Hobart, C. J. (1987). The role of cueing and organization in children's memory for events. *Journal of Experimental Child Psychology, 44*, 1–24.

Smith, D., Letourneau, E. J., Saunders, B. E., Kilpatrick, D. G., Resnick, H. S., & Best, C. L. (2000). Delay in disclosure of childhood rape: Results from a national survey. *Child Abuse & Neglect, 24*, 273–287.

Smith, S. M. (1988) Environmental context dependent memory. In G. M. Davies, & D. M. Thomson (Eds.), *Memory in context: Context in memory*. Chichester, UK: Wiley.

Snyder, L. S., & Lindstedt, D. E. (1995). Children's courtroom narratives: Competence, credibility, and the communicative contract. *Topics in Language Disorders, 15*, 16–29.

Somer, E., & Szwarcberg, S. (2001). Variables in delayed disclosure of childhood sexual abuse. *American Journal of Orthopsychiatry, 71*, 332–341.

Son, L. K., & Simon, D. A. (2012). Distributed learning: Data, metacognition, and educational implications. *Educational Psychology Review, 24*, 379–399.

Sorensen, T., & Snow, B. (1991). How children tell: The process of disclosure of child sexual abuse. *Child Welfare, 70*, 3–15.

Steller, M., & Koehnken, G. (1989). Criteria-based statement analysis. In D. C. Raskin (Ed.), *Psychological Methods in Criminal Investigation and Evidence* (pp. 217–245). New York, NY: Springer.

Steller, M., Wellerhaus, P., & Wolf, T. (1988, June). *Empirical validation of criteria based content analysis*. Paper presented at NATO Advanced Study Institute on Credibility Assessment, Maratea, Italy.

Sternberg, K. J., Lamb, M. E., Davies, G. A., & Westcott, H. L. (2001). The memorandum of good practice: Theory versus application. *Child Abuse & Neglect, 25*, 669–681.

Sternberg, K. J., Lamb, M. E., & Dawud-Noursi, S. (1998). Using multiple informants to understand domestic violence and its effects. In G. W. Holden, R. Geffner, & E. N. Jouriles (Eds.), *Children exposed to marital violence: Theory, research, and applied issues* (pp. 121–156). Washington, DC: American Psychological Association.

Sternberg, K. J., Lamb, M. E., Esplin, P. W., & Baradaran, L. (1999). Using a scripted protocol to guide investigative interview: A pilot study. *Applied Developmental Science*, 70–76.

Sternberg, K. J., Lamb, M. E., Esplin, P. W., Orbach, Y., & Hershkowitz, I. (2002). Using a structured protocol to improve the quality of investigative interviews. In M. Eisen, G. S. Goodman, & J. Quas (Eds.), *Memory and suggestibility in the forensic interview* (pp. 409–436). Mahwah, NJ: Erlbaum.

Sternberg, K. J., Lamb, M. E., Greenbaum, C., Cicchetti, D., Dawud, S., Cortes, R. M., Krispin, O. et al. (1993). Effects of domestic violence on children's behavior problems and depression. *Developmental Psychology, 29*, 44–52.

Sternberg, K. J., Lamb, M. E., & Hershkowitz, I. (1996). Child sexual abuse investigations in Israel. *Criminal Justice and Behavior, 23*, 322–337.

Sternberg, K. J., Lamb, M. E., Hershkowitz, I., Esplin, P. W., Redlich, A., & Sunshine, N. (1996). The relation between investigative utterance types and the informativeness of child witnesses. *Journal of Applied Developmental Psychology, 17*, 439–451.

Sternberg, K. J., Lamb, M. E., Hershkowitz, I., Yudilevitch, L., Orbach, Y., Esplin, P. W., & Hovav, M. (1997). Effects of introductory style on children's abilities to describe experiences of sexual abuse. *Child Abuse & Neglect, 21*, 1133–1146.

Sternberg, K. J., Lamb, M. E., Orbach, Y., Esplin, P. W., & Mitchell, S. (2001). Use of a structured investigative protocol enhances young children's responses to free recall prompts in the course of forensic interviews. *Journal of Applied Psychology, 86*, 997–1005.

Stevenson, K. M., Leung, P., & Cheung, K. M. (1992). Competency-based evaluation of interviewing skills in child sexual abuse cases. *Social Work Research and Abstracts, 28*, 11–16.

Steward, M. S. (1993). Understanding children's memories of medical procedures: "He didn't touch me and it didn't hurt!" In C. A. Nelson (Ed.), *Memory and affect in development* (pp. 171–225). Hillsdale, NJ: Erlbaum.

Steward, M. S., O'Connor, J., Acredolo, C., & Steward, D. S. (1996). The trauma and memory of cancer treatment in children. In M. H. Bornstein & J. L. Genevro (Eds.), *Child development and behavioral pediatrics. Crosscurrents in contemporary psychology* (pp. 105–127). Mahwah, NJ: Erlbaum.

Steward, M. S., Steward, D. S., Farquar, L., Myers, J. E. B., Reinhart, M., Welker, J., Joye, N., Driskill, J., & Morgan, J. (1996). Interviewing young children about body touch and handling. *Monographs of the Society for Research in Child Development, 61*(4–5, Serial No. 248).

Stobbs, G., & Kebbell, M. R. (2003). Jurors' perception of witnesses with intellectual disabilities and the influence of expert evidence. *Journal of Applied Research in Intellectual Disabilities, 16*, 107–114.

Stolzenberg, S. N., & Lyon, T. D. (2014). How attorneys question children about the dynamics of sexual abuse and disclosure in criminal trials. *Psychology, Public Policy, and Law, 20*, 19–30.

Stolzenberg, S. N., & Lyon, T. D. (2015). Repeated self-and peer-review leads to continuous improvement in child interviewing performance. *Journal of Forensic Social Work, 5*, 20–28.

Stolzenberg, S. N., & Lyon, T. D. (2016). "Where were your clothes?" Eliciting descriptions of clothing placement from children alleging sexual abuse in criminal trials and forensic interviews. *Legal and Criminological Psychology, 22*, 197–212.

Stolzenberg, S., & Pezdek, K. (2013). Interviewing child witnesses: The effect of forced confabulation on event memory. *Journal of Experimental Child Psychology, 114*, 77–88.

Storbeck, J., & Clore, G. L. (2005). With sadness comes accuracy; with happiness, false memory: Mood and the false memory effect. *Psychological Science, 16*, 785–791.

Strange, D., Garry, M., & Sutherland, R. (2003). Drawing out children's false memories. *Applied Cognitive Psychology, 17*, 607–619.

Strange, D., & Hayne, H. (2013). The devil is in the detail: Children's recollection of details about their prior experiences. *Memory, 21*, 431–443.

Stroud, D., Martens, S. L., & Barker, J. (2000). Criminal investigation of child sexual abuse: A comparison of cases referred to the prosecutor to those not referred. *Child Abuse & Neglect, 24*, 689–700.

Sullivan, P. M., & Knutson, J. F. (1998). The association between child maltreatment and disabilities in a hospital-based epidemiological study. *Child Abuse and Neglect, 22*, 271–288.

Sullivan, P. M., & Knutson, J. F. (2000). Maltreatment and disabilities: A population-based epidemiological study. *Child Abuse and Neglect, 24,* 1257–1273.

Summit, R. (1983). The child sexual abuse accommodation syndrome. *Child Abuse & Neglect, 7,* 177–193.

Sutherland, R., Pipe, M.-E., Schick, K., Murray, J., & Gobbo, C. (2003). Knowing in advance: The impact of prior event information on memory and event knowledge. *Journal of Experimental Child Psychology, 84,* 244–263.

Swanson, H. L. (1990). Executive processing differences between learning-disabled, mildly retarded, and normal achieving children *Journal of Abnormal Child Psychology, 18,* 549–563.

Swanson, H. L., & Trahan, M. (1990). Naturalistic memory in learning disabled children. *Learning Disability Quarterly, 13,* 82–95.

Sweet, R. C. (1966). *Educational attainment and attitude toward school as a function of feedback in the form of teachers' written comments* (Tech. Rep. No. 15). Madison, WI: Wisconsin Research and Development Center for Cognitive Learning.

Sweller, J., Van Merrienboer, J. J., & Paas, F. G. (1998). Cognitive architecture and instructional design. *Educational Psychology Review, 10,* 251–296.

Talwar, V., Lee, K., Bala, N., & Lindsay, R. C. L. (2002). Children's conceptual knowledge of lying and its relation to their actual behaviors: Implications for court competence examinations. *Law and Human Behavior, 26,* 395–415.

Talwar, V., Lee, K., Bala, N., & Lindsay, R. C. L. (2004). Children's lie-telling to conceal a parent's transgression: Legal implications. *Law and Human Behavior, 28,* 411–435.

Tannock, R., Purvis, K. L., & Schachar, R. J. (1993). Narrative abilities in children with attention deficit hyperactivity disorder and normal peers. *Journal of Abnormal Child Psychology, 21,* 103–117.

Tanweer, T., Rathbone, C. J., & Souchay, C. (2010). Autobiographical memory, autonoetic consciousness, and identity in Asperger syndrome. *Neuropsychologia, 48,* 900–908.

Teoh, Y. S., & Lamb, M. E. (2010). Preparing children for investigative interviews: Rapport-building, instruction, and evaluation. *Applied Developmental Science, 14,* 154–163.

Teoh, Y. S., & Lamb, M. E. (2013). Interviewer demeanor in forensic interviews of children. *Psychology, Crime & Law, 19,* 145–159.

Teoh, Y. S., Yang, P. J., Lamb, M. E., & Larsson, A. S. (2010). Do human figure diagrams help alleged victims of sexual abuse provide elaborate and clear accounts of physical contact with alleged perpetrators? *Applied Cognitive Psychology, 24,* 287–300.

Terr, L. C. (1988). What happens to early memories of trauma? A study of twenty children under age five at the time of documented traumatic events. *Journal of the American Academy of Child and Adolescent Psychiatry, 27,* 96–104.

Tessler, M., & Nelson, K. (1994). Making memories: The influence of joint encoding on later recall by young children. *Consciousness & Cognition, 3,* 307–326.

Testa, M., Miller, B. A., Downs, W. R., & Panek, D. (1992). The moderating impact of social support following childhood sexual abuse. *Violence and Victims, 7,* 173–186.

The Swedish Code of Judicial Procedures (SFS). (1942). The Swedish Code of Statutes (SFS). No. 740.

Thierry, K. L., Goh, C. L., Murray, J., & Pipe, M.-E. (2005). Effects of rehearsal and modality of test on children's source-monitoring performance. *Journal of Experimental Psychology: Applied*, *11*, 33–44.

Thierry, K. L., Lamb, M. E., & Orbach, Y. (2003). Awareness of the origin of knowledge predicts child witnesses' recall of alleged sexual and physical abuse. *Applied Cognitive Psychology*, *17*, 953–967.

Thierry, K. L., Lamb, M. E., Orbach, Y., & Pipe, M.-E. (2004, March). *The utility of anatomical dolls during interviews with alleged sexual abuse victims.* Poster session presented at the annual meeting of the American Psychology-Law Society, Scottsdale, AZ.

Thierry, K. L., Lamb, M. E., Orbach, Y., & Pipe, M.-E. (2005). Developmental differences in the function and use of anatomical dolls during interviews with alleged sexual abuse victims. *Journal of Consulting and Clinical Psychology*, *73*, 1135–1134.

Thierry, K. L., & Spence, M. J. (2002). Source-monitoring training facilitates preschoolers' eyewitness memory performance. *Developmental Psychology*, *38*, 428–437.

Thierry, K. L., Spence, M. J., & Memon, A. (2001). Before misinformation is encountered: Source monitoring decreases child witness suggestibility. *Journal of Cognition and Development*, *2*, 1–26.

Thompson, C. A., & Opfer, J. E. (2010). How 15 hundred is like 15 cherries: Effect of progressive alignment on representational changes in numerical cognition. *Child Development*, *81*, 1768–1786.

Thoresen, C., Lonnum, K., Melinder, A., Stridbeck, U., & Magnussen, S. (2006). Theory and practice in interviewing young children: A study of Norwegian police interviews 1985–2002. *Psychology, Crime and Law*, *12*, 629–640.

Titcomb, A. L., & Reyna, V. F. (1995). Memory interference and misinformation effects. In F. Dempster & C. Brainerd (Eds.), *Interference and inhibition in cognition* (pp. 263–294). San Diego, CA: Academic Press.

Tobey, A. E., & Goodman, G. S. (1992). Children's eyewitness memory: Effects of participation and forensic context. *Child Abuse & Neglect*, *16*, 779–796.

Toglia, M. P., Ceci, S. J., & Ross, D. F. (1989, April). *Prestige vs. source monitoring in children's suggestibility*. Paper presented to the Society for Research in Child Development, Kansas City, MO.

Tulving, E. (1972). Episodic and semantic memory. In E. Tulving & W. Donaldson (Eds.), *Organization of memory*. Amsterdam, Netherlands: Elsevier.

Tulving, E. (1983). *Elements of episodic memory*. Oxford: Oxford University Press.

Tulving, E. (2002). Episodic memory: From mind to brain. *Annual Review of Psychology*, *53*, 1–25.

Tulving, E., & Thomson, D. M. (1973). Encoding specificity and retrieval processes in episodic memory. *Psychological Review*, *80*, 359–380.

Tustin, K., & Hayne, H. (2010). Defining the boundary: Age-related changes in childhood amnesia. *Developmental Psychology*, *46*, 1049.

Tye, M. J. C., Henderson, S. A., & Honts, C. R. (1995, January). *Evaluating children's testimonies: CBCA and lay subjects*. Paper presented at meeting of CRIME CON: International Internet Conference on Crime and Criminal Justice, Little Rock, AR.

Uhl, E. R., Camilletti, C. R., Scullin, M. H. & Wood, J. M. (2016), Under pressure: Individual differences in children's suggestibility in response to intense social influence. *Social Development*, *25*, 422–434.

Underwood, B. J. (1969). Attributes of memory. *Psychological Review*, *76*, 559–573.

Undeutsch, U. (1982). Statement reality analysis. In A. Trankell (Ed.), *Reconstructing the past: The role of psychologists in criminal trials* (pp. 27–56). Stockholm, Sweden: Nordstedt & Sons.

Undeutsch, U. (1989). The development of statement reality analysis. In J. C. Yuille (Ed.), *Credibility assessment* (pp. 101–120). Dordrecht, Netherlands: Kluwer.

Ussher, J. M., & Dewberry, C. (1995). The nature and long-term effects of childhood sexual abuse: A survey of adult women survivors in Britain. *British Journal of Clinical Psychology*, *34*, 177–192.

Vallano, J. P., Evans, V.R., Schreiber-Compo, N., & Kieckhaefer, J. M. (2015). Rapport building during witness and suspect interviews: A survey of law enforcement. *Applied Cognitive Psychology*, *29*, 369–380.

Vicari, S. (2004). Memory development and intellectual disabilities. *Acta Paediatrica*, *93*(s445), 60–63.

Vizard, E., & Tranter, M. (1988). Helping young children to describe experiences of child sexual abuse: General issue. In A. Bentovim, A. Elton, J. Hildebrand, M. Tranter, & E. Vizard (Eds.), *Child sexual abuse within the family: Assessment and treatment* (pp. 84–104). Bristol: John Wright.

Vrij, A. (2000). *Detecting lies and deceit: The psychology of lying and the implications for professional practice*. Chichester, UK: Wiley.

Vrij, A., & Baxter, M. (2000). Accuracy and confidence in detecting truths and lies in elaborations and denials: Truth bias, lie bias and individual differences. *Expert Evidence*, *7*, 25–36.

Vrij, A., Edward, K., & Bull, R. (2001). Police officers ability to detect deceit: The benefit of indirect deception detection measures. *Legal and Criminological Psychology*, *6*, 185–196.

Vrij, A., & Fisher, R. P. (2016). Which lie detection tools are ready for use in the criminal justice system?. *Journal of Applied Research in Memory and Cognition*, *5*(3), 302–307.

Vrij, A., Fisher, R. P., Blank, H., Leal, S., & Mann, S. (2017). A cognitive approach to elicit verbal and nonverbal cues to deceit. In J.-W. van Prooijen & P. A. M. van Lange (Eds.), *Cheating, corruption, and concealment: The roots of dishonesty* (pp. 284–308). Cambridge, UK: Cambridge University Press.

Vrij, A., & Granhag, P. A. (2012). Eliciting cues to deception and truth: What matters are the questions asked. *Journal of Applied Research in Memory and Cognition*, *1*, 110–117.

Vrij, A., Harden, F., Terry, J., Edward, K., & Bull, R. (2001). The influence of personal characteristics, stakes and lie complexity on the accuracy and confidence to detect deceit. In R. Roesch, R. R. Corrado, & R. J. Dempster (Eds.), *Psychology in the courts: International advances in knowledge*. Amsterdam, Netherlands: Harwood Academic.

Vrij, A., & Van Wijngaarden, J. J. (1994). Will truth come out? Two studies about the detection of false statements expressed by children. *Expert Evidence*, *3*, 78– 84.

Wade, A., & Westcott, H. (1997). No easy answers: Children's perspectives on investigative interviews. *Perspectives on the memorandum. Policy, practice and research in investigative interviewing*. Aldershot, UK: Arena.

Wagland, P., & Bussey, K. (2005). Factors that facilitate and undermine children's beliefs about truth telling. *Law and Human Behavior*, *29*, 639–655.

Walker, A. G. (1993). Questioning young children in court: A linguistic case study. *Law and Human Behavior, 17,* 59–81.
Walker, A. G. (1994). *Handbook on questioning children: A linguistic perspective.* Washington, DC: American Bar Association.
Walker, A. G., Kenniston, J., & Inada, S. S. (2013). *Handbook on questioning children: A linguistic perspective* (3rd ed.). Washington, DC: American Bar Association.
Walker, A. G., & Warren, A. R. (1995). The language of the child abuse interview: Asking the questions, understanding the answers. In T. Ney (Ed.), *True and false allegations of child sexual abuse: Assessment and case management* (pp. 153–162). New York, NY: Brunner/Mazel.
Walker, N. E., & Hunt, J. S. (1998). Interviewing child victim-witnesses: How you ask is what you get. In C. R. Thompson, D. Herrman, J. D. Read, D. Bruce, D. Payne, & M. P. Toglia (Eds.), *Eyewitness memory: Theoretical and applied perspectives* (pp. 55–87). Mahwah, NJ: Erlbaum.
Walker, N. E., Lunning, S., & Eilts, J. (1996, June). *Do children respond accurately to forced choice questions? Yes or no.* Paper presented at the meeting of the NATO Advanced Study Institute: Recollections of Trauma: Scientific Research and Clinical Practice, Talmont Saint Hilaire, France.
Wandrey, L., Lyon, T. D., Quas, J. A., & Friedman, W. J. (2012). Maltreated children's ability to estimate temporal location and numerosity of placement changes and court visits. *Psychology, Public Policy, and Law, 18,* 79–104.
Wang, Q. (2016). Remembering the self in cultural contexts: A cultural dynamic theory of autobiographical memory. *Memory Studies, 9,* 295–304.
Wang, Q., Bui, V. K., & Song, Q. (2015). Narrative organisation at encoding facilitated children's long-term episodic memory. *Memory, 23,* 602–611.
Wang, Q., Peterson, C., & Hou, Y. (2010). Children dating childhood memories. *Memory, 18,* 754–762.
Warren, A., Hulse-Trotter, K., & Tubbs, E. C. (1991). Inducing resistance to suggestibility in children. *Law and Human Behavior, 15,* 273–285.
Warren, A. R., & Lane, P. (1995). Effects of timing and type of questioning on eyewitness accuracy and suggestibility. In M. S. Zaragoza, J. R. Graham, G. C. N. Hall, R. Hirschman, & Y. S. Ben-Porath (Eds.), *Memory and testimony in the child witness: Individual, social, and community issues* (pp. 44–60). Thousand Oaks, CA: Sage.
Warren, A. R. & McCloskey, L.A. (1997). Language in social contexts. In S. B. Gleason (Ed.), *The development of language* (4th ed., pp. 210–258). New York, NY: Allyn & Bacon.
Warren, A. R., & McGough, L. S. (1996). Research on children's suggestibility: Implications for the investigative interview. *Criminal Justice and Behavior, 23,* 269–303.
Warren, A. R., & Swartwood, J. N. (1992). Developmental issues in flashbulb memory research: Children recall the Challenger event. In E. Winograd & U. Neisser (Eds.), *Affect and accuracy in recall: Studies of "flashbulb" memories. Emory symposia in cognition, 4* (pp. 95–120). New York, NY: Cambridge University Press.
Warren, A. R., Woodall, C. E., Hunt, J. S., & Perry, N. W. (1996). "It sounds good in theory, but": Do investigative interviewers follow guidelines based on memory research? *Child Maltreatment, 1,* 231–245.
Warren, A. R., Woodall, C. E., Thomas, M., Nunno, M., Keeney, J. M., Larson, S. M., & Stadfeld, J. A. (1999). Assessing the effectiveness of a training

program for interviewing child witnesses. *Applied Developmental Science, 3,* 128–135.

Waterman, A. H., Blades, M., & Spencer, C. (2000). Do children try to answer nonsensical questions? *British Journal of Developmental Psychology, 18,* 211–225.

Waterman, A. H., Blades, M., & Spencer, C. (2001). Interviewing children and adults: The effect of question format on the tendency to speculate. *Applied Cognitive Psychology, 15,* 521–531.

Waterman, A. H., Blades, M., & Spencer, C. (2004). Indicating when you do not know the answer: The effect of question format and interviewer knowledge on children's "don't know" responses. *British Journal of Developmental Psychology, 22,* 335–348.

Wells, G. L., & Loftus, E. F. (1991). Commentary: Is this child fabricating? Reactions to a new assessment technique. In J. Doris (Ed.), *The suggestibility of children's recollections* (pp. 168–171). Washington, DC: American Psychological Association.

Wells, G. L., Turtle, J. W., & Luus, C. A. E. (1989). The perceived credibility of child eyewitnesses: What happens when they use their own words? In S. J. Ceci, D. F. Ross, & M. P. Toglia (Eds.), *Perspectives on children's testimony* (pp. 23–46). New York, NY: Springer.

Wesson, M., & Salmon, K. (2001). Drawing and showing: Helping children to report emotionally laden events. *Applied Cognitive Psychology, 15,* 301–320.

Westcott, H. L. (1991). The abuse of disabled children: A review of the literature. *Child Care, Health and Development, 17,* 243–258.

Westcott, H. L. (1992). The cognitive interview: A useful tool for social workers? *British Journal of Social Work, 22,* 519–533.

Westcott, H. L. (1993). *Abuse of children and adults with disabilities.* London: NSPCC.

Westcott, H. L., & Davies, G. M. (1993). Children's welfare in the courtroom: Preparation and protection of the child witness. *Children & Society, 7,* 388–396.

Westcott, H. L., Davies, G. M., & Clifford, B. R. (1991). Adults' perceptions of children's videotaped truthful and deceptive statements. *Children & Society, 5,* 123–135.

Westcott, H. L., & Kynan, S. (2004). The application of a "story-telling" framework to investigative interviews for suspected child sexual abuse. *Legal and Criminological Psychology, 9,* 37–56.

Westcott, H. L., & Jones, D. P. H. (1999). Annotation: The abuse of disabled children. *Journal of Child Psychology and Psychiatry, 40,* 497–506.

Wilgoren, J. (2003, January 10). Illinois expected to free four inmates on death row [Electronic version]. *The New York Times.*

Wilkinson, J. (1988). Context effects in children's event memory. In M. M. Gruneberg, P. E. Morris, & R.N. Sykes (Eds.), *Practical aspects of memory: Current research issues* (Vol. *1*; pp. 107–111). New York, NY: Wiley.

Willcock, E., Morgan, K., & Hayne, H. (2006). Body maps do not facilitate children's reports of touch. *Applied Cognitive Psychology, 20,* 607–615.

Williams, C. (1995). *Invisible victims: Crime and abuse against people with learning difficulties.* London, UK: Jessica Kingsley Publishers.

Williams, J. M. G. (1996). Depression and the specificity of autobiographical memory. In D. C. Rubin (Ed.), *Remembering out past: Studies in autobiographical memory* (pp. 244–267). Cambridge, UK: Cambridge University Press.

Williams, J. M. G., & Dritschel, B. H. (1992). Categoric and extended autobiographical memories. In M. A. Conway, D. C. Rubin, H. Spiner, & W. A. Wagenaar (Eds.), *Theoretical perspectives on autobiographical memory* (pp. 391–412). London: Kluwer Academic.

Wilson, J. C., & Pipe, M.-E. (1989). The effects of cues on young children's recall of real events. *New Zealand Journal of Psychology, 18*, 65–70.

Wissink, I. B., Van Vugt, E., Moonen, X., Stams, G. J. J., & Hendriks, J. (2015). Sexual abuse involving children with an intellectual disability (ID): A narrative review. *Research in Developmental Disabilities, 36*, 20–35.

Wolfman, M. (2016). *Understanding and addressing challenges faced by forensic interviewers in their work with children* (Doctoral dissertation, Victoria University of Wellington). Retrieved from http://researcharchive.vuw.ac.nz/handle/10063/5144

Wolfman, M., Brown, D., & Jose, P. (2016a). Taking stock: Evaluating the conduct of forensic interviews with children in New Zealand. *Psychology, Crime & Law, 22*, 1–18.

Wolfman, M., Brown, D., & Jose, P. (2016b). Talking past each other: Interviewer and child verbal exchanges in forensic interviews. *Law and Human Behavior, 40*, 107–117.

Wolfman, M., Brown, D., & Jose, P. (2017a). Examining forensic interviewers' perceptions of practice-focused supervision. *Australian & New Zealand Journal of Criminology.* 50, 566–581. First published date: July 5, 2016. DOI: 10.1177/0004865816655588

Wolfman, M., Brown, D., & Jose, P. (2017b). The use of visual aids in forensic interviews with children. Manuscript under review.

Wood, B., Orsak, C., Murphy, M., & Cross, H. J. (1996). Semistructured child sexual abuse interviews: Interview and child characteristics related to credibility of disclosure. *Child Abuse & Neglect, 20*, 81–92.

Wood, J. A., Schreiber, N., Martinex, K., McLaurin, K., Stork, R., Velarde, L. D., Garven, S., & Malpass, R. S. (1998, March). *Child interviewing techniques in two "ritual abuse" daycare cases: A quantitative comparison*, Paper presented at the American Psychology and Law Society conference. Redondo Beach, CA.

Wood, J. M., McClure, K. A., & Birch, R. A. (1996). Suggestions for improving interviews in child protection agencies. *Child Maltreatment, 1*, 223–230.

Woolley, J. D., & Ghossainy, M. (2013). Revisiting the fantasy–reality distinction: Children as naïve skeptics. *Child Development, 84*, 1496–1510.

Woolley, J. D., & Wellman, H. M. (1993). Origin and truth: Young children's understanding of imaginary mental representations. *Child Development, 64*, 1–17.

Wright, R., Guadagno, B. L., & Powell, M. B. (2009). An evaluation of a self-initiated practice exercise for investigative interviewers of children. *International Journal of Police Science & Management, 11*, 366–376.

Wright, R., & Powell, M. B. (2006). Investigative interviewers' perceptions of their difficulty in adhering to open-ended questions with child witnesses. *International Journal of Police Science & Management, 8*, 316–325.

Wright, R., Powell, M. B., & Ridge, D. (2007). What criteria do police officers use to measure the success of an interview with a child? *Psychology, Crime & Law, 13*, 395–404.

Wyatt, G. E., & Newcomb, M. D. (1990). Internal and external mediators of women's sexual abuse in childhood. *Journal of Consulting and Clinical Psychology, 58*, 758.

Yi, M., Jo, E., & Lamb, M. E. (2016). Effects of the NICHD protocol training on child investigative interview quality in Korean police officers. *Journal of Police and Criminal Psychology, 31*, 155–163.

Yi, M., Lamb, M. E., & Jo, E. (2015). The quality of Korean police officers' investigative interviews with alleged sexual abuse victims as revealed by self-report and observation. *Journal of Police and Criminal Psychology, 30*, 274–281.

Yii, S. L. B., Powell, M. B., & Guadagno, B. (2014). The association between investigative interviewers' knowledge of question type and adherence to best-practice interviewing. *Legal and Criminological Psychology, 19*, 270–281.

Young, K., Powell, M. B., & Dudgeon, P. (2003). Individual differences in children's suggestibility: A comparison between intellectually disabled and mainstream samples. *Personality and Individual Differences, 35*, 31–49.

Yuille, J. C. (1988). The systematic assessment of children's testimony. *Canadian Psychologist, 29*, 247–262.

Zajac, R., & Brown, D. A. (2017). Conducting successful memory interviews with children. *Child and Adolescent Social Work Journal.* Online first publication available from 15 December 2017. https://doi.org/10.1007/s10560-017-0527-z

Zajac, R., Gross, J., & Hayne, H. (2003). Asked and answered: Questioning children in the courtroom. *Psychiatry, Psychology and Law, 10*, 199–209.

Zajac, R., Jury, E., & O'Neill, S. (2009). The role of psychosocial factors in young children's responses to cross-examination style questioning. *Applied Cognitive Psychology, 23*, 918–935.

Zajac, R., O'Neill, S., & Hayne, H. (2012). Disorder in the courtroom? Child witnesses under cross-examination. *Developmental Review, 32*, 181–204.

Zajac, R., Westera, N., & Kaladelfos, A. (2018). The "Good Old Days" of Courtroom Questioning: Changes in the Format of Child Cross-Examination Questions Over 60 Years. *Child maltreatment*, in press.

Zaragoza, M. S., Dahlgren, D., & Muench, J. (1992). The role of memory impairment in children's suggestibility. In M. L. Howe, C. J. Brainerd, & V. F. Reyna (Eds.), *Development of long-term retention* (pp. 184–216). New York, NY: Springer.

Zaragoza, M. S., & Lane, S. M. (1994). Source misattributions and the suggestibility of eyewitness memory. *Journal of Experimental Psychology: Learning, Memory, & Cognition, 20*, 934–945.

Zaragoza, M. S., & Mitchell, K. J. (1996). Repeated exposure to suggestion and the creation of false memories. *Psychological Science, 7*, 294–300.

Zigler, E. F. (1969). Developmental versus difference theories of mental retardation and the problem of motivation. *American Journal of Mental Deficiency, 73*, 536–556.

Zigler, E. F., & Balla, D. (1982). Motivational and personality factors in the performance of the retarded. In E. F. Zigler & D. Balla (Eds.), *Mental retardation: The developmental-difference controversy* (pp. 9–26). Hillsdale, NJ: Erlbaum.

Index

abandonment 52
abuse
   children with intellectual
      disabilities (CWID) 138–40
   concealing 139
   generating event-specific labels
      for 22
   likelihood of 215–19
   pre-interview discussions of 163
   severity of 39
   see also sexual abuse; physical
      abuse
abusive experiences 16
accuracy 4, 111–12
   and autism spectrum disorder
      (ASD) 150, 152
   and children's age 114
   and children with intellectual
      disabilities (CWID) 144–5
   comparing witness and suspect
      account 112–14
   effect of visual aids on 97
   and free-recall response 59, 60,
      68–9
   and open-ended prompts 113
   and open-ended questions 59
   and option-posing prompts 113
   and suggestive prompts 113
   and supportive environment 89
   and "yes/no" questions 125
   and younger children 120
accurate responding 3
action cues 124, 125, 127, 131
actions
   ability to observe
      consequences 126
   distinguishing pretend from
      real 19
   suggestive 76
adaptability 18
ADHD *see* attention deficit/
   hyperactivity disorder
adolescents
   amount of reported
      information 15
   with ASD 150
   describing temporal aspects of
      events 45
   with intellectual
      disabilities 148–57
   recalling early life events 13
age
   and accuracy of reports 114
   and action-based cues 126

Tell Me What Happened: Questioning Children About Abuse, Second Edition.
Michael E. Lamb, Deirdre A. Brown, Irit Hershkowitz, Yael Orbach, and Phillip W. Esplin.
© 2018 John Wiley & Sons Ltd. Published 2018 by John Wiley & Sons Ltd.

age (cont'd)
  and allegation rates 162
  and children's understanding of ground rules 56
  and differences in eyewitness testimony 15–16
  and event memory 16–17
  and event recall 15–16
  and interaction with the interviewer 115–16
  and memory 4, 40
  and number of elicited details 123, 124, 127
  and quality of information provided 121
  and retrieval strategies 34
  and strategy use 22
  and suggestibility 29, 31
  and temporal concepts 126
  and temporal judgments 34–5
  and time-segmenting cues 126
  see also adolescents; younger children
allegations
  false 33, 174, 230–1
  implausible 218–20, 223
  likelihood of making 122, 181
  plausible 217–20, 223
  rates 162–3, 173–4, 220–1
  see also disclosure
ambiguous statements 155
American Professional Society on the Abuse of Children (APSAC) 4, 75
anxiety
  and establishing rapport 54
  and suggestibility 19
approach-withdrawal 18
APSAC see American Professional Society on the Abuse of Children
arousal, and memory 38–9
ASD see autism spectrum disorder
assertiveness 18
attachment 18
attainment of skills 13
attention deficit/hyperactivity disorder (ADHD) 154–6
  and coherence of narratives 155
  and event recall 155
  and maltreatment 154
  and NICHD Protocol 155
  and personally-experienced events 154–5
  and physical abuse 154
  and sexual abuse 154
  and suggestibility 155
Australia 82
autism spectrum disorder (ASD) 7, 149–54, 156
  and accuracy 150, 152
  and autobiographical memory 150
  and NICHD Protocol 151–4
  and option-posing prompts 152
  and suggestibility 150
  and suggestive prompts 152
  number and accuracy of elicited details 150–2
autobiographical memory 13
  and ASD 150
  and children with intellectual disabilities (CWID) 138
  development of 34
  retrieval strategies 120
  social interactionist perspective 14
  socio-cultural perspective 14, 27
avatars 208

behavioral re-enactment 14, 32
best-practice guidelines 235
body diagrams 7, 65, 193–4
  and NICHD Protocol 194–6
boys
  allegation rates 162–3
  with intellectual disabilities 139
brain regions 14

Canada
  evaluations of interviews 82
  NICHD Protocol study 105–6
case outcomes 221–3
CBCA see Criterion Based Content Analysis
child-centered interviews 8, 68
child development 3–8, 12–15
  and responsiveness to questions 16–17, 63
  see also developmental disorders
Child Guidance Centers 105
childhood 14

Index

children with intellectual disabilities
  (CWID) 111–12, 137–60
  ability to recall events 142–3
  accuracy of responses 144–5
  chronological-age matches
    (CA) 141–4, 146–8
  coherence of reports 145–6
  credibility of 140, 145, 157–9
  and cued invitations 144
  maltreatment 7, 138
  mental-age matches (MA) 141–4,
    146–8
  narrative and autobiographical
    memory skills 138
  and number of elicited details 145
  and open-ended questions 156
  perceptions of 158–9
  and physical injury 139
  prevalence of abuse
    against 138–40
  quality of reports 145–6
  questioning strategies 146–8
  recommendations for
    interviewing 156–7
  research on 141–8
  severity of disability 143–4
  and sexual abuse 139
  and specific questions 156
  and suggestibility 138, 142
  and suggestive questions 144
  and understanding of
    inappropriate behaviors 138
  see also intellectual disabilities
children's engagement 6
children's storybooks 19–20
CI see cognitive interview
coaching 9, 33
coercive interviewing 185
cognitive control 155
cognitive interview (CI) 7, 197–8
cognitive loading techniques 185
cognitive processes 161
cognitive strategies 34
coherence
  and attention deficit/hyperactivity
    disorder (ADHD) 155
  and children with intellectual
    disabilities (CWID) 145–6
  and NICHD Protocol 234–5
  and reluctance 179
  and supportiveness 179

communicative disorders 50
complicity 52
comprehension monitoring 130
computer-assisted technologies 206–8
contamination
  and directive prompts 131
  risk of 230–1
contextual clues 94, 196–9
  NICHD Protocol 197–9
contradictory information 215
  and option-posing 60–1
  and prompts 114
  and suggestive questions 60–1
  see also self-contradictions
conversational ability 26–8
conviction rates 222–3
coping styles 18
corroborative evidence 215
credibility
  assessment 213–20
  children with intellectual
    disabilities (CWID) 140, 145,
    157–9
  evaluation 133, 140, 145
  Criterion Based Content Analysis
    (CBCA) 214–19
critical thinking 203
cross-examination 18, 19
  use of an intermediary 159
  use of language 24
cued invitations 62, 94, 111, 122,
  124–32, 136
  and children with intellectual
    disabilities (CWID) 144
  and number of elicited details 124
  and younger children 121
cued-recall prompts
  and elicited temporal
    information 135
  and errors 59
  and temporal references 35
cues
  action-based 124, 125, 127, 131
  contextual 94, 196–9
  non-verbal 59
  objects as 14
  prior responses as 16
  time-segmenting 94, 121, 124,
    126, 127
  see also retrieval cues
culture 89, 236

daycare center cases 28, 29, 33, 119
depression 42
details
  from children with intellectual
    disabilities (CWID) 145
  erroneous 191
  event-specific 22
  false 23
  forensically-relevant 124
  inaccurate 150
  from individuals with intellectual
    disabilities 149
  memory for 36
  number of 113, 116, 120,
    123–4, 127
  peripheral 116
  and verbal abilities of
    children 145
  from victims 116–17
  from witnesses 116–17
developmental disorders
  and interviewing strategies 9
  and maltreatment 7, 138
  mitigating impact 50
direct experiences 31–2
directive prompts
  accuracy 113
  responsivity to 127, 130
  risk of contamination 131
direct questions 62
disclosure 33, 162–3
  delayed 163
  emotional support for 164–7
  to family members 164
  and fear of retribution and
    abandonment 52
  and free-recall prompts 125
  informal 163
  information about 99
  motivational factors 162
  parental reports of 52
  of physical abuse 174–5
  to peers 164
  and rapport 164–7
  and reassurance 165
  reluctant 52–4, 162–74
  and suggestive prompts 93
  and time of interview 48–9, 68
  and type of questions asked 110
  see also allegations
distress 54

dolls 7, 65, 89, 190–1
  anatomically-detailed 75–7
  suggestive actions 76
  technical suggestions 76
Down syndrome 149
"draw-and-talk" procedure 191
drawings 7, 191–3

early experiences 13, 14, 40
early memories 13–14
effortful control 19
embarrassment 41, 52
emotional intelligence 203
emotionality 18
emotional support 164–7
emotions
  expression of 180–1
  negative 180–1
empathy 171
encoding 22, 41
  and attachment 18
  and negative emotions 180
  and negative experiences 31–4
  and personal experiences 31–4
  strategies to strengthen 23
  and stress 41, 117, 226
erroneous answers 120
erroneous details 191
erroneous reports 29, 120
errors
  of commission 50
  and cued-recall prompts 59
  incorporated into memory 30
  of interviewers 55–6, 90
  intrusion 19
  of omission 50
  practices inducing 96–7
  and recognition prompts 59–60,
    62, 152
  source 22
event memories
  and age 16–17
  and predictions 35
  and repeated experiences 36
  see also event recall; events
event recall
  after delay 153
  and age 15–16
  and attachment 18
  and attention deficit/hyperactivity
    disorder (ADHD) 155

and children with intellectual
   disabilities (CWID) 142–3
effects of delay 41–6, 230
and fantasy 19–20
individual differences 17
and information processing
   skills 20
and intelligence 17
and knowledge 20–1, 40
and prior experiences 36
and severity of abuse 39
and source monitoring 21–2
strategy use 22–3
and stress 38–9, 41–2, 117
and temperament 18–19
and visual aids 65
see also event memories; events
events
   chronological organization 34–5,
      37–8, 45, 132, 135
   direct participation in 32, 116
   discussing 32–4
   distressing 38–42
   emotionally salient 3
   episodic accounts of 92
   everyday 40
   false 191
   forming general representations
      of 35
   forward projection of 126
   imagined versus experienced 19
   landmark 45–6
   memorable 14, 39
   mundane 40
   naturally occurring 3
   negative 18, 40
   neutral 40, 42
   non-experienced 69, 125
   nonverbal representations of 14
   number of occurrences 35, 37–8
   personally experienced 154–5
   positive 18, 40, 42
   repeated 34–8, 57
   reverse order of 126–7
   similar 35
   staged 3, 19
   temporal aspect 34–5, 37, 45–6,
      132, 134, 135
   traumatic 14, 16, 38–43
   see also event memories; event
      recall

event-specific details 22
evidence-based practice 4, 50, 68,
   201–2, 206, 227
executive function 155
experiences
   direct 31–2
   personal 31–4
   repeated 36–7
eyewitness testimony 3
   age differences in 15–16

false allegations 33, 174
false denials 33, 165
false details 23
false memories 21
false reports 90, 185, 193
   and supportiveness 164
false responding 3
false statements 90
family violence 42
fantasy 19–20
fear
   of abandonment 52
   of consequences for others 53
   of family disruption 53
   of not being believed 53
   of retribution 52
field interviews 64
field studies 4, 6, 101–18
Finland 83–4
focused recall prompts 59, 130
forward sequencing 35, 134
free narrative reports 16
free recall prompts
   accuracy 59, 60, 62, 68–9
   and contamination 62
   and disclosures 125
   and interviews with
      suspects 183–4
   and NICHD Protocol, 93–6
   and number of elicited
      details 123–4, 131
   and open-ended questions 94
   and temporal references 35, 135
   and younger children 93,
      120, 121

gender
   and allegation rates 162–3
   and expression of emotions 181
   and intellectual disabilities 139

general invitations 122
  and number of details elicited 123
girls
  allegation rates 163
  expression of emotions 181
  with intellectual disabilities 139
ground rules 5, 54–7, 79
  children's understanding of 56
  explaining 89–91
  future directions 232–4
  preparing the child for the interview 54–63
"ground truth" information 218
guilt 42
  and reluctance of disclosure 52

Home Office 79
hospital treatment
  memory of 41
  recall of 43–4
hurricanes 39, 41, 43
hyperactivity 154
hypermnesia 49, 50

images 20
imaginary objects 19
imagination-based processes 20
imagining 97
impulsivity 154
inaccurate reports 30
inappropriate behaviors 138
inattention 154
infantile amnesia 13–14
  and basic memory processes 15
  and emergence of a sense of self 15
  and language development 14
information-processing skills 20
informativeness 178
injuries 16, 40
  memory of 41, 43, 44
inoculations 40
insensitivity 175
intellectual disabilities (ID) 7
  adolescents and adults with 148–57
  developmental delay perspective 143
  and gender 139
  severity of 143–4, 157`
  see also children with intellectual disabilities (CWID)

intelligence 17
intermediaries 50, 159
interviewers 106–8
  ability to elicit information 4, 68
  behavior of 26, 122
  bias 58
  errors made by 55–6, 90
  establishing rapport 52–4
  feedback for 202–6
  interaction with victims/witnesses 115–16
  misclassifying own statements/questions 58
  and non-verbal cues 59
  personal characteristics 203
  self-reviews 209–10
  supervision of 203–5, 208
  training programs for 6, 202–11
  "train the trainer" approach 175
interviews
  child-centered 8, 68
  child-led exchange 62
  children's expectations 89
  and children with intellectual disabilities (CWID) 146–7
  delayed 153
  as a dynamic process 48
  evaluations of 69–86
  evidence-based practice 4
  informal 51–2
  interviewer-led exchange 62
  mock 207–9
  non-supportive style 54
  number of 49–50
  as a part of investigations 230–2
  practicing 5
  preparing the child for 54–7
  recommended practice 4, 6, 68–9, 88, 99, 108, 202–11
  repeated 157
  supervision and review of 7–8, 171, 177, 202–6, 208, 210, 236
  supportive style 53
  time after incident 48–9, 68, 95
  see also interviewers
intrusion errors 19
Israel 103–4, 112
  evaluations of interviews 70–4
  interviewing individuals with intellectual disability 138, 148
  interviewing suspects 182

likelihood of abuse 215–19
"Miranda warning" 186
Revised Suspect Protocol (RSP) 186
training programs 174–5, 181
Israeli Youth Investigative
    Service 103

Japan 105
joint transgressions 90

knowledge
    children's perception of 28
    and memory 20–1, 36, 40
Korea 81–2
    see also South Korea

laboratory-based studies 3, 29, 114, 116, 202–3
language deficits 138
    see also language development; language skills
language development
    delayed 23, 138
    and infantile amnesia 14
    see also language deficits; language skills
language skills 23–8
    children's vocabularies 23, 26
    conversational ability 26–8
    interpretation of words 25–6
    and memory performance 23–4
    productive 24
    receptive 24
    and suggestive questions 24
    see also language deficits; language development
legitimizing expressions 171
life events 13
linguistic style 24
    see also language skills
lying 33, 184–5

maltreatment
    and attention deficit/hyperactivity disorder (ADHD) 154
    and developmental disorders 7, 138
    and language delays 23
    repeated instances of 95, 132
manageability 18–19
medical examinations 18, 43, 218
    see also medical procedures

medical procedures 16
    and attachment 18
    children's accounts of 40
    children's memory of 32–3, 39
    see also medical examinations
Memorandum of Good Practice (MOGP) 79–81, 85, 104, 231
memory
    and age 4
    and arousal 38–9
    basic processes 15
    for details 36
    and direct experiences 31–2
    earliest 13–14
    enhancing 22
    individual differences 17
    and knowledge 36, 40
    and language competency 23–4
    long-term 13–15, 27
    non-verbal measures of 13
    and repeated experiences 36–7
    and stress 38–9, 41–2
    retrieval mechanisms 62
    traces 32, 44, 49–50
    "tunnel" 180
    see also autobiographical memory
mental context reinstatement (MCR) 196–200
meta-linguistic abilities 27, 34, 130
Miranda rights 186
misinformation 3, 22, 44
    and language skills 25–6
    post-event 29
    pre-event 28
    and repeated experiences 36
misleading questions 32, 33, 125
mock interviews 207–9
MOGP see Memorandum of Good Practice
mothers 51–2
motivational factors 162
MRC see mental context reinstatement
multiple incidents 95–7

narratives 27
    see also narrative skills; narrative training; personal narratives
narrative skills 34, 44
    and children with intellectual disabilities (CWID) 138, 145–6

narrative training 91–2
natural disasters 40
negative stereotypes 159
neurobiology 14
neurotransmitter systems 14
New Zealand 84
NICHD Investigative Protocol 2, 6–10, 88–100, 236–7
  accuracy of children's accounts 111–14
  adolescents and adults with intellectual disability 148–57
  attention deficit/hyperactivity disorder (ADHD) 155
  autism spectrum disorder (ASD) 151–4
  body diagrams 194–6
  break stage 97–9
  children with intellectual disabilities (CWID) 143–8
  closure stage 99
  coherence of narratives 27–8
  and contextual cues 197–9
  and credibility assessment 218–20
  and disclosure 99
  and drawings 192
  effectiveness of 102–18
  evaluation of 115–17, 237
  explaining purpose and ground rules 89–91
  follow-up questions 96–9
  free-recall phase 93–6
  future directions 232–7
  good practice 235
  introductory phase 89–91
  narrative-training phase 91–92
  practice of 'pairing' 63, 94, 96
  pre-interview considerations 88–9
  pre-substantive phase 89, 110
  questions to avoid 96–7
  rapport-building phase 91
  substantive phase 92, 106–8
  suggestive questioning 30
  supportive version 54
  training model 202–6
  use in other contexts 235–6
  see also Revised NICHD Protocol (RP)
nondisclosure 121
noninformative responses 130

nonverbal behavior 167
nonverbal cues 59
nonverbal experiences 14
Norway 84–5

open-ended invitations
  responsivity to 130, 131
  and younger children 121
open-ended prompts 5, 7, 9, 31, 59, 88, 93
  and accuracy of information 113
  and child-centered interviews 68
  and failure to respond 63
  and interviews with suspects 184–5
  and practice narratives 57
  see also open-ended questions
open-ended questions 4, 72
  accuracy of responses 59, 63
  and age of children 16
  and child's ability to answer 63
  and children with intellectual disabilities (CWID) 143, 156
  and directive questions 98
  and disclosure of abuse 110
  and failure to respond 63
  and free-recall 94
  and younger children 120
  see also open-ended prompts
optimism 171
option-posing 80, 97
  and accuracy 113
  and autism spectrum disorder (ASD) 152
  and children with intellectual disabilities (CWID) 144, 156
  and contradictory information 60–1
  and number of elicited details 123–4
  and recognition 62
  responsivity to 127, 130
  and use of NICHD Protocol 108
"outshining hypothesis" 196

"pairing principle" 63, 94, 96
parents
  abuse perpetrated by 139, 177
  of children with attention deficit/hyperactivity disorder (ADHD) 154

of children with intellectual disabilities (CWID) 138, 139
interviews with children 52
use of suggestive questions by 52
past experience 26–7
PCR *see* physical context reinstatement
pediatric examinations 43
   see also medical examinations; medical procedures
perceived responsibility 42
perpetrators 52, 102, 122, 139, 181–2
   see also suspects
personal experiences 31–4
personal narratives 14
   see also narratives
physical abuse
   and attention deficit/hyperactivity disorder (ADHD) 154
   by parents 163, 177
   and depression 42
   and reluctance to disclose 163, 177
physical context reinstatement (PCR) 197, 198, 199
physical injuries 139
   see also physical abuse
Piaget, Jean 126
planning skills 154
play 20
police officers
   characteristics of 203
   evaluations of interviews 78, 81, 121–2, 146–7
   training courses for 205–6
positive events 18
positive images 20
positive reinforcement 171
post-event contamination 62, 95
post-training practices 7
practice interviews 5
practice narratives 57–63
   and rapport building 57
   type of questions 59–62
pre-disclosed actions 121
pre-interview assessments 50–1
prepositions 26
prior knowledge 17
problem-solving skills 203
prompts
   and fantastic elements in children's accounts 20

focused-recall 59, 130
   see also cued-recall prompts; directive prompts; free-recall prompts; open-ended prompts; recognition prompts; suggestive prompts
prosecution 22

questions
   challenging 19
   closed 25
   directive 96, 98
   disclosure 110
   distribution of 64
   focused 58, 78, 80, 85, 88, 93–4, 96, 98–9, 189
   focused-recall 68–9, 131
   follow-up 96–9
   "forced-choice" 69, 120, 125
   forcing response 25
   funnel approach 64
   misleading 32, 33, 125
   option-posing 25, 144
   recognition 69
   responsiveness to 16–23, 108
   to avoid 96–7
   unanswerable 24, 25
   used in practice narratives 59–62
   "yes/no" 69, 97, 120, 125
   see also open-ended questions; specific questions; suggestive questions

rapport
   development and maintenance 54, 91, 168
   establishing 52–4, 91, 168
   and disclosure 164–7
   future directions in NICHD Protocol 234
   and practice narratives 57
   and suggestibility 91
real-life events 31–2
reassurance 165
recall
   contextual support 14
   and direct questions 62
   factors influencing 11–12
   and recognition processes 62–3
   see also event recall; recall memory

recall memory 4–5, 133
recognition memory 4–5
  and temporal attributes 133
recognition prompts 59–60,
    69, 131
  and errors 59–60, 62, 152
  and recall 62–3
Recommendations for Preliminary
    Investigations 78
rehearsal 23
reinforcement 29
reliability 3
reminders 14
reminiscence 49, 50
response bias 24, 62, 120
responsivity
  to directive prompts 127, 130
  to open-ended invitations
    130, 131
  to option-posing prompts
    127, 130
  to suggestive prompts 127, 130
  of suspects 183
  to temporal requests 133
  of young children 127, 130–2
retribution 52
retrieval cues
  access to 49
  and directive wh- questions 130
  generating 22, 50
  internal 34
retrieval skills 34, 58
retrieval strategies 42
Revised NICHD Protocol (RP) 88,
    91, 151, 161–85, 237–8
  and allegation rates 220–1
  and case outcomes 221–3
  development and
    evaluation 167–74
  further revision of 174–81
Revised Suspect Protocol
    (RSP) 186
routines 88
RSP *see* Revised Suspect Protocol

salience 42
Salt Lake City 221
Scotland 84
Scottish Executive Guidelines 84
self, emergence of a sense of 15
self-confidence 18

self-contradictions 24, 61
self-esteem 18
self-reviews 209–10
self-transgressions 90
sequencing 134
  see also forward-sequencing
sexual abuse 33
  and attention deficit/hyperactivity
    disorder (ADHD) 154
  and children with intellectual
    disabilities (CWID)
  effects of delay on recall 41
  factors influencing memory of 40
  parental reports of disclosures 52
  plausibility of 217–19
  and reluctance of disclosure 163
  repeated 34
  severity of 39
SFS *see* Swedish Code of Judicial
    Procedures
shame 41, 52
shyness 18
sketch-reinstatement-of-context
    procedure 153
skills, age of attainment 13
Skype 207
social challenges 138
social context 155
social pressure 29, 50
social support 42
source awareness 21
source errors 22
source monitoring
  errors 50
  and event recall 21–2
South Korea 106, 110
  see also Korea
specific questions 5
  and autism spectrum disorder
    (ASD) 150
  and children with intellectual
    disabilities (CWID) 142,
    146, 156
  and response bias 24
  and younger children 131
staged events 44
Statement Validity Analysis
    (SVA) 214
stereotypes 28
story-telling 145
strategy use 22–3

stress
  chronic 42
  and encoding 117
  and event recall 38–9, 41–2, 117
  management 203
substantive interviews 5
suggestibility 28–31
  and age 29, 31
  and anxiety 19
  and attention deficit/hyperactivity disorder (ADHD) 155
  and autism spectrum disorder (ASD) 150
  and children with intellectual disabilities (CWID) 142
  and executive function 155
  and number of interviews 49
  and rapport 91
  and repeated experiences 36
  and supportive interviewing style 53
suggestive interviewing 28–9
suggestive prompts 80, 97
  and accuracy 113
  and autism spectrum disorder (ASD) 152
  confrontational 31, 61
  and disclosure 93
  forms of 58
  interviewing suspects 184
  introductory 31, 61
  and number of details elicited 123–4
  and practice narratives 58
  responsivity to 127, 130
  and self-contradictions 61
  suppositional 31, 61
suggestive questions 3, 17, 30, 43, 63
  and autism spectrum disorder (ASD) 152
  and children with intellectual disabilities (CWID) 144
  and contradictory information 60–1
  and disclosure of abuse 110
  and erroneous answers 120
  and language skills 24
  by parents 52
  and recognition 62
  and response biases 120
  and self-contradictions 61

supportive environment 89, 164–5
supportive interviewer practices 41
supportiveness 168, 172, 178–9
  and coherence of children's accounts 179
  and false reports 165
  and informativeness 178–9
  see also emotional support
surgeries 18
suspects 7, 181–7
  and free-recall prompts 183
  and open-ended prompts 185
  responsiveness of 184
  and suggestive prompts 184
  see also perpetrators
SVA *see* Statement Validity Analysis
Sweden
  children with intellectual disabilities (CWID) 140, 147
  evaluations of interviews 77–9
  training courses 205–6
Swedish Code of Judicial Procedures (SFS) 78

temperament 18–19
temporal attributes 132–5
temporal concepts 126
temporal locations 134, 135
temporal reference points 121
temporal sequencing 135
theory of mind 26, 28
time
  concept of 126, 132
  patterns 134
  specifying 132
timing 135
time-segmenting cues 94, 121, 124, 126, 127
tools 189
  see also body diagrams; dolls; drawings
toys 89
training 7, 202–11
  computer-based 206–8
  programs 6, 175–7, 181
traumatic events 14, 16, 38–43
true statements 90
trustworthiness 159
truth telling 55, 56, 79, 90
tunnel memory 180

understanding 40
United Kingdom
    evaluation of interviews
        79–81, 121
    NICHD Protocol study 104–5
    registered intermediaries 50
    see also England
United States
    anatomically-detailed doll
        study 75–7
    court systems 37
    evaluation of interviews
        74–7, 121
    NICHD Protocol study 104

VCUG *see* voiding cystourethrogram
verbal ability 145
verbal recall 34
video clips 3
visual aids 7, 64–5, 97
    and children's accuracy 97
    and children's recall 65
voiding cystourethrogram
    (VCUG) 40, 43

Wales 79
"wh- prompts" 125, 130, 131, 136
words 20
working memory capacity 154

younger children 119–36
    ability to answer open-ended
        questions 63
    accuracy of reports 114, 120
    allegation rates 162
    amount of reported
        information 15–16, 72
    and body diagrams 193–4
    and cued invitations 121
    and dolls 190–1
    effect of delay on event
        recall 43
    effect of direct participation on
        memories 32
    encoding and retrieval
        strategies 34
    and focused-recall
        wh- questions 131
    and free-recall 93, 120, 121
    impact of questioning
        strategies 120
    interviewing 119–36
    language skills 23–8
    likelihood of making
        allegations 122
    memory of stressful
        experiences 41
    number of elicited details 116,
        120, 123–4, 127
    and open-ended questions 120
    and recognition prompts 131
    and recognition questions 69
    and references to temporal
        attributes 132–5
    responsivity 15, 127, 130–2
    and source monitoring 21–2
    strategy use 22
    and temporal concepts 35
    and "yes/no" questions 125
youth investigators 70, 74, 182, 218